2009.

Acting Between the Lines

Happy Car
All my Love
Sabine X

Acting Between the Lines

*The Field Day Theatre Company and
Irish Cultural Politics 1980–1984*

MARILYNN J. RICHTARIK

The Catholic University of America Press
Washington, D.C.

Library of Congress Cataloging-in-Publication Data
Richtarik, Marilynn J.
    Acting between the lines : the Field Day Theatre Company and
Irish cultural politics, 1980–1984 / Marilynn J. Richtarik.
        p.   cm.
    Originally published: New York : Oxford University Press, 1995–
    Includes bibliographical references and index.
    ISBN 0-8132-1075-5 (pbk. : alk. paper)
        1. Field Day Theatre Company.   2. Theater—Northern Ireland—
History—20th century.   3. Theater—Political aspects—Northern
Ireland.   I. Title.
PN2601.R53   2001
792'.09416—dc21   00-065663

Dedicated to my parents,
ALFRED and MARILYNN RICHTARIK, with love,
and to MR CHARLES E. HOLLEY,
the most devoted servant of the theatre I know.

Contents

Foreword to This Edition

THIS BOOK is a paperback reprint of *Acting Between the Lines*, which was first published in March 1995. Much, of course, has changed in Ireland, and especially in Northern Ireland, since then. Most significantly, the peace process facilitated over a period of nearly two years by former United States senator George Mitchell resulted in the Good Friday Agreement of April 1998, negotiated by the British and Irish governments along with representatives of various Northern Irish political parties and endorsed by the electorate of Northern Ireland in a referendum on 22 May 1998. This plan finally took effect on 2 December 1999 after a series of nerve-wracking disputes and delays. It provided for devolution of power over the province's domestic affairs to a Northern Ireland Assembly and a power-sharing executive made up of cabinet ministers from different unionist and nationalist parties, along with the establishment of both a British-Irish council and a North-South ministerial council and cross-border bodies. Immediately after legislation approving the transfer of authority from London to Belfast was passed by the British parliament, the government of the Republic of Ireland officially renounced its constitutional claim on the territory of Northern Ireland—thus formalizing the new relationship of trust and cooperation developed between the British and Irish governments, which had worked so hard to broker a solution to the crisis of Northern Ireland. Despite repeated close calls in the ensuing months, people remain hopeful that an end to the violence that has claimed more than 3,300 lives over a period of thirty years may be in sight.[1]

Field Day, too, has changed almost beyond recognition in the years since 1995. The Field Day Theatre Company I described in my book was a self-consciously Northern and Derry-based enterprise managed by six individuals (all artists, though several were academics as well) who reached out to a popular audience with

---

1. Alvin Jackson, *Ireland: 1798–1998* (Oxford: Blackwell, 1999) 396–417; Warren Hoge, "Northern Ireland Picks Up the Reins of Its Government," *New York Times* 3 Dec. 1999: A1.

pamphlets and challenging theatrical productions that tried, often through historical analysis or cross-cultural analogy, to broaden people's sense of what it could mean to be Irish. Today, two of the original six directors (Brian Friel and Tom Paulin) have resigned from the company's governing board, while two others (Seamus Heaney and David Hammond) remain as sleeping partners. "Field Day" is defined now by the interests of Seamus Deane and Stephen Rea, both of whom also maintain demanding careers apart from it (Deane as Notre Dame University's Keough Professor of Irish Studies, Rea as an international film star). Since both of them currently live in Dublin, the company's centre of gravity has shifted inexorably southwards. For years after it ceased annual play production in 1991 Field Day was allowed by the Derry City Council to keep an office rent-free in Derry, but, when the city began making plans in 1999 to sell the building that housed it, Field Day found itself on the brink of homelessness. When I spoke with Deane in June of 2000, he was in the process of locating office space for Field Day in Dublin. Moreover, he said, in order to maintain its tax-exempt status the company would have to be re-chartered in the South with re-written articles of association and a reconstituted Board that would probably be expanded to include several new members. Practical circumstances, he confided, were driving Field Day "into the arms of the Republic," but he was philosophical about that development.[2]

In the absence of a firm base and full-time administrator, Field Day has been increasingly less capable of mounting independent theatrical productions with extensive Irish tours; the last such project was its 1995 production of Chekhov's *Uncle Vanya* in a version by Frank McGuinness, and there had been a gap of over three years between it and Thomas Kilroy's *The Madame MacAdam Travelling Theatre* (1991). This gap was largely filled with controversy over the three-volume *Field Day Anthology of Irish Writing*, published late in 1991, and Field Day's largest ongoing commitment traces its origins to that debate. One of the most telling and persistent criticisms of the *Anthology* was that works by and about women were inadequately represented in it, and Deane (the general editor) quickly promised to make amends with an addendum in the form of a fourth volume that would concentrate on women's writing. Deane and Field Day are responsible for providing the

2. Seamus Deane, personal interview, 19 June 2000.

funding to make the addition a reality, but decisions regarding content are being made by a collective of eight female academics along with a small army of sub-editors.[3] Like every other aspect of the *Anthology*, this undertaking has grown exponentially in the years since its inception and taken much longer than expected to complete, but current plans call for "volume four" to be published (in two volumes) by Cork University Press in the fall of 2001.[4]

Nowadays, most of Field Day's activities are pursued in collaboration with other entities that provide the bulk of whatever logistical and administrative support is required. Thus, in 1998, Field Day paired with Belfast's Tinderbox Theatre Company to present Stewart Parker's *Northern Star* (directed by Stephen Rea) as part of the Belfast Festival. A longer-term endeavour, undertaken in cooperation with the University of Notre Dame Press in the United States and Cork University Press in Ireland, is "Critical Conditions: Field Day Essays and Monographs," a series edited by Deane. To date, nine monographs and collections of essays have been published, and several more are in press.[5] "Field Day" today, in short, operates like a trademark that the remaining directors can affix at will to any of their individual projects that seem to them to merit it.

Field Day's evolution raises interesting questions. It is self-evident that an artistic movement formed in reaction to the Northern Irish "Troubles" would be challenged to re-define itself by what may well prove to be the end of them. Moreover, as I argue in the following pages, Field Day's development has always been

3. Angela Bourke, Siobhan Kilfeather, Maria Luddy, Margaret MacCurtain, Gerardine Meaney, Máirín Ní Dhonnchadha, Mary O'Dowd, and Clair Wills, eds., *Field Day Anthology of Irish Writing* volume IV (forthcoming from Cork University Press, fall 2001).

4. Seamus Deane, e-mail to the author, 25 September 2000.

5. Titles already in print include Kevin Whelan's *The Liberty Tree: Radicalism, Catholicism and the Construction of Irish Identity 1760–1830* (1995), Luke Gibbons's *Transformations in Irish Culture* (1995), Joep Leerssen's *Mere Irish and Fíor-Ghael: Studies in the Idea of Irish Nationality* (1996) and *Remembrance and Imagination: Patterns in the Historical and Literary Representation of Ireland in the Nineteenth Century* (1996), Terry Eagleton's *Crazy John and the Bishop and Other Essays on Irish Culture* (1997), Harry White's *The Keeper's Recital: Music and Cultural History in Ireland, 1770–1970* (1998), Francis Mulhern's *The Present Lasts a Long Time: Essays in Cultural Politics* (1998), Marc Caball's *Poets and Politics: Reaction and Continuity in Irish Poetry, 1558–1625* (1998), and David Lloyd's *Ireland After History* (1999).

more pragmatic and improvisatory than either its supporters or its detractors wish to believe. The company, at any given time, is only whatever its directors decide it should be; it is (to quote myself) "a process, a practice, defined by what it does and, to a lesser extent, by what it says it is doing." And yet—when only two of the original six directors remain actively involved with the company, when the centre of operations has moved from Derry to Dublin, when the principal focus has shifted from touring theatre to academic publication (with the change in the target audience that implies)—in what sense can what is called Field Day now be the same as what went by the name of Field Day in the early 1980s? Perhaps the continuity derives from the type of issues that the company's various projects address: issues of Irish identity, history, and language that point to cultural tensions left unresolved by the new political arrangements in Northern Ireland. "Field Day" has also come to imply a political disposition that is, as Deane explains, Ae-mancipatory, intellectually stimulating and against everything that is dreary, propagandistic and vicious-like unionism, for instance.[6]

Despite Deane and Rea's determination to re-invent the company, Hammond acknowledges that "the corporate energy that fuelled Field Day for ten or twelve years no longer exists."[7] Even Rea, discussing Field Day in a recent interview for the Aer Lingus magazine, lapsed into the past tense: "I felt utterly focused with that company. We were taking what I believed to be important work to people who wouldn't normally go to the theatre. One of the achievements of Field Day was that it located an audience that was not a traditional theatre audience, but people who were concerned about the questions we were asking. That was exhilarating."[8] For me, too, the early years of Field Day's existence, years of populist idealism and conscious self-definition, remain its heroic age. The Field Day that Rea recalls with such nostalgia is the Field Day that is described and analyzed in this book.

Despite the many ways in which Ireland and Field Day have been transformed since 1995, because this study of Field Day's early years concentrates on a specific circumscribed period (1980–1984) most of it has not dated. There are a few references toward

---

6. Seamus Deane, e-mail to the author, 27 September 2000.
7. David Hammond, letter to the author, 17 September 2000.
8. Stephen Rea, quoted in Tony Clayton-Lea, "The Understated Actor," *Cara* 33.3 (May/June 2000): 30.

the beginning and end of the book to events that took place, for example, "fourteen" or "twenty-odd" years ago (counting from 1994, when the manuscript was first prepared for Oxford University Press). I have not attempted to update these, since any substitution would be equally outmoded by the time this reprint is published. Similarly, the reader should bear in mind that observations made in these pages about the "current" political situation in Ireland, north and south, have likewise been superseded by events. For the most part, though, this book tells a story about particular people acting at a particular time and in a particular place, a story that only gains in interest from the fact that the Ireland of the early 1980s has rapidly come to seem so distant.

—*Marilynn Richtarik*, October 2000

Acknowledgements

I WOULD like to thank Dr John Kelly for his constructive suggestions and enthusiasm, my family and friends for their encouragement and support, and Bob Lamb, who was there at the beginning. I also wish to recognize the assistance of the following: Julie Barber; Peter Bednekoff; Terence Brown; Sam Burnside; Marc Caball; Seamus Deane; Terry Eagleton; The Field Day Theatre Company; John Wilson Foster; Jason Freeman; Brian Friel; Georgia State University; David Hammond; Seamus Heaney; Lynda Henderson; Jesus College, Oxford; The John Hewitt Summer School; Jennifer Johnston and David Gilliland; Tim Kendall; The Killam Trust; Thomas Kilroy; Richard Kirkland; Modupe Labode; Brian Lacy; Bridget Lewis; The Linen Hall Library; The Lipman Seminar; Andrew Lockett; Edna Longley; James McCabe; David McGonagle; Brian McIlroy; Gary McKeone; Jerry Masinton; Ken Mills; Dan Murtaugh; Colette Nelis; Northern Arizona University Department of English; Finola O'Doherty; Bernard O'Donoghue; Tony and Ethel Ow; Tom Paulin; Bob Purdie; Joan and Peter Pyne; Stephen Rea; John Redmond; The Rhodes Trust; Robert Ritter; David Rudkin; Elizabeth Schultz; The University of British Columbia; George Watson; Susan Whimster; Brian Young.

Grateful thanks also to Seamus Deane and to Faber & Faber, Ltd. for permission to quote material for which they hold the copyright.

'Ireland is the old sow that eats her farrow.'

JAMES JOYCE

'in fact, I have never seen farrow eaten by a sow in my life: what usually happens is that the young pigs eat one another's ears.'

SEAMUS HEANEY

Introduction: Surveying the Field

FIELD DAY, a Northern Irish artistic and critical collective, has over the fourteen years of its existence come to be identified with a certain philosophical approach to the study of Irish literature and culture. This analysis centres on the idea of Ireland as a post-colonial country and of the violence in Northern Ireland as a lingering effect of colonial rule.[1] Field Day's success in popularizing this point of view has attracted the attention of well-known literary theorists, several of whom—Terry Eagleton, Fredric Jameson, Edward W. Said—have written under the Field Day banner. In their wake have followed a great many scholars, both Irish and international, who are at least as interested in Ireland as an exemplar of some more general theory as they are in the awkward particularities of the Irish situation itself. My own approach is different. The present study is a detailed examination of Field Day's first five years—its activities in that period and reactions to these both inside and outside the province of Northern Ireland. My focus is on contemporary views of the company and its relation to Ireland, north and south, because I believe that examining Field Day and its Irish context together may help to illuminate both. The time is ripe for an empirical study that takes into account those aspects of the Field Day project that make it unique—the interplay between local circumstances, political compromises, financial restraints, and personalities that finally make it possible to talk about 'a Field Day play' rather than simply 'a play Field Day has done'.

At various points in the following pages I will distinguish between three main critical spaces: the Republic of Ireland, Northern Ireland, and 'mainland' Britain. Geography is crucial in this case. The fact that Field Day is based in the north-west, in Derry, is extremely significant. For centuries, a major divide in Ireland has been that between east and west. The east coast cities of Belfast and Dublin, centres of population and commerce, enjoy easy access to Great Britain and the rest of Europe, while the west, officially revered as the last bastion of living Gaelic culture and the Irish language, has yet suffered acutely from lack of work, inaccessibility, and a steady loss of population. Derry, although it is a large city, shares with remote western areas the problem of unemployment and the feeling of isolation. Within Northern Ireland, the east–west divide demarcated by the River Bann is reinforced by sectarian and political divisions. These divisions are responsible for the more familiar separation of the island of Ireland into north and south. This boundary is human rather than geographical, but no less real for that. The border resulted indirectly from the resolute refusal of a critical mass of Protestants, centred in the north-east of the island, to have anything to do with a Home Rule government based in Dublin and bound to be dominated, in their view, by the Catholic Church. Thus in 1921 six of the thirty-two existing counties of Ireland, containing roughly one-third of the population and one-fifth of the area of the island, became known as Northern Ireland and remained under British rule, with a devolved government and parliament.

Partition did not solve the problem because Protestant and Catholic populations were mixed throughout the island. In the area which became the Republic of Ireland, Protestants comprised a small percentage of the population, and most of them who had any serious objection to the new regime simply left. In the North, however, the ratio of Protestants to Catholics was only about two to one, which meant that Protestants were able to dominate government and industry but never entirely to subdue the Catholic minority, which continued to desire political unification with the rest of the island. Ratios of population vary widely in various parts of the province, and people who live there have a highly refined territorial sense. In the eastern counties of Antrim and Down, there are four or five Protestants for every Catholic, although in Belfast the ratio drops to two to one. In counties Londonderry and Armagh there is a small Protestant majority, and in counties Tyrone and Fermanagh a small Catholic majority. In certain urban areas the balance of population differs from the surrounding countryside. Derry, Armagh, Newry, and Downpatrick, for example, are cities with Catholic majorities in counties with Protestant majorities. In Cookstown and Enniskillen this situation is reversed.[2]

Political differences in Ireland have long reflected underlying religious and cultural differences. Northern Protestants, on the whole, tend to favour the continuation of the political connection with Great Britain, whereas northern Catholics, by and large, are likely to prefer some form of united Ireland. Throughout this study I will be using the word 'unionist' to denote the former attitude and 'nationalist' to indicate the latter.[3] For most people in Northern Ireland, opinion on the 'national question' is less a purely political view than an article of faith, less an 'aspiration' than an assumption about who and where they are. The intractable difficulty of the Northern Irish situation is that these two world-views, translated into political goals, are incompatible. As long as Northern Ireland in its present state remains a province of either the United Kingdom or a future united Ireland, it will house a more or less permanently disaffected minority: at the moment largely Catholic and nationalist, perhaps in the future Protestant and unionist.

This impasse in the political realm has been garishly highlighted in the past twenty-odd years by organized violence, but military and paramilitary forces are only one factor in a highly complex system. The vast majority of people in Northern Ireland would not dream of killing anyone for the sake of their political or religious beliefs. It is when we realize, however, that the basic divisions in Northern Irish life take the form of actual physical violence only relatively rarely that we begin to grasp the true magnitude of the problem. Separation, more than confrontation, characterizes relations between Protestants and Catholics in the North. Even in such a small place (the population of Northern Ireland is about 1.5 million), it is possible to live with almost no contact, except of the most formal kind, with people from the other side. The poet Michael Longley has spoken of the 'invisible apartheid' that held sway in the province until the late 1960s,[4] and, although more widely recognized now as problematic, division between Protestants and Catholics is still a fact of life in much of Northern Ireland. One's religious and political background influences where one lives, with whom one associates, what sort of job one holds, what newspaper one reads, the type of education one acquires, where one goes for holidays or a night out, and, of course, what church one attends, and how one votes. All of this is, for most people, perfectly compatible with peaceful coexistence with neighbours of a different persuasion.

This idea of 'two communities' in Northern Ireland is necessary to an understanding of the pressure on each person in the province, but it is also a gross simplification. On either side of the main divide there are a number of communities, a political spectrum that ranges from the Ulster Defence Association (politicized unionist paramilitary) to the Reverend Ian Paisley's fundamentalist Democratic Unionist Party (DUP) to the Official Unionists to the centrist Alliance Party to the constitutional nationalist Social Democratic and Labour Party (SDLP) to Sinn Féin (the political wing of the Provisional IRA), with shades of opinion in between. In addition to these political communities there are the various regional communities, which are fairly well-integrated in some areas. Moreover, many individuals have resisted group pressure and work in various ways every day of their lives to pull down the barriers dividing people from each other. A large proportion of the North's writers, artists, and academics fall into this third major category, and several of them will feature prominently in the narrative that follows.

Many of the people involved with Field Day reached political awareness during the 1960s, at a time when anything seemed possible. The early movement for civil rights for Catholics represented for them a move away from the old, sectarian politics into a new age of co-operation; the intensification of violence toward the end of the decade demonstrated that the roots of civil discord ran deeper than they had supposed. Throughout the 1970s and early 1980s, as people lost confidence in political action, the idea of culture as an alternative to politics gained ground. The belief informing this approach was that it was necessary to change people's fundamental attitudes before there could be any real hope of political change. As early as 1972, the poet Seamus Heaney stated that he did not endorse the view that 'poetry makes nothing happen':

It can eventually make new feelings, or feelings about feelings, happen, and anybody can see that in this country for a long time to come a refinement of feelings will be more urgent than a re-framing of policies or of constitutions.[5]

Another poet, Derek Mahon, declared in 1986 that 'The function of the arts . . . is not to change maps but to change the expressions on the faces of men and women.'[6] Dramatist Stewart Parker remarked in the same year that

if ever a time and place cried out for the solace and rigour and passionate rejoinder of great drama, it is here and now. There is a whole culture to be achieved. The politicians, visionless almost to a man, are withdrawing into their sectarian stockades. It falls to the artists to construct a working model of wholeness by means of which this society can begin to hold up its head in the world.[7]

All three of these men have written plays for the Field Day Theatre Company, founded in 1980 with the intention of finding or creating a space between unionism and nationalism and proving by example the possibility of a shared culture in the North of Ireland. In its local aspect Field Day, especially in its early years, has been part of the more general attempt by artists and intellectuals to circumvent politics through culture. The difficulty with this programme was and is that culture itself in Northern Ireland is thoroughly politicized.

In order to examine the material in the detail I thought necessary to confront the complexities of the situation, I have limited my discussion to the first five years of the company. Although these were seminal years in which Field Day was defining itself and being defined by others, they have been strangely neglected by researchers. In the course of these years the architects of an artistic and cultural initiative, in an increasingly self-conscious manner, gradually formulated the policies and self-image that would shape its future activities. Obviously the company's emphasis and public perceptions of it have changed since 1985, but that seemed a natural place to stop since, on the occasion of its fifth anniversary, a number of articulate observers took the opportunity to assess Field Day's achievement to that date.

In discussing the reception of the Field Day plays I inevitably make extensive use of local and regional newspapers. In so far as local reviewers articulate the opinions of their communities, accounts printed in these papers are the only permanent record of what people in smaller venues around Ireland actually thought of Field Day at any particular time. Although newspapers in the North are usually associated with one 'side' or the other, it would be misleading to posit a rigid distinction or to assume that every item published in such papers is politically biased. In particular, the orientation of the newspaper for which they write does not seem to be an important factor in the critical judgements of local drama critics. Nevertheless, such context is something of which one should be aware.

The point of view of newspapers that regularly print editorials is usually fairly easy to identify. Many of the small weeklies quoted, however (and most Northern Irish papers, aside from those based in Belfast, are issued weekly rather than daily), avoid editorial comment and are principally devoted to local news: council politics, court and hospital notices, advertisements, and social and sporting events. In these cases, careful attention to items such as church notices, obituaries, weddings, club and society meetings, headlines, and the like reveals political and religious orientation. If, for example, a newspaper refers to Edward Daly as 'the R. C. bishop' of 'Londonderry' and to the Republic of Ireland as 'Eire', this indicates a generally Protestant readership.

The matter is further complicated by the fact that conflicting clues often appear in the same newspaper, reinforcing the idea that division, outside urban areas, is by no means absolute. In many papers, the local element appears to predominate over any sectarian or political slant. Taking this into account, I would place the newspapers most frequently cited into the following categories (I make a distinction between, for instance, a 'Catholic' paper and a 'nationalist' paper, meaning by the latter a publication with a clear political emphasis, generally finding expression in editorials):

unionist: *Londonderry Sentinel, Impartial Reporter & Farmers' Journal*
nationalist: *Derry Journal, Derry People & Donegal News, Strabane Chronicle, Ulster Herald*
Protestant: *Armagh Guardian, Coleraine Chronicle, Northern*

Constitution, Rathfriland Outlook, Ulster Gazette & Armagh Standard
Catholic: *Dungannon Observer, Fermanagh News.*

In Belfast the major newspapers are the establishment *Belfast Telegraph*, the working-class unionist *Belfast Newsletter* (and its sister paper, the *Sunday News*), and the nationalist *Irish News & Belfast Morning News*. All of these papers are published daily and read throughout the province. The national newspapers in the Republic of Ireland are the establishment *Irish Times*, the *Irish Press* group (including the *Evening Press* and *Sunday Press*) and the *Irish Independent* group (including the *Evening Herald* and *Sunday Independent*). The *Irish Press* was founded by Éamon de Valera and has historically been associated with his Fianna Fáil party, while the *Irish Independent* takes the Fine Gael line. I also refer fairly frequently to the *Sunday Tribune*, the newest Sunday paper. I have corrected misspellings and typographical errors except in headlines or where there was ambiguity.

Newspapers, like artistic enterprises, generally assume an audience even if they do not always reflect it. Field Day set itself the more ambitious goal of creating an audience. How the company initially proceeded and was received is the substance of the story I shall try to tell. At the very least the Field Day project is a declaration of faith in the only kind of 'opposition' that Stewart Parker believed the writer could offer to a factionalized political and social climate: 'an imaginative struggle to enfold human diversity and then to celebrate its wholeness in art. The act of imagination may not forestall the act of slaughter, but at least it bears witness to an alternative way of carrying on in the field of human relations.'[8]

'The Town I Loved So Well':
Derry and the Foundation of Field Day

THE seal of the city of Derry features, in addition to the red cross on a white background which commemorates its association with the city of London, a tower and a grinning skeleton. This symbolizes that Derry is a walled city that rose 'from the dead'. The visitor soon learns, however, that there are other stories told about the seal, including one about an avaricious Norman lord who was locked in the fortress by his relatives and left to starve to death. Like so many other fragments of Irish history, this legend strikes a resonant chord with events of more recent years in Northern Ireland where, over the past twenty-five years, civil division has yet again manifested itself in violence. Full of modern significance, too, is the grim joke locals tell about the grisly emblem. 'What we say,' the guard at the Guildhall explains, 'is that's a Derry man waiting for a job.'

The Field Day Theatre Company, based in Derry and founded in 1980 by the playwright Brian Friel and the actor Stephen Rea, has consistently concerned itself with the relationship between myth and present-day perception, history and politics. Over the last fourteen years Field Day has become such an established and important part of the cultural scene in Ireland that it is difficult now to recapture the sense of surprise that greeted Friel's announcement of his plans to take on the management side of theatre.

Considered by many to be Ireland's most important living playwright, Brian Friel was brought up in Derry and nearby Donegal and in 1980 lived just across the border from the city. The Field Day enterprise (which took its name, in part, from a certain linguistic affinity with 'Friel' and 'Rea') owed its existence to a convergence of circumstances. Rea, who had grown up in Belfast, had met Friel some years before during an English production of Friel's *The Freedom of the City*. His decision to approach Friel with the idea of touring an Irish play came out of a growing frustration with his London theatre work. Rea believed that 'an Irishman in English theatre is very conscious of belonging to a sub-culture rather than a culture proper. . . . I felt less expressed in terms of England than I did over here, but not in the narrow national way.'[1] Friel, as it happened, was in the process of finishing the script for *Translations*, and he proved receptive to the notion of an Irish touring project.

Both Friel and Rea were interested in learning more about the production aspects of theatre, and they shared a desire to make their work available to non-traditional audiences. What the company most emphatically was not was a commercial undertaking. As Friel put it, 'We accept that we are going to be out of pocket at the end of the venture.'[2] A crucial factor behind the formation of Field Day was the offer of the Arts Council of Northern Ireland to support Friel if he would get a professional production on the road. He noted that there was just one catch: 'They only fund existing establishments so we had to become an establishment.'[3] The Arts Council of the Republic of Ireland eventually contributed a smaller amount of money.[4]

Field Day, then, was formed on an *ad hoc* basis to produce *Translations*, and the impulse behind it was two-fold. Brian Friel and Stephen Rea shared what might be termed a populist goal for the company. They wished to bring professional theatre to people who might otherwise never see it. As an early press release made clear: 'every effort is to be made, through this and future productions, to reach the widest possible audiences.'[5] A quick glance at a list of the venues in which *Translations* played in the autumn of 1980 reveals that Rea and Friel meant what they said. Along with such established theatres as the Grand Opera House in Belfast and the Gate Theatre in Dublin, the play appeared in the Rainey Endowed School, Magherafelt; the Patrician Hall, Carrickmore; the Technical College, Armagh; and Enniskillen High School. In addition to the populist motive there was an aspect to the early Field Day project that may be called parochial in Patrick Kavanagh's sense of the word. Kavanagh draws a distinction between 'provincialism', which is always looking toward the metropolis, and 'parochialism', which is content in itself and feels no need to compare itself with more powerful or cosmopolitan areas.[6] In an interview after the opening of the show, Friel described what he saw as a new trend in the Irish theatre:

apart from Synge, all our dramatists have pitched their voice for English acceptance and recognition.... However I think that for the first time this is stopping, that there is some kind of confidence, some kind of coming together of Irish dramatists who are not concerned with this, who have no interest in the English stage. We are talking to ourselves as we must and if we are overheard in America, or England, so much the better.[7]

This self-confident localism was not merely Irish in character, although that was part of it. Field Day was more specifically a Northern enterprise. As a writer for the *Irish Press* noted, 'One thing that immediately strikes a person about the company is the number of people who either come from Derry or the North or have some relationship with the areas.'[8] On the simplest level this meant, as the *Belfast Newsletter* pointed out, that Field Day provided 'a new showcase for home-grown talent'.[9] Other people read a deeper meaning into the impact of *Translations*. In an editorial, the *Irish Times* applauded the 'self-help' spirit it saw emerging in the North: ' "Don't bother with anybody but the people in our own corner of Ireland" is the new desperate cry from the heart.... It may be only a concert, a debate, a dance, a lecture or an exhibition of some kind, but it does suggest a liveliness, a community needing to exert itself.'[10]

Ned Chaillet of *The Times* astutely noted that Field Day's 'occupation of Derry's Guild Hall was a dedication to their native Northern Ireland and a signal that a measure of normality, by whatever portion of normality that theatre occupies, had returned to the North'.[11] Along the same lines the *Irish Press* editorialized, 'Because of the bombs and the bombers, the North is often thought of as a cultural wasteland. The Derry experience has shown just how false is such a notion'.[12] Timothy O'Grady, writing for the *New Statesman*, put his finger on some of the energies underlying Field Day when he commented that Friel and Rea founded the company 'with the audacious intention of creating a new theatrical tradition in the north of Ireland. It is a bravado act of cultural politics, as much as of theatre.'[13]

Field Day's decision to rehearse *Translations* in Derry was largely a reflection of the fact that the action of the play takes place nearby. As the official synopsis had it:

The new play . . . is set in a hedge school in Donegal in 1833, when the new English Language National Schools are about to open, and the British Army is carrying out the first Ordnance Survey of the area. This involves finding English translations or phonetic equivalents for local place names. The main characters, English and Irish, stand at a moment of cultural transition, and the play explores their response to this crisis in their personal lives and in the historical life of the community.[14]

Using Derry as a home base made sense 'functionally and spiritually'.[15] When, in May 1980, Friel announced plans actually to stage the play there, the news was greeted with astonishment by the theatre doyens and delight by the 'second city'. Derry, a town in economic depression which lacked a civic theatre building, was an odd venue for a world première—especially by a dramatist whose last effort had opened on Broadway.

The city has been, as Social Democratic and Labour Party (SDLP) leader John Hume points out, 'a microcosm of the Irish problem'.[16] Historically, it is central to both the unionist and nationalist consciousness. For unionists, Derry, which withstood a lengthy siege by James II in 1689 to make possible the continuation of Protestant rule, is a symbol of their determination to remain British. For nationalists, who constitute a majority in Derry but a minority in the North as a whole, the gerrymandering that kept a Protestant minority in power in the city stands out as one of the most egregious of the official and legal discriminations practised against Catholics in Northern Ireland until recently.

Derry has also suffered from the current Troubles,[17] arguably more than any other Northern Irish town except Belfast. In order to appreciate the context in which Field Day performed it may be useful here to review some of the major events of the previous fifteen years, many of which took place in Derry, the 'cockpit of the Troubles'.[18] Perhaps as good a place as any to start is with the 1944 Education Act, which on the basis of examination results made a superior secondary education available to working-class children throughout the British Isles. The start of the civil rights movement in Northern Ireland may be largely attributed to the emergence of a Catholic middle class that was frustrated by discrimination in housing, voting, government, and employment. There were some hopeful signs in the early to middle 1960s—the IRA campaign of 1956–62 failed to attract and consolidate the support of the Catholic community in the North; Terence O'Neill, the Prime Minister of Northern Ireland, and Sean Lemass, the Taoiseach of the Republic, exchanged visits in 1965 with the aim of encouraging greater economic co-operation; Northern Ireland was gradually becoming a centre of the man-made fibres industry; and, in January 1965, the Nationalist Party decided to become the Official Opposition at Stormont, thus signalling a new willingness to work for their goals within Northern Ireland—but persistent problems of unemployment and political corruption remained. In the mid-1960s, Derry had the highest unemployment, four-fifths of it Catholic, for a city of its size in Western Europe.[19]

At the beginning of 1965 the suspicion was pronounced, and finally shared by unionists and nationalists alike, that the north-west of the province was being systematically downgraded by the government at Stormont.[20] By January, Derry had seen its sea links to Liverpool and Glasgow cut and the closure of the Royal Naval Air Station at Eglinton which had employed about 1,000 civilians. Monarch Electric Company, a major local employer, was threatening to lay off another 1,000, and the Joint Royal Navy–Royal Air Force Anti-Submarine Training School was likely to go the way of the Air Station. That month the Transport Tribunal approved the closing of the Londonderry–Portadown railway line, further limiting the city's access to the rest of the country. The O'Neill government's priority appeared to be development east of the Bann, with planning for the new town of Craigavon regarded as a case in point.

'Is it any wonder', a leader writer in the unionist *Londonderry Sentinel* inquired, 'that Londonderry people have become despondent over the past few weeks? Is it any wonder that they are becoming more and more convinced that the cards are stacked against them?' After a sideswipe at the nationalists who, it was alleged, had been blackening the reputation of the city in Great Britain, he concluded that 'Petty criticisms that have been hurled about in the past . . . must be cast aside, and there must be a unity of purpose and endeavour to get Derry back on the industrial map.'[21] The nationalist *Derry Journal* responded in kind:

It has taken the Unionists of Derry a long time to waken up to the fact that, where this city's vital interests are concerned, it is not a divided, but an isolated, city. If those who have held the reins of office here had not taken so long to realise that what this city wanted, and wants, from the powers-that-be in Belfast, is recognition of its grievous industrial needs, not the Mecca-like regard of adherents of certain principles, the economic cards might not have been so badly stacked against it as they are now.

Let's cut out the wailing and the moaning. The united purpose of the citizens in matters affecting the economic future of the city is beyond question. Let's get that purpose, that determination, working to good effect.[22]

One hope above all inspired the citizens of Derry at this time. It had been suggested in 1960 that Northern Ireland would soon need a second university to relieve the strain on the Queen's University, Belfast, and, besides its value as a mark of prestige and the immediate income from an influx of students, it was widely believed that the site of the new university would become a locus for industrial and commercial development. Most people in Derry believed that their city would be the obvious place for it. With a population close to 70,000, it was the second-largest city in the province and a centre for the entire north-west of Ireland. Modern hospitals in the area made it an attractive place for a medical school, and the natural environment of Derry offered a contrast to Belfast and provided ample scope for development in the biological sciences. Moreover, for the past 100 years the city had been the home of Magee University College, a two-year institution that sent students to finish their degrees at Trinity College, Dublin. Derry residents thought that the obvious way to get the new university off the ground immediately would be to grant university status to Magee and then work on expanding it. In 1962 the Londonderry Corporation, united for once, made formal application for the honour of having the university sited in the city. The eight-member Lockwood Committee was appointed in 1963 to study the educational needs of the province and make recommendations.[23] Originally it was only instructed to advise on the academic subjects that should be taught, but later, on its own initiative, it had its competence extended to include the question of location.

By the end of 1964, apprehension was growing in Derry that the decision of the committee would not be congenial. Many believed that opponents of Derry were slandering it as a city where party politics would hinder the development of the new university, and in order to counter this supposed objection the citizens mobilized in a striking display of unity. Leaders of the Roman Catholic, Presbyterian, Methodist, and Church of Ireland congregations issued a joint declaration in favour of Derry's claim, and local groups from the Unionist and Nationalist Parties to the Irish Transport and General Workers' Union, the Shirt Manufacturers' Federation, and the Licensed Vintners Association passed resolutions pledging their support.

On 8 February the interdenominational and inter-party University for Derry Committee, headed by local schoolteacher John Hume, convened a meeting in Derry's Guildhall attended by over 1,500 people 'representative of every political shade, all religious creeds and every facet of educational, professional, business and trade union life in the city'.[24] The Unionist mayor, Albert Anderson, expressed the view that a university would bring industries to Derry, 'which would help to unite the people in the North-West in a way they have never been united for generations', and the head of the Nationalist Party, Eddie McAteer, declared: 'They may be able to slap down the men of Derry; they may be able to slap down the men of Londonderry, but they have no chance at all of slapping down the combined team of Derry and Londonderry.'[25]

Two days later, the University Committee sent a deputation to O'Neill to present Derry's case yet again. That same morning, however, the Lockwood Report was issued, recommending, among numerous other things, that the university should be placed in Coleraine, a small and overwhelmingly unionist town on the north coast. A government white paper was issued along with the report, endorsing it. People in Derry were outraged and planned a mass lobby of Stormont.

On 18 February a large motorcade led by McAteer and Anderson began the eighty-mile trek to Belfast after being seen off by several thousand people in Guildhall Square. Other vehicles joined along the way, in Strabane, Omagh, and Enniskillen, and nearly 2,000 of them—limousines, furniture vans, coal lorries, bread vans, family cars—finally surrounded the Northern Irish Parliament building. They were met there by a sizeable crowd, including many Queen's students, and thousands watched as a petition was handed to the Prime Minister, along with a formal reply to the Lockwood Report. In Derry, where the mayor had ordered a public holiday, those who could not make the trip to Belfast observed two minutes of silence.

The government was unmoved. Not only did it put the party whip on Unionist MPs to vote for the adoption of the report, but it linked that vote to a vote of confidence in the government. When the Stormont Parliament voted to approve Lockwood by a vote of twenty-seven to nineteen, few were surprised though many were disgusted. Most of the members who participated in the debate on 3–4 March 1965 had named Derry as their preferred site for the university, and there was little doubt in the mind of anyone in the north-west that the site recommendation would have been rejected on a free vote. As one MP remarked in the course of the debate, 'One becomes increasingly nauseated by the two-faced attitude of the Government, who could continually praise the Maiden City, laud Derry's Walls and its "No Surrender" and, at the same time, stab it between the shoulder blades.'[26]

Unfortunately, the new solidarity of Derry did not long survive the frustration of its dearest hope. Even during the campaign old animosities occasionally surfaced. The dilemma of Unionists, torn between loyalty to the Party and the government and common regional cause with the Nationalists, was epitomized in the experience of E. W. Jones, MP for the city of Derry and Attorney General. He felt compelled, because of his position in the government, to vote against the city. At the annual meeting of the City of London-derry and Foyle Unionist Association—a meeting at which the members passed overwhelmingly (no debate being necessary) the resolution 'That this meeting calls on the Government of Northern Ireland to establish the second university for Northern Ireland in or near Londonderry'—he attempted to justify his position. Jones warned,

when the story of this affair is told one cannot but wonder how many of our political opponents are chortling and rubbing their hands because they may feel that they stood in a fair way to achieve the slaughter of at least two birds with one stone, namely a split in the Unionist ranks and the embarrassment of not only the Unionist Member for the Constituency but also a Member of the Government.[27]

An editorial in the *Derry Journal* was an indignant response to this insinuation: 'What hope is there to be for co-operation for a community's good in this area if it is to be destroyed by the sowing of dark suspicion and mistrust and an imputation of wooden horse tactics and sinister motives such as Mr. Jones has conjured up?'[28]

The unionists, however, did not have a monopoly on 'dark suspicion'. In an attempt to explain what seemed to them an irrational decree from Stormont, a 'faceless men' conspiracy theory quickly sprang up among Derry nationalists: certain prominent unionists, it was rumoured, had worked behind the scenes for their town's continued deprivation.[29] As Frank Curran, long-time editor of the *Derry Journal*, declared in 1986,

the hidden forces of extreme Unionism were adamant that a prize like the university could not be permitted to go to Derry, where it might well create a radical and largely anti-Unionist atmosphere that would render the continuance of the gerrymander virtually impossible, and make unchallenged Unionist control of the North less certain.[30]

The disappointment over the university is still remembered by many in Derry as the final straw, the real start of the present Troubles. The effect on nationalists was particularly devastating because the undemocratic way in which the matter was decided confirmed their worst fears about the processes of government in Northern Ireland at the very time when they were making tentative moves toward more extensive participation. John Hume recalls,

The university decision . . . electrified the people on the nationalist side, and I think was really the spark that ignited the civil rights movement, though I suppose nobody could have articulated it in those terms then. And when the university went to Coleraine, the chance of orderly change in Northern Ireland probably disappeared.[31]

The ill-fated crusade was, none the less, 'a form of dramatic, political, street education for the people of the city'.[32]

Seamus Heaney, who would later become active in Field Day, wrote of the mood of the province in 1966, 'Life goes on, yet people are reluctant to dismiss the possibility of an explosion. A kind of doublethink operates: something is rotten, but maybe if we wait it will fester to death.'[33] In Derry, the Unionists who controlled the Corporation were unwilling to alter the electoral boundaries or the city's limits, since that would destroy their artificial majority. This attitude hampered them in making improvements on the terrible housing situation. During this time of rising tensions, Brian Friel's father, Patrick Friel, was a Nationalist councillor for Derry.[34]

Large-scale lay-offs at the Monarch Electric plant precipitated a mass demonstration in Derry in November of 1966. When

Monarch closed altogether in January 1967, the unemployment total in the city climbed to over 5,000.[35] Soon there were civil rights marches as well. In February 1967, the Northern Ireland Civil Rights Association (NICRA) was formed to press for an end to gerrymandering, a fair allocation of housing and local government jobs, and 'one man, one vote' in local elections.[36] On 5 October 1968, NICRA planned a march in Derry that was banned by the Stormont government. The organizers decided to go ahead with the demonstration, and when the marchers reached and attempted to pass police cordons set up along their route, members of the Royal Ulster Constabulary beat them with batons, provoking rioting that lasted well into the night. About a hundred people were injured by the police, and the event received national and international news coverage.[37] In an article for *The Listener*, Seamus Heaney expressed the disillusionment of many Catholics at the fact that neither Westminster nor Stormont had ordered an investigation into the behaviour of the police:

Since the Cabinet have endorsed the actions of the police and still deny any notion of the injustice in a blatantly unjust situation, one can only conclude that their definition of 'improved relations' is 'the minority saying nothing to embarrass us'. . . . Indeed, a cliché-mongering movement begins to be discerned in Unionist speeches associating civil rights with 'communist and republican elements' and dropping the matter there—not that the rest of us are particularly reassured by the presence of Orangemen in the Cabinet.[38]

John Hume, together with other nationalist leaders worried about how to channel the protest in positive directions, founded the Derry Citizens Action Committee (DCAC) on 9 October. Local activist Eamonn McCann, however, 'stomped out' of the meeting that resulted in the formation of this group, denouncing its officers as 'middle-aged, middle-class and middle of the road'.[39] Over the next few weeks the DCAC organized a number of protests and sit-downs, culminating in a march on 16 November over the same route as before, in which 15,000 people participated. On 22 November, the Londonderry Corporation was abolished by the Northern Ireland government. Meanwhile, young leftists based around Queen's University, such as Bernadette Devlin and Michael Farrell, radicalized the student civil rights organization, People's Democracy (PD).[40]

The following year was one of mounting pressure, as extremists on all sides gained prominence. The first day of 1969 marked the start of a People's Democracy march from Belfast to Derry. On 4 January, near the end of their trip, the walkers were attacked at Burntollet Bridge by a group of hostile loyalists, including what were believed to be off-duty B-Specials (members of the exclusively Protestant part-time auxiliary police). There were rumours of collusion with the Royal Ulster Constabulary (RUC) as well. The incident sparked off extensive rioting against the police, who used water cannon to disperse several hundred people who had trapped the Protestant leader the Reverend Ian Paisley and his supporters in the Guildhall.[41] At 2 a.m. that night, a group of policemen invaded the Catholic Bogside area of the city where, as the Cameron Commission later appointed by the British government to investigate found, they were guilty of misconduct ranging from assault and battery to the use of provocative and sectarian slogans. No policeman was ever punished for participation in the harrassment, and residents of the Bogside immediately formed vigilante groups to protect themselves against law enforcement officials.

There was more rioting in the city during the weekend of 18–20 April, when the government banned another civil rights march, and on 29 April O'Neill resigned as Prime Minister. Sporadic disturbances continued through the summer, but the day that people regarded with most apprehension was 12 August, when the loyalist Apprentice Boys clubs from all parts meet for their annual march through Derry in commemoration of the lifting of the siege laid against the city in 1689 by James II. Catholics prepared for a major confrontation on that day—according to Bogside lore, the milkman is supposed to have received notes reading 'no milk, but leave 200 bottles'.[42] Rioting began early in the afternoon, and police forced Catholic rioters down into the Bogside where they retreated behind their barricades and began throwing petrol bombs. The RUC responded with CS gas, and the 'Battle of the Bogside' was under way. It lasted three days, and by the end of the first day 112 people had been treated in hospital. On 14 August, the government of Northern Ireland asked Westminster for help, and Prime Minister Harold Wilson and Home Secretary James Callaghan agreed that troops should be sent as a temporary emergency measure. The call for troops had had the support of such diverse leaders as John Hume and Bernadette Devlin, and the soldiers were greeted with enthusiasm by the Catholics of the Bogside. During the next few days, they were also deployed in Belfast. Although things calmed down upon the arrival of the army, both communities had already formed defence committees at the grassroots level which would become the nuclei for paramilitary groups.[43]

The year 1970 saw rearranging and renaming on a number of fronts. The SDLP was formed to replace the old Nationalist Party, the Ulster Defence Regiment replaced the discredited B-Specials, and, perhaps most important in determining future events, the Republican movement split and the Provisional IRA emerged. The civil rights rhetoric was beginning to give way to traditional republican demands.[44] After July 1971, when the first two Derry people were killed by the Army (the first British soldier had been killed in February of the same year), recruitment to the Provisional IRA rose dramatically. On 9 August 1971, the Northern Ireland government resorted to internment without trial of 'suspects', rounding up 346 prisoners, none of them Protestant, on the basis of outdated police lists.[45] The Provisionals responded with their bombing campaign against 'economic targets'.[46] The increased polarization of that time is reflected in a poem by Seamus Heaney which first appeared as an epigraph to his *Wintering Out* collection (1972). Dedicated to his Protestant friends Michael Longley and David Hammond, it opens with the visible signs of division and ends with something close to an acceptance of fate:

> Is there a life before death? That's chalked up
> on a wall downtown. Competence with pain,
> coherent miseries, a bite and sup,
> we hug our little destiny again.[47]

One of the most devastating episodes of the Troubles, particularly for Catholics in Derry, was Bloody Sunday, 30 January 1972. During a prohibited anti-internment rally in the city, British troops fired 108 live rounds in the Bogside, killing thirteen men, seven of whom were less than 19 years old (one more died later, and fourteen people were seriously injured). The army claimed to have been shot at first, but there was scant evidence of this. The report of the Widgery Tribunal, set up by the government to investigate these events, concluded that 'Soldiers who identified armed gunmen fired upon them in accordance with the standing orders in the Yellow Card. Each soldier was his own judge of whether he had

identified a gunman.' When the Widgery report was published in
April 1972 it was immediately rejected by the nationalist community as whitewash.[48] Ten years later, Brian Friel recalled that

It was really a shattering experience that the British Army, this disciplined
instrument, would go in as they did that time and shoot thirteen people. To
be there on that occasion and—I didn't actually see people get shot—but I
mean, to have to throw yourself on the ground because people are firing at
you is a very terrifying experience. Then the whole cover-up afterwards
was shattering too. We still have some kind of belief that the law is above
reproach.[49]

Another future Field Day director, Seamus Deane, writing shortly
after Bloody Sunday, expressed the emotions of the time in poetry:

> And when the storm passed
> We came out of the back rooms
> Wishing we could say
> Ruin itself would last.[50]

The IRA response to Bloody Sunday was to announce its intention to 'kill every British soldier [it] could'.[51] Civilians as well as
soldiers were killed, by Protestant murder gangs as well as by the
IRA, and 1972 became the bloodiest year to date of the Troubles,
with 474 left dead. On 24 March 1972, the British government
suspended the Northern Ireland government at Stormont and introduced direct rule from Westminster, an arrangement that persists to
the present day.[52] This was also the year that Derry's Guildhall was
bombed twice in the same week in June.[53]

The major political event of 1973 was the Sunningdale con-
ference in December, at which British, Northern Irish, and Irish
representatives agreed that the constitution of Northern Ireland
would not be changed without the consent of the Protestant majority. They also made plans to establish a power-sharing executive
for Northern Ireland of Unionist, SDLP, and Alliance Party members. This executive formally took office in 1974 but collapsed by
the end of May, brought down by the Ulster Workers' Council
strike of Protestant workers who objected to the 'Irish dimension'
insisted upon by the SDLP.[54] On the local level, in Derry, things
went rather better—local power-sharing arrangements made in
1973 have continued with a few interruptions until now, with the

SDLP claiming the largest share of the Council seats. Meanwhile, community divisions in Northern Ireland remained, and the violence continued and became a fact of daily life.

One of the more bizarre aspects of the plan to open an original Brian Friel play in Derry was the suggestion by the City Council that the company use the Assembly Hall of the Guildhall as an auditorium. This building had been a favoured target of the IRA precisely because it had symbolized so well Unionist domination of the city. When *Translations* opened on 23 September 1980, the Guildhall was barricaded against further terrorist attacks and was still covered with scaffolding used by workmen to repair damage done by the last bombers. An exquisite touch of irony, which did not go unremarked at the time, was that the Guildhall had been the setting for *The Freedom of the City*, a thinly veiled dramatization of the events of Bloody Sunday, in which three civil rights marchers are first trapped in the building and then shot as 'terrorists'. In that play, Skinner, played at one time by Stephen Rea, tells his fellow captives in the Guildhall 'this is theirs, boy, and your very presence here is a sacrilege'.[55]

But if it was a symbol the Guildhall was a multi-faceted one. In 1980 it represented not only a corrupt past, but a more hopeful present and future. The new power-sharing Council which had replaced the Londonderry Corporation was finally giving the Catholic majority a meaningful voice in civic affairs, and councillors were anxious to promote culture and peaceful pursuits in the city. The Guildhall had been used in times past as a location for amateur theatricals, although *Translations* was the first professionally cast play to be rehearsed and have its first showing there.[56] It had not been pressed into service in this capacity for about a decade (roughly corresponding to the duration of the Troubles), but it had once been, for some, 'a symbol of how two cultures could meet in peace and throw away their cares in front of the footlights'.[57]

The occasion of the opening of *Translations* in Derry was used by those local people who were pressing for a purpose-built civic theatre.[58] Friel himself had previously been a leading campaigner for this cause.[59] The necessity of using the Guildhall, with its unyielding design and poor acoustics, was a bitter reminder that 'Derry would already have a theatre if Northern Ireland's second university had been built there, as it should have been.'[60] Instead, the 'university and the civic theatre which should have been Derry's were shunted off to Loyalist Coleraine'.[61]

With this legacy of frustration implicit in the use of the Guildhall as a theatre, the whole-hearted enthusiasm evinced by the entire population for the *Translations* project takes on added significance. On 23 May 1980, the City Council agreed to donate the Guildhall as an auditorium and added a promise to provide lighting facilities and build a new stage for the production. The very next day councillors received a notice from the central government in London that no funds would be forthcoming from that source for anything not already in the budget. The Council decided to support the play itself, which it did to the tune of over £13,000.[62] In addition to this substantial contribution out of its own funds, the Council gave the company assistance with advertising, typing, and other general work, and councillors and council staff were present at every publicity function.[63]

The interest of the general public in the project was also intense. The decision to stage the show in Derry was announced in early June, and rehearsals began in mid-August. The local newspapers, principally the weekly *Londonderry Sentinel* and the semi-weekly *Derry Journal*, were assiduous in covering every conceivable aspect of the pre-production preparations—there were at least nine articles or photographs in these two papers in the two weeks before the play opened on 23 September. Much was made of Ann Hasson, an actress in the play who was a native of Derry, and of the fact that Ray McAnally, who played the hedge schoolmaster, was born in nearby Moville.[64] The *Derry Journal* featured an article on 'Derry Women in *Translations*', which, in addition to focusing on Ann Hasson, included interviews with Margo Harkin, the assistant stage manager, Finola O'Doherty, the administrative assistant, and Mary Friel (the playwright's daughter), who was helping with costumes.[65] On 10 September, the *Derry Journal* gave a comprehensive description of the installation of the stage and lighting equipment, in its loving attention to detail not omitting to mention the slope of the new stage. The *Londonderry Sentinel* countered next day with a slightly different angle on the same event. In an article whimsically entitled 'Councillors in the Dark', the paper recounted the disruption of the City Council Amenities and Leisure Committee meeting that ensued during the installation of the extra lighting, when normal Guildhall illumination was temporarily disconnected. The *Sentinel* then followed up on 17 September with a photograph of the new stage being built.[66] Photographs of rehearsals were also frequently printed in local and regional papers in the last weeks before the opening.

Apart from this widespread publicity, there were more direct contacts between the people involved in the production and the inhabitants of Derry. Members of the cast visited schools in the city and talked to children about the play and theatre in general. David Heap, the English actor who played Captain Lancey, helped to organize these visits and reported that they were warmly received.[67] The Irish critic Michael Sheridan commented on the community spirit surrounding the launching of Field Day's first production. According to the director, Art O'Briain, 'There is a vibrancy and vitality about this venture which no pure theatrical opening could ever hope to achieve. . . . we feel that we have become part of the community around us'.[68]

Friel was pleased to note that the play was attracting some positive coverage for Derry and that something other than tragedy and violence would be seen to be emanating from the city.[69] City officials were not oblivious to this aspect of the project. They also regarded the Guildhall production as an interim measure that would stimulate public interest in theatre while efforts continued to get a purpose-built theatre for Derry. In the light of all this, it became a matter of civic pride that the audiences should be large and enthusiastic. The *Derry Journal* reminded its readers on 19 September:

It is appropriate that this world première should be staged in Derry. The city is renowned the world over for its traditions in the field of culture and in the different art forms and its citizens are always on the market for first-class entertainment. The Council are convinced that the attendances at this new play by Brian Friel will bear witness to our great traditions in the cultural field.[70]

Lurking behind this exhortation must have been the awareness that what Derry was 'renowned the world over' for in 1980 was decidedly not 'its traditions in the field of culture'. Ticket sales were watched anxiously. By 12 September the opening night was sold out, and on 23 September the *Derry Journal* could report proudly that every ticket for every scheduled performance had been sold and an extra matinée had been added to accommodate the demand.[71]

Opening night was a highly emotional occasion. The real-life theatricality of the Derry opening was part and parcel of the impact of the original production, especially within Northern Ireland. An *Irish Press* editorial called it 'a unique occasion, with loyalists and nationalists, Unionists and SDLP, Northerners and Southerners laying aside their differences to join together in applauding a play by a fellow Derryman'.[72] After the play, the Unionist Mayor, Marlene Jefferson, led the audience in a standing ovation, and Friel was called on to the stage to receive its adulation in person. As the *Strabane Chronicle* described it a few days later, 'Tuesday's opening night was one of atmosphere—the likes of which even London drama critics who attended had never experienced at a world première.'[73] David Nowlan, veteran critic for the *Irish Times*, devoted his entire column to an account of the event, which he described as an 'electric love affair'. A review, he said, would have to 'await the cooler consideration of the grey Foyle morning'.[74] Paddy Woodworth, the company manager, said that if they had not already made plans to take the show on the road, they could have continued playing in Derry for a couple of months, and a council official told a reporter that he had 'not seen Derry so electrified by an event since Charlie Nash went up for the world title'.[75]

Perhaps others in the audience were reminded of another night, that of 8 February 1965, when Mayor Albert Anderson presided at a public meeting in the Guildhall:

In the emotional atmosphere there were no majorities or minorities, only Derry people who crammed into the Assembly Hall, the corridors outside and the stairs from the ground floor. Solicitor Arthur Jack told them that if the university was sited anywhere other than in Derry, it would be by the operation of influence and not justice.[76]

At least one observer experienced a feeling of *déjà vu*:

It was also a nostalgic occasion, with lots of seminal figures from the past, like John Hume, Mary Holland and Eamonn McCann trooping past Queen Victoria in the Guildhall foyer to the Unionist holy of holies, which made a rather echoey theatre. The audience's deep appreciation of the play, not just for its Derry author, convinced me again that the insult of the decision to site the second university at Coleraine was, in fact, the root of many of our ills.[77]

Translations would be a hit of major proportions throughout the British Isles and, indeed, the world. In Derry, however, civic pride, interdenominational co-operation, a troubled history, changing political configurations, and a defensive feeling common to the North as a whole about its international reputation combined to make the show's première of more than purely theatrical significance. Field Day was off to a rousing start.

2

Translations:
On the Page and On the Stage

THE critical response to *Translations* was generally as over-whelmingly positive as the popular reaction. The play was well received, not only in Derry, but everywhere it went on its two-month tour, which eventually grew to include fourteen cities and towns in both Northern Ireland and the Republic.[1] In a year of good new Irish plays, *Translations* was the smash hit of the Dublin Theatre Festival, with all seats at all performances, including two added shows, sold out.[2] It was not forgotten, either, in the end-of-the-year round-ups on both sides of the border. In Dublin, the *Evening Herald* proclaimed *Translations* the Best New Irish Play of the Year, while the *Sunday Independent* hailed the setting-up of the Field Day Theatre Company as the Theatrical Event of the Year. The *Belfast Telegraph* recognized Ray McAnally as the Best Actor of 1980 for his role in *Translations*.[3] A separate production opened the following year in London and was also extremely successful.

Since 1980 *Translations* has become a standard part of the repertoire of the Abbey Theatre in Dublin, where it has been produced several times. The play has been performed by dozens of amateur groups, particularly in Ireland, and has been seen by many thousands of people. The BBC has broadcast it twice as a radio play,[4] and Friel recalls that there have been productions in Norway, France, Germany, Finland, Australia, Canada, the United States, and Estonia, among other places.[5] Within a few years the play had acquired the status of a classic. *Translations* is now generally regarded as what Michael Sheridan declared it to be two days after it opened: a watershed in Irish theatre.[6]

How is one to account for the extraordinary and seemingly universal appeal of this play? Friel himself was taken by surprise by the overwhelming popularity of *Translations*, commenting that 'Nowadays, to write a three-act naturalistic play set in the 19th century in the Gaeltacht is a recipe for some kind of instant death, so its success astonished me.'[7] Certainly the production was excellent, and the simple fact that the play was produced at all meant a great deal to the people of Derry. Critics, however, both at the time and since, have referred too often to the play's 'theme' for us to ignore its actual content. What *Translations* was 'about' is a matter, clearly, of urgent concern. Accordingly, we will now turn to the published script of the play.[8]

Translations is set in a hedge school in County Donegal in 1833—about thirty years after the Act of Union with Great Britain. It is essentially a play of retrospect, in which Friel, a twentieth-century Irishman, imaginatively recreates a moment in time in which he perceives the beginning of the end of traditional Gaelic culture in Ireland. The audience looks in on Baile Beag,[9] an Irish village that has existed in the same way for centuries but is about to be changed forever. 'We like to think we endure around truths immemorially posited,' says one of the villagers (418), but hints of the new order abound. There are rumours of potato blight, a new national school is about to open in the neighbourhood to replace the hedge school, and British soldiers have been sent to the parish to work on the Ordnance Survey of the United Kingdom. One of the Survey's jobs is to translate the Irish place-names into English. In the world of the play this translation stands for colonial dispossession, because the history of places (as Friel's continuous interjection of etymological jokes and stories makes clear) is contained in the names they bear. As one of the characters observes, 'It's an eviction of sorts' (420).

As written, the play is a fairly balanced portrayal of the various tensions between the Irish and English characters that result from mutual misunderstanding and arrogance. The central character is Hugh, the drunken hedge schoolmaster and classical scholar. He looks down on English as a language of 'commerce' and tells one of the British officers, 'I'm afraid we're not familiar with your literature. . . . We feel closer to the warm Mediterranean. We tend to overlook your island' (399, 417). The director of the Survey in the area, Captain Lancey, is an uncultivated military man who treats the Irish people in the play like children because they do not speak English, although he himself cannot tell the difference between Irish and Latin.

Friel is at pains to avoid writing about 'rude peasants', but, if Lancey is a bit heavy-handed, he undermines the 'ruthless conqueror' stereotype as well through the introduction of Lieutenant George Yolland. Yolland is along as the survey's orthographer; it is his job to transliterate the place-names for the new maps. 'A soldier by accident' (stage direction, 404), he comes to regret his part in the project. In Baile Beag he found 'a consciousness that wasn't striving nor agitated, but at its ease and with its own conviction and assurance' (416). He loves Ireland, falls in love with an Irish girl, and wants to stay on in Donegal. Throughout the play he is trying to learn Irish, but wonders if he will ever stop being an outsider, confiding his fear that 'I may learn the password but the language of the tribe will always elude me, won't it?' (416).

Yolland's Irish assistant, Owen, is Hugh's returning son. He has made his fortune in Dublin and in a pragmatic, unsentimental way is willing to help the English drag Baile Beag into the modern world. There is, though, another side to Owen that recognizes the value of the old names and the culture they embody and is concerned about their impending loss. In a relatively early renaming scene, he and Yolland discuss the fate of 'Tobair Vree', a corruption of the Irish for 'Brian's Well'. Owen asks impatiently, 'do we keep piety with a man long dead, long forgotten, his name "eroded" beyond recognition, whose trivial little story nobody in the parish remembers?' 'Except you,' Yolland answers mildly, but Owen's firm rejoinder is 'I've left here' (420–1). Later in the play, however, Owen's approach to his job becomes markedly more conservative, as he translates 'the Murren' back to its original form, 'Saint Muranus' (431).

If Owen is the prodigal, his lame brother Manus is the loyal son who has stayed at the hedge school and helped his father over the years. Manus is the most stubborn adherent to the old ways, and although he knows English (as does Hugh) he refuses to speak it. He accuses Owen of betraying his tribe, and certainly some of Owen's 'translations' are dubious in the extreme.[10] Perhaps the most fundamental conflict in the play, although overshadowed by the more obvious one between the English and the Irish, is that between Owen and Manus. In this latent confrontation between brothers is epitomized the choice between a modern, Anglicized Ireland and a traditional, Gaelic one. In the end Manus hurriedly departs from 'Ballybeg'—there is no longer any place for him there. The field is thus left to Owen, but he himself is having second thoughts by this time.

The remaining characters, the pupils at the hedge school, include the mute Sarah, Jimmy Jack Cassie (the elderly 'Infant Prodigy' who talks to himself in Latin and Greek), Bridget and Doalty (less talented students), and Maire, who is the object of both Manus's and Yolland's affection. She is anxious to learn English in preparation for her impending emigration to America and thus represents the forces for change already working within Baile Beag itself.

The tragic aspect of the play is that it tells a story without villains in any obvious sense. There is no blind hatred between the Irish and the English on a personal level; the villagers like Yolland and are willing to give even Lancey the benefit of the doubt, and the soldiers are making, not war, but a six-inch map. However, no peaceful solution seems possible in this clash between two cultures. The difficulty of the situation is demonstrated by the renaming process. Naming is generally thought of as an either-or activity—a place will be called either one thing or the other. *Translations* asks what kind of compromise is possible in a case like that, when each side insists on the exclusive rights of its own vision of the world.

Nevertheless, things begin well enough, with both sides prepared to tolerate each other's idiosyncracies. Maire reports that the soldiers have even volunteered to help her family bring in the hay: 'I don't know a word they're saying, nor they me; but sure that doesn't matter, does it?' (389). The rest of the play attempts an answer to this casual question. Initially it appears that it does not matter. The soldiers are at first welcomed warmly by the students of the hedge school. As friends, Owen and Yolland work well together. An even more significant bridging is that achieved by Maire and Yolland. In their brief love scene they manage to overcome for an instant the barriers of language and culture. Ironically, the only words they share are the Irish place-names that Yolland is there to destroy, but they repeat them to each other like a litany.

Friel, however, does not give his audience licence to imagine that love conquers all. For him affection and mutual respect on the personal level cannot act as a panacea for the dislocations of cultural upheaval. Yolland and Maire connect, but their love has disastrous consequences: Manus leaves the village, Yolland disappears (the implication is that he has been abducted and killed by the mysterious 'Donnelly twins', delinquent hedge scholars), Manus will be suspected, and Lancey threatens reprisals against the whole village unless Yolland is found. Nothing is firmly resolved by the end of the play; we never find out what has happened to Yolland or what becomes of the village. As several reviewers commented, this open-endedness brings the concerns of the play into the present day.

None the less, the three main Irish characters—Hugh, Owen, and Manus—react to the new situation in ways that suggest three possible answers to the main question posed by the play: What should be the attitude of Irish people towards the fact of English domination? Manus tries to ignore the English; he leaves the fallen Ballybeg to take up a teaching job in a hedge school on Inis Meadhon, an island where the Gaelic culture still survives. The futility of this approach is evident, though. The Survey will be there, too, 'by December' (423). Owen, no longer the self-assured joker he was in the first act, rejects his role in the mapping project, symbolically letting the Name-Book drop to the floor and dismissing it to his father as 'my mistake—nothing to do with us' (444). In the end, he leaves to look for Doalty Dan Doalty, who had previously sworn, 'I've damned little to defend but he'll not put me out without a fight' (441).

Hugh, however, suddenly demonstrates an unsuspected ability to adapt. He waves aside Owen's apology for the Name-Book and announces that 'We must learn those new names. . . . We must learn where we live. We must learn to make them our own. We must make them our new home' (444). He cautions his younger son, 'it is not the literal past, the "facts" of history, that shape us, but images of the past embodied in language. . . . we must never cease renewing those images; because once we do, we fossilize. . . . To remember everything is a form of madness' (445).[11] After refusing to do so throughout the play, Hugh finally agrees to teach Maire English: 'But don't expect too much. I will provide you with the available words and the available grammar. But will that help you to interpret between privacies? I have no idea. But it's all we have' (446). In contrast to his earlier pronouncement about 'truths immemorially posited', he now tells Maire sharply that 'always' is 'not a word I'd start with. It's a silly word' (446). By giving Hugh in this frame of mind the last word, *Translations* becomes a play about living within the situation in which you find yourself, however much you may regret the circumstances that have forced such an accommodation on you. The final blackout is on Hugh reciting from the first book of the *Aeneid* the story of another great civilization that met an untimely end.[12] If any character in the play can be taken to speak for Friel, it is Hugh.

In *Translations* the playwright concerns himself consistently with language and what it means. As mentioned earlier, the displacement of one language by another in the play, epitomized by the changing of place-names, is a metaphor for the alienation experienced by Irish people under English rule. The two most remarkable features of the play, noted by virtually all contemporary reviewers from the most sophisticated London and Dublin critics to anonymous correspondents for small local papers, are: (1) the convention whereby the audience is led to believe that it is hearing both Irish and English spoken when in fact everyone is speaking English, and (2) the love scene between Maire and Yolland in which they manage to convey their affection for each other without the benefit of a common language.[13]

For many of the ideas informing his treatment of language in the play Friel was indebted to George Steiner, whose book *After Babel* he was reading while writing *Translations* and working on a version of Chekhov's *Three Sisters*. Friel acknowledged Steiner in the programme notes, and several of the play's most memorable lines are taken almost verbatim from this book. For example, Hugh's remark that 'it can happen that a civilization can be imprisoned in a linguistic contour which no longer matches the landscape of . . . fact' (419) is an echo of Steiner's dictum that 'A civilization is imprisoned in a linguistic contour which no longer matches . . . the changing landscape of fact.'[14]

Steiner's fundamental point is that translation is only a special case of communication in general. All human speech involves a large component of interpretation:

> Any model of communication is at the same time a model of translation, of a vertical or horizontal transfer of significance. No two historical epochs, no two social classes, no two localities use words and syntax to signify exactly the same things, to send identical signals of valuation and inference. Neither do two human beings.[15]

Perhaps his most radical suggestion is that 'communication outward is only a secondary, socially stimulated phase in the acquisition of language. Speaking to oneself would be the primary function.'[16] He argues that the greatest power of language is its capacity for 'counter-factuality' ('*Language is the main instrument of man's refusal to accept the world as it is*') and that 'Human speech conceals far more than it confides; it blurs much more than it defines; it distances more than it connects.'[17]

Steiner's model of communication is one of concentric circles spreading outwards from the most inner, private speech to a speech that includes larger and larger groups of people:

> We speak first to ourselves, then to those nearest us in kinship and locale. We turn only gradually to the outsider, and we do so with every safeguard of obliqueness, of reservation, of conventional flatness or outright misguidance. At its intimate centre, in the zone of familial or totemic immediacy, our language is most economic of explanation, most dense with intentionality and compacted implication. Streaming outward it thins, losing energy and pressure as it reaches an alien speaker.[18]

This substantial element of exclusiveness in language means that 'there is in every act of translation—and specially where it succeeds—a touch of treason'.[19]

In the debate between the 'universalists' (who believe differences between languages are surface phenomena) and the 'monadists', Steiner aligns himself more with the latter in maintaining that each language creates its own particular 'mapping' of conscious being, of 'reality'. Nevertheless, Steiner does not contend, as some extreme monadists have, that translation is therefore impossible. It would be logically inconsistent for him to argue this without arguing as well that communication of any kind is an impossibility. Instead he asserts that, though good translation is extremely rare and there is no such thing as perfect translation, there are 'examples which seem to approach the limits of empirical possibility'.[20] He seems to say, like Hugh at the end of *Translations*, 'It's all we have.'

Richard Kearney sees the contrast between two conceptions of language, 'one ontological, the other positivistic', as the central focus of Friel's play: 'The former treats language as a house of Being; the latter treats it as a mechanical apparatus for the representation of objects.'[21] He is impressed by Friel's refashioning of Steiner's scholarly work in popular terms, calling the play an outstanding example of how 'criticism may be retranslated back into imaginative practice'.[22] James Simmons agrees, 'the boldness and deftness that makes large audiences dwell on the subtle importance of changing the names of places is stunning'.[23] The diary Friel kept

while he was writing *Translations* records his struggle to incorp-
orate this linguistic theory without betraying the play itself. On 3
July 1979 he wonders, 'Are the characters only mouthpieces. . . . Is
the play only an ideas play? And indeed are those ideas amenable to
dramatic presentation?' On 6 July he isolates one of the problems
he faces as 'the almost wholly *public* concern of the theme. . . .
How long can a *society* live without its tongue?' and reminds
himself of his belief that the play should 'concern itself only with
the exploration of the dark and private places of individual souls'.[24]

Judging from the evident appeal of *Translations* to a large and
very diverse group of people, we might conclude that Friel over-
came these difficulties to write a play full of human interest. That
play none the less deals with theoretical linguistic questions. However, it is somewhat disingenuous to say, as Friel did once (and as
numerous people have quoted him as saying since) that 'the play
has to do with language and only language'.[25] When an Irish
playwright talks about language, it has a political edge. As Friel
remarked in another context, 'The problem with the Northern
situation is how you can tip-toe through the minefields of language
where language has become so politicized. You see, whenever you
have a war, language is always the first casualty.'[26]

This general problem is intensified in Ireland by the close association through many years of Gaelic revival and Irish nationalism.
The national self-consciousness that preceded and helped to shape
the movement for political independence was largely fostered by
the Gaelic League, founded in 1893. The classic statement of the
League's position was made the year before by its founder, Douglas
Hyde, in a speech before the National Literary Society in Dublin
entitled 'The Necessity for de-Anglicizing Ireland'. The gist of his
argument was that the 'failure of the Irish people in recent times
has been largely brought about by the race diverging during this
century from the right path, and ceasing to be Irish without becoming English'. He called special attention to

the illogical position of men who drop their own language to speak
English, of men who translate their euphonious Irish names into English
monosyllables, of men who read English books, and know nothing about
Gaelic literature, nevertheless protesting as a matter of sentiment that they
hate the country which at every hand's turn they rush to imitate. . . .

[W]e must strive to cultivate everything that is most racial, most smacking of the soil, most Gaelic, most Irish, because in spite of the little admixture of Saxon blood in the north-east corner, this island *is* and will *ever* remain Celtic at the core.[27]

Hyde went on to become the first President of Ireland, holding office from 1938–45. Many Republican activists, including Éamon de Valera and Ernest Blythe, received their first quasi-political experience in the Gaelic League. The membership of the League frequently overlapped with that of the Volunteers, Sinn Féin, and the Irish Republican Brotherhood.[28] As Ronan Fanning has pointed out, cultural nationalism became even more important after the creation of the Irish Free State: 'The collapse of an agreed political ideal in a partitioned, non-republican Ireland scarred by civil war made the government hold all the more fervently to an intact cultural ideal.'[29] After the adoption of the 1937 Constitution the issue of 'Gaelicization' became particularly sensitive because it was related to what might be regarded as the abandonment of the North. As de Valera said in February 1939, 'I would not tomorrow, for the sake of a united Ireland, give up the policy of trying to make this a really Irish Ireland'. In the same speech he nominated language revival as the keystone of that policy: 'I believe that as long as the language remains you have a distinguishing characteristic of nationality which will enable the nation to persist.'[30]

The combination, in *Translations*, of language and education would naturally be especially suggestive to politically sensitive Irish men and women because of the Republic's long-standing and ill-fated policy of language revival centred on the schools.[31] At first schoolchildren were taught through the medium of Irish for several hours each day, whether or not their home language was Irish. Gradually, in response to protests from parents and teachers who were worried about the effect this policy was having on students acquiring proficiency in other subjects, the line was modified. Today the emphasis is on including Irish language classes in the curriculum. Thus, although most citizens of the Republic have been exposed to Irish in school, if the goal of the original Gaelic Revivalists was to restore Irish as the everyday language of the people they must be said to have failed.

Nevertheless, Irish remains important for Irish writers on both sides of the border, if not as a medium then as a symbol. The decline of the language stands in a great deal of Irish writing for the loss or suppression of Gaelic culture as a whole. Tim Pat Coogan, in editing a recent supplement on the arts in Ireland, found the 'references to the Irish tongue, if not to the writing in Irish, remarkable—for Irish is commonly held to be a dying tongue, spoken daily as an original means of communication by possibly as few as 30,000 people'.[32]

The difficulties of writing in a language not somehow one's own is a theme stretching back at least as far as James Joyce's *A Portrait of the Artist as a Young Man*.[33] The poet John Montague uses the image of a 'grafted tongue' to express the dilemma of Irish writers in English:

> To grow
> a second tongue, as
> harsh a humiliation
> as twice to be born.[34]

Friel has stated that his concern in *Translations* is with 'the whole problem that the writers in this country experience: having to handle a language that is not native to him. . . . But I'm not talking about the revival of the Irish language. I'm just talking about the language we have now and what use we make of it'.[35] On another occasion Friel expressed the opinion that

There will be no solution [to the 'Irish problem'] until the British leave this island, but even when they have gone, the residue of their presence will still be with us. This is an area that we still have to resolve, and that brings us back to the question of language for this is one of the big inheritances which we have received from the British. . . . We must make English identifiably our own language.[36]

Regardless of Friel's own attitude toward language in Ireland, the fact remains that it is a politically loaded issue. Thus *Translations* might well be expected to suggest political interpretations to many people that may or may not have been what Friel intended to convey.

In addition to their public significance, the concerns of the play are deeply personal ones for Brian Friel. Both of his parents were native Irish speakers, his great-grandfather was a hedge schoolmaster, and the Ordnance Survey local headquarters was at Magilligan (very close to where the playwright was living when he was working on the script).[37] All of this is a reminder that *Translations* is not merely a 'language play'—it is also an historical fiction. Since the most incisive criticisms of the play have focused on the inaccuracy of its portrayal of history,[38] it seems reasonable to look now at the historical character of the institutions Friel treats dramatically in *Translations*, particularly hedge schools, National Schools, and the Ordnance Survey, and consider the use he makes of history in his re-creation of the 1830s.

The so-called 'hedge' schools were established during the reign of William III as a means of circumventing the penal laws forbidding the education of Catholics. Despite slight relaxations in government policy throughout the eighteenth century, these schools continued as largely secret, unlicensed institutions until the Catholic Emancipation Act of 1829.[39] The hedge schools were private schools, with payment often being made in kind (milk, butter, or sods for the fire). The schoolmaster plied his trade in a disused barn or purpose-built cabin, usually lodging around with the parents of his students. In 1824, 8 per cent of the total population of Ireland was attending school, and most of the Catholics who were receiving an education were doing so in the hedge schools.[40]

Hedge schools catered primarily to peasant children. Many contemporary observers commented on the common Irish people's thirst for education.[41] A notably high standard was attained in many of these schools, particularly in mathematics. In fact, a number of the civilian labourers hired by the Ordnance Survey had been trained in hedge schools. In 1853 the real-life Yolland wrote to a Major Walpole, 'The lower orders of the Irish have usually more of that particular class of information suited to the survey duties than the lower orders in England and Scotland.'[42]

Friel got most of his information about hedge schools from *The Hedge Schools of Ireland* by Patrick John Dowling. Dowling's is a fairly romantic view of hedge schools and schoolmasters, but it must be borne in mind that he is writing partly to debunk what appears to have been a popular negative view of them. His evidence is largely anecdotal, and he dismisses it himself when it does not support the image he wishes to project.[43] Dowling points out that many of the Irish language poets of the time were schoolteachers and stresses their role in preserving Gaelic culture. This would have been a political imperative in Ireland in 1935, when Dowling was writing, if one wished to paint a positive picture of any educational institution. He summarizes his point of view in his conclusion,

Writers have, many of them, described the Hedge Schools as poor, wretched, inadequate, mischievous. But let the worst be said of them, and it may still with truth be maintained that they represented a system of education truly democratic and truly national. With their passing, the last link with the ancient Gaelic schools of Ireland was severed.[44]

For other historians the past has another pattern. James Johnston Auchmuty, writing in 1937, states that 'it is held by some modern scholars that the Hedge Schoolmaster was largely responsible for "beating Irish out of the country" '.[45] In contrast with the Latin classics, Norman Atkinson notes, the Irish language was treated with 'increasing neglect, partly through lack of text-books, and partly through the realism of parents who recognised the social and economic advantages of equipping their children with a knowledge of English'.[46] Reports of surveys conducted by the Royal Dublin Society at the start of the nineteenth century confirm the inroads that English was making in the countryside.[47] Dowling himself, in the middle of his book, gives a more tempered account of the curriculum of the hedge schools:

The very least that was taught in the Hedge Schools included reading, writing and arithmetic. Other subjects found their way into the curriculum according to local needs, and in so far as the qualifications of the teacher would allow: history, geography, book-keeping, surveying and navigation. Latin and mathematics were commonly taught; sometimes Greek; and in Irish-speaking districts instruction in all these subjects was given in the vernacular. At the beginning of the 19th century, however, English as a medium of instruction was rapidly replacing Irish.[48]

This makes Friel's hedge school fairly exceptional, but well within the range of possibility. Hugh and Jimmy Jack are extra-ordinary characters, but such have existed in every time and place. Maire is more interested in English than in Latin and Greek (and quotes Daniel O'Connell to support her position), which makes her a fair representative of the internal pressures making for 'Anglicization'. Further, not all the hedge scholars in the play are academically inclined—Doalty has trouble with seven times nine— and truancy seems to be a problem for Hugh. Even some of Friel's more improbable touches have a basis in fact. Hugh tells Yolland

that he has written a book called 'The Pentaglot Preceptor or
Elementary Institute of the English, Greek, Hebrew, Latin and Irish
Languages' (419)—such a work was actually put together by
Patrick Lynch, an Irish schoolteacher who died in 1818. Lynch ran
a fee-charging school in a town, but he had himself been educated
in a hedge school.

It was partly the explosion of private pay schools that led to
the establishment by the British government of the Board of
National Education in 1831. In his presentation of the National
School initiative, Friel takes many more liberties than he does in his
depiction of a hedge school. The National Schools were not put in
place with the primary aim of getting rid of the Irish language—
economic incentives and the people themselves were doing that.[49]
The new schools were welcomed by the leadership of the Catholic
Emancipation Movement; O'Connell hailed them as a 'boon' that
would help to develop an educated Catholic electorate.[50] Séamas
Ó Buachalla has pointed out that the Commissioners went on
record in 1884 as saying that 'the anxiety of the promoters of the
National System was to encourage the cultivation of the English
language and to make English the language of the schools'.[51] This,
however, was a statement after the fact, when such organizations as
the Society for the Preservation of the Irish Language (founded
1876) had begun agitating on behalf of Irish. English was the
medium of instruction in the National Schools, and the long-term
effect of this on the conservation of Gaelic culture cannot be seen
as anything but negative, but this was largely a matter of con-
venience and did not depart significantly from the policy of the
hedge schools they replaced. The deterioration of the Irish language
would probably have been seen by some of the architects of the
National School system as a desirable side-effect of its institution, but this was not what was uppermost in their minds. Rather,
the principal motivation behind the National Schools was to
create a truly non-sectarian system of basic education in Ireland.
This aim was ultimately thwarted by the various efforts of all
the major religious sects, and the majority of the National
Schools ended up under the control of one religious group or
another.[52]

If this frustration of its primary purpose demonstrates anything more than the depth of sectarian feeling in Ireland, it is the
decentralized nature of the early National School system. Sean

Connolly remarks, 'What the national school system of the 1830s and 40s represented was not the imposition on local communities of an alien, centrally designed institution, but a massive state subsidy to an existing system of elementary education.'[53] In fact, a large proportion of the hedge school teachers were hired by the National Board to continue teaching (as Hugh applies to take over the new National School in *Translations*).[54] There was, regrettably, no provision for that part of the population who spoke only Irish,[55] but since many of the students attended school mainly to learn English this is a much more serious criticism from a twentieth-century perspective than it would have been in 1831. When pressure for Irish instruction began to build up among the population (beginning in the mid-1870s with the Society for the Preservation of the Irish Language), the school system responded. In 1879 the Board sanctioned the teaching of Irish as an 'extra' subject, similar to Latin and French, certified Irish teachers, and undertook to provide books at cost.[56] With the formation of the Gaelic League in 1893 dissatisfaction with this arrangement grew, and in 1900 the Board finally agreed to allow the teaching of Irish within class hours as a normal school subject (it was in this year also, incidentally, that English was first made obligatory in all schools).[57] After 1906 the government set up a number of bilingual schools in the Gaeltacht and trained teachers to work in them.[58]

In Friel's play, one of the characters says of the National Schools that 'you start at the age of six and you have to stick at it until you're twelve at least—no matter how smart you are or how much you know. . . . And every child from every house has to go all day, every day, summer or winter. That's the law' (395). This was not the case. It was not until 1892 that school attendance was made compulsory, and even then it was not required in rural areas unless the county council chose to approve the rule, which by 1908 ten had still declined to do.[59] In the interim, the National Schools appear to have been cursed with exceedingly poor attendance, with about 75 per cent of Irish children staying away from school. Most pupils had a short school life (from the age of 6 or 7 to about 12), and on any given day there was likely to be less than 40 per cent of the class present.[60] It thus seems reasonable to suggest that the National Schools would have proved extremely ineffective agents for 'imposing' English on the Irish people had there not been more powerful forces for change operating within the community itself (just as more recent efforts to revive Irish primarily through the school system have proved inadequate).

Nevertheless, Friel's distortion of the purposes and procedures of the National Schools is probably justified—in the context of his play. The 'anti-national' character of the National Schools must be acknowledged (if one takes 'the nation' to be Ireland). In those days of Union the aim was to erode any separate sense of Irish identity. The textbooks that the Commissioners produced 'were so devoid of national content or sentiment that they were successfully exported without change to the schools of Australia, Canada, the West Indies and New Zealand'.[61] P. S. O'Hegarty observes disgustedly that school reading books contained passages such as this: 'On the east of Ireland is England where the Queen lives; many people who live in Ireland were born in England, and we speak the same language, and are called one nation.'[62] Friel is expressing this sense of the National Schools in terms of his organizing metaphor: the loss of the Irish language. Although not all of what he says or implies is factually correct, the liberties he takes with history further the aims of his artistic creation. In *Translations*, Irish stands for the whole Gaelic culture that was rapidly disappearing by the 1830s, and place-names stand for the entire Irish language. This dramatic foreshortening allows Friel to comment in two hours upon historical processes that took centuries in reality. In his words, 'Drama is first a fiction, with the authority of fiction. You don't go to *Macbeth* for history.'[63] The problem with the appropriation of history for the purposes of literature becomes acute only when the historical fiction is taken literally. Unfortunately, audiences displayed a marked inclination to 'go to' *Translations* for history—about which more will be said later. First, though, it is necessary to examine one more matrix of historical context, that of the Ordnance Survey of Ireland.[64]

On 15 May 1979, Friel noted in his diary that he was reading and rereading, in addition to Steiner and Dowling, a book about the Ordnance Survey of Ireland by John Andrews entitled *A Paper Landscape* and a memoir of the parish of Templemore (including the city of Derry) that was produced by the Survey team.[65] As in Friel's play, the only survey of Ireland ever completed (1824–46) was performed by the Board of Ordnance and was, in that sense, a military operation.[66] The work of surveying the country was undertaken by the Royal Engineers partly out of a feeling that no Irish surveyors would be equal to the task[67] and partly because they had some expertise acquired in the process of surveying the rest of the United Kingdom.[68] The estimated cost of the Survey was £300,000; it ended up costing the government £820,000. The surveying itself was completed by 1842, and the last maps were published in 1846.[69] The main purpose for the Survey was land revaluation, which was an urgent need in 1824 as townland records were so hopelessly out of date that the cess (a local tax) sometimes bore ten times as heavily on one townland, per unit area, as on other townlands of the same quality.[70]

The head of the Survey Department for the whole United Kingdom was Colonel Thomas Colby. He saw the Survey as a monument for posterity and exhibited an 'obsessive' desire for accuracy.[71] Friel at one time considered writing a play with him as the central figure, but, as his vision of the play changed, Colby was subsumed in the character of Lancey.[72] Lieutenant Thomas Aiskew Larcom was appointed local head of the Survey in Ireland (where Colby spent as little time as possible). Larcom was a keen amateur antiquarian who shares many characteristics with Yolland in the play, although Friel does not identify him as being the inspiration behind the character. There were in fact officers named Lancey and Yolland working on the Survey, but Friel appears to have borrowed only their names.

In Friel's dramatic treatment of the Ordnance Survey there are a number of glaring misrepresentations. The inaccuracies cluster chiefly around his depiction of the British officers. As Andrews has pointed out, Yolland's courtship of Maire is implausible, though more from the standpoint of class than of race. Furthermore, that Lancey and Yolland cannot distinguish between Latin and Irish may be effective in the theatre, but it is completely unrealistic.[73] More misleading is the end of the play. Andrews recalls that he enjoyed *Translations* very much and felt himself carried along by the action despite a small 'jolt' now and then occasioned by such considerations as the above—until the actors reached the scene where Lancey threatens to shoot livestock and turn farmers out of their farms:

And that is when I wanted to start grumbling. ' "Prodding every inch of ground with their bayonets"!' I wanted to say, 'But they didn't have bayonets. Before soldiers went on Survey duty they had to hand in their bayonets'. . . . 'What audience', I wanted to say, 'would swallow the idea of a junior army officer violating the sacred rights of nineteenth-century property . . . by taking it on himself to evict the tenants from someone else's estate?' It really seemed like one of those terrible moments in the theatre, or in the lecture room, when the audience stops looking at the front and starts looking at each other. Anyway, that is what I did. I needn't have bothered. At that moment in the Gate Theatre every eye but mine was riveted on the stage. The bayonets, the shooting, the evictions: all my fellow play-goers were lapping it all up.[74]

In fact, as Andrews explains, the Survey's public relations were generally good.[75]

Most interesting, because most central to the dominant theme of the play, is Friel's treatment of the Survey's topographical department. As in the play, orthographers were hired to come up with standard versions of placenames to put on the new maps, but, contrary to the playwright's implication, the official policy of the Survey from 1830 on was to adopt the variant spelling that came closest to the original Irish form of the name (although this would not always by any means be the commonest form).[76] This was a bit complicated for an English speaker, but Larcom tried for a while to learn Irish, hiring John O'Donovan to teach him. In the end he decided it would be simpler to have a specialist carry out the necessary research, and O'Donovan was accordingly engaged in this capacity. The Survey was indeed fortunate to acquire O'Donovan's services, because he is recognized today as one of the foremost Irish scholars of the nineteenth century. He published an important Irish grammar in 1845, translated the Annals of the Four Masters, and was working on a translation of the Brehon Laws at the time of his death.[77]

O'Donovan's position with the Survey was that of 'toponymic field worker'. It was his job to go into the field to 'hear the names pronounced and interpreted by Irish-speaking residents and to study them in the context of local topography and antiquities'.[78] Half a dozen authorities, including local landowners, county records, clergy, schoolmasters, and existing maps, were typically consulted for each name.[79] O'Donovan's efforts were Herculean— he dealt with 144,000 names in 62,000 townlands.[80] Like Owen and Yolland in *Translations*, O'Donovan very often recommended changing the names of townlands completely,[81] but his motivation was to make a town's name accord as closely as possible with its Irish ancestor or equivalent. Local inhabitants would not have found this process particularly dislocating because the Survey placenames (especially the ones emended by O'Donovan) never really caught on. There was no index of townland names available until 1862, so the post office simply ignored the changes, as did almost everyone else.[82]

In addition to sending linguists into the field to collect variant spellings of place-names, the topographical department supported a team of library researchers to supplement the lists with spellings gleaned from historical documents.[83] Larcom (like Friel) believed that in finding the history of a name you come very close to finding the history of the place as well, and, once you have done so, you might as well write it up at government expense. By 1839 the department boasted a staff of eleven, including, besides O'Donovan, the poet James Clarence Mangan and the Irish scholar Eugene O'Curry, under the supervision of the well-known artist and archaeologist George Petrie.

For men such as these, the Survey provided a marvellous opportunity to investigate much more than the evolution of placenames. Larcom encouraged officers and men surveying in the field to record the customs of the people, their mode of living, and their habits, in addition to any information they came across on local antiquities.[84] In 1837 an officer was sharply reprimanded for failing to include a holy well on one of his plans.[85] The attention paid to detail by employees of the topographical department was nothing short of astounding, and Larcom followed all of their endeavours with avid attention. Eugene O'Curry wrote to him on 27 May 1837 that he had

succeeded in discovering a well on Glencullen Townland to which my attention was pointed by Mr. Petrie. . . . It cures sickness at the stomach and affection of the bowels, and continues in good, though declining repute.

They think it a lucky but not a blessed well. Washing dairy vessels with its waters is a certain specific against the loss of butter by witch-craft.[86]

Another time he reported that the 'finest holly tree . . . that ever I saw' was growing in a field west of an old church he was examining.[87]

The final destination of this material was to be a memoir

published for each parish in Ireland. In the event, the project was curtailed, but there was a memoir produced for the parish of Templemore which includes the city of Derry and which Friel read while he was writing *Translations*. This large volume marked the high point of the memoir scheme. Larcom wanted to prove that the Survey was capable of scholarly work as well as map-making, and in this he may have succeeded too well. As Andrews puts it, the memoir's many virtues (chiefly accuracy and comprehensiveness) were 'dwarfed by its enormous sprawling bulk'. Larcom and his colleagues

could not bear to leave anything out. In the end they needed more than 350 octavo pages to cover a single parish, instead of the half-dozen suggested as an average figure in the scheme originally submitted to the Irish government; and . . . they had spent . . . more than three times the original budget for a whole county. Not only that, but by choosing the kind of parish where the proportion of library work to field work was very high Larcom had dangerously exposed his flank, for it was now more obvious than ever that memoirs could not be written as a by-product of an ordinary survey.[88]

Despite the elaborate attempt at practical justification contained in the 'Preliminary Notice', it remains clear that much of the material included in the memoir is mainly of antiquarian interest. The book is broken into three main sections—Natural State, Artificial State, and General State—with a number of subdivisions in each one. The historical sections quote lengthy passages from contemporary documents and contrast different points of view for various events. Although the memoir is a wonderful resource for modern historians, it would have been difficult to pass off in 1837 as the mere odds and ends of a land survey.[89] A copy was sent to the Chancellor of the Exchequer, who was, rather predictably, dismayed:

That the ordnance officers should collect and be encouraged to collect much valuable information which cannot be given to the world in the shape of a map is quite true. That this should be published in the shape of a memoir . . . I admit. That we should pay for this I agree. But that we should undertake to compile regular county and city histories of all Ireland I cannot assent to.[90]

One of the Chancellor's concerns, in addition to the expense of the undertaking, was that the memoirs might 'open all the debatable questions in Irish party division'.[91] Derry, then as now, was a focal point in Irish politics, and Petrie, who did much of the historical writing for the memoir, was 'a catholic and a patriot'. His point of view was reflected in some of his remarks, which probably did not go down well with the loyalists who controlled the city.[92] In May 1842, the government received an anonymous letter from 'a protestant conservative' who claimed to have worked under Petrie and charged that most of the topographical staff were Catholic opponents of the government.[93] Shortly thereafter, the topographical department was shut down, with twenty-nine counties completed. Whether, as later nationalists would have it, 'the watchful Government, calculating that the work was evoking a spirit of Irish nationalism, suppressed O'Donovan's Department',[94] or whether, as the Chancellor observed at the time, its annual cost of £500 was 'a lot to pay for ascertaining the names of Irish townlands'[95] it would be difficult to say. What is clear is that the men of the topographical department preserved through their dedicated labour something that was rapidly disappearing in the 1830s. As an obituary of John O'Donovan (which appeared in *The Nation* on 14 December 1861) noted of his and O'Curry's work,

the circumstances of those eminent men having been employed on the Ordnance Survey—a work not likely to be reinstituted within any given period—and the facilities thus afforded for obtaining local and antiquarian information render their services to Irish history unique.[96]

In his treatment of the Ordnance Survey, then, Friel distorts the 'facts' more fundamentally than in his portrayal of Irish education, turning the intentions and legacy of the topographical department virtually upside-down for the purposes of his narrative.[97] Is this justifiable? Sean Connolly has asserted that '*Translations* represents a distortion of the real nature and causes of cultural change in nineteenth-century Ireland so extreme as to go beyond mere factual error,' and that Friel's version of the past is 'so unrealistic and idealised as to cast doubt, not only on his history, but also on his art'.[98] Andrews is more charitable, saying that the real subject of the play is 'the relation between authority and alienation' and that it was the dramatist's job to get as much of that into the script as possible, 'even in defiance of naïve historical realism'. He calls *Translations* 'an extremely subtle blend of historical truth and—

some other kind of truth'.[99] Friel himself apologizes for 'the tiny bruises inflicted on history in the play', and reminds critics that 'the imperatives of fiction are as exacting as the imperatives of cartography and historiography'.[100] Kearney, who believes that Friel is concerned almost exclusively with the 'crisis of language', argues that 'The charges of political nationalism and historical inaccuracy mistake the primary intent of Friel's work by reading it as a sociological tract.'[101]

In general there is nothing terribly wrong with changing history for the purposes of art. The very existence of fiction-writing as a respectable occupation rests on the premiss that telling a story is not the same as lying. The playwright is not, and is not expected to be, a historian as well. Fictionalizing historical events becomes a problem only when the fictional version is taken to be true, and here *Translations* becomes a case in point. As Connolly points out, '*Translations* has . . . become the basis for a widely-received view of the nature of cultural change in nineteenth-century Ireland'.[102] Here Field Day must be held partially culpable. The programme for the original production included extracts from the primary and secondary sources consulted by Friel during the writing of the play. These provided, as Ulf Dantanus has remarked, 'a strong aura of historical accuracy'.[103] In the absence of significant outside information on the part of most theatre-goers, these may have given *Translations* more historical authority than it deserved.

There is little doubt that Friel was aware that his creation was not 'history' in the strict sense of the word. On 22 May 1979 he jotted in his diary, 'The thought occurred to me that what I was circling around was a political play and that thought panicked me. But it is a political play—how can that be avoided? If it is not political, what is it? Inaccurate history? Social drama?'[104] A week earlier he had confided that one aspect kept eluding him, 'the wholeness, the integrity, of that Gaelic past. Maybe because I don't believe in it.'[105] It is tempting to speculate that what critics of the play have condemned as 'idealization' in its portrayal of Baile Beag resulted from Friel's attempt to convince himself of the self-confidence of the culture he was writing about. There is evidence that he was uncomfortable with the public response to the production. He was at pains to point out to an interviewer a few months after the play opened that 'I have no nostalgia for that time':

Several people commented that the opening scenes of the play were a portrait of some sort of idyllic, Forest of Arden life. But this is a complete illusion, since you have on stage the representatives of a certain community—one is dumb, one is lame and one is alcoholic, a physical maiming which is a public representation of their spiritual deprivation.[106]

However one chooses to judge the fact, in writing his play Friel was 'dreaming history'. Desmond Maxwell describes the dynamic behind Friel's plays thus, 'What might be, or might have been, is being asked to put its pressure on, and perhaps alter, actuality'.[107] In *Translations* Friel presents a version of the past which, though ultimately tragic, captures for a brief moment a vision of how two opposed groups could learn to appreciate each other. This possibility of mutual respect is undermined by violent men on both sides. It is in this sense that *Translations* may best be taken to be what Seamus Deane has called it: 'a parable of events in the present day'.[108]

Drawing on Hugh's final speeches, Kearney suggests that Friel is pleading for a 'discerning use of memory' that can distinguish between 'the past that liquidates by a narrow obsession with revenge, and the past which liberates into new possibilities of self-recollection'.[109] Dantanus feels that the inconclusive nature of the play's ending effectively extends the action into 'contemporary relevance' and expresses the opinion that 'it is sufficiently removed from the inflamed and entrenched politics of the contemporary situation to demand a hearing from everyone'.[110] Friel himself was more cautious, reminding an interviewer shortly after *Translations* opened, 'Politics are so obtrusive here.' Nevertheless, he stressed, 'We've got to keep questioning until we find... some kind of generosity that can embrace the whole island' and commented, 'Somebody asked me if it had a political message.... Well, if it has, I don't know what it is!'[111]

Friel himself might steadfastly refuse requests to assign a specific political interpretation to *Translations* (as he did), he might write an open-ended script resistant to easy allegorizing (as I would submit he also did), but that does not mean that *Translations* is not, or cannot in certain circumstances become, a political play. It is not even inconceivable that it could turn out to be more than one

political play with, not one, but several, messages, some of them
mutually exclusive. This is because the script, the words on the
page, of a play is only a part of what theatre is about.

Theatre is, in its essence, a collaborative art. The writer of a novel
or poem has a reasonable degree of control over the final form of
his creation, but the same cannot be said of the dramatist. His
vision is not realized until the play appears on stage, and to get
it there he is dependent upon producers, director, actors, stage
manager, lighting designer and technicians, set designer and build-
ers, costumers, and sound effects technicians, to name but a few of
the people associated with any theatrical production. Amid such a
complex configuration of talents and priorities, the writer's intention may dwindle almost to insignificance.

Brian Friel, after nearly twenty years in the professional theatre,
was unable to accept this fact with equanimity. As he told Ciaran
Carty shortly after *Translations* opened,

The dramatist ought to be able to exercise complete control over the
realisation of his characters. . . .

A director is like the conductor of an orchestra and the actors are the
musicians. They are all there to play the score as it is written.

Friel, Carty informed his readers, was 'a meticulous craftsman,
attending every rehearsal, never letting go of a play until it is a
reality on the stage'.[112] Perhaps this disposition of the playwright
was one consideration that led him into the management end of
theatre in founding the Field Day company.

However, even if a dramatist could somehow control all aspects
of the presentation of his play, all the myriad parts of the theatrical
collaboration, there is a vital term in the dramatic equation that
must remain beyond regulation. As Peter Brook, the influential
director, has stated, 'The only thing all forms of theatre have in
common is the need for an audience.'[113] This makes it, he claims,
unique among art forms. The necessity for an audience might
be said to be theatre's defining characteristic, and the reaction
of audience members at a play constitutes a secondary layer of
collaboration. Every person attending a performance brings his or
her own prejudices and preconceptions to bear upon the play, and
the product will be different in every case. A successful or popular
play may be one that does not rudely preclude too many of these
individual interpretations.

With these ideas about the nature of theatrical art in mind, we will now examine the contemporary critical reaction to *Translations* in three areas: Northern Ireland, the Republic of Ireland, and England. I believe that a reasonably clear pattern emerges in the response, and I will argue that the interpretations given in the different regions were so divergent as to suggest that audiences were watching, in effect, different plays. In the North, the ritual aspect of theatre was uppermost, with the act of performing and attending the play on a level with the dramatist's words themselves. In the Republic, the play was applauded in large part for what was seen as its nationalist political and social message. Finally, in London, it was the entertainment value of *Translations* that assured its success.

We have already remarked that in Derry, where the world première took place, the impact of *Translations* appeared to derive as much from the fact that it was produced in the city and was the result of a co-operative effort among people of many political persuasions as from the script itself. This is particularly notable in view of the fact that the play's subject-matter—the decline of the Irish language—was one with nationalist connotations which might be expected to provoke resistance from a sizeable percentage of Field Day's potential audience. Nevertheless, reviewers for the nationalist *Derry Journal* and the unionist *Londonderry Sentinel* were equally enthusiastic about the play. The *Journal*, reflecting on the poignance of the ending, quoted a comment overheard after the performance, 'They were speaking in different languages then and are still speaking in different languages now' and added, 'The play finishes with nothing really resolved and again there is a message for what is resolved more than a century later?'[114]

This basic pattern tended to repeat itself in the rest of Northern Ireland, where the majority of the venues were small towns without a tradition of professional theatre and where response to the play was as much a matter of civic pride as it was an aesthetic consideration. An interesting exception is Belfast, the first stop on the company's tour, where there seems to have been initial suspicion of *Translations*—probably because of the rousing reception accorded to it in Derry. On opening night, only 400 people turned out to populate a 1,000-seat theatre.[115] The reviews, however, were reassuring. Betty Lowry of the *Belfast Telegraph* saw the première in Derry and noted, in an unconscious echo of the *Derry Journal*,

'Nothing is resolved on stage, but then nothing has been resolved off stage more than a century later.' Her verdict was that it was 'an interesting play looking at the conflict between English and Irish from an unusual angle'.[116] Judith Rosenfield, who reviewed the play in Belfast for the unionist *Belfast Newsletter*, called it 'unusual and erudite' and expressed the view that Friel had given a fair portrayal of events: 'While he has painted one side of the approach by the British army to the villagers he has to some extent balanced it by Yolland's delight in the countryside and wish to live among the Irish and speak their language.'[117] Both women seemed a bit surprised by the historical revelations of *Translations*, but both mentioned the programme notes in defending the historical accuracy of the play. One criticism Edna Longley made some years after the première of *Translations* was that it did not include Ulster Protestants in its analysis of the origins of some of the problems in Ireland.[118] Perhaps the play was successful in the North partly because it did not take on that potentially divisive subject. At any rate, after a cautious welcome people in Belfast crowded to see the play just as people in Derry had done.

Having been performed in the two biggest cities in the North, *Translations* headed south for a two-week stint at the Dublin Theatre Festival, then back north for a series of one-night stands in a number of smaller towns. This type of tour is exceedingly hard work for cast and crew alike, as there is no time to rest and the suitability of the 'theatres' visited varies widely.[119] Field Day, however, was founded largely to bring theatre to precisely these places, and morale in the company was high.[120]

Throughout this politically polarized region, audience reaction was remarkably free of sectarian bias. The show played as well in 'Carrickmore of the four P's: plays, pubs, provos and poteen', where the 'kerbstones are all painted green white and orange' as it did in Enniskillen with its Protestant majority.[121] In Coleraine, three performances were booked out three days after bookings opened, and a fourth was added to help accommodate the demand.[122] The Carrickmore reviewer did express 'bitterness' for Maire's 'disloyalty' and called Lancey 'typical British officer material', but also 'experienced joy with [Yolland] at his gradual mastery of the Irish pronunciation and his growing love for Donegal and its people' and concluded that the script was 'historically competent and balanced'.[123]

Even this degree of political analysis was fairly unusual. Publicity for and reviews of *Translations* often barely mentioned what the play was about and almost never attempted to draw political lessons from it. Advance publicity for the Carrickmore performance, for example, read

There is really no need for the Mid-Ulster Drama Festival Committee to say any more about this upcoming production. Critics from all over the islands have said it all. Now's your chance to see this play which won for its author a standing ovation at the world première recently in Derry. . . . Now you can see it locally in . . . comfort and style in the New Patrician Hall, Carrickmore. The Festival Committee are re-creating the atmosphere for one night, with supper for patrons and a chance to see and meet the professional players afterwards.[124]

The arts writer for the *Armagh Guardian* voiced delight in welcoming Field Day, 'Armagh has not had the privilege of hosting such a distinguished company of professional actors and actresses in a long time'.[125] 'After the performance', added a writer in the *Ulster Gazette*, 'Festival patrons will have an opportunity to discuss the play and other Festival offerings at the Festival Club in Loudan's Hotel. It is hoped that members of the Field Day Company will be in attendance.'[126]

In Enniskillen the audience was given a much more extensive review than the play. The critic for the *Impartial Reporter* noted rather plaintively that 'nothing was resolved. The audience was left to draw its own conclusions—an increasing feature of contemporary drama', then went on to quote Mrs Janet Pierce, arts officer of the Fermanagh Council, at some length:

Everyone in the audience of 530 enjoyed it. There was a fantastic response from everyone and it was an outstanding event for the county. People came from both sides of the Border, including Monaghan and Sligo, and the actors were delighted with the response.

They said it was the best house they had played to, in terms of numbers and response. We have never had anything like it in Enniskillen . . . It bodes very well for the interest in drama for the future.[127]

Another article in the same paper pointed to the 'wonderful reception' given the play in Enniskillen, with a 'marvellous audience of 530 filling every corner of the assembly hall at the High School' and observed that 'If the spacious hall had not been available there would have been many disappointed playgoers.' The writer continued,

(In fact, quite a few who would normally have attended were away with a group from Enniskillen parish on a visit to Roscrea, Tipperary.) This reinforces the campaign for an Enniskillen theatre, apparently on the shelf for the time being. It is gratifying to see such good support. The play was enjoyable and the audience responded well.[128]

A few days after Field Day's visit, the *Fermanagh News* ran a page of photographs of audience members watching the performance.[129]

Some spectators apparently did not need to view the play as a political and theatrical metaphor in order to find contemporary significance in it. As a critic for the *Ulster Herald* commented, 'On a local and personal note, the Post Office who wished to number our countryside to the exclusion of the delightful, meaningful, mellifluous names of our townlands, would do well to see this play.'[130] A writer for the *Impartial Reporter* expressed similar sentiments, 'The subject is dear to our hearts in Fermanagh where we have been fighting to keep the old townland names.'[131]

It would probably be stretching the truth to suggest that reviewers for local papers in the North deliberately refrained from reflections on the origins of sectarian strife in Ireland. There does seem to have been a tacit avoidance, however, of political interpretation. Instead the performances of *Translations*, in Enniskillen and Carrickmore as in Derry, were occasions for the demonstration of local pride and solidarity. The 'black North' could, after all, produce something to excite admiration rather than disgust or pity.

While pre-production publicity had emphasized the Northern nature of the project, critics in the Republic proved only too anxious to get in on the act. There may have been uneasiness in some quarters at the way Friel was turning his back on the Dublin theatre establishment, but, if so, this was not explicitly stated. On the contrary, a number of reviewers focused on the cross-border and all-Ireland aspects of the production. An *Irish Times* editorial in August hailed the announcement that *Translations* would première in Derry: 'It is good to be reminded that, however jealously its different local traditions may be guarded, this island is all of a piece, each part interdependent with every other.'[132] Michael Sheridan of the *Irish Press* remarked that the 'transborder nature of the Field Day company' was reflected in a cast that included 'some of the most talented young actors from the North and South', and insisted that the occasion of the Derry opening was one that 'belonged to Irish theatre as a whole, and was executed in the manner which united the nation on a cultural level'.[133] Gerald Dawe believed that 'the play makes the North acceptable for most Irish people in cultural terms they are accustomed to and this familiarity is the play's *initial* strength and appeal'.[134]

Dawe's comment highlights the paradoxical foreignness of the North for many in the country which maintains a territorial claim on the province. Ronan Fanning has observed that the present Troubles have 'further reinforced the partitionist mentalities of a people few of whom would contemplate venturing north of the border'.[135] With what looks suspiciously like obliviousness to the local pride element of the play's opening, some Irish critics even suggested a neutralizing of Northern speech patterns, one writing, 'The acting throughout has a splendid natural quality, but the Northern accents may need to be toned down when the play comes south.'[136]

Overall, though, reviewers could hardly have praised *Translations* more. David Nowlan, the influential critic for the *Irish Times*, set the tone when he called the play a 'triumph' with 'near perfect' performances.[137] In *Translations*, he said, Friel was 'certainly trying to pose questions rather than to provide answers about cultural and linguistic identities'.[138] The reviewer for *Irish Catholic* agreed, 'Like all good plays, it does not answer all the questions it poses but leaves a good deal for the audience to puzzle over after the performance has ended.'[139] Con Houlihan was a lone dissenting voice when he called *Translations* a sentimental play bordering on 'melodrama'. He affirmed Nowlan's assessment, though, when he wrote that 'Mr. Friel does not take sides: this is a play that has no answers—only suggestions.'[140]

Not all of the critics were so circumspect. There was, in fact, much more willingness in the Republic than in the North to interpret the play in unambiguous political terms. Many of those who reviewed the play and, presumably, many of those who merely viewed it, took it for granted that *Translations* was about what Fintan O'Toole has referred to as 'the historical disjunction caused by the *forced* shift of Irish speech from the Gaelic language to English' (emphasis mine).[141] Colm Cronin of the *Sunday Tribune* called it one of 'the top ten plays of the last ten or twenty years' and summed up its theme as 'the rape of the local culture by the imported one ... the bastardisation of a heritage that stretched back to mythology'. The 'new schools and the new topography', he said, 'crowned the efforts of the Empire to kill off for all time both the language and the landmarks of the country'.[142] Michael Sheridan believed that Friel had painted a picture of 'a rural community with the hands of an empire at its throat and the boot of an imperial power at its chest' and excoriated the 'traitors' (Owen and Maire) 'in the midst of the community'.[143] Frank McGinley expressed the view in the *Donegal Democrat* that '*Translations* ... is about the transformation of a culture. It is about breaking down barriers in a spirit of enmity and conquest. It is about a failure to communicate, to understand—to translate'.[144] The Ordnance Survey and National School system, for McGinley, 'signalled the beginning of the final attack on the Irish nation'.[145] An Irish-language review in the *Irish Times* informed readers that the play looked back to that 'terrible period of Irish history when official and institutional consolidation was made on the decline of our language and culture and another language and culture were to be put in their place henceforth',[146] and John Jordan admitted in *Hibernia* that 'whatever one has of racial consciousness is touched to the quick'.[147]

A number of critics gave every appearance of having taken the play's version of history disturbingly literally. That is to say, they took Friel's hedge school, plausible in itself, as completely representative of hedge schools in general. Michael Sheridan thought that what Friel had demonstrated was that 'the English expression, far from bestowing a civilisation and knowledge, in effect robs the people of a tradition of learning which embraced intimate acquaintance with Latin and Greek'.[148] Desmond Rushe of the *Irish Independent* found the play to be 'an astonishing evocation of a time when the flashing-eyed Athene of Grecian saga was as familiar to Donegal peasants as the Grainne of Irish legend'.[149] McGinley confessed that 'I, at any rate, was confronted with an Ireland which despite my reading of history, I had not realised existed'. He continued, with no apparent irony,

mountainmen quoting liberally in Latin, men in coarse báinín discussing the Classics as if they were university professors—the hunger and respect for knowledge purely for its own sake, that was manifest in the ordinary peasant—this is the Ireland I cannot imagine, for it is so unlike our own time.[150]

Occasionally a note of self-reproach mingled with the nostalgia and the anger at England's cultural imperialism, reflecting at least a partial awareness that pressures making for change within the peasant communities were at least as effective in causing the decline of Irish as any that could be imposed from London. After characterizing the Survey and the school system as the 'cruel imposition of a dominant rich colonial culture upon an older civilisation', Gus Smith of the *Sunday Independent* moralized sadly,

The consequences as we have seen (though this is not Friel's argument) have been disastrous for us socially, culturally and politically. At least the less impressionable Welsh people have struggled to maintain their language; we did not—and have not.[151]

Colm Cronin agreed that 'The whole play is a poetic essay on the failure of a people to cherish and preserve the riches of their culture in transformation from one ethos to another. . . . [Friel] makes it clear where our characteristic weakness lies'.[152]

Martha McClelland, reviewing for *An Phoblacht*, the IRA newspaper, would tolerate none of this wishy-washy liberalism. Though the paper found itself in the unaccustomed company of the *Belfast Newsletter* and the *Londonderry Sentinel* in praising *Translations*, its critic drew radically different conclusions from the play. She focused on '[o]pportunist' Owen, 'a clever slave', and traced his 'political consciousness' as it develops from beginning to end. Owen is, quite simply, a 'collaborator', while Yolland is 'politically naïve, but basically decent'. The unhappy outcome of his affair with Maire only goes to prove that 'the social and political conflict of interest between colonisers and colonised cannot be resolved through good community relations'. Doalty emerges as the unexpected hero of the piece, as

Faced with his home being tumbled, a fully-conscious Owen now throws his lot in with Doalty, the salt-of-the-earth student who cannot translate Latin nor Greek but easily translates the Brit language of occupation. . . . and goes off to organise resistance.

It is Doalty who knows how to deal with the present and defend culture most effectively. His clarity of mind contrasts sharply with the old schoolmaster who . . . counsels the now-militant Owen, '*We must learn these new names; we must make them our new homes.*'

The play, McClelland concluded, 'deals powerfully with a number of themes of particular interest to Republicans'—'*Translations* needs no translation in the occupied six-counties'.[153]

There is a sense in which this review is only the most extreme statement of a strain that runs through much of the contemporary Irish response to *Translations*. A note by John Boland in the *Evening Press* on 17 January 1981 was probably partly a rebuttal of this current in the national reaction. The immediate occasion was the decision of the Irish-American Cultural Institute to award Friel a prize for *Translations*. The Institute, declared Boland, seemed undecided as to whether its award was for artistic or ideological merit. He took particular issue with a statement in the Institute's official press release that *Translations* was for 'the divers peoples of this planet who are suffering a rape of their traditions . . . if there is a national neurosis in Ireland it would be the not-surprising outcome of the imposition of foreign ideas and values over a period of centuries'. Boland proceeds to demolish this diagnosis:

> That is a very odd statement, implying that Ireland was somehow once a pure, homogeneous country, unsullied by 'foreign ideas and values': values which, you will recall, were brought over by the Fir Bolgs, the Celts, the Danes, the Normans, the British, the French and, yes, the Americans. All these ideas and values have gone to make us (as Bord na Gaeilge would say) part of what we are. To free ourselves of the effects of such 'impositions' we would have to get rid of our ancient monuments, most of Dublin, Cork, Galway, Limerick, Kilkenny and Waterford, our entire parliamentary process and much of our art and literature.[154]

I would hazard to suggest that, like this comment, much of the thoughtful criticism of *Translations* that was published often several years after the fact was a response to the initial Irish reception as much as a reaction against Friel's play itself. Friel may or may not have been refurbishing an 'old myth', as Edna Longley has accused him of doing, but some of his admirers certainly were. It is not only the words of dead men that are 'modified in the guts of the living'.[155]

If this is what *Translations* is really about, though, its success in England would seem unlikely, to say the least—yet successful it was. The play arrived in England to critical acclaim. Martin Esslin in *Plays and Players* stated that it put Friel in the 'very front rank of contemporary dramatists'.[156] Michael Coveney, reviewing for the *Financial Times*, called it 'the most moving, most reverberative and most important new Irish play for years'.[157] Irving Wardle of *The Times* had 'never been more certain of witnessing the première of a national classic',[158] and his colleague Ned Chaillet felt that 'it deserves to be judged a masterpiece, a play that will reward repeated visits'.[159]

English reviews came in three waves. The first few were by critics who attended the opening in Derry or who saw the play at the Dublin Theatre Festival. The second group of reviews were of the production at the Hampstead Theatre in London which opened in mid-May 1981, and the third appeared when the English production transferred to the National Theatre early in August. Only the first set of notices compare directly with the reviews looked at so far (which were also of the Irish production), but the others are interesting for what they say about the play's themes and as illustrations of how changes in the production entailed corresponding shifts in the weight of the play.

The earliest reviews reflected the novelty of a world première in Derry. Stephen Dixon set the scene for readers of the *Guardian*:

Derry in the drifting, drenching September mist. Green-uniformed RUC men cluster in doorways. From time to time an Army Land Rover squelches past, with the inevitable man riding machinegun at the rear. The outside of Derry Guildhall, where Brian Friel is adding the final polish at rehearsals of his new play, *Translations*, is forbidding: a high wire fence all around and a gauntlet to run of locked gates and security men.[160]

In the words of James Fenton of the *Sunday Times*, 'A great deal of the pleasure of the occasion derived from the sheer achievement of assembling a new company of Irish talent and staging a world première in such surroundings.'[161] Fenton had some reservations about the play's historical basis ('I would have believed more readily in the historical accuracy of the picture had the English officers been less oafishly unlatined'), but he was prepared to take the piece as 'a vigorous example of corrective propaganda'. 'But propaganda for what?' he wondered. 'The audience at the Guildhall in Derry included most political viewpoints, and it was an official Unionist who initiated the standing ovation. . . . the bulk of the response was local and without apparent sectarian bias'.[162]

Other English reviews of the Irish production also stressed what they regarded as the play's conciliatory nature. Yolland, wrote Michael Coveney, was not only 'sympathetically written by Mr. Friel, but sympathetically played by Shaun Scott'. He 'wants to learn the language, loves the countryside, admires the school. He is also, of course, an agent of destruction. But that is left unsaid.'[163] Ned Chaillet identified the theme of the play as 'the loss of the Irish language to an English invasion that had affection as well as militarism to it',[164] and Ian Hill remarked that the 'apparent idyll' of the village school 'inevitably crumbles' when an 'idealistic officer falls for a local girl and is dealt with by the terrorist/freedom fighters'.[165]

Does it matter, asks Friel quietly? Yes, he answers. But is it entirely without benefit? he prompts. Ray McAnally, in a splendid speech as the schoolmaster, talks of words which are signals of a civilisation imprisoned in a linguistic contour which no longer matches the map of facts.[166]

Hill could have had a lively discussion with the Irish critic who believed that one of the messages of the play was that 'the loss of Irish and its associated culture, however ragged, was a blow from which Ireland never recovered'.[167]

In their reviews of the original production, as of the later London one, English critics were prone to regard *Translations* as documentary. As Michael Coveney put it, 'That vanished world . . . is evoked with clear-eyed assurance.'[168] Even when accepting the same set of 'facts', however, and praising the play, the English reviews strike one as far removed in spirit from most Irish ones. Greater detachment was possible for English critics. For them, the past was past. Only with such an outlook could one write, as Victoria Radin did in the *Observer*, that

The pay-off is the violence that the English were then still capable of inflicting on Ireland, and Hugh's realisation that his country must cede to Englishness. . . .

Friel shows how closely the Irish temperament has absorbed English culture by casting this play about the quality of being Irish in the English language.[169]

Critical response to the English production continued in much the same vein when *Translations* opened at the Hampstead with a new director and a largely new cast. Stephen Rea was still in the company, playing Manus this time instead of Owen, and Shaun Scott stayed on in the role of Yolland. When the show transferred to the National in August, Scott was the sole survivor from the original Irish cast. Throughout this time, Ireland remained very much in the news as the hunger strikes at the Maze prison dragged on. Nevertheless, despite the fact that the Troubles dominated English front pages as *Translations* played in London, the English production appears to have lacked the political resonance of the play in Ireland. This is not to say that English reviewers did not see *Translations* as a political play, but they were impressed by different features than were their Irish counterparts.

Given the sensitive political context, a number of the London critics were anxious to counteract a potential chariness on the part of English theatre-goers. Eric Shorter conceded in the *Daily Telegraph* that

What is so hard to do with a play like Brian Friel's *Translations* . . . is to make it sound attractive to the average English playgoer. For it is all about Ireland in the early 19th century—Irish culture, Irish pride, Irish independence and Irish desperation as a colony.[170]

Shorter was eager to reassure his readers: 'You suspect a metaphor for modern Ireland? You may be right. You sniff propaganda? You would be wrong.' Other reviewers were equally quick to point out what *Translations* was not. Mark Amory of the *Spectator* observed that 'There is enough conflict here to fuel several plays, one of them a passionately felt and over-written denunciation of English violence. This, thank heavens, is not that.' He pointed to the familiar contrast between Lancey and Yolland as support for the idea that the play was a balanced portrayal: 'though the English captain is conventionally insensitive and prepared to be ruthless, his lieutenant is sympathetic, if naïve.'[171] The *Guardian*'s Michael Billington called it 'A powerful story; and one that a downright polemicist would have used as a straightforward example of English cultural rape.' Friel, however, 'is a deeply intelligent ironist whose prime concern is with the chameleon nature of language'.[172] (The reader will recall that 'rape' was precisely what more than one non-English reviewer thought the play portrayed.) A note of weariness crept into the review of B. A. Young for the *Financial Times*, who tried to abstract the play completely from its Irish context: 'I can't bring myself to talk about the rights and wrongs of Irish politics. Call the two parties Montagues and Capulets if it makes things easier; but this is as tragic a play as we are likely to see for a long time.'[173]

Young's review illustrates a notable feature of the English criticism. The weight of the play appears to have shifted away from Hugh, Owen, and Manus and towards Yolland and Maire. Shaun Scott and Bernadette Shortt (who played Maire) received almost universal accolades for their performances, and there seems to have been a general tendency to see *Translations* as a love story with complications. Scotsman Ian Bannen appears to have made of Hugh a much more conventional 'stage Irishman', playing the part in a top hat that one reviewer noted made him look like W. C. Fields (he sounded like him, too, if this critic is to be believed).[174] Ned Chaillet regretted the fact that Hugh was now portrayed as 'a drunkard, rather than as a drunkard grasping on to intellect and the sobriety of reason'.[175] Other critics applauded Bannen's acting, but the casting does seem to have created a certain amount of confusion. As Amory put it, 'it is hardly his fault if he is less Irish than the others'.[176]

Perhaps the most consistent element of the English criticism was its praise for the way *Translations* captured the atmosphere of a vanished time. This focus on the literal over the metaphorical elements of the play may have been partly a way of dodging unpleasant political reflections, but it probably had more to do with English ignorance of Irish history and culture. Then, too, there was the influence of Eileen Diss's set, which was 'so realistic, you receive a weird impression akin to that of looking at Victorian photographs through a stereoscope'.[177] Whatever the cause, English lauding of the play's educational value is striking. The critic for *Drama* said that '*Translations* . . . has the advantage of telling us much that maybe we did not know (I certainly did not) about Irish history.'[178] Amory found the most 'immediately enjoyable' aspects of the production to be 'the documentary interest of how they lived then and the pleasure of getting to know these sympathetic people'.[179] B. A. Young summed up this attitude when he told potential audience members, 'Never mind the plot. . . . It's the evocation of the sight and the feeling of the time that makes *Translations* so wonderfully moving.'[180]

Occasionally critics misread the history behind the play (Young, for example, believed that the hedge schools had sprung up to 'atone for the total lack of education provided by the British government',[181] a perception which softened considerably the reality of the penal laws), but there was remarkably little criticism of Friel's depiction of the historical phenomena in *Translations*. Fenton, with his objection to 'unlatined' British officers, was virtually alone, and even he accepted the play's distortions as 'corrective propaganda'. This lack of comment is intriguing when one remembers that *Translations* did contain factual misrepresentations that were not insignificant. English reviewers, by and large, accepted Friel's version of the past with equanimity; for them, it was just a play about something that happened 150 years ago, and a vague colonial guilt combined with a dearth of objective knowledge to make criticism of the play's history seem in poor taste. As the Englishman, Haines, calmly replies to a provocative comment by Stephen Dedalus in the first episode of James Joyce's *Ulysses*, 'I can quite understand that. . . . An Irishman must think like that, I daresay. We feel in England that we have treated you rather unfairly. It seems history is to blame.'[182]

English reviewers did, however, take every benefit of the doubt left by the play's ending. As Irving Wardle observed, 'None of this violence is shown. We are left to guess the lieutenant's fate, and the chances of the British carrying out their threat.'[183] While Irish critics had rarely hesitated to assume the worst, the English continued to hope for the best. Owen's action at the end of the play raised completely different questions for some of them than it had for reviewers 'across the water'. Martin Esslin believed that several of the villagers knew that Yolland had been murdered by 'local Irish nationalist rebels'; the British threat was that the entire village would be punished unless the matter was cleared up. Thus, when Owen dashed out at the end of the play Esslin wondered, 'Will he save the village by betraying the nationalists with whose cause he is in sympathy? We are left with that question.' For him, Friel had brilliantly highlighted 'the moral dilemma of those in Ireland who desire independence and national freedom but abhor violence in any form'.[184] This interpretation contrasts starkly with that given in *An Phoblacht*, for example.

In short, while the tragedy of poor Yolland and Maire came through quite clearly in London, the cultural and linguistic tragedy that preoccupied critics in the Republic remained an abstraction. Ned Chaillet wrote that

In Ireland the play was a muted Irish tragedy, a chronicle of the final incursions of English culture into the backwaters of Gaelic Ireland. In London, the tragedy is less muted, but it is shared with the English and is much more clearly a masterful effort to chart the gulf of incomprehension that exists between the two peoples.[185]

My own examination of the Irish and English reviews of *Translations* leads me to a rather different conclusion: that Chaillet did well to leave the 'gulf of incomprehension' in the present tense.

Six Characters in Search of an Author(ity): The Field Day Board of Directors

THE enthusiasm generated by *Translations* was something that a number of interested observers believed should not be allowed simply to dissipate. Seamus Heaney recalls, 'The excitement which that play caused was palpable and its gratifications had to do with a feeling that the dramatic form had allowed inchoate recognitions, both cultural and historical, to be clarified and comprehended. Most people talked about it with relish, some with resistance, all with awakened attention.'[1] He remembers, 'I was very much encouraging Brian Friel just after the production of *Translations* to do something . . . to keep the energy rolling because my sense of that moment and that play was that this was what theatre was supposed to do'.[2]

Brian Friel insisted in 1982 that Field Day had no grand plan at the start:

It hadn't any formal beginnings . . . in that Stephen and I sat down and said 'now what we must do for the next three or five years is this, and we must attempt it in this kind of way'. It began more casually, where a group of people with a kind of intuitive understanding of various things found themselves coming together on the enterprise.[3]

This 'group of people' included Friel, Rea, and Heaney, along with David Hammond, Seamus Deane, and Tom Paulin, who were formally announced as the Board of Directors of the Field Day Theatre Company in September of 1981.[4] The immediate reason for having a board was pragmatic. As Hammond recollects, he received a telegram in 1981 explaining that in order to obtain charitable status the company needed a board of directors and asking him to be on it:

I was delighted to join the company. I had known Brian Friel for fifteen or sixteen years before that and I also knew that Seamus Heaney had been invited and he and I had been friends for years. I didn't know the other new recruits so well, but we were certainly not strangers.

So, it was a combination of more or less like-minded people. But there was no clear idea at the start what we wanted to do, except give Brian Friel and Stephen Rea our support. Then we had to invent a vision for Field Day, to try to articulate a policy and a progress.[5]

Heaney and Friel were old friends, as were Heaney and Deane, who had been pupils together at St Columb's College in Derry. Paulin had reviewed *Translations* in London and believes it was partly as a result of this that Friel asked him to be a director. He remembers that Friel and Rea emphasized the fact that they wanted both religious traditions represented on the board, which would be made up of three Catholics and three Protestants.[6]

Dictated by the tax laws though it was, the board was not envisaged as a merely token body. Friel remarks, 'Here we had friends not involved in theater who were so enthusiastic about our project, it seemed wasteful not to make use of their talents.'[7] According to Heaney, 'There was some hope that the poets might deliver a play or two and that the activities of the company could contribute to the general opening up of a debate on the relation between culture and politics that had developed in Ireland during the 1970s.'[8] Friel had expressed his belief in the need for such engagement as early as 1972:

I do not believe that art is a servant of any movement. But during the period of unrest I can foresee that the two allegiances that have bound the Irish imagination—loyalty to the most authoritarian church in the world and devotion to a romantic ideal we call Kathleen—will be radically altered. Faith and Fatherland; new definitions will be forged, and then new loyalties, and then new social groupings. It will be a bloody process. And when it has subsided, the Irish imagination—that vivid, slovenly, anarchic, petulant, alert to the eternal, impatient with the here and now instrument—will have to set about shaping and interpreting the new structure in art forms.[9]

In keeping with the Northern emphasis of the *Translations* project, Friel told Fintan O'Toole in 1982 that he thought the 'important defining thing' about the members of the board was that 'they're all Northern people'. He said that a sense of 'rootlessness and impermanence' might well be 'the inheritance of being a member of the Northern minority': 'the difficulty is what to re-claim. You can't deposit fealty to a situation like the Northern situation that you don't believe in. Then you look south of the border and that enterprise is in so many ways distasteful. And yet both places are your home, so you are an exile in your home in some kind of sense.' That 'sense of exile . . . brings with it some kind of alertness and some kind of eagerness and some kind of hunger. . . . And I think those are the kind of qualities that maybe Field Day can express.'[10] Friel was speaking as a Northern Catholic, yet what he says may apply equally well to Ulster Protestants. They, too, are aware of themselves as a minority (in the entire island of Ireland) and feel equally insecure in their present political and cultural situation, thinking of themselves as more British than Irish but suspecting the British government of wanting to pull the rug out from under their feet, identifying themselves with much that is Irish but unwilling to acknowledge this allegiance too openly for fear of encouraging those who would claim them for 'Ireland' without their consent.

Friel himself was publicly in favour of a united Ireland, and in trying to contribute to a cultural revival in the North he saw benefits accruing to the whole island. The Republic, he said, 'could be adjusted and I think it could be made very exciting. . . . But I think it requires the Northern thing to complete it. I'm talking about the whole Northern thing.'[11] Derry, for him, epitomized the 'Northern thing'. As he remarked in 1981,

I believe in a spiritual energy deriving from Derry which could be a reviving breath throughout the North. I think there is more creative energy here than anywhere else. Derry doesn't look to either Belfast or Dublin, but to itself, that's why I want to work here. . . .

[t]he dispossessed are coming into their own and if this island is to be redefined the essence of redefinition could come from here.[12]

If a sense of dispossession and spiritual exile was the common heritage of inhabitants of Northern Ireland, most of the members of the new Field Day board were exiled physically as well. With the exception of Hammond, they had all left the North. Deane and Heaney lived in Dublin, Paulin and Rea in England, and Friel in Donegal just across the border from Derry. All of them had spent significant time outside Ireland, which helped to give them a wider perspective on events in their home province.

This displacement had political as well as spiritual implications. Together with many other Irish intellectuals, the members of the board were motivated by an acute feeling of crisis, engendered by the Troubles, to re-examine their own assumptions about nationality. Seamus Heaney recalls their first meeting:

We believed we could build something of value, a space in which we would try to redefine what being Irish meant in the context of what has happened in the North over the past 20 years, the relationship of Irish nationalism and culture. We were very conscious that we wanted to be quite independent of the British influence exercised through Belfast and the equally strong cultural hegemony of Dublin.[13]

The members of the Field Day board, in their individual creative work as in the project they were embarking upon together, were looking for ways to respond artistically to the political and social upheavals that surrounded them. Heaney has remarked that from the moment the violence began in 1969 'the problems of poetry moved from being simply a matter of achieving the satisfactory verbal icon to being a search for images and symbols adequate to our predicament'.[14] A new crisis had been reached in 1980, when republican prisoners in the Maze Prison, who had been denied special category status after the end of internment in 1975, began a 'fast unto death' in support of their claim to be considered political prisoners. This protest was called off at New Year, but in March 1981 Bobby Sands began a new hunger strike campaign. He was joined at regular intervals by other hunger strikers, many of whom continued the fast after his death on 5 May. British Prime Minister Margaret Thatcher refused to consider their demands, and by the time the hunger strike ended in October ten prisoners had died, including two men from Derry.[15] A despairing editorial in the independent Belfast review *Fortnight* assessed the impact of the H-block crisis, which the writer believed had 'done more to polarise the two communities here than any other element in thirteen years of "troubles" ': it had legitimized the IRA cause (tarnished before by their violent actions), created an upsurge in recruits for them, and allowed Sinn Féin seriously to challenge the SDLP for the leadership of Northern nationalists. Most damaging, the hunger strike had made the struggle look once again like a simple case of the Provisionals versus the British, resulting in the collapse of any middle ground within the province.[16]

It was against this background of profound nationalist alienation and dangerously intensified feelings on both sides that the Field Day board was assembled. At a talk in Derry in 1985, Deane was reported as saying that, in 1981,

One of the basic assumptions of the group was that neither the North or South's political establishments had long to survive and that in a comparatively brief historical period the whole island would be radically altered.

Field Day felt that as writers it was part of their responsibility to help create in advance of these changes an idea of Irish culture and tradition which would be more generous than any of the essentially sectarian visions of Irish literature which had previously existed.[17]

Deane's willingness to regard the Republic as well as the North as politically unviable is a distinctive feature of the Field Day approach. This might be seen as either a progressive, new way of regarding the political impasse or as a throwback to traditional Northern nationalism (adherents of which have always been loath to believe that the government in the South could survive indefinitely without them). The directors, as Northerners, were fascinated and disturbed by the ambivalent response to the Troubles in the South.

For many in the Republic of Ireland, events north of the border seemed as distant as contemporary occurrences in Vietnam or Afghanistan. Word of the violence was ubiquitous—on television, on the radio, in newspapers and magazines—but the attitudes that engendered it seemed strange and foreign. There had been sympathy for the civil rights movement and some excitement, especially at the beginning, that things appeared to be coming to a head. During the Battle of the Bogside, before British troops were sent as a peacekeeping force, the Irish government even made oblique threats to intervene.[18] As the violence continued, however, with no end in sight, the Republic distanced itself from events north of the border. In May 1970, for example, two ministers (including Charles Haughey) were forced to leave the cabinet for allegedly conspiring to import arms and ammunition for the IRA. The Dublin government foreswore the use of force to assist the Catholic minority in the North.[19] Public opinion in the Republic also edged further away from the embattled Northern minority. Southerners had their own problems, chiefly economic, and they were mainly concerned that the anarchy they saw threatening to engulf the North should not cross the border.

A contrary indication was the reaction to Bloody Sunday, after which a wave of anti-British sentiment swept the Republic and the British embassy in Dublin was burnt down, surrounded by a crowd of 20,000–30,000 people.[20] This mood, however, did not last. As Seamus Deane saw it in 1979,

The year 1972 saw a very definite turn on the part of the Republic from its earlier attitude to Northern Ireland. Despite Bloody Sunday and the proroguing of Stormont, Dublin was politically muted. The burning of the British Embassy was no more than a gesture, an allowed release of energy after which attention turned to the real consequences of those late January days—the effects upon the Republic's trade and tourism.[21]

Their reluctance to get involved in the Northern conflict forced Irish people in the Republic to re-examine some of their most cherished assumptions—for example, that the entire island of Ireland was one natural unit. In light of the fact that people were killing each other in the North, how seriously did they take their stated aspiration to a thirty-two county state? Conor Cruise O'Brien stated the problem most vividly for Southerners: 'the Irish nation' and 'the people of Ireland' were not synonymous terms. The 'nation' included only those who thought of themselves as belonging to it, and this group was overwhelmingly Catholic. The Ulster Protestants presented an intractable problem to Irish nationalists, because they by and large did not think of themselves as belonging to the 'nation', but they were an established part of the population of Ireland. Thus, for O'Brien, nationalism itself was a threat that few who lacked experience of the opposing factions in Northern Ireland could comprehend:

The nationalist aspiration has deep historic roots. So also has the tradition that resists that aspiration. To push that aspiration against that tradition is to push towards civil war. But most of those who push that aspiration, or give their assent to its pushers, are by no means prepared to pay any of the price of civil war. The strength of the aspiration is far from being proportionate to the length of its roots, or to the extent of its diffusion.[22]

This view of the perfunctory nature of the territorial claim to the North in the Republic is convincingly supported in a study by Clare O'Halloran of the policies of the Irish Free State in the formative period 1922–37. Taking off from Ronan Fanning's idea that effective achievement of sovereignty over the twenty-six counties was more important to the leaders of the newly independent Ireland than the aspiration to unity, she argues that the picture of the early years that emerges is 'less of an unambiguous irredentism than of pragmatic partitionism mediated through a manipulative national-ist rhetoric and common to all political parties'. In an epilogue to her historical study, O'Halloran concludes that in the years since 1937, the 'trend towards greater separation, freely chosen by southern governments, was accompanied by an intensification and refinement of the irredentist rhetoric'.[23]

By the early 1970s, though, some of those politicians still serious about reunification were starting to realize that the accommodation of a significant Protestant minority would require changes in the Republic itself. O'Brien, as a Labour member of the Dáil, suggested in 1971 that the thirty-two county Socialist Republic he supported could only be achieved gradually through improved understanding between Catholics and Protestants. He maintained that the stand-ing claim of the Dublin government to the whole island (Articles Two and Three of the 1937 Constitution) was a positive barrier to such understanding. Noel Browne, another member of the Dáil, urged that the Republic should seriously consider establishing a secular constitution and state in the South in the hope of easing the apprehensions of Northern Protestants about a united Ireland.[24] Garret FitzGerald, in his 1972 book *Towards A New Ireland*, stated that the time had come to consider 'ways in which it might prove possible to overcome the obstacles to reunification that have been strengthened in the past half-century, reinforcing the basic inter-community hostility that initially led to Partition'. Acknowledging that the Northern Protestants were most afraid of the influence of the Catholic Church on affairs in the Republic, FitzGerald suggested a federal solution with an autonomous Northern Ireland region. Further, he listed steps that the Republic should take unilaterally to convince contemporary unionists of its good will to change. These included repealing the constitutional provisions giving the Catholic Church a 'special position' in the Republic and outlawing divorce, amending the anti-contraception laws, modifying the censorship policy, and removing the Irish language requirements for public service jobs. The result, he hoped, would be a 'non-sectarian, pluralist, united Ireland'.[25]

Later in 1972 the Republic did, in fact, repeal the clause giving the Catholic Church a special position, a largely symbolic action in a country where 95 per cent of the population was Catholic.[26] Meanwhile, the irredentist clauses remained. In 1981, as Taoiseach, FitzGerald became the leader of a 'constitutional crusade' to argue for changes in the Constitution that would remove its sectarian ethos and make it more acceptable to Northern unionists. Ironically, the crusade foundered in the face of a successful counter-campaign for a denominational anti-abortion amendment to the Constitution (eventually passed in 1983).[27]

In short, in 1981 there did not appear to be any real consensus for change in the Republic. The attitude of Southerners seemed to be that the North's problems belonged to the North and they would prefer to be left out of them. Conor Cruise O'Brien's influential *States of Ireland* (1972) had emphasized internal tensions in Northern Ireland, particularly the strained relations between Catholics and Protestants, shifting the focus away from the ancient feud between the Irish and the English.[28] Such an interpretation may well have reinforced negative Southern stereotypes about both communities in Northern Ireland that were older than partition itself.[29] W. B. Yeats had felt a similar distaste in his own day for the denizens of the North and their politics, telling Lady Gregory, 'I have always been of the opinion that if such disagreeable neighbours shut the door, it is better to turn the key in it before they change their mind.'[30]

The fanaticism on both sides that was so evidently a component of the violence in the North provoked some soul-searching in the universities as well. To what extent was Irish nationalism, hitherto seen as a good and necessary thing, to blame for the present crisis? People began to take another look at history. Was it really the chronicle of 800 years of struggle against the English, or was the truth more complicated than that?[31] Thus the movement in Irish historiography known roughly as 'revisionism' gathered momentum with the Troubles.[32]

A sign of the times was the publication of 'The Canon of Irish History—A Challenge' by Father Francis Shaw. The author questions the received view of the Easter Rising of 1916 as the glorious prelude to national independence. He points out that only a tiny minority of the Irish population at the time supported the extreme separatists who instigated the Rising and that the armed rebellion was universally unpopular until the British government committed blunders (executing the leaders and threatening conscription) that gained sympathy for the insurgents. Shaw draws attention to some of the more unsavoury aspects of Padraig Pearse's philosophy, including an implacable hatred of England, a belief in the sanctity of warfare and bloodshed, and an insistence on an exclusively Gaelic Irish identity. In Shaw's view, the Rising, by confirming unionist intransigence, did more to divide than unite Ireland and led directly to partition and indirectly to the Civil War of 1922–3.

Shaw's article was originally completed in 1966, during the year that marked the fiftieth anniversary of the 1916 Rising, but was not printed then because the critical tone of the piece was felt to be unsuitable for a commemoration. It was not published until 1972, by which time the mood of the country had changed considerably. The editor of *Studies* magazine introduced the 'Challenge' thus:

Although this article was not written as a tract for the present troubled time in Ireland . . . it may very well be read as such. In 1966 it seemed likely that a new chapter was opening in relations between Ireland and England, with special reference to the unity of this country. . . . The hopes of six years ago have been dashed, and today a new terror is abroad, a new violence in spirit and in deed.

It is the theme of the article which follows that insofar as this violence on one side seeks its inspiration in a certain interpretation of Ireland's patriotic past it cannot be justified as either Christian or truly patriotic.[33]

Throughout the 1970s and after, other books and articles by writers such as R. F. Foster, Terence Brown, F. S. L. Lyons, A. T. Q. Stewart, and T. W. Moody challenged the idea that Irish people are, or should be, exclusively Gaelic and Catholic. In various ways they searched in the past for more inclusive models of Irish identity. This intellectual current was an important influence on future members of the Field Day group, who were themselves critical of the status quo in both parts of the island.

At this point we must take a closer look at the individual members of the Field Day co-operative and at what they had been doing before being brought together on the board of directors. Field Day, unlike many other theatre companies, is not organized around a core group of actors. It is not characterized by any particular style of acting or direction. As a touring company, it does not have its own theatre building. It is, as Michael Sheridan has called it, 'a theatre company where the writer reigns'.[34] The only factor that has unified the activities of the company since 1981 is the board of directors, members of which either write the plays themselves or commission or select the work of other writers. Field Day is, at any point in time, only what the members of the board think it should be, so it is important to have some sense of who these men are. Furthermore, they are people trying to come to terms with a particular political situation, some knowledge of which is essential to an understanding of the pressures upon them. Since, as Heaney says, one goal of the company was to help redefine 'the relationship of Irish nationalism and culture', we shall focus particularly on this issue with respect to each of the directors.

There are at least two competing misrepresentations of the Field Day board, which I hope to challenge. The first, more naïve, view is that the members of the board are somehow representative of the larger political and cultural configurations in Northern Ireland, that the board balances evenly Protestant and Catholic concerns. This is an impression of the group more likely to be held by people outside the province—for example, the two *Newsweek* reporters who wrote in 1986 that

Field Day's board of directors consists of three men from the Catholic tradition and three from the Protestant, a fact that signals a hopeful truth about the artistic community in Ulster: it has strived to transcend sectarian differences, not simply wish them away.[35]

When another journalist made the happy suggestion to David Hammond that it was 'interesting, and perhaps significant, that the Field Day board members got along so beautifully although they were from "the two traditions"—three Protestants and three Catholics', he said, 'Yes, true', and added, 'All lapsed'.[36] In fact, none of the board members is particularly representative of the community from which he comes. This general observation is more true of the Protestant members than of the Catholic—there are no unionists on the Field Day board.

The other popular misapprehension about Field Day is that it has a covert political programme for Northern Ireland and that everything the company does advances a definite, but unstated, aim. This conspiracy theory has more adherents within the province and is held particularly by critics of the group who see it as a nationalist organization. W. J. McCormack, who has done Field Day the honour of stating that it 'has set the terms for the current debate in

Irish criticism', is certainly mistaken when he refers to the members of the board as a 'tightly structured team of polemicists'.[37] Field Day is a process, a practice, defined by what it does and, to a lesser extent, by what it says it is doing. Its aims are constantly evolving and change over time. Although the company has always insisted that it is engaged somehow with politics, the precise nature of this engagement has never been spelled out. This is deliberate. The Field Day directors have not promulgated a political 'platform' partly because they want to be free to change their emphasis as circumstances and the general political climate change, and partly, perhaps more important, because they could not agree on a single political position among themselves. David Hammond describes the protocol for early Field Day board meetings:

The meetings were irregular and infrequent, maybe four or five a year. But in those early days we were seeing each other as individuals, as companions, at all kinds of occasions so we were closely in touch. The meetings usually lasted a couple of days, maybe in Friel's house or a local hotel, and they were times of great pleasure. We seemed to be tireless, full of energy and laughs, very bold and allowing each other vast areas of disagreement.

There was never a proper chairman or anything like that so that the meetings would have appeared to an outsider as completely un-business like and wasteful of time. But they were important to us—the atmosphere allowed plenty of scope for ideas to generate, plenty of time for discovery. Although we did not often see eye to eye we always ended up by coming to a decision without ever having to vote.[38]

This conviviality has had the effect of distracting observers—and doubtless at times the directors themselves—from their 'vast areas of disagreement'. As Seamus Heaney says, each of the directors 'has a different version or vision of the thing'.[39] Each brought his own experience and preoccupations to the Field Day project, and Field Day itself is more a loose coalition than a disciplined party cell.

The pre-eminent director in 1981 was Brian Friel. It was his previous work and the philosophy implicit in it that had inspired Stephen Rea to approach him with the idea for a touring company. As the actor remarked in 1983, 'Everybody has to make a pilgrimage at some time and I made mine to Brian Friel.'[40] Friel himself had made a long pilgrimage to the theatre. Born in Omagh in 1929, he moved to Derry with his parents when he was 10 years old. His father was a schoolteacher and a Nationalist Party member of Derry Corporation, and Friel grew up in 'a very traditional, Catholic, nationalist home'.[41] He attended St Columb's College in Derry and at the age of 16 went to Maynooth College to study for the priesthood. He left after two and a half years without finishing. It was, he recalled in 1964, 'an awful experience, it nearly drove me cracked. It is one thing I want to forget. I never talk about it—the priesthood.'[42] Instead of devoting himself to the Church, Friel spent a year at St Joseph's Training College and began teaching mathematics in Derry, a career he would pursue for ten years. During those ten years he married, began writing short stories after school (he was under contract to the *New Yorker* for a time), and started, as he puts it, 'to survey and analyse the mixed holding I had inherited—the personal, traditional and acquired knowledge that cocooned me, an Irish Catholic teacher with a nationalist background, living in a schizophrenic community, son of a teacher, grandson of peasants who could neither read nor write'.[43]

In 1960 Friel left his teaching job and became a full-time writer. He soon decided to concentrate his efforts on dramatic writing. The BBC had already accepted two of his radio plays, and in 1962 his play *The Enemy Within* was performed at the Abbey Theatre in Dublin.[44] It tells the story of St Columb, the Irish monk who established a monastery on Iona, off the coast of Scotland. Friel dramatizes in him the dilemma of the person who must choose between the demands of home and tribe and the pure devotion to work of the priest or the poet.

Tyrone Guthrie, the distinguished Irish director, was impressed enough by *The Enemy Within* to invite Friel to come with him to Minneapolis, Minnesota, where he was going to open the theatre that would bear his name. Friel seized the opportunity, since he had found himself embarked somehow on a theatrical career while being 'almost totally ignorant of the mechanics of play-writing and play-production apart from an intuitive knowledge'. He took his wife and two children and moved to America for six months in 1964. This time was crucial both personally and professionally. Friel recalls,

I learned a great deal about the iron discipline of theatre, and I discovered a dedication and a nobility and a selflessness that one associates with a theoretical priesthood. But much more important than all these, those months in America gave me a sense of liberation—remember this was my first parole from inbred claustrophobic Ireland—and that sense of liberation conferred on me a valuable self-confidence and a necessary perspective so that the first play I wrote immediately after I came home, *Philadelphia, Here I Come!* was a lot more assured than anything I had attempted before.[45]

It was also Friel's first big hit, playing in Dublin, New York, and London within a few years. The play records the last night young Gar O'Donnell spends in his home village of Ballybeg before going to live with his crass Irish-American aunt in Philadelphia, with the action alternating between encounters on that night with his family and friends in the village and flashbacks to scenes of their previous relationships. Friel splits the character of Gar into a public and a private self to illustrate the lack of real communication between people who have known each other all their lives. Gar Public is guarded and taciturn, while Gar Private is inventive and loquacious.

Philadelphia, Here I Come! is well representative of Friel's best work. He takes a typically Irish theme—emigration—and deals with it in a highly personal way. The failure of communication and personal relationships, the contrast of cultures (in this case, Irish and American), the verbal power and complexity, are all typical of Friel. So, too, is the device of the split character. In the future, Friel's formal experiments would be part of an ongoing attempt to make play-goers feel the pressure of a wider truth without denying or diminishing the particular truths (often contrary to fact) of his characters; his best drama gives a sense of truth behind and between what characters are saying, but never allows the audience complacently to assume that it knows what that truth is. Critical events happen off-stage, or even far removed in time and space from the action of the plays, so the record is usually left tantalizingly incomplete. His characters may be consciously truthful, even when they give completely different versions of the same event, but no single character has access to the whole truth, the absolute that one is none the less made to feel as a real force in the world.

'Objective' observers in Friel's plays likewise miss significant aspects of this larger truth. The idea of personal or subjective reality is one that Friel holds very dear. In his 'Self-Portrait' he asks himself, 'What is a fact in the context of autobiography?' and answers,

A fact is something that happened to me or something I experienced. It can also be something I thought happened to me, something I thought I experienced. Or indeed an autobiographical fact can be pure fiction and no less true or reliable for that.[46]

Philadelphia, Here I Come! is not about Ballybeg or even about Gar's life there—it is about Gar's memory of his life there, his regrets about it, the things left unsaid. It is this that gives the play its power and poignancy. Even as Gar goes through the last, disappointing motions with the people who have constituted his life until now, he knows that he will idealize his birthplace as soon as he has left it behind him: 'Just the memory of it—that's all you have now—just the memory; and even now, even so soon, it is being distilled of all its coarseness; and what's left is going to be precious, precious gold . . .'.[47] Memory is the hidden or ostensible subject of most of Friel's plays. In *The Loves of Cass McGuire* (1966), old people in a nursing home find refuge in their own distorted versions of their past lives; the *Winners* and *Losers* in Friel's double-act, *Lovers* (1967), are winners and losers only in the light of things that happen outside the frame of the narrative; Fox, the showman in *Crystal and Fox* (1968), is driven by a self-destructive wish to return to a less encumbered past.

Friel generally captures his main characters on the threshold of death or of a new life. Fintan O'Toole writes, correctly I think, that Friel 'is essentially a writer dealing with change'.[48] Friel's stated ambition in 1970 was 'to write a play that would capture the peculiar spiritual, and indeed material, flux that this country is in at the moment'. He believed this would have to be done 'at a local, parochial level, and hopefully this will have meaning for other people in other countries'.[49] *Philadelphia, Here I Come!* had introduced theatre-goers to Friel's fictional County Donegal village. Most of his subsequent plays would also be set in Ballybeg, which he has compared with William Faulkner's Yoknapatawpha County.

Donegal is a usefully inclusive frame for an Irish playwright because, as a north-western border county, it is a focus for social tensions in both parts of the island. The problem of Irishness has been one that has interested Friel for a long time. As he explained in 1972, it is very difficult for an Irish writer to find his faith: he is born into a certainty that is cast-iron and absolute. The generation of Irish writers immediately before mine never allowed this burden to weigh them down. They learned to speak Irish, took their genetic purity for granted, and soldiered on. For us today the situation is more complex. We are more concerned with defining our Irishness than with pursuing it. We want to know what the word native means, what the word foreign means. We want to know have the words any meaning at all. And persistent considerations like these erode old certainties and help clear the building site.[50]

Friel's plays, taken together, are a fairly comprehensive investigation of the Irish Catholic psyche, in characters of different ages, classes, and historical epochs.

This questioning of national identity was intensified by the Troubles. Friel's party political involvement was in the 1960s, in the old Nationalist Party, but he found it a dreary, 'hopeless' organization.[51] After the outbreak of violence in 1969, his work departed for a time from the themes of his early memory plays in favour of more political comment. This latest sectarian outbreak in the North and the response, or lack of it, from the South demonstrated the worst of both Irish worlds. Characters like Gar and Cass were pathetic but sympathetic; it would be harder to find anyone to like in *The Mundy Scheme* (1969) or *The Gentle Island* (1971), both dark, bitter plays.

The Mundy Scheme is a heavy-handed satire on the materialism of the Republic and records the conspiracy of various members of the government in collusion with rich American business men to make the west of Ireland into an international graveyard (they consider 'The West's A Wake' as an advertising slogan). An opening voice-over asks,

What happens to an emerging country after it has emerged? Does the transition from dependence to independence induce a fatigue, a mediocrity, an ennui? Or does the clean spirit of idealism that fired the people to freedom augment itself, grow bolder, more revolutionary, more generous?

Friel's answer to the latter question appears to be an emphatic 'no', as Dan Mahon, the Minister for Development, defends the government's actions with the immortal words, 'Even if we did sell half the country to America we got top prices for it.'[52]

If he was critical of the modern Republic, Friel was no starry-eyed romantic about the Western Isles. *The Gentle Island* (dedicated to David Hammond), which exposes the underlying savagery of a group of inbred islandmen, is a deeply disturbing play because it so completely subverts the audience's expectations.[53] The play begins with an almost stereotyped exposition of the end of an era. Virtually all of the inhabitants of Inniskeen ('the gentle island') have decided to leave it for good and live on the mainland. Only Manus Sweeney, his son Joe, and his son and daughter-in-law Philly and Sarah have elected to stay on the island. The conventional sentimental response is to applaud these people who are keeping a tradition alive. This is the reaction of Peter, a visitor from Dublin who finds the Sweeneys hospitable and friendly. His travelling companion (and lover?) Shane is not so sure. Of Manus he says, 'The place and his way of life and everything he believes in and all he touches—dead, finished, spent.'[54] Throughout the play there are hints of brutality that cast doubt on the viability of the island culture. Manus is handicapped as the result of a fight years before with his wife's uncles during which they cut off one of his arms with herring knives, Sarah's mother nags her husband to drown the dog before they leave for the mainland, boys tie two cats together and throw hot water on them for amusement, and the young Sweeney men beat Shane merely for something to do. This disturbing undercurrent finally explodes into the open near the end of the play when Sarah claims to have seen her husband and Shane having sex in the boathouse. Manus reacts by taking down his gun—although Sarah is the one who ends up shooting Shane, wounding him severely. The play ends with Joe's decision to leave the island.

The Gentle Island is a shocking play, more so than anything else Friel has written. In brief outline, the plot is almost identical to that of *Translations*. The setting is remote, western, and rural, inhabited by Irish people who live in a traditionally Irish way. Strangers come and make friendly overtures to the natives, but they represent disruptive modern currents and encourage a restlessness in their hosts. A sexual transgression occurs involving one of the strangers, and the result is violence that heralds the end of the old way of life. The main difference, of course, is that in *Translations* the visitors are English and in *The Gentle Island* they are Irish. While in *Translations* the action could be interpreted as the subversion of a noble and pristine culture by malignant outside forces, in the earlier play it is the obduracy of the islanders in refusing to make any concession to the world outside that is questioned and criticized. The fact that the repression involved is homosexual is carefully calculated to produce the maximum unease in the audience. Had Friel continued in this mode it is difficult to imagine what he would have produced.

Friel's next play, *The Freedom of the City* (1973), was inspired by a particular incident, and he has said that, in retrospect, 'the experience of Bloody Sunday wasn't adequately distilled in me. I wrote it out of some kind of heat and some kind of immediate passion that I would want to have quieted a bit before I did it.'[55] The play does, however, capture admirably the emotions and public and private debates of the time. The incident about which the drama is constructed is the shooting, by the British Army, of unarmed civilians who have taken refuge in the Guildhall after a banned civil rights march. Friel surrounds three solid main charac- ters and their version of their lives with a multiplicity of public voices, including a judge, a police constable, a sociologist, a priest, a balladeer, a brigadier, an RTÉ commentator, and expert wit- nesses. Michael is an unemployed young man who has a basic faith in the justness of the civil rights movement and believes that if people like himself can show the authorities 'that we're responsible and respectable . . . they'll come to respect what we're campaigning for'. Skinner, in contrast, is a radical and a cynic who believes the basic issue is an unfair economic system, not political rights: 'It has nothing to do with doctors and accountants and teachers and dignity and boy scout honour. It's about us—the poor—the majority—stirring in our sleep. And if that's not what it's all about, then it has nothing to do with us.' Lily, the mother of eleven, admires both of them for their political conviction (although they disagree strongly with each other), but her reasons for marching are entirely personal. She has a mongol child, and she marches for him: 'Isn't that stupid? You and him and everybody else marching and protesting about sensible things like politics and stuff and me in the middle of you all, marching for Declan.'[56] The motivations we never hear mentioned by any of the principals are sectarian resent- ment and devotion to straightforward republicanism. These are imposed on them by outside authorities—news reporters, army officers, a priest, a writer of patriotic songs—and commended or condemned depending on the point of view of the observer. The official report, quoted at the end of the play, directly contradicts what the audience has witnessed. Even sympathetic accounts of the deceased, such as that given by reporters up from the Republic, do not reflect the characters as we have come to know them. Authorities prove once again to be unreliable. Political explanations do not, for Friel, answer the questions that are really worth asking about people.

Friel's *Volunteers* (1975) are likewise people for whom a political description is inadequate. They have all been interned for revolutionary political activity, but their reasons for joining the republican movement are very different. Smiler was imprisoned for leading the protest when a friend of his was interned; the elderly Knox joined the 'subversives' for companionship; Butt, rather like Michael in the earlier play, is a plain man who finally lost patience with injustice and discrimination; Keeney had been a leader of the movement, but has been rethinking his position in prison. They are also volunteers in a second sense—they have gained temporary release from prison in order to help with an archaeological excavation. On this, the last day of the dig, they find out that a kangaroo court of their fellow prisoners has sentenced them to death as traitors for collaborating with the state enemy. Whatever they do, whether they try to escape or return to prison, they will be killed. The play is dedicated to Seamus Heaney, and, as Heaney had done in *North*, Friel makes a 'symbol perfected in death' of a long-dead and anonymous person, in this case a skeleton with a hole in his skull and a rope around his neck. The prisoners identify themselves with 'Leif' and wonder how he died, speculating that he, too, was caught in a sectarian conflict, 'a war/Between Jesus and Thor'. Or maybe, as Keeney suggests, 'he was a casualty of language. . . . which of us here isn't?'[57] In this the plight of the volunteers may be a metaphor for the position of the artist in the minefield of language which is contemporary Ireland. Just as the dig site is about to be covered by a hotel, so the particular histories of the volunteers will be covered up and lost. The play, like Leif's skeleton, remains, a monument to their small part in the larger horror of the Troubles.

Living Quarters (1977) and the two scripts of 1979, *Aristocrats* and *Faith Healer*, mark a move away from the public divisions that had occupied Friel for a time and back into personal, intrafamily conflict. In this trio of plays, among Friel's most powerful, he is preoccupied by the question of how the past determines the present and is in turn changed by it through memory. Indeed, this was the question that had exercised Friel throughout his career, from Gar's daydreaming that remembers a love his father felt but was never capable of expressing, to the playwright's creation, through re-creation, of Baile Beag. Given his personal view of the way the world and the human mind work, it is hardly surprising that Friel was interested in historiography and revisionist history. He had always been committed to the re-examination of subjective images, whether of the national or the personal past. This inevitably had political implications, whether the politics were on the surface of the play, as in *The Freedom of the City*, or below it, as in *Aristocrats*. Ultimately, though, his plays resist the clarity of political discourse.

If Friel had a political programme at this point, it was to be found less in the subject-matter of his plays than in the process of creation itself. As a writer, he had come to see the political problem of Ireland's relation with Britain as a problem of language:

it's our proximity to England, it's how we have been pigmented in our theatre with the English experience, with the English language, the use of the English language, the understanding of words, the whole cultural burden that every word in the English language carries is slightly different to our burden.

Since the problem originated in language, Friel also believed it might be

solved by language in some kind of way. Not only the language of negotiations across the table. It's going to be solved by the recognition of what language means for us on this island. Whether we're speaking the kind of English that I would use, or whether we're using the kind of English that Enoch Powell would use. Because we are in fact talking about accommodation or marrying of two cultures here, which are ostensibly speaking the same language but which in fact aren't.[58]

Friel had spoken in 1980, during the run of *Translations*, about the need to find an authentic Irish voice in English: 'Perhaps this is an artist's arrogance, but I feel that once the voice is found in literature, then it can move out and become part of the common currency.'[59]

The politics, then, was in how the writer chose to deal with his subject, in the language he employed to articulate his view of the world. As for his themes, these had to come from within in order for him to avoid becoming 'a propagandist, or a megaphone for the more raucous element of [his] tribe' or betraying his 'inner spirit structure that must always refuse a worldly or public subscription'.[60] As Friel emphasized to Fintan O'Toole, he never began a play with the intention of making a statement:

I don't think you start from that premise. . . . You don't have anything to say about anything. You delve into a particular corner of yourself that's dark and uneasy, and you articulate the confusions and the unease of that particular period. When you do that, that's finished and you acquire other corners of unease and discontent.[61]

Stephen Rea's political beliefs were more clearly defined. He had deliberately moved away from his origins to become a republican. As he told a reviewer in 1982, 'My beliefs are not unionist, I think we need a new Ireland.'[62] Rea grew up in a Protestant area of Belfast, one of four children of a bus-driver, and decided he wanted to make a career in the theatre when he auditioned for the BBC Northern Ireland children's radio show 'I Want To Be An Actor'.[63] At Queen's University in Belfast he read English and French, but the only thing that really interested him in the curriculum was the story of the Irish Renaissance and the early Abbey Theatre. Rea remembers, 'My ambition was to tour Ireland doing plays. . . . The original Abbey was an inevitable influence for me. What else can you name that had that total connection with what was going on around it? It was opening wounds.'[64] Rea was not involved in the Dramatic Society—'I regarded them all as poseurs'—but helped to form the Young Irish Theatre Company, a 'self-consciously nationalist operation' performing works by Synge and Lady Gregory, 'reviving plays that probably didn't deserve to be revived. . . . a kind of Celtic twilight rather than modern social realism'.[65] The other major influence on Rea at university was meeting and talking with radical republicans. He says, 'The only good thing for me at Queen's was these Border Catholics coming in and seeing the whole thing as a sham. The austerity of Michael Farrell and the appropriate disrespect of Eamon McCann, took the place and showed it to be a pile of shit.'[66]

As soon as he finished his studies, Rea moved to the Republic and auditioned for the Abbey Theatre.[67] He was terribly disappointed by what he found, since 'I went consciously looking for the old Abbey, for the Irish nation. And of course it wasn't there.' In particular, he failed to find the dynamic partnership between theatre and politics that he had expected. His first Abbey production was an M. J. Molloy play set in sixteenth-century Ireland, but he did not learn until Molloy's speech on the opening night that the play was written 'to explore what it was like to live behind an iron curtain'. Rea recalls,

It's a moment that's burned into my head. Here was the author telling us that his intention had been overtly political, while the production had been a shambles, just thrown on and never addressed in any intellectual fashion, I didn't know until the curtain speech what the play was about. I should have gone out into the rain that night and not come back.[68]

It was not long before Rea did leave the Abbey for London. He met Jack MacGowran, a former Abbey actor who had made a similar escape years before and who offered Rea a part in his production of Sean O'Casey's *The Shadow of a Gunman*.[69] From this start, Rea went on to work on the Fringe, with companies like The People Show, Freehold, and the political touring group 7:84.[70] Richard Eyre spotted him for Trevor Griffiths' *Comedians*, which played at Nottingham, then at the Old Vic. With Griffiths Rea formed the first of his friendships with playwrights—others would be with Sam Shepard, Stewart Parker and, of course, Brian Friel. He believes that the relationship between actor and playwright is vital and that the best theatre happens when they 'meet half way'. He quickly moved on to the National Theatre, where he made a hit as *The Playboy of the Western World* in 1975. Rea enjoyed working at the National, where he felt the actor was placed above the director, and the Royal Court, whose productions seemed to him 'to touch the core of English life and society'.[71]

It was at the Royal Court that he met Friel, while acting in a production of *The Freedom of the City*. Rea remembers,

There was an instant rapport between us, we seemed to be thinking about the same kind of things. Then I hardly saw him for the next six years. In 1979 I gave him a call. We met and had a chat about things. It was purely instinctive. We both wanted the same things and we decided to work together to achieve them.[72]

In terms reminiscent of Friel's, Rea described in 1983 his own sense of the political and cultural climate in Ireland and what he hoped to accomplish through his work:

I think Ireland's beginning to try and throw off the old colonial thing so that we can get on with it ourselves. In the end, you know, it's really up to the artists. They're often the only ones that can do it. . . .

I think [the political situation is] desperate, and at the end of the day you can do very little about it. That's why I feel that Field Day is it for me. It's a political statement because we insist on being northern, and we insist on being all Ireland as well, you see, so you can't get more political than that. And we believe that the energy of Ireland at this moment in time is coming from the North, and this is our expression of it.[73]

He says, 'At the end of the day I have to believe what a play is saying before I can take part', and adds 'I don't know how people with left wing views can act a right wing part, or the other way around. I do not know what kind of schizo they are to be able to work like that.'[74]

Seamus Deane was likewise by 1981 committed to a political goal in his work as a teacher and critic, and his aim was the destruction of nationalist shibboleths. Born in Derry in 1940, he grew up in the Catholic ghetto of the Bogside.[75] With the help of the Education Act, he studied at St Columb's College in Derry, Queen's University in Belfast, and Cambridge University, and then spent several years in America at Reed College in Oregon and Berkeley in California, after which he returned to Ireland to continue his academic career. In 1981 he was Professor of English and American Literature at University College, Dublin, where he had been teaching since 1968.

He had early dedicated himself to a life of letters. By 1981, Deane had published two full books of poetry, *Gradual Wars* (1972) and *Rumours* (1977). In addition to being a creative writer, Deane was an influential literary and social critic. He was particularly interested in the intersection between politics and literature. In the introduction to his edition of *The Adventures of Hugh Trevor* by the eighteenth-century writer Thomas Holcroft, one of his first major academic projects, Deane writes, 'The merits of *Hugh Trevor* as a piece of fiction are a good deal less than the book's importance as a document in the development of one strain of radical, Dissenting thought in England.'[76] This statement is entirely characteristic, both in Deane's evident sympathy for Holcroft's radical critique of contemporary society and in his own attraction to literary works with a pronounced political content or undercurrent.

In his poem 'A Fable' Deane warns against the tendency to aestheticize the violence in the North, to see it as a tragedy from which it is impossible for Ireland to escape. Deane acknowledges that it is tempting to see a relentless Fate at work in the story of a Belfast house-painter who jumped through a window to escape from an assassin only to be shot through the head by a gunman on the other side. It would be more productive, though, to consider 'the stricter question|of hate. Who fired the gun?' 'Don't think of it as Fate', he urges,

> Don't try to be doubly kind
> to killer and killed.
>
> If all hold it in mind
> that killers will be killed, that
> the clear-sighted see the blind
> inscrutable face of Fate
> swarming with acne
> and adolescent hate, then all should find
> truer reason for despair
> in the story. . . .
>
> .   .   .   .
>
>   He has to be got,
> that unfinished youth who fires the shot.
> I write to finish the job.[77]

In other words, in order to address the disorders of Northern Ireland it is essential first to see them as human problems and then to think about the roots from which they spring.

For Deane, the most obvious source of the Northern minority's discontent was inequality and discrimination. Having grown up when and where he did, he saw plenty of things to criticize about society in the North. In 'Derry' he writes,

> The unemployment in our bones
> Erupting on our hands in stones;
>
> The thought of violence a relief,
> The act of violence a grief;
>
> Our bitterness and love
> Hand in glove.[78]

In Northern Ireland, the problem of economic deprivation is complicated by the tribal element. When Deane was a boy in Derry advancement was blocked for Catholics and the ancient grudge between the Protestant civic leaders and the Catholic citizen majority gained new life in each generation. The existence of the 'other side' fostered ties within each community. Continuity and a sense of belonging, partly predicated on resentment of those who did not belong, was reinforced by community rituals. Deane focuses on this aspect of the problem and the lingering effect of such formative experiences on his own perception of the Northern crisis in a later poem, 'Bonfire'. One of the biggest tribal celebrations in Northern Ireland is Derry Day, 12 August, when loyalists from all over the province (and the world) meet to march through Derry. To counter this display, Catholics in the city traditionally affirm their own solidarity on 15 August, with bonfires ostensibly laid in commemoration of Our Lady. In 'Bonfire', the poet acknowledges his ties with his people and suggests that present violence may be an unavoidable consequence of past injustice. His education and the distance he has travelled from Derry have equipped him with a desire to be objective, but he doubts whether he has the ability. Is it, he seems to ask, having considered the circumstances from afar, wrong after all to take sides?

> Had I not been then so shone upon
> I might have learned a milder wisdom.
> Yet I have burnt each hand
> In unison with all those damned
> Who warmed themselves each year
> By the hot wood and I fear
>
> The colder temper that we gained
> Endures more stress than we have strained
> To give it. I cannot understand or pray

That what others think should weigh
More than it does. A tree that crashes
Weighs no more, burnt, than its ashes.

I wish there were avoiding it
For the condemned
And for the wise.
But who would pretend
Now to advise?
For there must be burning once the fire's lit.[79]

Deane, in common with working-class poets of other nationalities (the English poet Tony Harrison, for example), was alienated from his childhood surroundings by his education and the doors that opened to him. This general unease was compounded by the fact that the deliverance from conditions of deprivation came from the very State he was bred to distrust. His education was the instrument both of his freedom and of his isolation as an individual. For the artist this alienation is often fruitful, but also painful, as he is torn between the wish to participate fully in his world and his recognition of the need for detachment to render it effectively in language. The separation of the writer from the things he is writing about is mirrored by a division in himself. Deane's enigmatic poem 'The Victim', written for Brian Friel, may be read as a parable on his own estrangement from his roots at the very time that he mastered the linguistic resources to write about them. The people and places of home

interfused with each resolve
To leave until a covert language took
Possession of my mind and made me feel
The foreigner who yet possessed the real
Touch for love the native always knows,
The tang of territory, the zodiac
Of signs, gangland's sudden close

Upon an enemy as though God had made a sign
That this guy's language wasn't theirs or mine,
Though he said nothing other than what he wore
Which cut his body out for other classes
Or sliced his face in two with horn-rimmed glasses.[80]

The speaker of the poem and the 'enemy' in horn-rimmed glasses, the 'native' and the 'foreigner', are both Seamus Deane.

In 1969 Deane joined forces with Derek Mahon, W. J. McCormack (also known as Hugh Maxton), Augustine Martin, and Michael Gill to start a review called *Atlantis*. Brian Friel and Seamus Heaney were among the 'founder sponsors', along with the likes of Samuel Beckett, Donald Davie, Brian Moore, and John Hewitt. The idea was to provide a focus for 'informed commentary' on 'current events, tradition, the arts'. The team declared in their inaugural editorial,

Part of our aim is to see Ireland in an international perspective, to lift its drowsy eyelid and disturb it into a sense of relationship and awareness. . . .

Atlantis will be a literary magazine, but not exclusively so. Literature is about life (it is, in a sense, life;) and the obsessive tedium of so much Irish writing is a reflection on the society which engenders it. We must, therefore, examine that society, and the larger human society of which it forms such a minute part, in an attentive and critical spirit. To this extent *Atlantis* will be a political magazine also. Recent events in Northern Ireland have revealed that our old lunacies persist, which is profoundly depressing; but also what is at last almost exhilarating, that there is a new awareness of the need for radical change, and an urgent need to expose the real polarities of Irish life.[81]

Atlantis published a great deal of new Irish writing, including work by John Montague, Francis Stuart, Brian Moore, William Trevor, Thomas Kinsella, John Banville, James Simmons, and virtually every other notable Irish writer of the time. Another speciality of the magazine was translation, along with critical articles by commentators as different as Roy Johnston, once Marxist theorist for the IRA, and Conor Cruise O'Brien.

In the second issue of *Atlantis* (October 1970), Deane published a review of several new books on Northern Ireland notable for the insight it provides into his own analysis of the Troubles at that time. The first element he examines is that of ethnic nationalism, which he describes as a nation's attempt to define its essence in terms of genetic purity. This, he warns, leads easily on to racism: 'It seems clear, at this point in time, that the ethnic roots of Catholic and Protestant dreams of unity [with the rest of Ireland or with Great Britain] must be pulled.' In his view, 'The people of both parts of Ireland are in need of each other and therefore in need of a solution which goes beyond the current nationalist remedies.'[82]

Deane praises warmly a book by Liam de Paor called *Divided Ulster*. De Paor's interpretation, with which Deane concurs, is that 'Northern Ireland is a standard colonial problem whose idiosyncrasies are cast into high and somewhat false relief by the glossy sheen of the consumer ethic typical of advanced capitalism'.[83] For Deane, the real root of the problem is economic, and his prescription in 1970 is a movement toward the left:

To quote Marx—probably a silly thing to do in Ireland, but nevertheless—'Right can never be higher than the economic structure of society and its cultural development conditioned thereby'. Forty years of unemployment and injustice and impoverishment in the Bogside make that sound like a very pungent truism.[84]

These three ideas—the threat posed by ethnic nationalism, the colonial nature of Ireland's problems, and the economic basis of violence in the North—would remain important elements of Deane's social thinking.

Atlantis became a journal increasingly devoted to public affairs. By the fifth issue it was bursting at the seams as a literary magazine, with 70 out of 136 pages devoted to articles on the 'New Ireland Concept' in which different writers outlined the kind of Ireland they would like to see in the future. An editorial distinguished between 'reformist' and 'revolutionary' approaches to the New Ireland, espousing the latter,[85] and contributors followed through with a generally Marxist approach to social and economic problems. In 1974 *Atlantis* ceased publication after four years and six issues. McCormack explains the reasons for the shut-down, chief among them being the huge increase in printing and paper costs and the fact that the editors were no longer living close together, since conducting business on paper rather than in person highlighted their different priorities.[86] Certainly the tone of the final editorial differed from the breezy confidence of the first one:

Despite the speed with which public affairs develop and mature, we have little confidence that, by the time this issue of *Atlantis* reaches the public, Ireland will have significantly advanced in its politics. There has been change certainly—a new President and a new government in the south, and a new kind of parliament in the north—but this is only the minimal superficial change which effectively blocks the way to any profound adjustment in our society.[87]

Another, longer-lived, journal with which Deane was closely associated was *The Crane Bag*, started in 1977 by Richard Kearney (a former student of Deane's at University College, Dublin) and Mark Patrick Hederman, with Deane as a member of the editorial board. In lieu of creative writing, *The Crane Bag* published mainly social and literary criticism along with interviews with prominent intellectuals and politicians. Each issue of *The Crane Bag* looked at one subject or theme in various ways. Contributors spanned the political spectrum. The editors tried to avoid adopting one position for the magazine, which they envisioned as a container for many different views. Kearney and Hederman used the idea of 'the fifth province' to explain what they wanted *The Crane Bag* to be. Modern Ireland consists of four provinces, yet the Irish word for a province means 'fifth'. This anomaly led the editors to posit a new kind of unity in the fifth province, one that would transcend the divisions between the four historical provinces: 'The purpose of *The Crane Bag* is to promote the excavation of unactualized spaces within the reader, which is the work of constituting the fifth province. From such a place a new understanding and unity might emerge.'[88]

The notion the magazine attempted to challenge was more fundamental than any particular political view; it was, in fact, 'the assumption that art and politics are two quite separate areas: the former a matter of the yearly visit to gallery or concert; the latter, an item of daily news, but other people's business'. In *The Crane Bag*, the editors hoped, 'the creativity of art and the commitment of politics might converge'.[89] Kearney's keynote contribution to the first issue made the case for a positive relationship between politics and art:

Art has always been considered non-political by virtue of the age-old prejudice that it is opposed to reality. In its most fundamental dimension, however, art may become intimately related to reality, not just as 'imitation' (Mimesis) but as 'creation' (Poesis). Thus viewed, art is reality in excess, ahead of itself, over-reaching its traditional boundaries towards the horizon of possibility: ultra-reality.[90]

The notion of a fifth province above the fray of national politics and the conviction that art could shape as well as reflect society would become central to the Field Day enterprise. Other ideas that would surface time and again in various Field Day projects were also floated in *The Crane Bag*. In the second issue, for example, the theme explored was the 'sense of nation', with the editors concluding, on the evidence, that there was a 'deeply rooted schizophrenia in the Irish psyche', a result, at least in part, of the 'English colonization of Ireland'.[91] The third issue started from the premiss that modern Irishness is 'predominantly bourgeois, Catholic and nationalistic' and asked 'Is there an alternative way in which Irish people can develop and cultivate a sense of identity? Can we go beyond the idioms of religious sectarianism, nationalist self-righteousness and bourgeois preoccupation with "the greasy till"?' (The editors concluded that 'the mythic experience of openness may serve as counterpoint to any modern "nationalist" experience of enclosure'.)[92]

Meanwhile, throughout the 1970s, *The Crane Bag* was only one of many journals to which Deane contributed, reordering Irish literary history in the process.[93] He was especially fascinated by the Irish Literary Revival and by the contemporary 'Northern poets'. As a critic he concentrated on 'the relation of poetry to national feeling in Ireland'. As he wrote in 1975, although the response of twentieth-century writers to politics might vary in different periods, 'all preoccupations are related to nationalism—the need to join with it or escape from it; with Ireland, and the need to create identity on its terms or to dictate identity on the poet's own'.[94] He identified the writers of the Revival, from Yeats and Synge to Pearse, Joyce, and O'Casey, with a late manifestation of the Victorian-Romantic struggle against middle-class utilitarianism. In various essays Deane explored the 'literary myths' of the Revival: the idea of 'Celtic' distinctiveness, inherited from Matthew Arnold, which he regarded as largely responsible for the insidious racialism behind ethnic nationalism; a tendency to idealize the writer or exceptional individual, coupled with a wistful nostalgia for community and haunted by guilt over betrayal of the group; and a shared eagerness to replace a disorderly history with historical fictions that were actually disguised aesthetic theories. Although he regarded many of these fictions as dangerous when they were taken by the unwary as fact, Deane believed that the encounter of the Revival writers with history had been, on the whole, an enabling one. The comparatively little interest he displayed in Irish writers of the thirties, forties, and fifties may be attributable to the fact that they seemed to him more determined to avoid the demands of politics. With the renewed outbreak of violence in the sixties, however, Northern poets were confronted with a public crisis that it was impossible to ignore. In his writings on these poets of his own generation, from John Montague to Derek Mahon, Deane focused on their response to the political situation in the province, regarding that as the central challenge of the times to art. When he joined the Field Day board in 1981 he was one of Ireland's most controversial critics, eager to carry the debate outside of academe. Field Day, for him, might be a way to answer the self-rebuke in his 1977 poem 'Scholar II':

> I remember at times
> How irresponsible I have
> Become. No ruling passion
> Obsesses me, although passions
> Are what I play among.
> I'll know the library in a city
> Before I know there is a slum.
> I could wish the weight of
> Learning would bring me down
> To where things are done.[95]

If Seamus Deane would prove to be the most influential addition to the Field Day project, Seamus Heaney was the best known. Born in 1939 in County Derry, Heaney was the eldest of nine children of a Catholic farmer and cattle-dealer. Like Deane, he attended St Columb's College in Derry and Queen's University, Belfast, where he was a member of the informal 'Group' whose mentor was Philip Hobsbaum.[96] After completing his degree he taught for several years at St Thomas's Secondary School and St Joseph's College of Education in Belfast before taking a position as a lecturer at Queen's, which he held from 1966 until 1972. During this period he spent one academic year (1970–1) at the University of California in Berkeley, then a centre of student unrest. In 1972 he moved to County Wicklow in the Republic and worked for several years as a freelance writer and broadcaster. From 1975 to 1981 he lectured at Carysfort College in Dublin, moving to the city in 1979. By 1981 he had published *Death of a Naturalist* (1966), *Door Into the Dark* (1969), *Wintering Out* (1972), *North* (1975), *Field Work* (1979), and various other pamphlets and limited editions. Faber's issue, in 1980, of both *Preoccupations: Selected Prose 1968–1978* and *Selected Poems 1965–1975* confirmed Heaney's reputation.

In contrast to Deane, who in his criticism made the case for an international, comparative approach to the history and literature of Ireland, Heaney strove to reach universal truths by probing more and more deeply into limited, personal experience. As a man and as a poet he was doubly divided—between his Irish cultural inherit- ance and his English literary heritage and between the beliefs and prejudices of a Northern Catholic and the tenets of his liberal education. Both of these divisions were brought into sharp focus by the Troubles, and some of Heaney's most compelling poetry is enriched by the tension between various aspects of his own personality. Central to his writing persona is an awareness of the nature of the sectarian divide in Northern Ireland. In 1984 Heaney would say that his 'quietist' approach to the 'sectarian thing' was largely a result of growing up in the country: 'in a rural community of small farmers, the cooperative element is always there. You can't really fall out, you can't live two lives. You can't live a life of sectarian resentment and, at the same time, neighbourly cooper- ation. I suppose it is possible—but we didn't, anyway.'[97] Lack of 'resentment', however, does not imply that one is unconscious of difference, and sectarianism was more of a shaping force for Heaney than at times he would like to admit. Gravity in Northern Ireland pulls the individual inexorably toward one of the two main communities, Protestant or Catholic. Heaney has gone so far as to say that there is really no such thing as a private person in Ireland, that 'the first person singular is ratified by a family life and a place in the community, that each person has a kind of public profile, no matter how small the public happens to be'.[98]

In *Death of a Naturalist*, Heaney's first full-length collection, 'Docker' sticks out. Among love poems and poems about his child- hood in the country, it focuses on a Protestant dock worker (tra- ditionally one of the most sectarian occupations in the North) for whom 'God is a foreman with certain definite views':

> That fist would drop a hammer on a Catholic—
> Oh yes, that kind of thing could start again ...[99]

Heaney recalled in 1977 that this was one of the very first poems he wrote: 'my first attempts to speak, to make verse, faced the Northern sectarian problem. Then this went underground and I

became very influenced by Hughes and one part of my temperament took over: the private county Derry childhood part of myself
rather than the slightly aggravated young Catholic male part.' This
Catholic part, a social and political as much as a religious identification, never really left him, though:

I think that poetry and politics are, in different ways, an articulation, an
ordering, a giving of form to inchoate pieties, prejudices, world-views, or
whatever. And I think that my own poetry is a kind of slow, obstinate,
papish burn, emanating from the ground I was brought up on.[100]

If most of *Death of a Naturalist* was concerned with the poet's
personal past, it also includes poems like 'At a Potato Digging'
and 'For the Commander of the "Eliza"' that indicate Heaney's
identification with an ancestral past that would become more and
more the subject of his poetry. He is as careful with his blame as
with his praise, however, aware that he will be regarded as speaking
for more than just himself. As he says,

Everybody in the north is born with a sense of solidarity with one or other
group. . . . So the emergent self grows up carrying responsibility for the
group—holding the line, keeping up the side. But as you come to different
awareness you know there are complicated concessions to be made, truths
to be told beyond the official shibboleths. Yet the minute you do set
down . . . betrayals . . . you become consciously aware that you aren't just
yourself, you *are* part of the group. I suppose a lot of self-censorship goes
on.[101]

Through most of the 1970s Heaney was affirming and exploring
his specifically Irish heritage, while the activity that was becoming
the centre of his life—writing poetry in English—ensured that he
could never forget the British dimension of himself. As a writer,
politics and language were inextricably linked for him. Heaney's
study of Irish gave him a strong sense of an alternative tradition,
and this attempt to link himself with Irish roots was 'congruent'
with 'the political disaffection from Unionism'.[102] The effort
to effect a reconciliation between the two would be an abiding
concern for him. In the placename poems of *Wintering Out*
('Anahorish', 'Toome', 'Broagh') Heaney believed he had achieved
a breakthrough 'that convinced me that one could be faithful to the
nature of the English language—for in some senses these poems
are erotic mouth-music by and out of the anglo-saxon tongue—

and, at the same time, be faithful to one's own non-English origin'.[103]

Around the same time, Heaney was discovering a poetic image that would allow him to hint at complexities beyond the Irish–English dichotomy. The bog appears in Heaney's work in the last poem of *Door Into the Dark*, 'Bogland', where 'Every layer they strip | Seems camped on before.'[104] Heaney pointed out in 1975 that the word 'bog' is one of the few words in English taken directly from Irish, where it means 'soft'. In the area where Heaney grew up, the bog was also called 'the moss', and 'moss' is a word with Norse origins probably carried to Ireland by Scottish planters. The linguistic mesh of 'bog' and 'moss' thus carried in it the Irish, English, and Northern European points of reference in some of Heaney's best-known poems.[105] The language, like the bog itself, preserves the past. In 'Navvy' (*Wintering Out*), Heaney elaborates on the bog as an embalmer, this time in the more sinister guise of a history that claims us whether we regard it or not:

> . . . The morass
> the macadam snakes over
>
> swallowed his yellow bulldozer
> four years ago, laying it down
> with lake-dwellings and dug-outs,
> pike-shafts, axe-heads, bone pins,
>
> all he is indifferent to.[106]

In later poems such as 'The Tollund Man', 'The Grauballe Man', 'Punishment', and 'Strange Fruit', victims of ancient tribal violence have been wedded to the 'goddess' for so long that they have become a part of the bog, with 'pods' for eyelids, wrists like 'bog oak', an instep 'cold as a swan's foot | or a wet swamp root'. In Heaney's poetry they undergo a second transformation in art, and the brutal nature of their deaths is distanced as they are seen in the context of a history extending behind and before them. This distancing, however, is compromised in each case by an implicit comparison with the present day, which cannot be contemplated with equanimity. If the poems offer the consolation that violence is nothing new to the twentieth century and contemporary conflicts will be forgotten someday just as the bodies in the bog have been absorbed into the land, the parallels between present and past undermine the comforting objectification of the bog bodies and force the poet to see them as human. In 'Punishment', for example, the speaker addresses the corpse of a girl who was executed for adultery and draws a connection between her plight and that of Catholic girls in his own Northern Ireland who were abused for dating British soldiers. The force of the poem derives from his own ambivalence toward his subject:

> I almost love you
> but would have cast, I know,
> the stones of silence.
>
> .   .   .   .   .
>
> I who have stood dumb
> when your betraying sisters,
> cauled in tar,
> wept by the railings,
>
> who would connive
> in civilized outrage
> yet understand the exact
> and tribal, intimate revenge.[107]

Throughout the early 1970s, Heaney was gradually facing up more directly to his own sectarian resentments, residues in himself of which his education told him to be ashamed. His time at Berkeley had given him an enhanced awareness of poetry as 'a mode of resistance'—*North* was one of the fruits of this.[108] Another was *Stations* (1975), a pamphlet of prose pieces embodying experiences Heaney compared with Wordsworth's 'spots of time'. Beginning in 1970–1 in Berkeley and finishing in May and June of 1974, Heaney excavated 'moments at the very edge of consciousness which had lain for years in the unconscious'. He says, 'I wrote each of them down with the excitement of coming for the first time to a place I had always known completely', and 'the sectarian dimension of that pre-reflective experience presented itself as something asking to be uttered also'.[109] In 'Kernes', a Protestant boy exchanges taunts with the speaker and his friends, who throw sods at him and then disappear 'down lanes and over pads'. A young boy resists the beauty of 'Sweet William' flowers because of the sectarian associations of their name. 'July' reverberates with the menacing drums of Protestants preparing to celebrate the anniversary of the Battle of the Boyne: 'Through red seas of July the Orange drummers led a chosen people through their dream.'[110]

Not all of Heaney's poems dealing with the sectarian divide simply record it. Sometimes the moment depicted is an awkward attempt to bridge the gap. One of these, also in *Stations*, is 'Trial Runs', in which a Protestant neighbour returning from the Second World War brings the speaker's father rosary beads as a present. The two men make uneasy jokes about it, and 'Their laughter sailed above my head, a hoarse clamour, two big nervous birds dipping and lifting, making trial runs over a territory.'[111] This neighbour recalls the one in 'The Other Side', who is confident and dismissive on his own side of the stream, but shy and diffident on the other. At the end of the poem the speaker surprises him in their yard, waiting for the rosary to end before he knocks on the door for a visit:

> . . . I stand behind him
> in the dark yard, in the moan of prayers.
> He puts a hand in a pocket
>
> or taps a little tune with the blackthorn
> shyly, as if he were party to
> lovemaking or a stranger's weeping.
>
> Should I slip away, I wonder,
> or go up and touch his shoulder
> and talk about the weather
>
> or the price of grass-seed?[112]

Heaney was trying in these years to overcome his reticence on the subject of the Troubles. In 'Whatever You Say Say Nothing' (*North*), he repudiates the conspiracy of silence in Northern Ireland, where ' "Religion's never mentioned" ':

> O land of password, handgrip, wink and nod,
> Of open minds as open as a trap,
>
> Where tongues lie coiled, as under flames lie wicks,
> Where half of us, as in a wooden horse
> Were cabin'd and confined like wily Greeks,
> Besieged within the siege, whispering morse.[113]

The speaker is still afraid that he is 'incapable' of springing a leak in these 'great dykes'. The desire to be fair without being false was something that Heaney had expressed as his concern as early as 1972:

On the one hand, poetry is secret and natural, on the other hand it must make its way in a world that is public and brutal. . . .

At one minute you are drawn towards the old vortex of racial and religious instinct, at another time you seek the mean of humane love and reason. . . .

You have to be true to your own sensibility, for the faking of feelings is a sin against the imagination. Poetry is out of the quarrel with ourselves and the quarrel with others is rhetoric. . . .

One half of one's sensibility is in a cast of mind that comes from belonging to a place, an ancestry, a history, a culture, whatever one wants to call it. But consciousness and quarrels with the self are the result of what Lawrence called 'the voices of my education'.[114]

By 1977, the twin fault lines in Heaney's writing personality—between an Irish and a British cultural inheritance and along the sectarian divide in the North—were merging into one in his thinking. He told Seamus Deane in an interview in *The Crane Bag* that

I always thought of the political problem . . . as being an internal Northern Ireland division. I thought along sectarian lines. Now I think that the genuine political confrontation is between Ireland and Britain. Yet it is my own sensibility and heritage of feeling which is the basis for the feeling of the poems, and I never had any strong feelings, for example, about the British army; it was always the R.U.C., the B Specials, and so on.

Acknowledging that the recent English language tradition seemed to tend towards 'the insulated and balanced statement', Heaney none the less expressed his belief that 'major poetry will always burst that corseted and decorous truthfulness'. In doing so, it was bound to be 'one-sided': 'the poet incarnates his mythos and must affirm it.' The mediation between the balance of form and the imbalance of feeling was 'the very root and intimacy of the poet's act'. His poem 'Hercules and Antaeus' was, he said, a metaphor for this tension, where 'Hercules represents the balanced rational light while Antaeus represents the pieties of illiterate fidelity.' In the case of 'almost every Northern poet, the rational wins out too strong'.[115] Heaney saw himself as no exception. His Antaeus is 'raised up' by 'the challenger's intelligence':

out of his element
into a dream of loss

and origins—the cradling dark,
the river-veins, the secret gullies
of his strength,
the hatching grounds

of cave and souterrain,
he has bequeathed it all
to elegists.[116]

In *Field Work*, Heaney's 1979 collection, the rational seems to win out even more conclusively, as the poet tries to step back and find some perspective beyond taking sides. He quotes Coventry Patmore approvingly in 'The Harvest Bow': *'The end of art is peace.'*[117]

Seamus Heaney had moved literally as well as figuratively away from his 'origins'. In 1972, when he decided to take his family to live in County Wicklow, Ian Paisley's *Protestant Telegraph* pronounced good riddance to the 'well-known papist propagandist' on his return to 'his spiritual home in the popish republic', while the *Irish Times* welcomed him with an editorial.[118] Heaney recalls, 'it wasn't a matter to me of rejecting anyone but of my own growth. The crossing of the border had a political edge to it because we were opting to go into the Republic. But I was quite content in a way to accept and undergo that political dimension because I had never considered myself British.'[119]

The move was nevertheless a wrenching one. The raw hurt of uprooting comes through clearly in the poems of 'A Northern Hoard' (*Wintering Out*). At one point the speaker declares, 'I'm cauterized, a black stump of home.'[120] If Heaney did not believe he had betrayed 'Ulster', he sometimes wondered whether he had not betrayed himself. This worry finds poignant expression in 'Exposure', the final poem in *North*. The poet, in Wicklow, attempts to justify himself to himself:

> I am neither internee nor informer;
> An inner émigré, grown long-haired
> And thoughtful; a wood-kerne

Escaped from the massacre,
Taking protective colouring
From bole and bark, feeling
Every wind that blows;

Who, blowing up these sparks
For their meagre heat, have missed
The once-in-a-lifetime portent,
The comet's pulsing rose.[121]

One suspects that much of the appeal of the Field Day enterprise for Heaney was its Northern slant. Involvement in the company would be a focus for his thoughts on the continuing crisis of his birthplace and a way for him to affirm his identity as a Northerner. Fortunately, he had never fully severed his roots.

David Hammond, unique among the Field Day board members, had not left Northern Ireland to live elsewhere but had stayed on even through the worst of the Troubles. Born in Belfast in 1928, Hammond's first career (like Brian Friel's) was as a teacher. He taught in both primary and secondary schools and was principal for a time of a centre for handicapped adults. In 1964 Hammond joined the educational department of the BBC, where he served as a radio producer, a television producer, a maker of documentary films, and as head of education, winning a Golden Harp award in 1972 for 'Dusty Bluebells', a film study of children's street games in Belfast.[122] Another particular enthusiasm of his was folk music, and he had been in charge of a number of radio and television programmes dealing with various aspects of folklore and music. He also collected and performed songs, recording four albums of traditional Irish songs himself, producing three albums of music performed by others, and publishing a book of Belfast songs.[123] Hammond had begun singing publicly in 1956 and since then had performed under the auspices of Orange Lodges, Gaelic football clubs, and government departments.[124] In 1980 Hammond was still with the BBC, though growing restive with its institutional nature, and he may have looked to Field Day as a less formalized mode of contributing to the cultural life of Northern Ireland.

Hammond's interest in folk culture is connected with his belief that the idea of two 'separate, intact communities at loggerheads' in Northern Ireland is belied by history. 'I don't believe,' he says,

that there are two things: a Planter culture and a Gaelic culture. I think it
was a great mistake by the Arts Council in the 1970s to send round two
poets, one called John Hewitt and one called John Montague, and call it
Planter and Gael. I think that's reinforcing some kind of crippled vision of
what Ireland was, you know. As if . . . half of the people remained truly
Gaelic and part of the people remained truly Planter. I think it's awful. I
think it's terrible. It's to do with the feeling that all Celts are Catholic and
all Planters are Protestant.[125]

Hammond asserts that the real story is much more complicated
than this. He likes to point out, for example, that Maginnis and
Paisley are Celtic names, while Hume and Fitt are British names,
and that the vast majority of the men who work in the Belfast
shipyards are Protestant Celts, with Irish surnames. Hammond
remarks, 'I have spent a lot of time . . . with vernacular speech,
vernacular song, architecture, the folklife of the country. Folklife is
only another name for history. Folklife is the people's own version
of their own lives, where they came from. History is a kind of
official version of that.' At the grassroots level, he believes, 'There
is less difference—I'm not saying that the difference doesn't
exist, for God's sake people are killing each other because of the
difference—but there is not as much difference as that Planter-
Gael thing encourages.'[126] Like Friel, Hammond is fascinated by the
idea of language as the emblem for a whole culture, and the
language he wants to capture in some lasting form is the language
of 'the street and the kitchen' before it is 'driven out' by formal
education.

Despite his interest in history, Hammond believes that it is time
for Ireland to look toward the future. He says it is unfortunate that
Irish artists have been encouraged in 'a kind of nostalgia, an eternal
fixation with the past'. He feels that 'In a country which has the
highest proportion of young people in Europe, many of them
without employment, that approach is simply not realistic any
more.'[127]

Hammond says Field Day grew out of 'despair with unionist and
nationalist outlooks' and a 'mistrust of politicians, political systems'. He saw the chance to promote 'some kind of alternative
outlook on the island' which would be 'apart from either unionism
or nationalism'.[128] Hammond himself has never belonged to any
political party and has always eschewed the doctrinaire.[129] He

acknowledges, however, 'some kind of wish for a self-determining style of government. Something to do with the feeling that we ought to be able to do it ourselves. It isn't anti-English. . . . It's just a feeling that we can do it ourselves.'[130]

Tom Paulin, like Stephen Rea, came from a Protestant background and called himself a republican. He, however, had reached that position comparatively recently in 1981. As he recalled a few years later,

Until about 1980 I took a different view and believed what most Ulster Protestants still believe—that Northern Ireland was, and ought to remain, permanently wedded to Great Britain. Although I had always hated Ulster Unionism very bitterly and supported the Civil Rights movement from the beginning, I believed that civil rights and greater social justice in Northern Ireland could be achieved within the context of the United Kingdom. . . . I believed that to oppose the partition of Ireland was necessarily to espouse a violent and simplistic nationalism. . . .

Belatedly, I've come to believe that class politics and proper democracy will only be possible in Ireland once the 'national question' has been answered. . . . In my view it is impossible to achieve a wide and cultivated cosmopolitan outlook without beginning . . . from the idea of a secular republic.[131]

Paulin was born in Leeds in 1949 and brought up in Belfast, his mother's birthplace. His grandfather had been a Presbyterian elder, and his grandmother served as a nurse in Carson's Army, which helped to resist the home rule tide and kept Ulster (or at least part of it) British. His father, however, was an outsider, an Englishman who had moved to Belfast to become headmaster of a school there. Paulin's parents were middle-class liberals who opposed the Unionist regime at Stormont and always voted Labour before politics in the province became completely polarized. The entire household took a keen interest in political affairs. One of the poet's earliest memories is of his father asking him in 1956 (when he was seven years old) who he thought the new leader of the Conservative Party would be.[132]

If Paulin did not fully participate in unionist culture, he did identify strongly with Northern Ireland. Despite the fact that he had attended Hull and Oxford Universities and that he was teaching at Nottingham University in 1981, Paulin's writing still focused on the North. His family ties continued to draw him back to the province, and he was married to a Northern Irish woman of Indian origin.[133] In 'Surveillances', the poet surveys the contemporary Northern Irish landscape, complete with prison camp and circling helicopter, and concludes,

> You know this is one
> Of the places you belong in,
> And that its public uniform
> Has claimed your service.[134]

By 1981 Paulin had already published two full-length collections of poetry, *A State of Justice* (1977) and *The Strange Museum* (1980), and three shorter poetry books, *Theoretical Locations* (1975), *Personal Column* (1978), and *The Book of Juniper* (1981). In 1983 Seamus Deane would call him 'the only political poet writing in Ireland at the moment'.[135] The first poem in his first book is called 'Cadaver Politic', which gives some idea of his tone. Paulin tended to focus on the banal, sordid aspects of everyday personal and political life, and a streak of anti-authoritarianism ran through much of his poetry. 'A Just State', for example, is described in these terms

> Its justice is bare wood and limewashed bricks,
> Institutional fixtures, uniforms,
> The shadows of watchtowers on public squares,
> A hemp noose over a greased trap.[136]

Northern Ireland, for Paulin, was an especially unnatural creation. One poem opens on the 'stretch of water' separating Ireland from Great Britain, and continues,

> Any state, built on such a nature,
> Is a metal convenience, its paint
> Cheapened by the price of lives
> Spent in a public service.[137]

The speaker of 'A Partial State' reflects on the past injustices of Stormont, about which the British overlords did not wish to know too much, and concludes with the motto: '*What the wrong gods established | no army can ever save*'.[138]

In his political poetry, Paulin had made several different approaches to his Northern Irish subject. In 'Manichean Geography I' and 'Manichean Geography II', for example, he explores by analogy the colonial roots of the problem. Both are set in vaguely tropical, colonial landscapes and register the absurd, degrading side of imperialism, in which the colonized lands have become 'Images of our own disgust'. Links to the unionists in Northern Ireland are made through a few charged words, as, for example, 'chosen' and 'orange' in the following passage. The imperialists can offer only crass materialism and consumer goods like Black and Deckers and calico:

> And the chosen people will serve
> Themselves with orange jube-jubes
> In a brand-new discount warehouse.[139]

In an earlier poem, 'A New Society', Paulin makes obeisance to the economic roots of Ireland's troubles and expresses the desire for a fairer system. Describing the demolition of a slum district, he imagines a replacement:

> Where rats are destroyed and crawlies discouraged,
> Where the Law is glimpsed on occasional traffic duties
> And the streets are friendly with surprise recognitions.[140]

It was, however, in rummaging among his own antecedents for some clue to the political and social failures of the North that Paulin found his true subject. In 'Settlers' he exposes what he sees as the violence latent in unionist persistence. His settlers (modelled, it would seem, on his own grandparents) come to Belfast from Glasgow:

> He manages the Iceworks, is an elder of the Kirk;
>   She becomes, briefly, a cook in Carson's Army.
> Some mornings, walking through the company gate,
>   He touches the bonnet of a brown lorry.
> It is warm. The men watch and say nothing.
>   'Queer, how it runs off in the night,'
> He says to McCullough, then climbs to his office.
>   He stores a warm knowledge on his palm.
>
>   Nightlandings on the Antrim coast, the movement of guns
> Now snug in their oiled paper below the floors
>   Of sundry kirks and tabernacles in that county.[141]

Just as Seamus Deane categorized Bogside nationalism as a ghetto version of Irish nationalism and stated that the biggest problem facing both main communities in the North was how to 'join with history',[142] Paulin believed that the Protestants did not have a proper sense of themselves as a distinct people with a historical identity. Rereading history, he fastened upon the abortive revolution of 1798 as an opportunity Protestants missed to unite with Catholics in a shared Irish identity. Modern-day unionists, he felt, were insufficiently aware of the radical republican element of their heritage. He told John Haffenden shortly before he joined the Field Day board that

what I find at the moment is a real sense of how fundamentally ridiculous and contradictory it is to be an Ulster Protestant. It's a culture which could have dignity, and it had it once—I mean that strain of radical Presbyterianism, free-thinking Presbyterianism, which more or less went underground after 1798. I pretty well despise official Protestant culture, and can't now understand how people can simultaneously wave the Union Jack and yet hate the English, as many Protestants do. I think there really *has* to be a united Ireland, and I don't mean in any way that I'm committed to bloodshed—but it is a fundamentally absurd political state, and it's got to go.[143]

'Desertmartin' captures Paulin's sense of the cultural inadequacy of Ulster unionism:

> It's a limed nest, this place. I see a plain
> Presbyterian grace sour, then harden,
> As a free strenuous spirit changes
> To a servile defiance that whines and shrieks
> For the bondage of the letter: it shouts
> For the Big Man to lead his wee people
> To a clean white prison, their scorched tomorrow.[144]

As Deane and Friel were committed to a re-examination of traditional Irish nationalist assumptions in an effort to find a more inclusive model for a future Ireland, likewise Paulin, having rejected his own heritage, was determined to look to the past his ancestors had discarded for a more enabling model of Northern Protestantism. This cultural concern, coupled with the zeal of the converted which he brought to his own version of Irish republicanism, would be his chief contribution to Field Day.

As the foregoing discussion has demonstrated, the Field Day board members assembled in 1981 were individuals with very different priorities. Together they were, as they liked to say of themselves, 'six characters in search of an author'.[145] What, then, did they have in common? First, they were friends. Second, all except Rea were or had been teachers. Third, all but Hammond were, as Heaney says, 'northerners living outside Northern Ireland'. He explains that this displacement was 'only an outward sign of a condition common to most self-aware people, north and south of the border—namely, that everything was shifting, that the older norms and intellectual arrangements had to be examined in the light of new political upheavals'.[146] This sense of imminent change implied for them a need to re-examine the past in search of opportunities for social harmony lost, perhaps not irretrievably. As writers, they were particularly interested in how language had been used and abused to embalm orthodoxies. They sought to make people aware of unexamined barriers to imagination and creativity in order to look more positively toward the future. As Friel put it, their spiritual exile gave them a sharp sense of alienation from both the Republic and the United Kingdom, and this sensibility was not the end but rather the beginning of their joint enterprise:

we are trying to make a home. . . . We don't think that exile is practical. We think that exile is miserable in fact. . . . one of the problems for us is that we are constantly being offered the English home, we have been educated by the English home and we have been pigmented by an English home. . . . And the rejection of all that, and the rejection into what, is the big problem.[147]

Many of the questions the members of the board asked themselves were thus the same; the answers they might find would probably be different. None the less, their views were similar enough to enable them to come together on a major project. Broadly speaking, it would be fair to say that each of the board members favours a united Ireland of one sort or another, although they have arrived at that position from very different starting points. This political conviction, however, is an individual and private thing for each of them and has not been made an explicit part of the company's brief.

The desire to avoid associating Field Day with any particular political position was especially marked in the beginning. It did seem necessary, however, to have some sort of general statement of purpose. This, in 1981, was kept very general and was much the same as it had been for *Translations*:

firstly, to forge a Northern-based theatre company which would rehearse and tour in the North and then tour throughout the whole of Ireland; secondly, to concentrate on smaller venues, where theatre is rarely seen; and finally, to perform plays of excellence in a distinctively Irish voice that would be heard throughout the whole of the island.[148]

Of course, as Rea pointed out, to insist both on a Northern and on an all-Ireland context for their work was making a clear political statement, but the politics at this stage was implicit in how the company was carrying on its business. Otherwise, they were simply writing, producing, and performing plays.

Friel appeared to be particularly anxious to dispel the impression that Field Day had some sort of hidden agenda. *Translations*, as we have seen, had been received in some quarters as a political play, leading to speculation about the nature of his next project. A columnist for the *Evening Herald* wondered in January 1981, 'What is he doing? He wouldn't say—and one is sure that Friel is involved in a dramatic production of major political impact for Ireland.'[149] This sort of talk made Friel extremely uncomfortable. In 1980, as *Translations* opened, he had stated that there was 'no question of the new company or the play . . . being part of a crusade for anything'.[150] In 1981 he did not seem inclined to revise this position. When Elgy Gillespie asked him to be more specific about Field Day's 'artistic and political aims', he replied that he was not sure what those two things were or how they moved in relation to each other: 'I'd love to be preachy but I'm not sure what the sermon is. We can only define afterwards what the sermon is.'[151]

The choice of *Three Sisters* as the company's second production was presumably intended, in part, to confound observers who were already pinning labels on Field Day. Friel said that he and Rea 'wanted a classic, we felt a classic would be what Field Day needed at this point. We're still defining ourselves by exploration and we both still feel this development is an integral part of our career.'[152] It is significant, too, that Friel had completed his version of the play before *Translations* was staged, so rather than being custom-written for Field Day it reflected Friel's own fascination with

Chekhov and his desire to make the play more accessible to Irish audiences.

Another thing that Friel insisted upon in 1981 was the impermanence of the company. He distanced himself from the Derry theatre campaign and emphasized that Field Day's plans went no further than the current season: 'If a great new play emerged tomorrow, specially if it was a Northern play, we'd jump at it. Or else we might put out a magazine or do something completely different.'[153]

The assembling of the board, though, indicated the intention of the company to function in one form or another for some time. It could be that different members of the board had different ideas about what their role and the role of Field Day was to be. It cannot be denied that, in 1981, those who followed the activities of the company were receiving mixed-signals. Officially—that is, in the programme notes for *Three Sisters*, which most of those interested enough in Field Day to attend a performance would have read—the company appeared determined to have a mission. The keynote was sounded in Seamus Deane's introductory note, 'What is Field Day?' It was, he said, 'a political gesture, smacking of Northernness' that involved 'a double secession—from the North and from the Republic'. It was 'like the Abbey in its origin in that it has within it the idea of a culture which has not yet come to be in political terms. It is unlike the Abbey in that it can no longer subscribe to a simple nationalism as the basis for its existence.' Field Day 'breaks new ground not in stage convention, not in theatrical language, but in the idea of breaking down the calcification of the theatrical audience'. It was 'inventing an audience'.

Deane baffled the uninitiated with abstruse references to the Théâtre Libre, the Free Theatre of Berlin, Brecht's theatre, and Grein's Independent Theatre, and sentences like 'The audience which believes itself to be witnessing "art" or "theatre" in Mullingar or Magherafelt also has, along with this stylised media-conception of what it is doing, a recognition that it is itself part of that theatre.' With sideswipes at the 'hallowed and hollowed tradition of the Abbey' and 'the spurious aestheticism of the Lyric', he unnecessarily affronted much of the theatrical establishment in Ireland. Finally, with his declaration of allegiance to 'a culture which has not yet come to be in political terms', he alarmed the suspicious—if 'simple nationalism' were no longer enough, would a more complex, subtler nationalism suffice?[154]

What, though, did all of this have to do with a Hiberno-English version of an 80-year-old Russian play? Despite his praise in passing of 'the idea of a theatre without a roof over its head', I suspect that Deane was theorizing in a context much larger than that of the 1981 Field Day tour. It was too early to answer the question he posed himself. What Field Day was and whether it could deliver the things he had promised would have to be proved in the practice.

4

'Talking to Ourselves': The Early Years

FIELD DAY'S press release for *Three Sisters* announced that it was a 'translation' in the deepest sense of the word. Friel interprets Chekhov's masterpiece for contemporary audiences in conveying not only the meaning of the original words but also the essence and significance of Chekhov's vision. He illuminates for us the complexities and confusions of life in Ireland today.[1]

Perhaps the best place to begin a discussion of the 1981 tour is to reflect upon what was meant by that. What drew Friel to *Three Sisters*, and what made him and Rea decide that Field Day should produce an Irish version of it?

A pragmatic answer to the second question may be advanced. Field Day needed a script, and Friel's treatment of Chekhov's *Three Sisters* was available, completed even before *Translations*. Possibly, too, the directors felt that doing a classic might reduce the pressure of expectations on the company and lessen the impact of what Friel called 'the second novel jinx'.[2] Friel also believed that the classics of world theatre were not performed often enough in Ireland,[3] and, since a major part of the company's purpose was to create an audience for theatre in places that had no real theatrical tradition, naturally he wanted to expose this new audience to the best of world drama. *Three Sisters* was one of Friel's personal favourites (it had been in the repertoire of the new Guthrie Theatre in Minneapolis during the time he had spent there as an 'unpaid observer' and apprentice dramatist[4]), and he described his work on the play as 'a labour of love'.[5]

In addition to his affection for this particular play, Friel had long been an admirer of Anton Chekhov. They had a great deal in common. Both of them came from the submerged classes of their respective countries but strove to achieve a more open and cosmopolitan outlook; both wrote short stories in addition to plays; each attended rehearsals if possible, distrusted directors, and was positively suspicious of theatre as an artistic medium; both were sceptical men. Perhaps the strongest attraction for Friel was Chekhov's character. When the Russian was still a young man he wrote to his patron Aleksey Suvorin that there was a great distinction to be made between *'solving a problem* and *stating a problem correctly.* It is only the second that is obligatory for the artist.'[6] He shunned political labels: 'I am not a liberal, not a conservative, not a gradualist, not a monk, not an indifferentist. I should like to be a free artist and nothing more, and I regret that God has not given me the power to be one.'[7] Later in life, though he remained wary of politics, he changed his mind somewhat about the need for absolute objectivity in art:

Remember that the writers whom we call eternal or simply good and who intoxicate us have one very important characteristic in common: they move in a certain direction and they summon you there too. . . . The best of them are realistic, and paint life as it is, but because every line is permeated, as with sap, by the consciousness of a purpose, you are aware not only of life as it is, but of life as it ought to be, and that captivates you. And we? [the artists of his generation]. . . . We have no politics, we don't believe in revolution, we have no God, we are not afraid of ghosts, and I personally am not afraid even of death and blindness. One who desires nothing, hopes for nothing, and fears nothing cannot be an artist.[8]

In his private notebook, Chekhov tried to reconcile his feeling that he was incapable of more than accurate representation of life with his growing conviction that the highest art has a conscious purpose behind it: 'Man will only become better when you make him see what he is like.'[9]

If Chekhov did not believe he was able to do more in his literary work than point out what the problems were, in the rest of his life he did what he could to try to alleviate some of them. There were in effect two Chekhovs—Chekhov the writer and Chekhov the doctor. As he put it, 'Medicine is my lawful wife and literature my mistress'.[10] He wrote in his notebook, 'A Mussulman for the salvation of his soul digs a well. It would be a pleasant thing if each of us left a school, a well, or something like that, so that life should not pass away into eternity without leaving a trace behind it.'[11] Chekhov lived in accordance with this philosophy. He was active in his district organizing relief for famine victims, giving peasants free medical treatment, supervising a campaign against an impending epidemic of cholera, and helping to plan and finance the building of schools in three villages. In 1890 he paid his 'debt to medicine' by spending three months on the prison island of Sakhalin, conducting a detailed census of the entire population and talking with as many people as he could. He collected material for a documentary work on the Siberian penal system, which he laboured at for several years and eventually published as *The Island of Sakhalin*. Upon his return to Moscow he wrote to Suvorin,

God's world is good. Only one thing isn't good: ourselves. How little there is in us of justice and humility, how poor is our conception of patriotism! The drunken, bedraggled, good-for-nothing of a husband loves his wife and child, but what's the good of that love? We, so the newspapers say, love our great country, but how is that love expressed? Instead of knowledge—inordinate brazenness and conceit, instead of hard work—laziness and swinishness; there is no justice; the concept of honor does not go beyond 'the honor of the uniform,' the uniform which is the everyday adornment of the prisoners' dock. What is needed is work; everything else can go to the devil. The main thing is to be just—the rest will be added unto us.[12]

Chekhov's artistic restraint combined with his personal passion must have been inspiring to Brian Friel. With Field Day he was trying, like Chekhov, to accomplish something in the world outside the theatre, and the example of the Russian was proof that a writer could be socially committed without losing his artistic integrity. The programme for the Field Day production of *Three Sisters* contained a poem by Seamus Heaney, prompted, he said, by talks with Friel and entitled 'Chekhov on Sakhalin'. Heaney celebrates the conscience of Chekhov, who felt so keenly

> . . . the burden of his freedom
> To try for the right tone—not tract, not thesis—
> And walk away from floggings. He who thought to squeeze
> His slave's blood out and waken the free man
> Shadowed a convict guide through Sakhalin.[13]

Artistically as well as personally, Chekhov was exemplary. What one writer has said of Chekhov's mature drama is equally true of Friel's. The playwright

concentrates on the effect of a single *theme* upon the thoughts and emotions of a group of finely drawn and subtly counterpointed characters. . . . The conventional protagonist is . . . replaced by an ensemble, and his protracted struggle of will against an opposing force is supplanted by the epiphany of a collective pathos before an oppressive inevitability.[14]

Nicholas Moravčevich has described Chekhov's shift from 'natu-ralistic veracity to impressionist selectivity'. Chekhov, he main-tains, was able to accomplish far more with this technique in his plays than in his fiction because in drama the audience is privileged to know simultaneously what *does* happen on stage, what the various characters *think* has happened, and how the individuals' perceptions determine their parts in the action as it unfolds.[15]

In Friel's best theatrical work, as in Chekhov's, the dramatic interest is in the differing interpretations that various characters give to the same events. This is especially true of Friel's masterpiece, *Faith Healer* (1979), which consists of four monologues spoken by three characters, each recounting the story of their life together and its abrupt end. Each monologue reveals a different, but entirely convincing and internally consistent, version of the story. One is both mesmerized by each tale in turn and tantalized by the possi-bility of a higher plane of truth upon which all of them would be reconciled.

Chekhov's influence had also been noticed by reviewers of Friel's other 1979 play, *Aristocrats*, to which the adjective 'Chekhovian' is often applied. Behind it lie Chekhov's major plays, especially *Three Sisters* (1901) and *The Cherry Orchard* (1904). *Aristocrats* focuses on a decaying aristocratic family in a backward, provincial area and records their struggles with their environment and their own delusions. The plot, such as it is, is similar to that of *The Cherry Orchard*, for *Aristocrats* captures the moment when an era comes to an end, with the family house (like the orchard in Chekhov's play) symbolizing the past that must finally be put to rest. Like the auction in *The Cherry Orchard*, the death of Father pinpoints this moment of loss, although it is also a kind of liberation for his children, who will now be free to live their own lives without the burden of familial obligation to hold them back.

Georgy Tovstonogov writes,

Chekhov was the first Russian playwright to see the complexity and even impossibility of mutual understanding, to see man's difficulty in expressing all he thinks and feels. I think that the themes of spiritual loneliness and isolation, and of the futility of trying to reach another human soul, were suggested by Chekhov to the many foreign authors in whose writings they later appeared.[16]

Brian Friel should be counted among their number. Certainly human loneliness, the difficulty of vital connection between human beings, and the unreliability of words as a conduit of meaning have been major themes for Friel as for Chekhov.

One can only speculate as to what convinced Friel and Rea that the play was an appropriate one for Field Day, but *Three Sisters*, with its concentration on frustrated expectations and thwarted lives, must have found plenty of sympathetic hearers in Northern Ireland, where people felt likewise stuck in a stultifying situation. Like the North in 1981, Chekhov's Russia was going through a 'period of discouragement with political action following upon the failure of the inchoate radical movement of the seventies'.[17] Seamus Deane has characterized the Northern situation in terms that recall the three sisters' yearning for Moscow:

Once one or other community achieves its ideal—an Ulster secure from its enemies, a 32-county Republic—then and only then will all be well and will people have restored to them all those rights—the right to life, the right to housing, work, legal justice—which have necessarily been suspended in the meantime. So the whole culture stagnates while it waits for the great day of constitutional reckoning. When that day dawns, our political leaders will feel free to grant what the existing situation will not allow. But in the meantime—nothing. For the Northern minority, everything will be fine when they accept the State; for the rest of Ireland, particularly its minorities, everything will be liberalised when peaceful reunification takes place. But neither acceptance nor reunification are remote possibilities. So the present is determined by the promise of an unrealisable future.[18]

There are other parallels to be made between the Russian and the Irish situations. Both countries had largely peasant economies (over 81 per cent of the Russian population at the end of the nineteenth century belonged to the peasant class) with a gentry whose cultural importance was out of all proportion to their numbers. Both were on the edge of Western Europe, late to develop industrially, and conscious of their backwardness. The two countries were overwhelmingly rural, with few large towns. Ronald Hingley notes that 'Less tactful foreigners, and some Russians too, described Moscow itself . . . as one vast village,' an observation that has often been made about Dublin as well.[19] The three sisters, like Friel's audience in Derry, were thus living in a provincial town within what many regarded as a provincial country.

There is abundant evidence that Chekhov took the horrors of provincial life seriously. As he wrote despairingly in his notebook, 'In the life of our towns there is no pessimism, no Marxism, and no movements, but there is stagnation, stupidity, mediocrity.'[20] Towards the end of *Three Sisters*, Andrey (in Friel's version) rages against the conditions of his life:

Look at this town. One hundred thousand people—all indistinguishable. In the two hundred years this town has been in existence, it hasn't produced one person of any distinction—not one saint, not one scholar, not one artist. Just one hundred thousand identical, drab people, eating, sleeping, working, eating, sleeping, dying. Isn't it puzzling? And in order to invest their drab lives with some little excitement, they gossip and drink and gamble and take each other to court for broken fences and for slander actions—because if they didn't, they'd die of overwhelming boredom. Yes, die of it. That's why wives deceive their husbands—not for pleasure but just to reassure themselves they are still alive. And that's why husbands pretend they hear nothing and see nothing. Their very pretence is an activity, an assertion—no, a faint whisper—that they're alive too. Isn't it ridiculous? And into this charade children are born with their own hopes and their own dreams and then in time succumb like the rest of us to this living death, become spectres like the rest of us.[21]

Chekhov explained that the actor who played Andrey 'must almost threaten the audience with his fists' while delivering this speech.[22]

For at least some members of Field Day's audience in remote areas of Ireland, the oppressive sense of the people on stage that the real, good life is elsewhere must have struck a chord. So, too, must Chekhov's characters' attempts to find meaning in their suffering. This was a question that tormented Chekhov. He wrote in his notebook, 'Let the coming generations attain happiness; but they surely ought to ask themselves, for what did their ancestors live and for what did they suffer.'[23]

To be sure, much of the suffering in *Three Sisters* is highly subjective and perhaps unnecessary. It has been described as 'an absurd play about three grown-up women who spend four acts not going to Moscow when they have the price of the ticket'.[24] Throughout the play, some characters suffer through having things that other characters suffer through not having. Irina admires Olga's busy life while Olga longs to stay at home and keep house; Masha finds the passionate love that Irina dreams is waiting for her in Moscow, but in the end it brings her mostly pain and adds to her feeling of exile and loss; the sisters deplore the fact that they must live in the provinces and want to return to Moscow, while Vershinin is glad to escape from the bustle of the city into the more relaxed countryside; Masha has the husband that Olga desires desperately—and is bored stiff by him. The dream of Moscow itself is called into question repeatedly. With one line an elderly servant casts doubt on the sisters' image of Moscow as the great good place. During the fire in Act III he remarks to Olga, 'Did you ever hear tell, Miss, that in the year one thousand, eight hundred and twelve Moscow was burned down too—just like this' (68).

Yet the sisters' aspiration to go home to Moscow cannot simply be dismissed as ridiculous. We may suspect, with Vershinin, that once they are living there 'it'll mean nothing' to them (54), but at least they have a dream, they have not given up hope that life can be made better. Chekhov did not give up this hope, either. 'From the days of my childhood', he said, 'I have believed in progress.'[25] Constantin Stanislavski was bothered by 'something missing' in the original Moscow Art Theatre production of *Three Sisters* until he suddenly realized that

The men of Chekhov do not bathe, as we did at that time, in their own sorrow. Just the opposite; they, like Chekhov himself, seek life, joy, laughter, courage. The men and women of Chekhov want to live and not to die. They are active and surge to overcome the hard and unbearable impasses into which life has plunged them.[26]

Chekhov was too much of a realist, however, to subscribe to a facile optimism. As Sean O'Faolain explains, such a man 'finds his recompense in Time, in the past, present and future, in that shadow which guarantees to everybody with a historical sense the pleasure and pain of memory, intense interest in the present, some hope and frequent despairs for the future'.[27] Thomas Kilroy in a programme note for the Field Day production of *Three Sisters* referred to Chekhov's 'acute historical sensibility', and this was undoubtedly one of the things that attracted Brian Friel, also a playwright with a keen sense of time passing, to the Russian's work.

At the centre of *Three Sisters* is a debate about the future, with the two sides taken by Vershinin and Baron Tusenbach. Vershinin believes that 'in two or three hundred years time, in a thousand years time . . . a new kind of life, a truly happy life, will have evolved'. This view of the life to come is the analogue of the sisters' longing for Moscow, because it assumes as its corollary that happiness in the present is impossible. The Baron argues, in contrast, that life in the future will be essentially the same as life today, 'as difficult and as mysterious and as joyous and as exuberant as it is now' (47). By locating the two perspectives in different characters, Chekhov is able to examine them both at an ironic distance. Both, however, imply an active striving toward something better. 'Work', as the Baron proclaims, 'is the answer' (27). The 'revelation' that Irina experiences at the start of the play is that 'man must work. . . . Work—work—work; that's the only thing that gives life purpose and meaning. That's the only thing that guarantees contentment and happiness' (13). The events of the next five years teach her that nothing guarantees contentment and happiness, but that purpose and meaning are valuable for their own sake. Broken and disillusioned by her drudgery in the post office and local government, she recalls her agreement to marry the Baron: 'And the moment I made that decision, the moment I said yes to him, a lot of the confusion seemed to lift and I felt a great sense of relief and the old passion for work, work, work suddenly possessed me again. Life had acquired a fresh pattern; a new shape was emerging' (94).

In the triumphant ending of the play, Olga achieves for the sisters a creative synthesis of the two positions debated throughout the preceding acts. The only way to keep going is to hope and prepare for the future while living determinedly in the present, never forgetting that the end of human life is mystery:

Just listen to that music. It's so assured, so courageous. It makes you want to go on, doesn't it? Oh my God! Yes, of course we will die and be forgotten—everything about us, how we looked, how we spoke, that there were three of us. But our unhappiness, our suffering, won't be wasted. They're a preliminary to better times, and because of them the people who come after us will inherit a better life—a life of peace and content and happiness. And they will look on us with gratitude and with love. But our life isn't over yet. By no means! We are going to go on living! And that music is so confident, so courageous, it almost seems as if it is about to be revealed very soon why we are alive and what our suffering is for. If only we knew that. If only we knew that. (113–14)

Friel was quick to explain that he had not adapted the play, changed it to an Irish setting, or tried to underline specifically Irish meanings. Nor was his work a translation in the usual sense, because he readily admitted that he did not know a word of Russian.[28] What he had produced was a 'translation' from the English-language versions (mainly English and American) already available into the kind of English that is spoken in Ireland today. As he explained, 'What I did was simply to put six texts in front of me and tackle each line at a time, to see first of all what was the meaning of it, then what was the tone and then eventually what was the sound. It took nine months in all.'[29]

Friel's reasons for wishing to do a version of *Three Sisters* in the Irish vernacular were both philosophical and political. The translations in existence did not seem to him adequate to an Irish understanding of Chekhov:

Somehow the rhythms of these versions do not match with the rhythms of our own speech patterns, and I think that they ought to, in some way. Even the most recent English translation again carries, of necessity, very strong English cadences and rhythms. This is something about which I feel strongly—in some way we are constantly overshadowed by the sound of English language, as well as by the printed word. Maybe this does not inhibit us, but it forms us and shapes us in a way that is neither healthy nor valuable for us . . .[30]

He explained elsewhere:

I wrote this play in an Irish idiom because with English translations Irish actors become more and more remote. They have to pretend, first of all, that they're English and then that they're Russians. I'd like our audience to see Captains and Lieutenants who look as if they came from Finner or Tullamore. The decolonisation process of the imagination is very important if a new Irish personality is to emerge.[31]

Friel did not want to change Chekhov. What he was trying to do was to make the Russian's work more accessible to Irish actors and audiences.

In practice, Friel's adjustments are obvious only in a few roles. As one reviewer noted, 'The lines are not remarkably Irish or even Synge-an; only one part is peppered with Irish expressions, in the bejapers and begorrah vein'.[32] This is Natasha's, whose lower social status means that her language is richer in colloquialisms and local expressions. She says she's 'thick as poundies' (71), exclaims 'Jesus, Mary and Joseph! You put the heart across me!' (111), refers to her

child as a 'wane' (104) and to herself as an 'eejit' (36), and declares
that the carnival has the servants 'astray in the head altogether'
(38). Besides being laden with such phrases, Natasha's speech is full
of specifically Irish constructions, as in 'sure aren't we all?' (69).
Other characters are also given the occasional Irish expression or
construction, as when Kulygin announces that Chebutykin has
decided to 'go on the hammer' and ended up 'Footless!' (72) or
when the doctor himself reiterates his view that 'sweet damn all it
matters' (114) at the end of the play. Such use of language probably
did help Irish audiences to equate the characters in the play with
personality types with which they were already familiar. Nuala
Hayes, the actress who played Natasha, was of the opinion that
'Friel's translation locates the play better, making it a more "social
play". The differences in the language of the Prozorov family and
other characters are more apparent in this interpretation.'[33]

The Irish aspect of Friel's version, however, does not consist
solely of the skilful deployment of localisms. A more subtle dimension is given where Friel manages to convey the sense of a line with
Irish resonances. For example, when Natasha threatens to throw
the elderly servant, Anfisa, out of the house, she shouts, 'She's a
peasant and that's where she belongs—out in the bogs!' (70)
Most other versions say 'country'. When Andrey bemoans the fact
that their town has produced no men of note, he fumes, 'not
one saint, not one scholar, not one artist' (103). In Ireland, the
'Land of Saints and Scholars' renowned in more recent times for its
writers, that line conveys an acute sense of being out of the cultural
mainstream.

In other places, Friel slants the lines slightly to reflect experience
in Northern Ireland, where people have worse problems than mere
boredom and provincial stagnation with which to contend. He adds
a line for Kulygin (not particularly important in the context of the
conversation in which it is uttered): 'The most wonderful thing
about the human spirit is its resilience' (30). Friel's Vershinin remarks, 'God alone knows how the way we live will be assessed. To
us it's—it's how we live, our norm. But maybe in retrospect it will
look anxious and tense. Maybe even . . . morally wrong. Well . . .'
(22). An early translator of the play, Jennie Covan, rendered this
line as 'And it may happen that our present mode of life with which
we are so satisfied, will in time appear strange, inconvenient, stupid, unclean, perhaps even sinful . . .'. Elisaveta Fen, in an English

version that Friel admired, wrote, 'It may well be that in time to come the life we live to-day will seem strange and uncomfortable and stupid and not too clean, either, and perhaps even wicked . . .'.[34] Near the end of the play when Andrey dreams, in a parody of Vershinin's utopian predictions, of a world free from the mundane realities of everyday life, 'this endless round of vodka and cabbage-and-bacon and gossip and pretence', Friel adds a serious line for him: 'we must keep believing in a future for our children that is open and honest and free. Because the very fact of clinging on to that belief is in itself the beginning of a release, a liberation. Maybe the only liberation available to us . . .' (104).

One generally unfortunate result of Friel's labour is its tendency to expand and make wordier a play which is already very long. Where Ronald Hingley translates an early speech of Vershinin thus:

I lived in Nemetsky Street at one time. Used to walk to the Red Barracks from there. You cross a gloomy-looking bridge on the way and you can hear the water rushing underneath it—a depressing place when you're on your own.[35]

Friel writes:

I used to live in Nyemetsky Street. I could walk to the Red Barracks from there. And on the way you had to cross this black bridge and underneath you could just hear the water—a kind of throaty, strangled sound. It was so—hah!—it wasn't the liveliest place to pass on your way to work every morning by yourself. (21)

Later, when Andrey asks the servant Ferapont if he has ever been to Moscow, Friel has the man reply, 'Me! Oh, God, no. Moscow? Oh, never, never. If it had been the will of God I would have been, though. But there you are' (42). Fen's translation is more restrained: 'No. It wasn't God's wish.'[36] Taken singly these expansions may work quite well, and this verbosity could even be considered typically Irish. In a play as long as *Three Sisters*, however, the cumulative effect of such additions is to overweight the script in performance.

Friel made a few other adjustments to the play. Some, such as the addition of homosexual undertones to the relationship between Roddey and Fedotik, two minor characters, seem to serve no real purpose and merely provide the opportunity for some heavy-handed comedy. Other Friel touches add to the play usefully. In Act

II he interpolates a whole episode built around the random observation of Dr Chebutykin that 'Balzac was married in Berdichev town.' Berdichev was 'a town proverbially known as the dullest in the whole of Russia', leading David Magarshack to suggest that the phrase implies 'that one need not seek happiness in Moscow seeing that one of the greatest writers of France found it in Berdichev'.[37] In the original, Irina absently repeats this phrase and that is the end of it, but in Friel's version she, Fedotik, and Roddey start improvising a song to fit the words:

Pause. There is a sense that this moment could blossom, an expectancy that suddenly everybody might join in the chorus—and dance—and that the room might be quickened with music and laughter. Everyone is alert to this expectation; it is almost palpable, if some means of realising it could be found. VERSHININ moves close to MASHA. If the moment blossoms, they will certainly dance. FEDOTIK moves close to IRINA (to Roddey's acute annoyance); they, too, will dance. TUSENBACH sits at the piano.

The Baron, however, 'is all thumbs' and complains, 'I can't play without music.' Thus, 'The moment is lost' in 'an atmosphere of vague embarrassment' (50–1). As an illustration of the difficulty these people have with living in the present and behaving spontaneously and as a metaphor for the possibility and difficulty of art, these seconds of tension are central to Friel's vision of the play. A reviewer from *The Times* who generally disapproved of Field Day's *Three Sisters* called this 'the one passage where the production really flowers. . . . a genuine addition to the Chekhov heritage'.[38]

Similarly, in Dr Chebutykin's drunk scene, in which he faces up to the emptiness of his life and his sense of self-disgust, Chekhov (or, at any rate, other translators of Chekhov) has him soliloquize in ordinary fashion, referring to himself as 'I'. In Friel's version, he addresses his reflection in the mirror in the second person singular: 'Maybe you're the reality. Why not? Maybe this *[body]* is the image. Maybe this hasn't arms and legs and a head at all. Maybe this has no existence . . . just pretends to exist . . . just pretends to walk about and eat and sleep . . . I wish that were true. I wish you *[reflection]* were the reality, my friend.' The rest of the speech is likewise delivered to 'you' (73). This device is an extremely effective way of dramatizing the doctor's deep alienation from himself and his world. In moments such as these, Friel makes the play his own without ever straying far from the spirit of Chekhov.

Field Day announced that it would be returning with another production by mid-January 1981, at which time negotiations had already begun with the two Arts Councils and the City Council to provide financial and logistical support.[39] By the end of that month, the choice of play had been made.[40] The mayor of Derry, Councillor Joseph Fegan, officially welcomed the company back to the city in June. Referring to *Translations*, he said,

A world première of a new play was a new experience for Derry, never before did we get the opportunity to play host to such a prestigious occasion. . . . Derry responded magnificently to that great occasion. . . .
    Brian Friel and Stephen Rea, when they left Derry on a nationwide tour last year, said they would be back, and today they are back.[41]

The *Derry Journal* reported that 'Following on the pattern established last year, the play will be rehearsed in Derry and open in the Guildhall in the second week of September.' The City Council would be happy to support Field Day, hopeful that 'the people of Derry and the North-West will respond in the way that they came to support *Translations*, and that the occasion will demonstrate once again that the city can support professional theatre and that we need purpose built facilities that can accommodate it'.[42]

Field Day eventually succeeded in acquiring a business manager, Derryman Noel McKenna, as well as grants from both the Northern and Southern Irish Arts Councils.[43] At the end of June the *Sunday News* informed its readers that a 'huge move is afoot to recruit as many Ulster actors as possible for the all Irish cast' of *Three Sisters*.[44] The fourteen actors eventually chosen were mainly, though not exclusively, from the North. Olwen Fouere, who played Irina, was from Galway, and the 'big challenge to her in the play' was 'adapting to the Northern Irish idiom'. Stephen Rea would direct, despite the fact that his only experience in that line was 'a couple of short plays, in London eight years ago'.[45] He left the English production of *Translations* when it transferred to the National Theatre in order to return to Derry to begin five weeks of rehearsal on the new play.[46] Kevin McCaul, Principal Amenities Officer of the Derry City Council, believed it was important that Field Day 'are not just here on a one night stand. They have been here now for six weeks, rehearsing, living with us, working with us, building up a relationship.'[47] Brian Friel, as was his habit, attended all the rehearsals.[48] The tour arranged for *Three Sisters* was very similar to that followed by *Translations*.[49] Michael Sheridan commented, 'The small towns and less fashionable centres, both North and South are by implication as important to the progress of Field Day as the densely populated urban areas which define the popular acceptance of the arts.'[50] Mary MacGoris remarked that 'For practically anybody in this country, but certainly for those in those towns, it should at least make a nice change from politics.'[51]

Professional theatre in Derry was still something of a novelty, and several writers from outside the province underlined the distinctive features of cultural life in Northern Ireland: security checks at the Guildhall, the army helicopter that nearly drowned out the dialogue during Act III on opening night, and the car bomb that forced the cancellation of the dress rehearsal. For Brian Friel, 'The car bombs are more of an inconvenience than a worry. In fact, we chose Derry to open in, not only because of my own association with the city, but because in a way it is outside the political implications of either Dublin or Belfast.'[52] Visitors found it difficult to be so blasé. Dónall Ó Gallchóir, in an article entitled ' "Drama" in Derry' (written in Irish for the *Irish Press*), described his trip North for readers in the Republic. He had made plans to visit Derry for the first time in ten years, intending to see *Three Sisters*, because he had been told that things were finally back to normal there. The first sign of 'normality' was the British army checkpoint at the border, which unnerved him somewhat but did not prevent his entering the city and attempting to find a parking space. As he was about to leave his car, he happened to glance across the River Foyle just in time to see a building blown up before his eyes, upon which he quickly decided to drive closer to the Guildhall and cancel his ticket. He was prevented from this by a bomb scare in the Guildhall itself, so turned tail and drove away, getting caught on the bridge in a crowd of police and soldiers, from one of whom he managed to ascertain the way to Moville: 'and the curtain fell on Derry behind me. I had enough drama à la Derry to do me for the next ten years.'[53]

Fortunately for Field Day not all potential audience members were so easily deterred, and the première of *Three Sisters* was a kind of muted replay of the *Translations* euphoria. The Guildhall audience on 8 September 1981 included the same sort of political, religious, and artistic celebrities who had turned out in such force the previous year, and though, as David Nowlan noted, the 'voltage' was inevitably lower the second time around, 'there was still a fairly electric buzz', and the play received 'a respectful hearing with prolonged and warm applause at its conclusion'.[54] Critical reaction was mixed. In general, the translation received better reviews than the production. One thing that almost everyone agreed upon was that the performance ran on far too long. The first night curtain did not come down until four hours after it came up, leading one reviewer, looking on the bright side, to remark that 'The audience certainly received good value for their money.'[55] Several reviewers detected a lack of direction or complained that the acting was uneven or lacked subtlety.[56] Many of these same critics, however, agreed that 'Friel has indeed increased Chekhov's accessibility for Irish audiences'.[57] John Keyes advanced a justification of Friel's efforts that must have pleased the dramatist:

An Irish company, and dialogue in places colloquially Irish, does not make the play an Irish play. What it does is to enlarge our understanding of Russian mores by making us recognise those which we share with them and by exhibiting those aspects of mankind which remain universal and unchanged by time or place.[58]

Not everyone agreed that Friel had achieved his aims, however. Desmond Rushe complained in the *Irish Independent* that he had succeeded in making the play more accessible only to Northern Irish people, since his 'vernacular is often so localised that it threatens to become irritatingly intrusive'.[59] A writer in the *Londonderry Sentinel* found the whole project patronizing and wondered where it would lead: 'Are we next to have the beauty of Shakespeare's language translated into Irish phrases and repeated in various blends of an Irish brogue?'[60]

During its Irish tour Field Day's *Three Sisters* covered fifteen towns both north and south of the border. In 1983 Stephen Rea recalled the response to the play around Ireland: 'In places of no theatrical sophistication, the audience loved it. They simply followed the story. In some cases they hadn't seen a play for 30 years. But in centres of theatrical pretension, we were criticised for "tampering with the classics".'[61] For 'centres of theatrical pretension' read 'Dublin'. *Three Sisters* was performed at the Gaiety

Theatre there during the annual theatre festival, and it was not celebrated by the critics. Colm Cronin expressed the 'humble opinion' that 'it didn't do much for Chekhov's original which hardly needed to be clarified or made more relevant for Irish audiences by being colloquialised to a degree that was more laughable than comic at times'.[62] The reviewer for the *Sunday Journal* believed that 'Friel has made his characters Irish to the extreme and, in my opinion, overstated their every move',[63] and the critic for *The Times*, in town for the festival, found it a 'coarsely reductive exercise in Irish Chekhov, which comes as a crashing disappointment from the group that created *Translations*'.[64] Gay Byrne reported, 'It's one of the few occasions at a theatre when I've actually heard a man snoring loudly, until eventually a woman had to thump him awake. The rest of us felt she should have left him in peace and we could have joined him.'[65]

Though the performance had been cut down to three hours since the Derry opening, it was still considered by many people to be too long. The company was particularly distressed by the fact that significant numbers of its audience members were leaving before the end of the play each night. Nevertheless, Rea 'vowed that he would not cut it any further', implying that people just wanted to get to the pubs before they closed. The festival director, Brendan Smith, offered a more charitable, and probably more accurate, interpretation of this rude behaviour, attributing it to 'the tyranny of the last bus'.[66] Years later, the Dublin reception of *Three Sisters* still rankled with Rea. In a 1985 interview he noted that, since the Field Day production, the Abbey had performed a 1983 version by the English playwright Michael Frayn, which seemed to him 'a complete avoidance of responsibility'.[67]

Mixed reviews or not, *Three Sisters* proved at least one thing— *Translations* was not to be an isolated phenomenon. Field Day had a life of its own and a sense of purpose that extended beyond one wildly successful production. Friel and Rea were still cagey, though, about what exactly they had in mind for the future. Friel confided to an interviewer in August 1981:

Ideally, of course, we would like to do a brand new play, preferably an Irish one, preferably a new Northern play. But, then, on the other hand, we feel very strongly that if there isn't something we want to do and believe in fully, we will just do nothing.

We haven't an institution that we have to serve and we don't want to acquire a roof. We want to be transient in the aesthetic sense as well as in the practical sense, which gives us independence.[68]

As he put it in another place,

This could be our last play, or we could go on for another twenty years. . . .

It's part of the fluxiness to not know if we'll be doing something or not, and we feel fluxiness is the most important thing for us now.[69]

'Fluxiness' aside, the *Derry Journal* was able to report, on 25 June 1982, that Field Day would indeed be returning with another production, this time a farce by Brian Friel entitled *The Communication Cord*. 'Following the pattern of previous Field Day productions', rehearsals would be held in Derry, leading up to a first performance in the Guildhall followed by an extensive Irish tour (fifteen towns in about six weeks). The Mayor of Derry, now Alderman William O'Connell, offered as before the support of the City Council:

The name of Field Day Theatre Company is synonymous with Derry since the time, two short years ago, when it burst upon the Irish theatrical scene with its first production.

Their commitment to theatre for the province is something for which we should be grateful and the fact that the company is Derry based, is something of which we all should be proud.

It was still hoped that the enthusiasm of Derry audiences for Field Day would 'demonstrate the need for a purpose-built theatre in the city'.[70]

Field Day began 1982 with serious money worries. *Three Sisters*, an austere classic, had not had the broad appeal of *Translations*, and its fourteen-member cast and bulky set had put a huge strain on the organization.[71] If the company was to have a chance to continue, it now needed a popular success. As Lynda Henderson, former editor of *Theatre Ireland*, explains, 'at that stage Field Day needed a pot-boiler'.[72] Early pre-production publicity assured potential theatre-goers that there would be nothing heavy this time around. Friel told reporters that 'Unlike my other plays, I have written it [*The Communication Cord*] primarily to give pleasure.'[73] 'Last year', he remarked, 'I think people would have been a little wary of a classic such as Chekov's *The Three Sisters* but this new comedy should appeal to most people.'[74] The main thing he wanted, he said, was that people should find it funny: 'I don't mind if it's slapstick at all as long as people laugh at it. If they don't, then in some way I've failed. There might be a chance you could take more out of it, but you wouldn't need to.'[75]

In other interviews, though, particularly as the date of the opening approached, Friel hinted at other levels to his play. He explained to Ray Comiskey,

a farce is a very serious enterprise. It's supposed to entertain and be very funny, and if it isn't it has failed as a farce. . . .

But then, I think that it's a perfectly valid way of looking at people in Ireland today, that our situation has become so absurd and so . . . crass that it seems to me it might be a valid way to talk and write about it.[76]

The Communication Cord is set in a thatched cottage in Ballybeg, County Donegal, where Tim and Jack, a university lecturer (without tenure) and a lawyer, plan to spend at least part of the weekend. The place belongs to Jack, but Tim is to pretend that it is his for a few hours in order to impress his prospective father-in-law, Dr Donovan, a politician and amateur antiquarian described by Richard Kearney as 'a caricature of all that is sentimental and sententious in the modern bourgeois Republic'.[77] Complications arise in the shape of a nosey old neighbour, Nora Dan (Jack calls her the 'quintessential noble peasant—obsessed with curiosity and greed and envy'[78]) who is convinced the house is legally hers; a German who wants to buy the cottage; an old girlfriend of Tim's, Claire; his present girlfriend, Susan; and Evette, a young Frenchwoman who comes for a weekend with Jack and turns out to be Donovan's mistress. As its title suggests, the play is about the difficulties inherent in any act of communication. The twists in the plot are the result of misunderstandings, misidentifications, and misinterpretations. The farce could be said to constitute an illustration of the hazards of translation in George Steiner's sense of the word.

The most serious element that appears to have been intended by Friel is an implicit comparison with *Translations*. That play, he believed, had been treated 'much too respectfully':

You know, when you get notices especially from outside the island, saying 'If you want to know what happened in Cuba, if you want to know what

happened in Chile, if you want to know what happened in Vietnam, read
Translations', that's nonsense. And I just can't accept that sort of pious
rubbish.[79]

He wanted, he said, *The Communication Cord* to be seen 'in
tandem' with *Translations*.[80] In the words of Seamus Heaney,
'There was something unmistakable about the vehemence of *The
Communication Cord*; it was a punitive exercise against stereotypes
which he had played with' directed 'first of all at himself, I think, in
some ways': 'The genre of farce was corrective to the genre of
romantic-historical.'[81]

When asked to describe more precisely the target of Friel's wit,
Heaney replied, 'I suppose it would be directed at a relatively
complacent nationalist middle-class inhalation of the balmy myth
of the lost Irish past.'[82] In *The Communication Cord*, the image of
that Irish past that had taken on flesh and blood for many who had
seen *Translations* is presented as sentimentalized and sanitized to a
ludicrous degree. The house itself becomes the symbol of this
factitiousness. Friel establishes the tone in his first stage direction:

Every detail of the kitchen and its furnishings is accurate of its time (from
1900 to 1930). But one quickly senses something false about the place. It
is too pat, too 'authentic'. It is in fact a restored house, a reproduction, an
artefact of today making obeisance to a home of yesterday. (11)

Donovan is delighted to see that the old posts and chains have been
retained in the kitchen, proving to him that Tim knows his 'heritage', but seems oblivious to the reality they represent—animals
sleeping in the same room as their owners. When he locks himself
to the wall at the end of the first act and cannot free himself, he is
caught and punished by the past about which he knows so much
but understands so little. When Jack, on the other hand, extols the
virtues of the 'ancestral seat of the McNeilis dynasty', he does so
with his tongue securely in his cheek: 'This is where we all come
from. This is our first cathedral. This shaped all our souls. This
determined our first pieties. Yes. Have reverence for this place' (15).
His attitude is cynical rather than sentimental, but not any more
attractive than Donovan's. Tim tries to enter into the spirit of the
deception, but he cannot escape the impression that the house hates
him: 'Maybe it's because I feel no affinity at all with it and it knows
that. In fact I think I hate it and all it represents. And it senses that.
And that's why it's out to get me' (43).

The inability of these modern-day Irish people to possess their own past unselfconsciously is only one aspect of the play's parodic relationship with *Translations*. Another is the way in which Friel treats some of the same themes—naming and the difficulty of communication—in a farcical way. Fintan O'Toole notes, for example, that 'The delving into the historical derivation of names in *Translations* is mirrored here by Donovan's ludicrous attempts to explore the recesses of meaning contained in the names which Tim desperately invents for the locals.'[83] When Donovan sees Jack swimming down on the beach, Tim identifies him as 'Jack the Cod', a fisherman. Donovan gushes, 'Jack the Cod! I love that. Call a man Jack the Cod and you tell me his name and his profession and that he's not very good at his profession. Concise, accurate and nicely malicious. Beautiful!' (46) Tim has told Susan that the motorbike outside (really Jack's) belongs to Nora Dan and that she uses it to scramble on the sand dunes. When Susan refers to her later as 'Nora the Scrambler' Donovan racks his brain trying to figure that one out: 'Give me a clue. Has it to do with eggs? You keep hens!' (47) As in *The Gentle Island*, the urban Irish are as much outsiders here as characters like Barney the Banks, the German who wishes to buy the house. Nora Dan, the only genuine local, calls the cottage 'a byre by right' in which people with any self-respect would not deign to live (44). As she says, though, 'You know the way strangers get queer notions about a place like this; and foreigners is the worst' (23–4).[84]

It would be a mistake, however, to place too much emphasis on social criticism in *The Communication Cord* or to doubt Friel when he says that the play was written 'for laughs'.[85] He had his own reasons for wanting to write a non-serious play, as he explained to Fintan O'Toole. After *Faith Healer*, *Translations*, and *Three Sisters*, he felt that

I was being categorised in some sort of a way that I didn't feel easy about, and it seemed to me that a farce would disrupt that kind of categorising. . . . It's a form to which very little respect is offered and it was important to do it for that reason, not to make it respectable, but to release me into what I bloody well wanted, to attempt it, to have a go at it.[86]

The *Irish News* reported a few days before the play opened that Friel 'says that for his part he did not deliberately intend the play to be full of symbolism but he adds with a grin that no doubt some people, particularly the academics will find symbolism in the work'.[87] He was not wrong about that. For Richard Kearney, 'Friel seems to be suggesting that his confusion of each character with the other is a logical consequence of the historical translation, documented in *Translations*, of the native Irish language and culture into the contemporary babel of the International European Community.'[88] Seamus Deane, in a programme note, wrote that, in *The Communication Cord*,

the most sterile of all illusions is exposed—that of a heroic past which has dwindled to a most unheroic present. The belief in a heroic past almost inevitably produces a farcical present because it gives free rein to cheap attitudes, ranging from facile nostalgia to hard-boiled cynicism. Such attitudes beget stereotyped behaviour and when such behaviour is dominant a culture becomes a caricature.[89]

Tom Paulin, to whom the play was dedicated, found in its 'apocalyptic ending' (Tim and Claire, reunited, are so busy kissing they do not notice that they are knocking over the beam that holds up the ceiling of the kitchen) a 'conclusion whose comic pragmatism redresses or counterbalances some of the more *völkisch* pieties which *Translations* inspired'.[90] Fintan O'Toole's praise, though more restrained, strikes me as just and perhaps more in the spirit of the work itself: '*The Communication Cord* is the funniest new Irish play for a very long time. It is a slight work, one that need not be taken too seriously and one that should not tempt the unwary into exaggerations, but it is very easy to enjoy.'[91]

The play was certainly a popular success. Nearly 3,500 people saw it during the seven nights it played in Derry, and the company reported 90 per cent business almost everywhere else that they went.[92] By the end of its run the production had attracted 23,000 people.[93] The first-night audience was the usual mix of civic, artistic, religious, and theatrical leaders, 'from all sides of all divides'.[94] Michael Coveney, visiting from London, noted, 'You couldn't move at the bar for poets, politicians and assorted theatre folk.'[95] David Nowlan, the *Irish Times* critic, mused enviously, 'Maybe we could persuade some of those Dublin Councillors to make the journey northwards to see how much their Derry counterparts enjoy Irish theatre?'[96] Response on the road was similar. In Omagh, for example, 'the audience loved it, and never missed a line or a laugh'.[97]

For a farce, *The Communication Cord* was slow to get moving. Several critics agreed with Desmond Rushe that Friel 'should plunge into capricious action sooner . . . the lecturer and the barrister talk for a full 15 minutes before the complications commence, and it is too long in a relatively short play'.[98] This, however, did not seem to detract from audiences' enjoyment of the production. Reaction from Newry was fairly typical: 'After a somewhat subdued opening ten minutes any niggling doubts about the Field Day Theatre Company were soon dispelled and a laugh a minute was guaranteed to the end of the performance.'[99] This initial wordiness was probably unavoidable given Friel's conception of the play. He had stated that the farce was 'to some extent an attempt to illustrate a linguistic thesis',[100] and the beginning of the first act is where Tim explains his research into the 'response cry' as a particular example of the more general problem of human communication. His thesis is that communication is extremely difficult and contingent on numerous conditions. As Friel explained, 'In the case of *Translations* we were talking about the function of a fractured language, an acquired language and a lost language. In this case it's saying . . . that perhaps communication isn't possible at all.'[101] Throughout the play, the response cries used by the different characters—Tim's 'O my God', Susan's 'It's unbelievable', Claire's 'Yes'—take on completely different meanings in different situations, leading Tim and Claire to conclude that 'Maybe the message doesn't matter at all then. . . . It's the occasion that matters. And the reverberations that the occasion generates' (92).

Much of the humour of the play derives from Friel's playing with and on the subject of Tim's thesis. Opinion was divided over whether this much verbal joking was suitable in a farce. Gus Smith felt that 'Friel's richness of language slows the action', and Mary MacGoris detected a 'superfluity of words'.[102] For David Nowlan, on the other hand, this was what made the play worth seeing a second time: 'there is more than mere farce in this play. But even the farce itself is as much verbal as mechanical: the confusion arises as much from the words as from the situation. The jokes come in on several different levels: what worked on just one level first time around is now getting home on a higher plane.'[103] Ray Comiskey recognized in the play's 'underlying linguistic concerns' some common ground with *Translations* and commented that 'it fits in with the emerging interests of Field Day'.[104] Frankie McGinley, for one, was not sure what was expected of him: 'when the hero, who is writing a thesis on Linguistics (a special interest of Friel's) begins explaining in convoluted jargon his apparently abstruse theory on conversation—I found the explanation interesting rather than ridiculous; I believe I was supposed to find it ridiculous.'[105] Other reviewers took both the serious and the silly in their stride. One wrote that 'Friel appears to poke fun' at Tim, but realized that 'the play is also a demonstration of his theory about "shared context" and "response cries". We are offered a way of looking analytically at the misunderstandings which pile up relentlessly and at the one-word despairing exclamations which mark the breaks in the action.'[106]

The element of satire in the play was also noted by several reviewers. The critic for the *Limerick Leader* saw in Friel's characters 'a microcosm of the post-1960s Ireland', modern 'Irish Types who verbalise themselves into personal, social, professional or political fantasies'.[107] David Nowlan recognized that

this new farce is virtually a send-up of the sentiments so movingly expressed in its author's own *Translations*. In that fine play about the plunder by stealth of a community's cultural identity, both culture and identities were lovingly drawn and painfully clear. In *The Communication Cord* all is confusion as phoneys fall over each other in their stampede to assert their mock cultural identities.[108]

As James Simmons put it, more crudely, 'There is something heroic and liberating about an author pissing on his own monument.'[109]

As Field Day made its third tour in as many years, onlookers renewed their attempts to categorize the company's activities. This was not an easy task because, as one writer pointed out, the actors changed, the directors changed, the type of drama changed, and the venues changed.[110] Lynda Henderson and Paul Hadfield remarked in *Theatre Ireland* that, since the company did not opt for 'the well-recognised advantages of establishing a "core"' group of actors, 'the greater burden of carrying the philosophy of Field Day has fallen upon the play chosen for performance'.[111] Field Day was still identified almost exclusively with Friel and Rea. Nowlan remarked that the 'annual opening of a new Friel play produced by the author's own company, Field Day, has become a major event not only for Derry but for the whole Irish world of theatre'.[112] Maggie

Stanfield reported that 'Friel wrote Tim Gallagher's part with Stephen very much in mind' and asserted, 'it seems to have become an understood commitment that the young Belfast-born actor will take the lead in a Friel play per year'.[113]

The official description of Field Day had not changed substantially: 'a Northern based touring company aiming to "perform plays of excellence in a distinctively Irish voice that will be heard throughout the island"'.[114] Friel explained to Ray Comiskey that this meant, in practical terms, rehearsing and opening in Derry, having mostly northern people around, and touring North and South 'from Coleraine to Kerry'.[115] This brief was already beginning to be regarded as politically suspect in certain quarters of Northern Ireland. Rea commented on the initially lukewarm reception in Belfast, where *The Communication Cord* did not fill the house on opening night despite good reviews,

Belfast seems scared of Field Day and what we stand for. There is something intrinsically political about what we are trying to do in that we stress our Northern but also our Irish, identity, and that bothers a lot of people. . . .

When we say we want to give some kind of expression in dramatic form to the Irish people, that scares a lot of people.[116]

Observers of whatever political orientation were starting to look for a more specific political line from Field Day. This would not necessarily be expected from a theatre company, of course, but public statements and programme notes by the directors encouraged the view that Field Day was on an ideological crusade, although it was by no means clear exactly what aims the directors had in mind. It was easier to tell what they were against—chiefly the idea of Northern Ireland as being simply another part of Britain. Through their theatrical work they asserted their right to, first, a uniquely Northern identity and, second, a share in an Irish culture as distinct from the British one in which they also had a stake.

Tom Paulin, in his programme note to *The Communication Cord*, affirmed

there is in Derry an effort at civil definition which appears to be absent, or at least less keenly felt, in Belfast and Dublin. Imaginatively, Derry is the most advanced city in Ireland and the Guildhall is a temple which joins the stained, bright images of empire to the idea of a new *res publica*. . . .

Like Bostonian patriots, the members of Field Day are separatists, but separatists who also hunger for Europe. . . . We hope that there is now in this island the possibility of a shared *civilitas* and conscience which can be given coherent form.

In words that must have rung alarm bells for those with unionist leanings, Seamus Deane speculated:

If a congealed idea of theatre can be broken, then the audience which experiences this break would be the more open to the modification of other established forms. Almost everything which we believe to be nature or natural is in fact historical; more precisely, is an historical fiction. If *Field Day* can breed a new fiction of theatre, or of any other area, which is sufficiently successful to be believed in as though it were natural and an outgrowth of the past, then it will have succeeded. At the moment, it is six characters in search of a story that can be believed.[117]

These programme notes raised eyebrows all around Ireland. Four of the five writers of the 'collective review' of *The Communication Cord* in *Theatre Ireland* (January 1983) adverted to them, generally in an uncomplimentary fashion. James Simmons liked the play but commented,

In the beautiful programme, articles by scholar-poets Seamus Deane and Tom Paulin might have been written in drunken euphoria on holiday from Academe (and common sense). Like Seamus Deane's offensive attack on that older, sister project, The Lyric Theatre, Belfast, in last year's programme, these make claims for the company and the play that may be responsible for the surprising number of people I have talked to since who dismiss the whole enterprise because the play has a very modest satirical or intellectual content.[118]

Gerald Dawe agreed that

too much attention has been given to *Field Day's* significance (cultural and otherwise) and not enough time allowed for it to be left alone like any touring theatre company to find its own feet, making ends meet while, in the process, opening our eyes a little bit more to the world around us.[119]

Noting that there were 'a number of eminent intellectuals and men of letters' on the company's board and that 'in contributory essays to the programme' they had made 'major assertions about the company's significance', Paddy Woodworth asked Stephen Rea where Field Day was headed. Rea replied,

Look, it started as an instinct between Brian and me. These guys, some of the most creative brains in the country, are helping to define what we are doing. We're always looking for ways they might become more active in the actual productions, it's quite deliberate that they're not theatre people, their presence broadens our outlook considerably.[120]

Field Day's self-conscious iconoclasm may account in part for the hostile reaction it occasionally provoked from the local theatre establishment. Hadfield and Henderson critically assessed the company's first three years, detecting 'elitism' and 'crescent self-satisfaction' in the group. They expressed the view that Field Day had not been altogether good for Irish theatre, in that 'a lot of attention has been given to and hopes raised by an enterprise which has promised more than it has been able to deliver' and worried that the association was having a negative effect on Brian Friel's work for the stage. In conclusion they offered some unsolicited advice to the company:

In weighing up their progress to date they should give a greater priority than has hitherto been evident to their solid work-a-day achievements in rural tours; recognise that the defensive/arrogant tendency to closedness is doing them harm both in limiting their access to creative and developmental ideas and in the public reception of their work; and expend less energy on semi-mystical formulations of their own meaning.[121]

Field Day directors had recently begun to appropriate publicly the notion of the 'fifth province'. Friel stated in September 1982,

Field Day is not about changing the North—I hate using grandiose terms like this—but in some way the very fact that it's located in the North and has its reservations about it, and that it works in the South and has its reservations about it, it's like, as somebody said, an artistic fifth province.[122]

The following month, in an interview with Fintan O'Toole, Friel referred approvingly to the idea that Field Day was 'a kind of an attempt to create a fifth province to which artistic and cultural loyalty can be offered'. When O'Toole asked him directly, 'Doesn't the whole Field Day project then depend on political nationalism and on the achievement of a united Ireland?' Friel answered,

I don't think it should be read in those terms. I think it should lead to a cultural state, not a political state. And I think out of that cultural state, a possibility of a political state follows.[123]

Taking O'Toole's point that Field Day raised the question of art's power to affect society, Friel responded to the criticism that the company was speaking only to the usual middle-class theatre audience:

There are other theatre groups who are into something else. If you're into agitprop or if you're into political theatre or if you're into street theatre— that's their enterprise. We're not into that kind of enterprise. I think what we're saying is: we'll go to the people who are there but we'll talk to them in a certain kind of way. You know, we're living with what we have. We're trying to talk to them in a different voice and we're trying to adjust them to our way of thinking.

Besides, Friel added,

We're not in fact speaking to the same people apart from Dublin. This is one of the reasons why—we're happy to go to Dublin and play for a week and the only reason we would go and play for four weeks would be to make money which would fund us then next time round. It's not a question at all of turning your back on the capital city but we're into something else I think.

The people in the small towns that Field Day visited were listening: 'I think they hear things in theatre because they haven't been indoctrinated in the way a metropolitan audience is. They hear different sounds in a play. They are great audiences in a different kind of way to a Dublin theatre audience.'[124]

Despite Field Day's commitment to larger goals, however loosely defined, future plans remained tentative. Finance was a 'perennial problem'. The company received about two-thirds of its funding from the Arts Council in Belfast, with most of the remainder coming from its counterpart in Dublin. There were also much smaller amounts from the Northern Ireland Tourist Board, Irish Shell, and subscriptions from programme advertisers. Money had to be solicited annually, which meant a 'hand to mouth' existence for Field Day. Friel was philosophical,

Of course, I worry endlessly about it [finance], but in the long term I don't really worry all that much, because I think we'll survive as long as we need to survive. . . . If we were getting a million dollars tonight it would be great for this year. But we're not looking to an endless future. That's what I'm really saying.[125]

For Rea, too, it was a matter of principle that 'if the impetus fails, if the creativity dies, we won't prolong it'.[126] Most of the time, though, his enthusiasm was uppermost, 'It's hard not to sound pretentious about the whole thing, but I find the experience wonderful and just want to keep it going year after year.'[127]

'Not Just A Little Touring Company':
Field Day Further Afield

FIELD DAY'S reputation in the first few years of its existence had depended mainly on the talents of its founders, Brian Friel and Stephen Rea. On 15 September 1983, the company launched a new venture that would engage more extensively the energies of its other directors, who had hitherto confined their public activity to the penning of controversial (some said pretentious) programme notes on the plays.[1] Seamus Heaney recalls,

> *Translations* was a moment in theatre when you could feel a relationship between the activity of a single dramatist exploring a theme, and the condition of the country. That play went intravenously into the consciousness of the audiences and the country. . . . I suppose what we were searching for were other ways in which that kind of stirring and self-inspection could be extended beyond theatre.[2]

Field Day, the board had decided, would produce pamphlets as well as plays, ideally a set of three every six months.[3] The first three titles were by three of the directors themselves. Tom Paulin's *A New Look at the Language Question* provided a theoretical context for the work of the company to date, Seamus Heaney in *An Open Letter* objected to being included in an anthology bearing the title *The Penguin Book of Contemporary British Poetry*, and Seamus Deane analysed the stereotype of the English and the Irish as *Civilians and Barbarians*.

The title of Paulin's pamphlet sets the keynote for the entire series. The 'language question' has been since the end of the last century one of the basic tenets of Irish nationalism, and the content of the pamphlet bears out the initial impression that the views expressed in it are certainly not going to be unionist. However, Paulin promises a 'new look' at this old question, a phrase that implies either a new vision of the Irish nation and its language, a critique of traditional Irish nationalism, or both. He begins his essay with some observations on the link between language and nationality: 'The history of a language is often a story of possession and dispossession, territorial struggle and the establishment or imposition of a culture. Arguments about the "evolution" or the "purity" of a language can be based on a simplistic notion of progress or on a doctrine of racial stereotypes.' The danger of such arguments is that they are too often based on a 'mystic and exclusive idea of nationhood', a 'chimerical idea of racial purity'.[4] He then provides a brief history of the English language and various attempts to standardize it, concluding, with reference to lexicographers from Samuel Johnson to H. W. Fowler, that 'Fundamentally, the language question is a question about nationhood and government', so much so, in fact, that 'a Unionist who retains a marked Irish accent is either an unconscious contradiction or a subversive ironist' (7, 5).

Through the story of Noah Webster, Paulin explores the identity crisis of a nation without its 'own' language. In the midst of the American Revolution, in 1780, Webster decided that 'As an independent nation, our honor requires us to have a system of our own, in language as well as government' (9). For Paulin, Webster's *Dictionary of American English* is 'a great originating work, the scholarly equivalent of an epic poem or of a prose epic like *Ulysses*' (8). The American rejected Jonathan Swift's dream of one, integrated English-speaking culture in favour of a separatist idea. As evidence for the considerable influence of this idea Paulin cites the *Scottish National Dictionary*, the *Dictionary of Canadianisms on Historical Principles*, and the *Dictionary of Jamaican English* (10).

Webster's concept of American English made the language appear to be a 'native growth'. In Ireland, as in America, English has become thoroughly naturalized, and yet the situation there is more complicated. This is because, in Ireland, English has been regarded as an 'imposed colonial tongue'. Whatever the social and economic incentives to speak English, Irish 'was not completely suppressed or rejected, and it became central to the new national consciousness which formed late in the 19th century' (10). As a result of independence, Irish was restored as the national language of the country and became an important part of the school syllabus in the Republic and in Catholic schools in the North. According to Paulin, attitudes toward Irish reflect social divisions in Ireland:

Traditionally, a majority of Unionist protestants have regarded the Irish language as belonging exclusively to Irish catholic culture. Although this is a misapprehension, it helps to confirm the essentially racist ethic which influences some sections of Unionist opinion and which is also present in the old-fashioned nationalist concept of the 'pure Gael'. As a result, Unionist schools are monolingual while non-Unionist schools offer some counterbalance to English monolingualism. Put another way, state education in Northern Ireland is based upon a pragmatic view of the English language and a short-sighted assumption of colonial status, while education in the Irish Republic is based on an idealistic view of Irish which aims to conserve the language and assert the cultural difference of the country (10–11).

Paulin's choice of adjectives leaves little doubt as to which he considers preferable, although a unionist might well take offence at the implication that state schools in Northern Ireland are 'monolingual' simply because they do not all offer Irish. In these days of European integration, he might argue, is it not as useful to learn French or German as Irish? Furthermore, our hypothetical unionist might add, Northern Ireland is not a 'colony', but a part of the United Kingdom.

Paulin does not dwell on the old opposition between the Irish and English languages. Instead, he turns his attention toward English as it is actually spoken in Ireland today, which he refers to variously as 'Hiberno English', 'Ulster English', and 'Irish English'. He judges this 'language' to be 'in a state of near anarchy'. The disorder is a problem mainly for writers and their readers:

Spoken Irish English exists in a number of provincial and local forms, but because no scholar has as yet compiled a *Dictionary of Irish English* many words are literally homeless. They live in the careless richness of speech, but they rarely appear in print. When they do, many readers are unable to understand them and have no dictionary where they can discover their meaning. The language therefore lives freely and spontaneously as speech, but it lacks any institutional existence and so is impoverished as a literary medium (11).

Part of the difficulty, Paulin contends, is 'the absence of a classic style of discursive prose', citing as examples of degeneration the 'slack and blathery manner' of Owen Dudley Edwards and the prose style of F. S. L. Lyons which, in Paulin's view, is 'drawn from the claggy fringes of local journalism' (11). Perhaps the best alternative, he muses, would be a modern version of Swift's 'ideal, international English': the 'stateless' language of Samuel Beckett. Paulin rejects that suggestion almost as soon as he makes it, however, claiming that 'Most people ... demand that the language which they speak has a much closer contact with their native or habitual climate' (12).

His fascination with dialect makes Paulin sympathetic to the separatist ideas of Ian Adamson, whose *The Identity of Ulster*, with its account of an ancient Cruthin (British) people in Ulster before the Gaels, has been an important influence on the Ulster nationalism now propounded by the Ulster Defence Association (UDA). Adamson argues that if all the people of Northern Ireland would only recognize their common identity as Ulster men and women and acknowledge the fact that they have more in common with each other than with either the Republic or Great Britain, they might finally transcend the religious divide and build a new, independent Northern Ireland together.[5] Paulin finds him 'in some ways the most interesting of recent loyalist historians because he writes from the dangerous and intelligent edges of that consciousness'. He is especially taken with the chapter on 'The Language of Ulster', in which Adamson describes how the original language of the area, Old British, was displaced by Irish in much the same way that Irish was later crowded out by English. 'In this way', writes Paulin, 'he denies an absolute territorial claim to either community in Northern Ireland and this allows him to argue for a concept of "our homeland" which includes both communities' (13).

This sounds reasonable enough, but in his next paragraph Paulin crosses into more questionable territory:

Where the IRA seeks to make a nation out of four provinces, the UDA aspires to make six counties of one province into an independent nation. Official Unionism, on the other hand, tries to conserve what remains of the Act of Union and clings to a concept of nationality which no longer satisfies many of the British people whom the Unionists wish to identify with (13).

By referring to the two paramilitary organizations in a manner which could be interpreted as approving and to the Official Unionists in a way that makes it clear that he considers their position the most irrelevant of the three, Paulin was bound to offend a large segment of unionist sentiment.

The next passage reinforces the idea that Ulster is not British—at least not in any straightforward way. 'Adamson's historical myth', notes Paulin, 'necessarily involves the concept of a national language, and he is deeply conscious of the need to prove that he speaks a language which is as indigenous—or as nearly indigenous—as Irish.' He does this by arguing that since both English and Lallans (Ulster Scots) were modified by the Gaelic speakers who learned them, with these changes later being adopted by the entire population, neither is now really a 'foreign' language. Paulin quotes Adamson, 'The dialect of Belfast is a variety of Ulster English, so that the people of the Shankill Road speak English which is almost a literal translation of Gaelic.' Adamson's view of the language of Ulster seems to Paulin 'part of a worthwhile attempt to offer a historical vision which goes beyond traditional barriers' (14), and he refers benignly to the historian's dream of an Independent Ulster within which both Irish and Lallans would be preserved, an 'alternative to both the Irish Republic and the United Kingdom' (15).

Paulin, however, would have Adamson take his argument one step further:

one of the weaknesses in his argument is an uncertainty about the status and the nature of the English language in Ireland. He sees Ulster Scots as oppressed by educated 'Ulster English'—the provincial language of Official Unionism, for example—but he lacks a concept of Irish English. This is because Adamson . . . is unwilling to contemplate the all-Ireland context which a federal concept of Irish English would necessarily express. Such a concept would redeem many words from that too-exclusive, too-local, usage which amounts to a kind of introverted neglect. Many words which now appear simply gnarled, or which 'make strange' or seem opaque to most readers, would be released into the shaped flow of a new public language. Thus in Ireland there would exist three fully-fledged languages— Irish, Ulster Scots and Irish English. Irish and Ulster Scots would be preserved and nourished, while Irish English would be a form of modern English which draws on Irish, the Yola and Fingallian dialects, Ulster Scots, Elizabethan English, Hiberno-English, British English and American English. A confident concept of Irish English would substantially increase the vocabulary and this would invigorate the written language. A language that lives lithely on the tongue ought to be capable of becoming the flexible written instrument of a complete cultural idea (15).

This paragraph must have left many of its original readers reeling. What exactly does Paulin mean by 'a federal concept of Irish

English', and why does such a thing 'necessarily' entail an 'all-Ireland context'? How can something as abstract as a 'concept' suddenly 'redeem' local dialect from its function as local dialect? By what fiat would the 'new public language' come into being? Paulin says that there 'would' exist three fully fledged languages in Ireland, but he leaves it to the reader to imagine what would have to happen first to make this possible if such is not the case now. It makes very little sense to say that Irish English 'would' be a form of English drawing on everything from the Yola dialect to American English—either it is already or it is not, and what it may be in the future is unlikely to be determined by either polemical pamphlets or Acts of Parliament.

Underlying Paulin's logical leap here, though not stated directly, is the assumption of the inherent desirability of a united Ireland. In a pamphlet the whole thrust of which has been to emphasize the connection between language and political power, between national languages and national constitutions, the association in the reader's mind of a federated, united Ireland with Paulin's 'federal concept of Irish English' is unavoidable. In vain might Paulin protest, with Jonathan Swift, that his pamphlet is 'no politicks, but a harmless proposall about the improvement of the English tongue'.[6] Paulin's 'complete cultural idea', like Friel's 'cultural state', is a coy reference to a political aim.

This aim is never made explicit. Instead, Paulin retreats behind the literary barricade and returns to an issue raised earlier and upon which he is well-qualified to speak: the problems of an Irish writer who wishes to use words common in Irish speech but not included in the Oxford English Dictionary:

the writer who professes this language must either explain dialect words tediously in a glossary or restrict his audience at each particular 'dialectical' moment. A writer who employs a word like 'geg' or 'gulder' or Kavanagh's lovely 'gobshite', will create a form of closed, secret communication with readers who come from the same region (15 – 16).

An interesting observation, but Paulin sees no way out of the dilemma he illustrates. Too much dialect becomes a gimmick; avoidance of it altogether is an impoverishment; Standard British English, he claims, is 'impossible for any Irish writer'. Cosmopolitan English might be an option for some creative writers, though not for discursive ones, who 'must start from a concept of civil duty and a definite cultural affiliation' (16). Thus Paulin hastily draws together the threads of his various insights, and the pamphlet ends—not with a bang, but a whimper:

Unfortunately, the establishment of a tradition of good critical prose, like the publication of A Dictionary of Irish English or the rewriting of the Irish Constitution, appear[s] to be impossible in the present climate of confused opinions and violent politics. One of the results of this enormous cultural impoverishment is a living, but fragmented speech, untold numbers of homeless words, and an uncertain or a derelict prose (16–17).

In the second pamphlet of the series, Seamus Heaney takes a more humorous look at the connection between language and politics. His *An Open Letter*, like *Translations*, takes as its theme the significance of names and is prompted by the inclusion of several of his poems in *The Penguin Book of Contemporary British Poetry*, edited by Blake Morrison and Andrew Motion.[7] The pamphlet is a tongue-in-cheek verse letter in the form of thirty-three stanzas after the manner of Robert Burns, in which Heaney objects to the adjective 'British' as applied to himself. Towards the beginning he offers the editors a brief review of the historical distinction between the two islands:

> Caesar's Britain, its *partes tres*,
> United England, Scotland, Wales,
> *Britannia* in the old tales,
>   Is common ground.
> *Hibernia* is where the Gaels
>   Made a last stand
>
> And long ago were stood upon—
> End of simple history lesson.   (23)

After identifying himself with the downtrodden Gaels, Heaney admits that his reservations might appear to some absurd or arbitrary—he has been called a British poet before without protesting publicly, and a large proportion of his audience is British—but, he admonishes,

> . . . don't be surprised
> If I demur, for, be advised
>   My passport's green.

> No glass of ours was ever raised
> To toast *The Queen*.
>
> .   .   .   .   .   .
>
> You'll understand I draw the line
> At being robbed of what is mine,
> My *patria*, my deep design
>   To be at home
> In my own place and dwell within
>   Its proper name—   (25–6)

It would be possible for a reader to take Heaney's point and yet still believe that the issue was a fairly trivial one. After all, Morrison and Motion probably did not intend to make a political statement with the title of their anthology. Perhaps, indeed, they were only looking for a more inclusive word than 'English' with which to describe the poetry.[8] Heaney attempts, in the last third of his letter, to explain why it matters so much to a Northern Irish person whether he or she is called 'British' or 'Irish'.

Much of the delicacy of the problem stems from the anomalous position of Northern Ireland midway between two countries with different cultures, neither of which is fully committed to the province and to neither of which it entirely belongs. The old nationalist view of partition and the recurrent Troubles in the North as a wholly English imposition does not comprehend the real complexity of the situation:

> The hidden Ulster lies beneath.
> A sudden blow, she collapsed with
> The other island; and the South
>   's been made a cuckold.
> She has had family by them both,
>   She's growing old
>
> And scared that both have turned against her.
> The cuckold's impotent in Leinster
> House. The party in Westminster,
>   All passion spent,
> More down-and-out than sinister,
> Just pays the rent.   (27–8)

There are a great many people from Northern Ireland who consider themselves British, although Heaney does not happen to be one of them. Do the people of Great Britain, however, consider them to be equal citizens? Heaney suggests that the fervour with which the British label is insisted upon by unionists is a measure of their insecurity:

> *Ulster is British* is a tune
>   Not quite deceased
>
> In Ulster, though on 'the mainland'—
> Cf., above, 'the other island'—
> Ulster is part of Paddyland,
>   And Londonderry
> Is far away as New England
>   Or County Kerry.   (28)

In conclusion Heaney refers to a poem by Miroslav Holub, 'On the Necessity of Truth', in which a man creates a disturbance in a cinema when a beaver in a film is mistakenly dubbed a muskrat by the narrator. Heaney sees the poem as a '[f]able of proper naming':

> Names were not for negotiation.
> Right names were the first foundation
>   For telling truth.
>
>   .   .   .   .
>
> Need I go on? I hate to bite
> Hands that led me to the limelight
> In the Penguin book, I regret
>   The awkwardness.
> But British, no, the name's not right.
>   Yours truly, Seamus.   (29)

His tone throughout is self-deprecatory and apologetic, but Heaney makes his point. Demonstrating that there were no hard feelings, he later assigned the Morrison and Motion anthology to a class he taught at Harvard—'British and Irish Poetry, 1930–1980'.

An Open Letter was not Seamus Heaney's only contribution to Field Day in 1983. On 10 November the company, in association with the Glens of Antrim Historical Society, launched his *Sweeney Astray*, a translation of *Buile Suibhne*.[9] Julie Barber, the new Field Day administrator, explained that

Cushendall was chosen for the launch as the Glens of Antrim are in the heart of Sweeney Country, and Field Day was chosen as the publisher as their first production, Brian Friel's *Translations*, was similarly about old ways of life being displaced by the new.[10]

Buile Suibhne is a medieval Irish narrative with sources in tradition dating from the seventh century. Sweeney, a king of Ulster, insults St Ronan and is cursed by him. During a battle soon afterward he goes mad and is transformed into a bird. *Buile Suibhne* records his wanderings and brief interludes of sanity and ends with his forgiveness by another saint, Moling, who writes down his story and has him buried in hallowed ground upon his death. Sections of the story had been translated before, most famously by Flann O'Brien in *At Swim-Two-Birds*,[11] but this was the first time anyone had attempted the entire body of poetry. Heaney had been working on his version for ten years.[12]

Heaney was drawn to *Buile Suibhne* for several reasons, as he explains in his introduction to *Sweeney Astray*. There was, first of all, the conflict between two ways of life, one old and one new, though the struggle underlying the medieval text is one that makes present quarrels between Catholic and Protestant or English and Irish, hundreds of years old though they may be, seem recent in comparison. Heaney observes, 'the literary imagination which fastened upon [Sweeney] as an image was clearly in the grip of a tension between the newly dominant Christian ethos and the older, recalcitrant Celtic temperament'.[13] Mad Sweeney is also, for his twentieth-century translator, 'a figure of the artist, displaced, guilty, assuaging himself by his utterance', and the tale of his woeful adventures is 'an aspect of the quarrel between free creative imagination and the constraints of religious, political and domestic obligation' (p. viii). '[I]n a more opportunistic spirit,' Heaney writes, it is possible 'to dwell upon Sweeney's easy sense of cultural affinity with both western Scotland and southern Ireland as exemplary for all men and women in contemporary Ulster, or to ponder the thought that this Irish invention may well have been a development of a British original, vestigially present in the tale of the madman called Alan' (p. viii).[14] Heaney maintains, however, that his 'fundamental relation' with Sweeney was 'topographical': 'His kingdom lay in what is now south County Antrim and north County Down, and for over thirty years I lived on the verges of that territory, in sight of some of Sweeney's places and in earshot of others' (p. ix). As one reviewer pointed out, in making the translation Heaney had 'shifted his gifts into the territory of deepest memory, the tradition of *dinnseanchas*' in which the poet was enjoined to equip himself with particular legends and stories that 'married him irrevocably to his native landscape'.[15]

In an interview by Mitchell Harris for the American magazine *An Gael*, Heaney referred to this explicitly as part of his motivation for translating *Buile Suibhne*:

Part of my intention of doing *Sweeney* was in the deepest (and least, I hope, offensive) sense political. I wanted the Unionist population to feel that they could adhere to it, that something could be shared. For example, names and landscapes. And that's why I changed all of the place names into their modern equivalents. This is hopefully very subtle . . . Glens of Antrim, Dunseverick, Bushmills, Strangford, County Down, . . . these are all places which are kind of sacral Unionist sites in some ways. So [there is] a little subversive intent saying beneath this layer, there's Sweeney. . . . I wanted the *Sweeney* to be a help; something that Ulstermen of both persuasions could have some identity with. You see, the problem with translations from the Irish is that, on the whole they have been perceived—and *Sweeney* will too, of course—be perceived as a . . . declaration of Sinn Fein culture. But I think Sweeney's different because he's from the North, he's from Antrim, I did him, and he's got all these places. . . . [I]n a hundred years' time . . . ideally, [*Sweeney*] would be part of some united Ulster mythology.[16]

Not everyone approved of Heaney's tactics, particularly his use of Anglicized place names. Purists such as Proinsias O Drisceoil felt that 'The internal consistency of the translation is affected . . . by the . . . anachronism', and that colloquial language and 'references to the counties (post-Elizabethan creations) . . . serve to remind the reader that the book is a twentieth century translation and break the suspension of disbelief'.[17] Others agreed with John Montague, who thought that the use of current place names was 'a marvellous notion' and remarked, 'now no one has an excuse for ignoring our early Tarzan'.[18]

In general, the critical split was between those who believed that Heaney had not been faithful enough to the original[19] and those who, like Eavan Boland, saw it as 'a poem not so much with roots as about roots', an attempt 'to put some shape and organization on one of the oldest archetypes in European literature: the dislocated creative individual'.[20] Perhaps the last word is best left to Bernard O'Donoghue, an Irish scholar, medievalist, and poet in his own right. He saw that 'Just as *North* was not primarily about preserved bodies but about contemporary history, so *Sweeney* is not about the seventh-century lunatic but about the conscientious, displaced modern poet.' *Sweeney Astray*, he wrote, should be regarded as 'a work of the greatest literary note'.[21]

Seamus Deane's contribution to the first set of Field Day pamphlets, *Civilians and Barbarians*, has a much less cautious and conciliatory feel to it than Heaney's *Open Letter*. He begins with the proposition, which he identifies as 'the nucleus of modern European theories of freedom', that 'Those who live under the law are civilians; those who live beyond it are barbarians' and points out that the weakness of this formulation is that it fails to mention whose law 'compels men to be free'.[22] Thus, he argues, the Irish have been branded as barbarians through the centuries because they have often shown little deference toward English law, which English observers have interpreted as lack of respect for Law itself. With reference to Edmund Spenser's *View of the Present State of Ireland* (1596), *Discovery of the True Causes why Ireland was Never Entirely Subdued* (1612) by '[o]ne John Davies', and an unfinished account by Samuel Coleridge (1814) of the failures of English policy in Ireland from Henry II's time to the Act of Union, Deane contends that several features of the English view of Ireland remain constant:

Most pronounced among these are the assumption that the strife in Ireland is the consequence of a battle between English civilization, based on laws, and Irish barbarism, based on local kinship loyalties and sentiments; that the added complication of religion helps to intensify that Irish barbarism by fostering ignorance and sloth, disrespect for English law and respect for Papal decrees in its stead, conspiracy and rebellion by cherishing foreign connections hostile to England (35).

According to Deane,

The wisdom of English commentators on Irish affairs has always been vitiated by the assumption that there is some undeniable relationship between civilization, the Common Law and Protestantism. Ireland has remained a permanent rebuke to this assumption, and has been subjected to vilification on that account. The assumption has remained unquestioned (35).

Deane's vigorous, combative style and penchant for esoteric references tends to obscure the fact that this statement, coming where it does, is a gross generalization ('always') based upon three examples pre-dating 1815. The rest of the pamphlet, however, enlarges upon this thesis.

After a brief digression on English reaction to the French Revolution (the French revolutionaries, being, like the Irish in later times, Catholic and nationalistic, were regarded with similar suspicion by English writers—seen, even, as *'inferno-human* beings'), Deane turns his attention to nineteenth-century social movements in Ireland, especially the temperance movement. Here he records 'a curious reversal of the conventional Protestant/Catholic attitudes':

In Ireland, the Protestant has tended to turn to law and the State even in matters of social and moral attitude, because Protestantism and the State have been for so long in a defensive alliance with one another. The Catholic, on the other hand, has turned to conscience and the Church (increasingly the same thing in the modern period), seeking from the Church rather than the State legitimisation for social and moral issues (37).

Throughout the 1800s a whole range of English social legislation was being implemented in Ireland with 'a highly Spenserian aim in view—the civilisation of the wild natives' (38). The dispensary system of health care, the national school system, the Ordnance Survey—anyone who had seen *Translations* would appreciate the significance of Deane's positioning of Field Day's most famous production within the more general framework of his argument—the legal system of Resident Magistrates, and the creation of a nationally controlled paramilitary police force all reflected social thinking also prevalent within England at the time, although it was applied more consistently in Ireland. 'All of these schemes', Deane points out, 'were, in effect, pieces of preventive legislation':

A whole range of conditions—like the condition of being drunk, or illiterate, or from somewhere unheard of or unknown, or vagrant, or disaffected—was now realised as being beyond (not exactly against) the law (38).

The underlying aim was to inhibit the development of a condition of mind—that of *'homo criminalis.'* The Irish mind was merely one variant of this more general category, but it was to the English mind . . . ineluctably criminal because of the very simple fact that it tended to show remarkably consistent disrespect for English law and, therefore (!) for the Law as such. The stereotypes of the Irish person— the quaint Paddy or the simian terrorist—arise quite naturally from the conviction that there are criminal types, politically as well as socially identifiable to the police and to all decent citizens (39).

Although he has been at some pains here to point out that the general belief in criminal 'types' is located in a particular historical moment, is a 'theoretical construct of the great age of scientific criminology, the detective novel and high industrial capitalism', Deane begins his next paragraph with the bland assertion that 'This brings us to the doorstep of our own time' (39). He believes that 'The language of politics in Ireland and England, especially when the subject is Northern Ireland, is still dominated by the putative division between barbarism and civilization', and he devotes the remainder of his pamphlet to an examination of the contemporary 'rift between the competing discourses of the civilian and the barbarian' (39).

In the past century, aspects of barbarism earned a certain cachet, so the label was no longer a completely derogatory one. In literature, 'barbarism' became 'primitivism' and 'represented a vigour lost to the sophisticated art of the civilised world' (39). The problem with this, Deane thinks, is that

The essential issues have . . . been 'displaced' into literature in such a manner that their reality has been further attenuated in the minds of the Irish people. The writer as barbarian, the audience as civilian—that is an easily accepted exercise in role playing. But the romanticisation of writing involved in this is not nearly so important as the humiliating conquest of the audience. For such an audience is tamed; it has learned to be submissive to the massive system of controls which the modern political machine operates. Among those systems of control is the image of the writer as licensed barbarian—a sort of wild Irish native performing in an English court. But, beyond that, there is the much more concentrated manipulation of the civilian audience's reaction to the other kind of outsider—the criminal type and, above all, the *politically* criminal type, your friendly neighbourhood terrorist (40).

This is where Deane would probably have lost many of his readers. Leaving aside the dubious implication that literary theory conditions the way most people look at the world, one might well resist the suggestion that 'the civilian audience' must be manipulated in order to be outraged by terrorist activity. Deane goes on to describe the 'stereotype' of the Irish terrorist:

This stereotype has all the classic faults of the barbarian as seen from the view of the English civilian. First he is Irish; next Catholic; and, if not Catholic, then an extreme Protestant, a Dissenter of the old, troublesome Calvinistic or Ranter type; in addition he is from a working-class background and is unemployed (unemployable); therefore he draws money from the benevolent state which he intends to subvert and by which he is oppressed as he was also educated and fed free milk by it. He is from an area of dirt and desolation, not to be equalled in Western Europe, a blot on the fair face of the United Kingdom. He drinks a lot for, since the Fenians, it has been a standard piece of English lore that all Irish guerilla groups meet in pubs when they are not blowing them up. Sometimes, they manage to do both. Finally, and worst of all, he is sometimes a she. Locked in a poverty trap, lost in a mist of sentiment and nostalgia, exploiting the safeguards of laws they despise, faithful to codes other than those of the English rite, they are the perfect reproduction, with some nineteenth century romantic tints, of Spenser's wild Irish. Most important of all, they are not only barbarians, they are criminals. Their opponents, who wear uniforms, and live in barracks, and drive armoured cars, operate checkpoints, etc. etc., kill with impunity, because they represent, they embody the Law. The terrorist embodies its denial. The brutal exploitation of events by both sides demonstrates over and over again the endlessness of the battle for supremacy of one kind of discourse, one set of political attitudes over another (40).

The situation in Northern Ireland, Deane maintains, is complicated by the fact that 'modes of discourse other than the political' also become involved, particularly the moral mode (41). He notes a qualitative difference between the appeals made by the churches to terrorists and those made to 'the forces of Law and Order':

The first are made to individuals, loners, to come in out of the moral cold, to cease disgracing the cause they ostensibly represent; the second are made to a corporate body, not to the individual. The 'barbarians' are always 'men and women', or specific, even named, individuals. They enjoy the privilege of individuality precisely because they will not be granted the status of a corporate force within civil society. The ground of the appeal, however, is that of the universal condition of mankind, redeemed and unredeemed, saved and damned, or, if you like, civilian and barbarian. The moral and religious idiom, which claims this universality, has in fact been incorporated into the political idiom which *appears* to be more local in its range. The moral idiom therefore is no more than a reinforcement of the political while appearing to be independent of it (41).

Deane finds the distinction between moral and political idioms in Northern Ireland to be a spurious one because, to his mind, they operate so often in collusion. He cites as an example the Peace Movement, which he calls 'one of the most successful of all political exploitations of a moral code which was in fact a political code' (41). It is generally forgotten, he writes, 'that the incident which sparked the movement off began with the killing of an IRA man, who was driving a car, by a British soldier—who was himself in no danger':

The charismatic movement in Catholicism and the evangelical movement in Protestantism combined to display, in front of the cameras, the longing for peace by a population disturbed by the guerillas within their ranks— not by the army, or the police, or the unemployment, housing conditions and so forth. As farces go, it was one of the most successful of modern times (41).

The failure of the Peace Movement to change anything only reinforced the 'demonising mythology'. So, says Deane, did the dirty protest at the Maze Prison and the hunger strikes. Perhaps, he suggests, people's images of themselves are so limited by the dichotomy between civilians and barbarians that they are incapable of seeing the world in any more constructive way. 'Of all the blighting distinctions which govern our responses and limit our imaginations at the moment,' he concludes, 'none is more potent than this four hundred year-old distinction between barbarians and civilians. We may ask, with Bishop Berkeley in *The Querist* "Whether the natural phlegm of this island needs any additional stupefier?"' (42)

Deane's intention in writing his essay was clearly to help people get beyond this 'blighting distinction'. As he puts it, 'Political languages fade more slowly than literary languages but when they do, they herald a deep structural alteration in the attitudes which sustain a crisis' (42). Nevertheless, in attempting to deconstruct one stereotype Deane himself perpetuates another one. At the start of his essay the civilians and barbarians of his title are identified, respectively, with the English colonizers of Ireland and the native population; in the middle the barbaric category has narrowed to include only those Irish who are intractable to English law; and by the end there are only two types of barbarian left—the artist and 'your friendly neighbourhood terrorist'. This progression of his argument lends Deane's tone a peculiar ambiguity. He seems, by some sleight of hand, to identify the Irish population generally (at the beginning of his pamphlet) with the Provisional IRA (by the end). Then, in his eagerness to redress the balance of legitimacy between 'civilians' and 'barbarians', or to make the point that legitimacy is in the eye of the beholder, he sides with the oppressed barbarians in a way that, in the context, makes him sound like a terrorist sympathizer.

The impact on readers in Northern Ireland would be rather like that of Paulin's unfavourable comparison of the Official Unionists with what he sees as the cultural commitment of the IRA and the UDA. In fact, Deane's analysis proved even easier for many people to reject out of hand because it seemed obviously to come from a Catholic and nationalist point of view. This was ironic, for Deane considered himself a fierce critic of traditional Irish nationalism. How could he be interpreted in a way so contrary to his intentions?

The biggest problem with *Civilians and Barbarians* is that, in playing off the 'Irish mind' against the 'English mind', Deane leaves the mind of the Ulster unionist out of his neat series of oppositions. Any discussion of that would obfuscate his argument since, as he has defined the terms, civilians are Protestant and English while barbarians are Catholics of some other nationality. His acknowledgement of the Protestants who are also by now indigenous to Ireland is confined to a couple of glancing references to the United Irishmen and the fear so created among English observers of 'the combined forces of Popery, Dissent, and Unbelief, fighting under a political flag' along with an aside in his catalogue of the English person's Irish terrorist, who is 'if not Catholic, then an extreme Protestant, a Dissenter of the old, troublesome Calvinistic or Ranter type' (36, 40).

What is especially unclear is whether the Northern Irish Protestants belong in the category of 'civilians' or 'barbarians'. When Deane contrasts Protestant and Catholic attitudes they seem to belong in the former category, but when he mentions them in connection with groups of rebels or outlaws they appear to go with the rest of the 'wild Irish'. The symmetry of Deane's argument compels him to speak as little as possible about divisions among people within Ireland, because when he talks about 'civilians' and 'barbarians' he is really talking about 'English' and 'Irish'.

The difficulty here is that these categories were not always easily distinguishable even in Spenser's time, and they certainly are not now. The concept of Britishness and the Ulster unionists' adherence to it makes the Irish–English division an analytical tool of only limited utility when it comes to Northern Ireland. Unionists do not consider themselves 'English' or, in any simple sense, 'Irish', and Deane refuses to call them 'British'. Thus their status is indeterminate, and the resulting uncertainty does considerable damage to his case.

Deane might argue that he is more interested here in the attitudes of 'the English civilian' on the 'mainland', who may make little distinction between the two groups in Northern Ireland. It is odd, in that case, that we are not given a single contemporary example of English reaction to the problems of Northern Ireland. He mentions the calls of the churches and the abortive Peace Movement, but these are both reactions from within the province. All we have to represent the English point of view is his own enumeration of what he takes to be English attitudes. It was hardly surprising, then, that many of his readers should regard Deane's vision of the English as at least as caricatured as the opinion of Irish people he imputes to them.

This was the considered feeling of a number of critics concerning the pamphlet series as a whole. In Ireland the pamphlets were generally taken as straightforward nationalist statements and greeted with approbation or disgust depending upon the political opinions of the reader or reviewer. This must have surprised and dismayed their authors. Shortly before the series was launched, Seamus Heaney had told the *Irish News* that it was aimed at breaking the mould of traditional nationalist thinking.[23] If what they were saying was new, though, very few people seemed to notice.

One of the most scathing reviews was by Maire Mhac an tSaoi and appeared in the *Irish Press*.[24] She singled Deane out for special rebuke:

I am made distinctly uneasy by the thought that Seamus Deane is a Professor of English Literature, so patent and so obsessive, in this essay, is his need, perhaps subconscious, to conduce to hatred of the eponymous people, an appreciation of whose thought and language it is his profession to impart.

She believed that the biggest weakness in Deane's analysis was that his readers were given

no inkling that the dichotomy in his title is as old as time. A barbarian was initially a person whom an ancient Greek couldn't understand—not that he would want to anyway—but there is no society, no culture that we can apprehend, no matter how remote in time or space, in which the germ is not latent. Our most pressing need today, if our planet is to survive, is to control these manifestations in ourselves rather than, as in Professor Deane's diatribe, to isolate them in others.

She quoted with amusement the 'stereotype' of the Irish terrorist and remarked, 'I would have thought that passage the perfect identikit picture of your rank-and-file I.R.A.-man. Not so; it is intended as heavy irony.' Her response to Deane's bleak conclusion was that 'in our given historical circumstances a little phlegm might be no bad thing'.

Moving on to Paulin's pamphlet, Mhac an tSaoi stated that 'his quality of being a poet equips him particularly well to understand the dilemma of the writer from the sub-culture', but expressed the opinion that his 'projected linguistic atlas and guide reflect and describe only the landscapes of a self-indulgent cloud-cuckoo-land'. Worse, she feared his pamphlet would 'encourage in their toxic and pathetic fantasies those Ulstermen who would out-Fenian the Fenians and fabricate for themselves an ancestry distinct from, and even more romantic than, any other available in our islands, tracing descent from the legendary Picts or Cruithin, as being the epitome and distillation of authentic, autochthonous, British stock'.

Heaney was the only pamphleteer to escape Mhac an tSaoi's censure:

Where the other Seamus vituperates and agonises in the throes of wounded identity, Seamus Heaney transcends the condition by dint of artistry and generosity and maintains his essential dignity as an individual and as an Irishman the while. Tom Paulin sweats verbiage over the blue-prints for a literary vehicle that will be quintessentially Ulster. Seamus Heaney serenely imposes his personal idiolect on the reader by the authority of the poetic word.[25]

Owen Dudley Edwards took a similarly dim view of the series, which he dubbed 'Wrongs antique-dealt and served up trite, | With sparkling whine'. Nor, gratuitously insulted by Paulin, did he resist the temptation to respond in print:

> To think that I, who ring these rhymes,
> Am singled from *The Irish Times*
> To symbolise stylistic crimes
>   By angel-weeper,
> Guardian of language in these climes:
>   My blather's keeper!
>
> .   .   .   .   .   .
>
> Taking soup from the next tureen,
> To taste a puker shade of green
> Imbibe Professor Seamus Deane
>   And all he hated
> Writ out in prose like vaseline
>   Regurgitated.

Edwards, too, regarded Heaney's pamphlet as the one 'pearl among the swine'.[26]

Heaney did not escape so easily the sharp eye of Eavan Boland. Writing in the *Irish Times*, she commented, 'Seamus Heaney has been in and around anthologies of English poetry for nearly fifteen years. . . . I cannot believe that the sudden appearance of the word "British" on the title page came as a rude shock. He has either changed his mind or changed his friends, and neither process is completely safe for poets.' She acknowledged that

This may seem unsympathetic to what, after all, may be the beginnings of a new Ulster nationalism. Yet therein lies the rub. A new Ulster nationalism is not my idea of what Irish poetry needs, but I would be quite willing to lay aside this prejudice if the new nationalism contained all the voices, all the fragments, all the dualities and ambiguities of reference; but it doesn't. Judging by the Field Day pamphlets here in front of me, this is green nationalism and divided culture. 'Whatever we mean by the Irish situation,' writes Derek Mahon, 'the shipyards of Belfast are no less a part of it than a country town in the Gaeltacht'. Would that this were true; or, at least, would that it were real. The danger is that underneath the new words we will have the old wounds.

Boland chided Heaney for his insistence upon something which she believed had very little to do with poetry: 'Poetry is defined by its energies and its eloquence, not by the passport of the poet or the editor; or the name of the nationality. That way lies all the categories, the separations, the censorships that poetry exists to dispel.'[27]

Robert Johnstone, reviewing the pamphlets for *The Honest Ulsterman*, agreed with Boland that 'under the new gloss is the old wood of green nationalism'. He dealt humorously with Paulin and Heaney—'Who, apart from Tom Paulin, says "gulder" unself-consciously?' and 'Perhaps Blake and Andrew should have called it *The Penguin Book of West European Archipelagean Poetry*'— but Deane's pamphlet he found more seriously disturbing. 'Most worrying', he wrote, 'is that at some point in his argument "Irish" becomes synonymous with "Provo".' Referring to Deane's description of the dirty protest in the Maze, he remarked,

It is an effective literary image, but one which ignores the reality of the choices and forces involved. As Unionists and the Northern Ireland Office understood very well, it was impossible to accede to the prisoners' demands without conferring legitimacy on their 'armed struggle'. The Provos had engineered a situation in which the British were unable to absorb them into the Pale of civilisation, a process which the British at least have been on occasion prepared to attempt, without admitting defeat. . . .

For Deane it is deep-seated prejudice which prevents the English considering the Provos' demands, or republican demands, seriously. Might it not be that those demands have been considered and dismissed? Might it not be that the means by which those demands are advocated have debased them?

Johnstone acknowledged that 'there is anti-Irish racism in England', but he was more struck by 'the blatant and much less discriminate anti-English racism of republican spokesmen and publications'. He agreed with Deane that it was probably 'time to wield a scalpel on the corpse of republican mythology—a task for which the Field Day pamphleteers seem eminently qualified, but sadly disinclined, on the evidence so far, to undertake'.[28]

Paulin's response, in the next issue of the magazine, was that 'In my view, neither Deane, Heaney nor myself adopt a position which a generation of revisionist historians has influentially undermined.' 'Significantly', he added, 'Johnstone suggests that I refer to Ian Adamson as a "protestant" historian. I do not. I call him a "loyalist" historian—but it is characteristic of Johnstone's essentially sectarian cast of mind that he should misquote me in this way.' Johnstone replied that, while he agreed with much of what Paulin had argued in his pamphlet, he questioned what he took to be the basic premiss of the series as a whole:

it is true that it's very easy to talk in sectarian terms when one lives in Northern Ireland. . . . I think our main problem is not British imperialist attitudes—the drift of the first three Field Day pamphlets—but our own sectarianism. Imagining that British withdrawal would turn us into enlightened United Irishmen seems naïve and dangerous. . . .

It is too comfortable and too easy to initiate a project such as yours by laying it all on the Brits. And it is strange to say the least that your pamphlets look fixedly eastwards while selling mainly on this side of the Irish Sea.[29]

Terence Brown, however, writing in *Fortnight*, rejected the idea that Field Day stood for green nationalism:

That is to over-simplify. Paulin is as concerned about Ulster Scots as he is about Irish or Irish English; Heaney, in several key, highly elliptical stanzas, is complicating his awareness of Ulster's political and social dilemmas beyond the rather crude versions of these found in 'Ocean's Love to Ireland' and 'Act of Union' . . . ; while Deane's concerns are specifically the analysis of modes of consciousness in colonial conditions which involve all parties in diminutions of human possibility.[30]

Genuine green nationalists perceived that Field Day was not toeing the line. Pádraig Ó Conchúir, for example, dismissed Paulin's pamphlet as 'ten pages of blather about the creole dialects of English on the island of Ireland'.[31]

Other commentators saw no reason why Field Day should have to apologize for 'Irish national feeling'. Maurice Harmon, writing in the *Irish University Review*, remarked approvingly on the way the pamphleteers 'distance themselves from the London, British, imperialist centre by emphasising differences of language, identity and patria', but made no mention of the second part of Field Day's brief, that of distancing itself from Dublin as well.[32] Breandán Ó

Doibhlin noted what seemed to him the remarkable vehemence of Maire Mhac an tSaoi's attack on Seamus Deane:

I suspect that Séamus Deane's sin lies in the topical reference of his thesis, in his permitting himself to feel with his fellow Northern Catholics both the whips and the scorns of British and colonist. His failure 'to control these manifestations' sorts ill with Máire Mhac an tSaoi's irreproachable liberalism, but then it is rooted in a couple of generations of minority alienation, while all liberalism tends simply to be conformity with the dominant ethic. The distinction between barbarians and civilians insinuates itself into many an unlikely place.

If anything, he felt, the pamphlet writers may not have gone far enough:

For, while Séamus Deane rightly criticizes the colonialist assumption of a relationship between civilization, the Common Law and Protestantism, he might surely have added in all logic the colonialist assumption of an undeniable relationship between civilization and the English language. Perhaps even, to be fair to the English, it may be difficult for them to see why a neighbouring island which has long since accepted their language and cultural dominance should continue to make such a song and dance about political separation. When we use English as 'our' language, particularly for the purpose of moulding the chaos of our country into the order of art, have we not acceded to civility? Have we not acquiesced in Seamus Heaney's 'rude forcing' of our identity, turned our ravishment into a feckless romp and forfeited an ancient love? Am I pushing the metaphor too far, or does some such secret scruple worry at the guts of all our most conscientious writers in English?
   Or if it doesn't, should it?[33]

   Richard Kearney and Ronan Sheehan, another former student of Deane's, also wrote to defend him against the ravages of Maire Mhac an tSaoi and Owen Dudley Edwards:

for demonstrating that some Englishmen promulgated colonialist views which branded Irish people as barbarians, Deane is himself accused of promoting hatred. In fact he is doing the very opposite: exposing hatred which masquerades as literature, legislation or journalism. Must we now regard *any* critique of British colonialism as a symptom of the corruption of nationalism?[34]

In another context Kearney isolated the 'common concern' of the three authors:

the use and abuse of language as a powerful, if all too often ignored, means of remembering our past, defining our present and projecting new images for the future. Without such critical attention to the worlds we inhabit, no political reshaping of the world can be totally successful.

'To be sure,' he acknowledges,

these are not 'penny pamphlets' written for the man in the street; they are two-pound-fifty pamphlets written by intellectuals for intellectuals. But it is an auspicious beginning nonetheless. For the translation of these high-minded and crucial debates into idioms more available to the wider public, there are, of course, the Field Day plays.[35]

This was a dubious proposition, given Friel's stated refusal to think of drama in programmatic terms, but this was how a great many people began to see the Field Day project. Idiosyncratic though they were, the first three Field Day pamphlets set forth several of the ideas that had governed Field Day's practice. Each of the plays, in a different way, had demonstrated a preoccupation with language and an insistence that language has a political dimension. *Translations* had been an illustration of the vital connection between language, culture, and self-determination. The 'two' languages on stage pointed up the function of shared speech as a mark of community, and the trauma of the on-stage disintegration of the hedge-school society symbolized the historical undermining of the Irish language. Friel's *Three Sisters* looked past the wreckage to a new assertion of cultural distinctiveness—Irish people could be Irish even while speaking English—while *The Communication Cord* showed up the ludicrousness of a backward-looking cultural ideal.

The company's tours had always taken place in an all-Ireland context, and people could draw what conclusions they would from that. Some might have detected politically suspect undertones, too, in Stephen Rea's explanation of the thinking behind Field Day in October of 1983: 'We are looking for areas to discuss amongst ourselves, as Irish people, instead of looking to England or else-where for approval, as Irish writers of the past felt they had to do.'[36] All of this could have been disregarded by people who simply wanted to see a play. As Rea himself said, 'Nobody could describe our plays as overtly political'.[37] With the inauguration of the pamphlet project, though, some of the more obscure references in the programme notes began to take on a life of their own. Those looking for an explication of the company's 'mission' would henceforth seek for it there.

Perhaps the reception of the first set of pamphlets had given the directors a heightened sense of the difficulties facing the company. In a discussion printed in the *Sunday Independent* a few months later, Deane admitted that

It's no good just performing our plays and selling pamphlets to people we know. There's no point in continuing unless we can get through to Unionists. We must seek an audience of people in [the] North who would be put off just by our names, by [the] fact that two of us are called Seamus. We must find a way of convincing these people that Field Day is for them, that it's not subversive.[38]

As 1983 drew to a close, Field Day, together with *The Crane Bag*, was presented with a *Sunday Independent* Arts Award. The citation in that newspaper on 1 January 1984 read:

putting forward art and ideas as integral elements in the contemporary political debate, the *Crane Bag* magazine in the south ... and Field Day ... through its plays, poetry and pamphlets have succeeded (from their different geographical and cultural originals) in postulating a 'fifth province' of the mind where the divisions of the four political provinces might be confronted and resolved.[39]

There were significant parallels between the work of the *Crane Bag* editors and that of the Field Day directors. Both organizations professed an interest in creative interchange between art and politics and both claimed to be in the business of shaking off old conceptions of Ireland and 'Irishness' in order to look forward to a richer, more inclusive notion of Irish identity. Seamus Deane had been active in both enterprises.

It came as no great surprise, then, when Field Day announced the publication of its second set of pamphlets in May 1984 to find that two of them, the first contributions to Field Day by people who were not directors of the company, were by Richard Kearney and Declan Kiberd, both *Crane Bag* veterans and lecturers with Deane at University College, Dublin (the third was written by Deane himself).[40] Kearney, Kiberd, and Deane had also been featured in a series of lectures delivered at University College, Dublin, and televised by RTÉ in the Republic. These lectures were subsequently published by the *Crane Bag* as *Ireland: Dependence & Independence*.[41] Their pamphlets for Field Day—Deane's *Heroic Styles: The Tradition of an Idea*, Kearney's *Myth and Motherland*, and Kiberd's *Anglo-Irish Attitudes*—were in part developments of ideas also aired there.[42]

In his RTÉ lecture, 'Remembering the Irish Future', Deane had argued that both communities in the North look at a future in which one of them will have won and the other lost. Besides the insecurity engendered in both groups, which is a 'recipe for permanent strife', this state of affairs encourages on both sides a kind of utopian thinking in which people believe that everything would be all right if only (for unionists) the Northern Catholics would finally accept the State or (for nationalists) the Northern majority would allow peaceful reunification to take place. Since neither outcome is likely in the foreseeable future, Utopia is converted into Eden as Irish people 'remember' a time when all was as it should be. In Deane's view, this makes Ireland a backward-looking place with 'a conservative politics' and 'a Romantic literature'.[43] He insists that

The moment for utopianism is past. It brought great gains—a great theatre, a great literature, above all, a stable Republic. But all of these gains were dogged and tainted by exile, emigration, censorship, provincialism, civil war in the South, anti-Catholic pogroms in the North. Since the sixties, if not earlier, the dark side of the achievement has predominated.[44]

In particular, '[n]ationalism . . . was reduced in this century to a caricature of itself because it could not reconcile its conservative cultural vision of itself with the economic demands of modernisation'.[45] People in Ireland, says Deane, should strive to free themselves from the past and begin to construct their future on their own terms, instead of acceding to the determinism inherent in the idea of a pre-existing national essence that is either responsible for political and social problems or prevented from expressing itself by the political stalemate:

If the Irish could forget about the whole problem of what is *essentially* Irish, if they could be persuaded to see that this does nothing but produce an unnecessary anxiety about a non-existent abstraction, they would have recovered some genuine independence. Irishness is the quality by which we want to display our non-Britishness—or our anti-Britishness or, Britishness is the quality by which we display our non-Irishness. Both are forms of dependency. The idea of what is British continues to govern the idea of what is Irish. Both should be allowed to lapse back into the arms of the nineteenth century in which they were cradled.[46]

Deane intended *Heroic Styles*, his second pamphlet for Field Day, to be a further damnation of romantic nationalism as he believed it to have been promoted in the writings of the Irish Literary Revival. In it, he attacks 'the myth of Irishness, the notion of Irish unreality' and 'the notions surrounding Irish eloquence' as 'political themes upon which the literature has battened to an extreme degree since the nineteenth century when the idea of national character was invented'.[47] In a colonial situation, he suggests, one is always forced to choose whether or not to align oneself with 'the nation', and this in turn often implies an acceptance of the idea of racial distinctiveness. The resultant stereotyping 'is itself an alienating force. To accept it is to become involved in the spiritual heroics of a Yeats or a Pearse, to believe in the incarnation of the nation in the individual. To reject it is to make a fetish of exile, alienation and dislocation in the manner of Joyce or Beckett' (57–8). Deane believes that 'both Joyce and Yeats are troubled by the mystique to an extent that, in contemporary conditions, we cannot afford. The dissolution of that mystique is an urgent necessity if any lasting solution to the North is to be found' (58). Earlier, sounding oddly like Conor Cruise O'Brien, Deane had warned,

The acceptance of a particular style of Catholic or Protestant attitudes or behaviour, married to a dream of a final restoration of vitality to a decayed cause or community, is a contribution to the possibility of civil war. It is impossible to do without ideas of a tradition. But it is necessary to disengage from the traditions of the ideas which the literary revival and the accompanying political revolution sponsored so successfully (56).

Deane's criticism of old-fashioned nationalism, however, was not acknowledged or even perhaps recognized by many of the early reviewers of the pamphlets. In fact, Deane himself was branded a green nationalist. The reason for this can be traced to structural flaws in the essay itself which make it extremely confusing—and possibly to a certain ambivalence in Deane's own thinking.

The most basic problem with the pamphlet is that Deane never really explains what he means by 'style'—or, rather, that his use of the word changes subtly in different contexts. He begins with the proposition that there have been two main literary-historical modes of regarding Irish culture: Romantic and modern, represented by Yeats and Joyce respectively. Neither of these, he asserts, is adequate to the task of interpreting contemporary Irish reality: 'The problem which is rendered insoluble by them is that of the North.' Deane even makes the extraordinary assertion that 'In a basic sense, the crisis we are passing through is stylistic. That is to say, it is a crisis of language—the ways in which we write it and the ways in which we read it' (46).

It would seem, then, that the 'heroic styles' of the title are Romantic and Modernist. Soon, though, this particular distinction is lost as Deane compares the work of Yeats and Pearse and points out that 'to the extent that we prefer one as literature to the other, we find ourselves inclined to dispossess it of history, to concede to it an autonomy which is finally defensible only on the grounds of style' (47). Here, rather than as a descriptive convention ('Romantic'), 'style' functions in another sense as an individual hallmark or technique, the way in which a writer imprints his personality on the world. It is strange, at this juncture, that Deane does not examine in detail a poem by either Pearse or Yeats, presumably assuming a complete knowledge of both on the part of his readers. Curiously, in a pamphlet that takes style as its subject, there is no close textual analysis whatsoever.

Deane does not continue to talk about 'style' in this sense, though, but quickly returns to the opposition of Romantic and Modernist world-views, this time adding a new twist. Yeats and Pearse were both romantics, according to Deane, because

They were men who asserted a coincidence between the destiny of the community and their own and believed that this coincidence had an historical repercussion. . . . Whatever we may think of their ideas of tradition, we still adhere to the tradition of the idea that art and revolution are definitively associated in their production of an individual style which is also the signature of the community's deepest self (52–3).

Joyce's writing, in contrast, is less a 'style' than 'a polyglot mixture of styles' (52). The stylistic conflict, the 'battle between style as the expression of communal history governed by a single imagination . . . and Joycean stylism, in which the atomisation of community is registered in a multitude of equivalent, competing styles' is no less than 'a battle between Romantic and contemporary Ireland' (53).

Deane uses 'style', then, in a rather eccentric way to mean 'essence'. Understanding this illuminates his argument somewhat, but a puzzle remains. If the problem is 'univocal, heroic, Yeatsian style' (52), then why is not Joyce's pluralism an adequate response? Deane appears to be in two minds himself. On the one hand, he repudiates the 'mystique' of Irishness and condemns Yeats for disseminating it, but on the other he is not quite able to let go of the idea that there is, or should be, something distinctive about Irish people by virtue of their being Irish. He acknowledges that Joyce's attempts to 'free himself from set political positions' did allow him to give 'a certain harmony to varied experience', but, Deane worries, this might simply be

the harmony of indifference, one in which everything is a version of something else, where sameness rules over diversity, where contradiction is finally and disquietingly written out. In achieving this in literature, Joyce anticipated the capacity of modern society to integrate almost all antagonistic elements by transforming them into fashions, fads—styles, in short (56).

'Style' thus acquires yet another meaning—the one it commonly has in a consumer society—as far as imaginable from the Yeatsian sense of style with which he began.

In fact, style (whatever Deane means by it) is not the main issue. He is ultimately concerned less with 'style' than with the 'idea' of the second part of his title. He formulates this idea at the beginning of the essay:

When the language is English, Irish writing is dominated by the notion of vitality restored, of the centre energised by the periphery, the urban by the rural, the cosmopolitan by the provincial, the decadent by the natural. This is one of the liberating effects of nationalism, a means of restoring dignity and power to what had been humiliated and suppressed. This is the idea which underlies all our formulations of tradition (47).

Deane identifies two variations of the idea: adherence and separation. For proponents of the first (Deane mentions Yeats), 'the restoration of native energy to the English language is seen as a specifically Irish contribution to a shared heritage' (47). Other writers, such as Joyce, follow the second route of 'separation as a

means to the revival of suppressed energies' (50). Deane attempts
to assign political values to these two cultural positions—he refers
later in his essay to 'the variations of adherence (i.e. politically
speaking, unionism) and of separation (politically speaking, republicanism)' (57)—but the equation does not quite work because, in
real life, Yeats was the nationalist and Joyce the anti-nationalist.
The contortions Deane performs in implying the opposite would
lead a number of critics to wonder whether he himself were not still
operating under the sway of some limiting sectarian assumptions.

The most fatal ambiguity in the whole essay appears in Deane's
treatment of Yeats. He seems unable to make up his mind whether
he is condemning the poet for being a romantic nationalist or for
identifying with the Protestant Ascendancy. Noting that Yeats
regarded his work as part of a larger English-language tradition,
Deane charges that his '[c]ultural nationalism is thus transformed
into a species of literary unionism' (47). He dismisses the nationalist sentiments of the Anglo-Irish leaders of the Irish Literary Revival
as 'recruitments by the fading class of the myths of renovation
which belonged to their opponents. Irish culture became the new
property of those who were losing their grip on Irish land' (47–8).
In Deane's view, 'All the important Irish Protestant writers of the
nineteenth century had, as the ideological centre of their work, a
commitment to a minority or subversive attitude which was much
less revolutionary than it appeared to be' (48). Whatever the connection of Yeats's programme for Irish literature with nationalism,
'it was not, finally, a programme of separation from the English
tradition' (49).

This statement begs the question of whether Deane regards such
a separation as a necessary part of honest Irish national feeling. He
certainly does nothing to dispel such suspicions with his long quotation from 'A General Introduction for my Work' (1937) by Yeats:

The 'Irishry' have preserved their ancient 'deposit' through wars which,
during the sixteenth and seventeenth centuries, became wars of extermi-
nation; no people, Lecky said . . . have undergone greater persecution, nor
did that persecution altogether cease up to our own day. No people hate as
we do in whom that past is always alive . . . Then I remind myself that
though mine is the first English marriage I know of in the direct line, all
my family names are English, and that I owe my soul to Shakespeare,
to Spenser and to Blake, perhaps to William Morris, and to the English

language in which I think, speak, and write, that everything I love has come to me through English; my hatred tortures me with love, my love with hate . . . This is Irish hatred and solitude, the hatred of human life that made Swift write *Gulliver* and the epitaph upon his tomb, that can still make us wag between extremes and doubt our sanity (49–50).

Deane characterizes this as the 'pathology of literary unionism' (50) and uses it to prove that Yeats regarded 'the central Irish attitude as one of self-hatred' (49).

Another way of looking at this passage, however, is as evidence less of self-hatred than of genuine self-division. In a sentence Deane cuts from the quotation (coming after 'my hatred tortures me with love, my love with hate') the poet writes, 'I am like the Tibetan monk who dreams at his initiation that he is eaten by a wild beast and learns on waking that he himself is eater and eaten.'[48] Is not Yeats making a persuasive case for the impossibility of total separation from England as a cultural and political programme? It would seem that he was tempted by such an extreme nationalist position but had come to reject it. Was not Yeats simply recognizing what Friel acknowledged over forty years later in *Translations*: that, for better or worse, the impact of England on Ireland has been profound and that one of the effects of it has been that educated Irish people are more likely to come to an awareness of literature through the medium of English than of Irish? That, as Deane himself had repeatedly argued, there is no such thing as a 'pure' or 'essentially' Irish tradition? Long before Field Day, Yeats was proclaiming the falseness of the rigid separation between ideas of Englishness and Irishness. He embodied it. Does Deane's apparent inability to see it this way stem from an unwillingness on his part to acknowledge Yeats's claim to be as Irish as Deane himself is?

At any rate, after contrasting the approaches of Joyce and Yeats, Deane concludes that they have more in common than would at first appear. Their narratives (Pearse is thrown in as well, for good measure) 'are all based on the ideological conviction that a community exists which must be recovered and restored. These communities—of the family in Joyce, of the Ascendancy in Yeats, of the revolutionary brotherhood in Pearse—underwent their restoration in literature which is self-consciously adversarial.' The danger is that 'these narratives continue to send out their siren signals even though the crises they were designed to describe and overcome have long since disappeared. The signals have been at last picked up in Northern Ireland—for so long apparently immune to them— and are now being rebroadcast' (53). Both Northern communities 'pride themselves on being the lone and true inheritors of their respective traditions', and together they have 'become stereotyped into their roles of oppressor and victim to such an extent that the notion of a Protestant or a Catholic sensibility is now assumed to be a fact of nature rather than a product of these very special and ferocious conditions' (53–4).

Deane unites the various strands of his argument by remarking that:

In such a situation, nothing is more likely to perpetuate and even galvanise these stereotypes than the dream of a community's attaining, through a species of spiritual-military heroics, its longed-for destiny. Each begins to seek, in such a climate, a leadership which will definitively embody the univocal style which is the expression of its inner essence or nature. But in such a confrontation, style is no less than a declaration of war. It is the annunciation of essence in a person, in a mode of behaviour, in a set of beliefs (54–5).

In terms that must have outraged a great many unionists, he identifies Ian Paisley as 'the most remarkable incarnation of the communal spirit of unionism. In him, violence, a trumpery evangelicalism, anti-popery and a craven adulation of the "British" way of life are soldered together in a populist return to the first principles of "Ulsterness"' (55). He acknowledges a bit more complexity on the other side: 'John Hume acts as the minority's agent of rational demystification and the IRA as its agency of millennial revenge' (55).

In conclusion, Deane argues that the time has come to break away from an 'abstract idea of essence', to dissolve 'the mystique of Irishness' (57):

One step towards that dissolution would be the revision of our prevailing idea of what it is that constitutes the Irish reality. In literature that could take the form of a definition, in the form of a comprehensive anthology, of what writing in this country has been for the last 300–500 years.... Everything, including our politics and our literature, has to be rewritten— i.e. re-read. That will enable new writing, new politics, unblemished by Irishness, but securely Irish (58).

It must be emphasized, to his credit, that Deane did not hesitate to put his money where his mouth was. He may not have foreseen it in 1984, but he would spend the better part of the next seven years of his life putting together just such an anthology.

Richard Kearney's study of mythic and secular attitudes is Deane's contrast between romantic and modern Ireland in a different form, and, like Deane, he moves easily back and forth between politics and literature. The theme was not a new one for Kearney. He had frequently explored it in lectures and articles (five of which he footnotes in his Field Day pamphlet). His RTÉ lecture, 'Faith and Fatherland', had outlined the way in which the Catholic Church in Ireland moved after Independence to appropriate 'a certain idealised, some would add clichéd, version of Gaelic nationalism'. Kearney explained in his talk how social legislation in the Republic enforcing the moral code of the Catholic Church arose partly out of an equation of sexual with national purity, and he concluded with a call to both Catholics and Protestants in Ireland to reconsider their respective religious heritages. What was needed, he said, was not the jettisoning of 'our most deeply rooted myths and ideals', but rather a critical distinction 'between those which discourage and those which encourage a more open and creative understanding of our national identity'.[49] This idea also lies behind *Myth and Motherland*.

Kearney begins his Field Day pamphlet with the arresting statement by an American Jesuit, Daniel Berrigan, that those seeking to understand a society should begin by visiting its prisons and reading its poets. He glosses Berrigan's statement thus: 'it is often in its deviant or dissenting voices that a community expresses those hidden aspirations or alienations which frequently find no place in our more established modes of expression.'[50] While prisoners fall beneath the law, poets are thought to go beyond it in a creative rather than a destructive way. Both 'refuse the current consciousness of reality by invoking *something else* which precedes or exceeds it, which remains, as it were, sub-conscious or supraconscious' (61). This 'something else' is defined as myth. In his pamphlet Kearney examines a particular mythic structure, that of sacrificial martyrdom, operating behind the words and actions of both prisoners and poets in Ireland, chiefly the Maze hunger strikers and the writers of the Irish Revival.

In defining the terms of his discussion, Kearney quotes Mircea Eliade to show that myth is sacred history, the repeatable and exemplary acts of the founding fathers that exist in circular rather than linear time. Man, '[b]y *imitating* the exemplary acts of mythic deities and heroes ... detaches himself from profane time and magically re-enters the Great Time, the Sacred Time'. These mythic acts constitute 'what generally goes by the name of *tradition*' (62). The relevance is clear to the situation in the North, where 'the two traditions' is a catch-phrase. Kearney summarizes the mythic attitude as one of piety, 'a sense of dutiful allegiance to the claims of father and fatherland' (62). The opposite of piety, he says, is the secular attitude: 'If the former pertains to the sacred time of myth, the latter pertains to the profane time of our ordinary experience' (63). In short,

under the rubric of mythic piety might be listed the following properties: unity, eternity, permanence, faith, repetition, ancestry, tradition, essence. Under the rubric of historical secularity we could enter the contrasting values of plurality, temporality, change, reason, innovation, individuality, freedom, arbitrariness and experiment (63).

There follows an epitome of current philosophical debate on the nature of myth, with some thinkers (Eliade and Carl Jung) defending it as a necessary part of being human and others (Kearney cites Emmanuel Levinas, Rudolph Bultmann, and Jürgen Moltmann) favouring the 'rational' critique of 'a *mythos* of irrational mystification which is considered subversive not only of individual liberty but of our humanistic civilization as a whole' (65).

With this in mind, Kearney proceeds to a description of the 'prison discourse' of the H-Block campaign in which he demonstrates how it invokes a long sacrificial tradition that includes

Pearse's funeral oration at O'Donovan Rossa's grave in 1915; the reply by the volunteers in 1916 to the British call to surrender, that they 'had gone there to die not to win'; the victory achieved by the rebels not when they shot *at* the British from the General Post Office but when they were shot *by* the British in Kilmainham jail; and the celebrated maxim of Terence McSwiney, the Sinn Féin Lord Mayor of Cork who died on hunger strike in 1920: 'It is not those who can inflict the most, but those who suffer the most who will conquer' (66).

Ballads, one of the most popular responses to such events, are 'like myths, . . . often authored by nobody yet known to everybody' (67). Nor, Kearney maintains, has the 'propaganda power of mythic logic . . . been lost on the IRA leadership' (67):

The prison campaign showed that the Republican movement operates in terms of two distinguishable, if not always distinct, discourses. On the one hand, there is a rhetoric that leans towards the Gaelic Catholic Nationalist idioms of myth, tradition, piety and martyrdom. On the other hand, there is the secular discourse of military action, political electioneering and social work (69).

That is why Kearney believes that 'it is simplistic to declare that a vote for Sinn Féin is always a vote for violence. Unless, that is, one means a vote for violence "suffered" rather than violence "inflicted"' (68).

The Republican movement is not the only place in Irish politics, according to Kearney, where the 'tension between mythic and anti-mythic discourse' can be found:

In the Unionist camp . . . one might cite the opposition between the 'tribal' Ian Paisley and the more 'liberal' Robert McCartney. In the Forum of constitutional nationalism, one found differences emerging between the Haughey-Mallon wing and the Fitzgerald-Hume-Spring wing (69).

The old opposition between militant and constitutional nationalism fits the same pattern, as does the choice between De Valera's 'traditional' Ireland and Lemass's 'modern' one. The basic distinction is that between 'a *mythologising* form of politics which interprets the present in terms of a unifying past (sacred tradition) and a *demythologising* form of politics which interprets the present in terms of a pluralising future (secular progress)' (69).

Having dispensed with the prisoners and politicians, Kearney moves on to the poets. In a by now familiar scenario, Yeats and the Modernists (Joyce, Beckett, Flann O'Brien) emerge as the main antagonists. Kearney mentions the attraction the idea of 'the sacred rite of blood-sacrifice' had for Yeats (70), but he takes a more sympathetic view than Deane of the poet's cultural programme:

Yeats' recourse to the legendary images of Celtic mythology may . . . be interpreted as an attempt to make peace between the opposing interests of class, creed and language. It was a plea for a cultural *continuity* based on a homogenous Ancient Irish Sect which *preceded* all contemporary disputes. In its way, it was a plea for Tone's ideal of a common Irish tradition embracing 'Protestant, Catholic and Dissenter' (71).

Nevertheless, Irish writers of the more secular variety have been inclined to reject Yeats's mythologizing as 'sanctimonious claptrap' (71). Beckett, for example, found the notion of a National Literature absurd. He admired writers who 'began with their own nothingness and wrote about the impossibility of ever translating this nothingness into something else' (72).

Kearney seems most interested in the approach of Joyce, who wanted not only to 'Europeanise Ireland' but also to 'Hibernicise Europe':

In *Ulysses*, Joyce uses one kind of myth to demythologise another. . . . By playing mythic archetypes off against mythic stereotypes . . . Joyce was suggesting that we can be liberated from our pre-established narratives of identity without capitulating to the modernist cult of solitary individualism. What Joyce found attractive about the Greek mythology of Ulysses (Bloom)/Penelope (Molly)/Telemachus (Stephen) was its *foreignness*—its ability to offer us alternative models of universality whose very otherness to our native models would enable us to redefine our experience in a new way, in a way untrammelled by the restrictive pieties of the motherland (73).

For Kearney, Joyce's experiments show that 'myth need not be the suspension of the individual, as Yeats and Beckett believed. For myth can only survive in and through the multiple re-inventions of different individuals and these individuals can best communicate through the universalising idioms of myth' (74).

In order to demonstrate that the political and literary discourses frequently overlap, Kearney turns to the myth of motherland as exemplified in the writings of Padraig Pearse. Pearse had three mothers—mother church, motherland, and mother-tongue—but he often managed to conflate all of them in his 'conjugation of the Catholic and mythological idioms of martyrs sacrificing themselves for the sake of the Eternal Mother' (75). In fact, affirms Kearney, this image contained 'the overall *mythos* of the 1916 Rising which gained common currency in the popular imagination' (75), and he speculates at some length as to whether such 'mythic idealisations of Irish womanhood might be somehow related to the

social stereotypes of the Irish woman as pure virgin or equally pure
son-obsessed mother' (76). Perhaps

Woman became as sexually intangible as the ideal of national independence became politically intangible. Both entered the unreality of myth.
They became aspirations rather than actualities. Thus it might be argued
that a sociological transposition of Irish women into desexualised and
quasi-divine mothers corresponds somehow to an ideological transposition
of Ireland from a Fatherland (the term *an t-athardha* was used to denote
Ireland in much bardic poetry up to the 17th century) into idioms con-
noting a Motherland. As psychoanalysis reminds us, the mother has always
been a powerful unconscious symbol for one's forfeited or forbidden
origins (76).

He completely ignores the social and economic factors making for
late marriages and sexual continence in a country that had not only
recently experienced a devastating famine but where sons often did
not inherit their fathers' land until they were in their mid-thirties or
older and contraception was not available. Nevertheless, the idea is
an intriguing one.

In the last section of his pamphlet, Kearney moves from the
description of how he sees myth working in Ireland to 'the ethical
question'—how it *should* work (78). He terms this a valid consideration 'when literary myth spills over into political myth':
'There can be no poetic licence for political barbarism. *Mythos* can
never be insulated from the ethical critique of *Logos*' (78). Both
mythos and *logos* are essential, though. 'Myth', says Kearney, 'is a
two way street':

It can lead to perversion (bigotry, racism, anti-semitism, fascism, totali-
tarianism); or it can lead to the projection of genuine utopias whereby
individuals, communities and indeed the community of nations as a
whole, can identify with the goal of *universal* liberation. If we need to
demythologize, we also need to remythologize. It is our ethical duty therefore to use our powers of *logos* to discriminate between the authentic and
inauthentic uses to which *mythos* is put in our culture. . . . And this is not
as simple as uncritically assuming that our established division between
poets (as an instance of emancipation) and prisoners (as an instance of
incarceration) has done the job for us. There are prisoners behind bars who
should not be there and some poets who should be there (79).

Like Deane, Kearney appears to present a choice between a

backward-looking and a forward-looking philosophy, with the argument weighted in favour of the latter, but he manages to avoid any conclusive statement. He advocates the rational critique of myth, but, if genuine myth is 'sub-conscious or supra-conscious', is it really open to that kind of scrutiny? When it ceases to be something believed and becomes something merely talked about, perhaps—but is that still myth? Perhaps what is actually needed is a realization that some of our most basic assumptions *are* myths and a decision as to whether or not they are worth keeping as conscious beliefs.

Kearney concludes with a veiled reference to *Translations*:

> Without mythology, our hopes and memories are homeless; we capitulate to the mindless conformism of fact. But if revered for its own abstract sake, if totally divorced from the challenge of reality, mythology becomes another kind of conformism, another kind of death. We must never cease to keep our mythological images in dialogue with history; because once we do we fossilise. That is why we will go on telling stories, inventing and re-inventing myths, until we have brought history home to itself (80).

It thus slowly emerges that the important choice is not between piety and secularity (the IRA has one foot in each world) but among an infinite number of ideas. It is the content of these ideas, not their mythic or anti-mythic formulations, that matters in the end, and here we are offered only vague guidelines: 'What is required is a radical interrogation of those mythic sedimentations from our *past* and those mythic aspirations for our *future* which challenge our *present* sense of ourselves, which disclose other possibilities of being' (79). What Kearney has to say is always interesting and elegantly presented, but he tries to give the impression of providing a practical programme for action, which he does not. *Myth and Motherland* finally succeeds on the descriptive rather than the prescriptive level.

Declan Kiberd's pamphlet, *Anglo-Irish Attitudes*, also operates on two levels with different degrees of success. It is, in effect, two pamphlets, the first an entertaining and well-documented discussion of several famous Irish plays, the second a frontal assault on Ulster unionism. The literary and political tracts make strange bedfellows. As a modern literary critic, Kiberd abhors the mode of thought that makes people into types, but, in the part of his essay in which he focuses on contemporary politics, he betrays a stereo-typed view of Ulster Protestants that is blatant and unapologetic.

He begins with a summary of his argument:

The English did not invade Ireland—rather, they seized a neighbouring island and invented the idea of Ireland. The notion 'Ireland' is largely a fiction created by the rulers of England in response to specific needs at a precise moment in British history. The English have always presented themselves to the world as a cold, refined and urbane race, so it suited them to see the Irish as hot-headed, rude and garrulous—the perfect foil to set off British virtues. The corollary of this is also true. The Irish notion of 'England' is a fiction created and inhabited by the Irish for their own pragmatic purposes.[51]

In the literary part of the pamphlet he proceeds to demonstrate this thesis, drawing his examples primarily from *The Importance of Being Earnest* by Oscar Wilde and *John Bull's Other Island* by George Bernard Shaw.

'Antithesis', Kiberd asserts, 'was the master-key to the entire Victorian cast of mind' (85). This was the mental habit that sustained rigid dichotomies between country and city, male and female, child and adult, good and evil, English and Irish. Wilde in his drama challenged this way of thinking, subverting his audience's expectations by having his characters display qualities one would normally expect in their opposites. Indeed,

Far from being an exponent of the witty paradox, Wilde is interested in the moment of modernism when the ancient antithesis dissolves to reveal an underlying unity. Like Yeats, he could see that talent perceives differences, but only genius discerns unity (86).

In his life as in his art, Wilde defied stereotypes: 'The ease with which [he] effected the transition from stage Irishman to stage Englishman was his ultimate comment on the hollowness of the antithesis, on the emptiness of both notions' (86).

For Kiberd, Shaw 'was another writer who treated England as a laboratory in which he could define what it meant to be an Irishman' (88). In *John Bull's Other Island*,

the English and Irish are identical peoples, who have nevertheless decided to perform extreme versions of Englishness and Irishness to one another in the attempt to wrest a material advantage from the unsuspecting audience of each performance (90).

By making two of the main characters 'a romantic Englishman and an empirical Irishman' Shaw challenges one stereotype, but that is not really the end of the story because

by his performance of absurd sentimentality, Broadbent effectively takes over the entire village on the terms most favourable to himself, while Larry Doyle loses his cynical self-composure in the face of the ruin of his people. . . . In the end, the Anglo-Irish antithesis is questioned, but only to be reasserted in a slightly modified form (90).

Perhaps, Kiberd suggests, that was why Edward VII broke his chair in laughing at the play. In fact, he submits,

Both Wilde and Shaw are finally English writers in the strict terms of Shaw's own definition of Englishness as a talent for keeping ideas separate in watertight compartments. The right side of the dramatist's brain never knows what the left doeth, and the plots of their plays are entirely at variance with the subversive one-liners and jokes (91).

Kiberd chooses to explain this contradiction away as 'a measure of the artistic constraints on any socialist dramatist who sought a career in the London of the time' (91).

In his RTÉ lecture, 'Inventing Irelands', Kiberd had rounded up the usual suspects. Ireland, he intimated, is burdened with an incomplete image of itself propagated by writers and politicians (chiefly Yeats and Éamon de Valera):

Look at any course on modern Irish literature and mark the dominant names: Wilde, Shaw, Yeats, Joyce, Synge, O'Casey, Behan. Ask who is the odd man out and the answer is Yeats, because all the others are self-proclaimed socialists. But you'd never suspect that to look at the themes which dominate the textbooks—Big House; violence and war; the image of the peasant; the idea of nationalism; the western island; the experience of religion; the oppression of writers and so on. Wherever you look you can see that Yeats is still calling all the shots. . . . We are asked to pretend that our literature is mystical, conservative and rural, when it is more often Protestant, socialist and cosmopolitan—the very opposite of what it has been made to seem.

Kiberd championed this alternative strand in Irish literature and politics, exemplified by men such as Joyce and James Connolly, for whom ' "revival" was less an assertion of traditions long-denied than an insistence that Irish people have the freedom to conceive of themselves'.[52]

Kiberd concentrates, in his Field Day pamphlet, almost exclusively on the 'socialist' writers. Yeats merits only a paragraph. Unlike Wilde and Shaw, he tried 'to express Ireland to herself rather than exploit her for the foreigner' (91). This sounds like an admirable project (it was, in fact, the Field Day programme), but Yeats was less interested in demolishing stereotypes, according to Kiberd, than in changing their value:

He accepted the Anglo-Irish antithesis, but only on condition that he was allowed to reinterpret it in a more flattering light. Whereas the English had called the Irish backward, superstitious and uncivilised, the Gaelic revivalists created an idealised counter-image which saw her as pastoral, mystical, admirably primitive. Yet such a counter-image was false, if only because it elevated a single aspect of Ireland into a type of the whole. 'Connaught for me is Ireland', said Yeats; but Ireland is not Connaught—rather she is a patchwork quilt of cultures, as she was before the Normans invaded (91–2).

That is why, Kiberd maintains, 'Subsequent writers came increasingly to question the legacy of Yeats and to turn instead for guidance to that socialist tradition of Irish writing initiated by Wilde and Shaw' (92), offering the examples of Sean O'Casey and Brendan Behan.

It is at this point that Kiberd makes the awkward leap from literature to politics:

In all of the plays discussed, opposites turn out to be doubles; clichés employed at the start by one side are appropriated by the other; and each time an Irishman meets an Englishman, he simply encounters an alternative version of himself. The Irish Question is really the English Question, and *vice-versa*. The Irish are accused of never forgetting, but that is because the English never remember. The Irish are accused of endlessly repeating their past, but they are forced to do so precisely because the English have failed to learn from theirs (93).

He quotes the final chapter of Oliver MacDonagh's history *States of Mind: A Study of Anglo-Irish Conflict 1780–1980*[53] to show that 'Epoch-making events like the Union of 1801 or the proroguing of Stormont in 1972 arose . . . from "an absorption in the immediate". "Each stroke was seen in terms of a current problem, in terms of breaking an impasse, of cutting a hopeless tangle"' (94).

Kiberd takes issue with earlier chapters of MacDonagh's book, though, for breathing new life into old stereotypes:

MacDonagh sees the English view of history as developmental—they take short views in the conviction that all things ripen in the fullness of time. The Irish he depicts as an ahistorical people who reject notions of chronology, see history as the endless repetition of familiar themes with no hope of resolution, and pay scant heed to the squatters' rights conferred by the centuries on the invading English. . . . MacDonagh adds such polish to the familiar cliché that the Irish are prisoners of their own past. But his final chapter explodes this opening thesis by proving that it is the English who force such dreary repetitions on the Irish (94–5).

Kiberd avers that it is really the English who are 'obsessed with their past, while the Irish are futurologists of necessity':

As British power and prestige decline, English leaders turn more and more to the past for comfort and consolation. . . . And while all this is going on, the Irish appoint a Forum to debate their own future. Like all colonised peoples whose history is a nightmare, the Irish have no choice but to live in the foreglow of a golden future. For them history is a form of science fiction, by which their scribes must rediscover in the endlessly malleable past whatever it is they are hoping for in an ideal future (95).

The most vulnerable aspect of Kiberd's argument is its over-reliance on psychological explanations for perceived differences between Irish and English people. He implicitly acknowledges the problem with this glancing reference to colonial history. However, as he himself says, 'In such a land, the word "history", like the word "Gaelic", means whatever you want it to mean, and therefore means nothing' (95). In repudiating the idea of national character, Kiberd is in danger of ignoring real social and cultural differences between the two islands. Wilde, he tells us, rejected the notion that 'upbringing and social conditioning determined consciousness' (86)—but surely they have something to do with it? Kiberd appears to recognize this in part when he remarks that 'The socialist dream was also the imperialist pretence—that the whole world could be recast in a single image—and it was this imperial pretence which caused a Gaelic poet to fear the imminent emergence of West Britain, "Saxa Nua darb ainm Éire"' (97). When pressed, Kiberd is no more happy than Deane with the idea that there is *no* real difference between English and Irish.

This ambivalence gives rise to a dilemma. Kiberd notes that many people with positive feelings toward Ireland also have clichéd views of its population (spontaneous, eloquent, pugnacious), and deems it 'not surprising that Irish writers and critics often bite the liberal English hand that feeds them'. However,

the sole alternative is to be told by the High Tories that West Belfast is like East Finchley. For better or worse, the audience of British liberals and leftists remains Ireland's most firm hope. (The notion that the Tories will initiate the final withdrawal, just as the Republicans and not the Democrats extricated America from Vietnam, is probably wishful thinking) (98).

Here Kiberd displays two highly significant assumptions. He presupposes, first, that Great Britain should sever its connection with Northern Ireland and, second, that it is for this that 'Irish' people hope. Readers who might have been wondering where the Ulster unionists belong in all of this playing of 'Irish' and 'English' or 'British'—which Kiberd mistakenly uses interchangeably—off against each other would now have their answer: nowhere. When Kiberd says 'Irish' he means 'nationalist'; when he says 'British' he means people on 'the mainland'. People living on the island of Ireland who yet prefer to think of themselves as British do not fit into either category.

How he regards them himself is soon made clear. Kiberd criticizes F. S. L. Lyons's *Culture and Anarchy in Ireland: 1890–1939*[54] for offering 'culture rather than cash by way of explanation' of the conflict in Ireland (99), but he praises him for documenting 'with rare descriptive power' 'that curious blend of resolution and hysteria, of barbarous vulgarity and boot-faced sobriety, which lies beneath the emotions of Ulster Protestantism' (100). One doubts whether the late Professor Lyons would have appreciated the compliment.

Nevertheless, Kiberd's fundamental criticism of Lyons's thesis is sound. He argues that it works well in a nineteenth-century context but is less convincing as an explanation of the contemporary situation:

Is it really true that the difference between Glenn Barr and John Hume is attributable to a clash of cultures? How vital is the Gaelic tradition to a Dublin Government whose Minister for Education cannot even speak the Irish language? How deep is the loyalty of insurgent Unionism to the Anglo-Irish tradition? And to England, for that matter? (101)

Kiberd champions an economic explanation such as that put forward by Michael Farrell and Eamonn McCann.[55] He admits that such socialist writers 'may be somewhat cavalier in their dismissal of culture as a potent source of distinctive symbols—symbols which reinforce and seem to legitimise the economic aspirations of the various Ulster factions. But it is at least arguable that they are a good deal nearer to the facts of the matter' than Conor Cruise O'Brien and F. S. L. Lyons (102).

Kiberd acknowledges that it should not be necessary to point to culture *or* economics as being exclusively responsible for the Troubles, but he also wonders 'why the British intelligentsia choose to believe one set of explanations rather than the other'. He shrewdly suggests a number of possible reasons for this preference and then asks

Or could it be that Ireland is still deemed 'interesting and different', a place where the unexpected always happens, where men kill and die for abstract images and evocative symbols? This reading of the Irish as martyrs to abstraction—a reading sponsored most notoriously in the poetry of Yeats—is the greatest single obstacle to a full understanding of the situation in Ireland today. It bedevils attempts by students, both native and foreign, to understand the masterpieces of Irish literature; but it bedevils also the attempts by British well-wishers to understand John Bull's Other Island (102).

In the immediate future, Kiberd announces, it is incumbent upon 'British liberals' to 'study Ulster Unionism and spell out to the English public the implications of its continuing support for such a régime' (102). It is apparently irrelevant to his argument that Northern Ireland has been ruled directly from Westminster since 1972. 'Unionist misrule', he writes, 'has exacted a heavy cost not just in terms of British lives and money, but also in terms of its effect in eroding many of the best features of British democracy,' as 'attempts by the English to root out corruption from their own body-politic have been hampered by their involvement in Ireland' (103).

Kiberd is clearly writing for London, not Belfast—so much for expressing Ireland to itself. He observes,

British commentators are rightly outraged whenever London is bombed by the IRA, and they ask, 'What kind of people could do such a thing?' But they never ask an equally pressing question—'What kind of people are we supporting in Ulster?' The ignorance of Ireland among English people is considerable, but the ignorance of Ulster Unionism among English liberals is almost total. The current crisis has prompted most Irish people to re-examine some of their deepest historical assumptions, but it has as yet given rise to no similar self-questioning in England. On the contrary, a bomb in Harrod's gives all the hoariest anti-Irish clichés a new lease of life. If British writers are serious in their attempts to contribute to a solution, they must break out of the current impasse. To do that, they must cure themselves of their longstanding fixation on Irish nationalism and apply themselves to the study of Ulster Unionism (104).

One might say of Kiberd's pamphlet, as he does of Shaw's play, that it 'is itself an artistic casualty of the vice of compartmentalisation which he satirises' (91).

The first set of Field Day pamphlets had been criticized as reflecting a nationalist political agenda. Many readers, in the words of Eavan Boland, had perceived the 'danger ... that underneath the new words we will have the old wounds'. This reaction to the initial pamphlets became itself an element in the response to the second set—reviewers of whatever political hue were on the alert for symptoms of nationalism or unappeased sectarianism. Supporters of the company in particular were already somewhat on the defensive. Dermot Moran, in a sympathetic review of the second set of pamphlets, asserted that

Criticism of Field Day has tended to argue that it claims too high a role for literature. Edna Longley, for example, has attacked the first series of Field Day pamphlets as a species of literary nationalism, which she sees as part of a movement to ally poetry with politics especially in Northern Ireland. She is wary of poets adopting a public voice, claiming to speak for the tribe, or reading the literary inheritance in terms of a restrictive concept of tradition.

He noticed, however, a contradiction in Longley's approach:

her demand is to separate literature from politics, yet she criticizes other poets in terms of their politics—especially Heaney.[56] For Edna Longley it is not that his poetry has no politics—it has the *wrong* politics. Her attempt to keep poetry pure is really an attempt to maintain the literary status quo; literature is art, it needs to be judged by professional, neutral academics like herself otherwise it gets into the hands of the mob and becomes dangerous. Her reaction against Field Day is really a reaction against the idea of a public.

Moran, on the other hand, believed it was

to the credit of Field Day that they have entered into the field of mediation and dialogue between poet and public, literature and politics. The pamphlet is the obvious medium for this encounter, and will push our literature and its criticism beyond outworn antinomies and stereotypes into more fruitful responses to the Irish reality.[57]

Other critics were more sceptical about exactly how much real questioning was going on. Terence Brown, who had enthusiastically reviewed the first set of pamphlets, had more doubts about the second, which he expressed in the *Irish Press*:

What exactly is a field day? In the North of Ireland one day of the year is especially associated with events in 'the Field' which serves for the Orangemen both as an arena of unfettered licence and metaphor of tribal victory. The 12th of July adds its own potency to the idea of having a field day. I don't suppose this was in the minds of the directors of Field Day when they chose that name for their theatrical and cultural enterprise. But there are features of their modes of thought revealed in the second batch of their pamphlets which suggest that the metaphor of the field as appropriated by the Orangemen has some application in their case also. History is where they have their field day, for it provides them both with an arena in which they can move with a creative freedom not possible in the drab givenness of the present and with metaphors of national possibility.

Referring to Kiberd's comment that history serves as a form of 'science fiction' for colonized peoples, he remarked that the Field Day writers certainly appeared to take that attitude toward it and complained that 'one might have hoped, given the first three pamphlets, for something a bit more genuinely historical and a little less fictional as a follow-up'. Nevertheless, he thought that 'What Kiberd actually has to say about Anglo-Irish relations themselves is much less remarkable than his combative prose postures would suggest: the English and the Irish have often regarded one another in stereotypical terms when in fact there has been a good deal of social interaction to the benefit of both.' It took Brown a while to get to what really bothered him about Kiberd's pamphlet:

Part of Kiberd's problem as a writer in this pamphlet is that he would like to be an ideologue on behalf of something, probably some form of social-ism ... but other things keep breaking through to disturb the ideological trajectory of his discourse—like nationalism for instance. So what one gets is a sense of ideological fervour without a very clear sense of its philosophic, propositional and logical origins.

More worrying still to Brown, given the fact that Kiberd set out to challenge stereotyped views, was the latter's own evident antipathy toward unionists. 'Isn't it time', he asked,

Field Day really got to grips with Northern Protestantism. To allow itself to be represented on the subject by Declan Kiberd's polemical, intemperate and misrepresenting gloss on F. S. L. Lyons ('that curious blend of resol-ution and hysteria, of barbarous vulgarity and boot-faced sobriety, which lies beneath the emotions of Ulster Protestantism') would be serious dis-service to what is, despite my reservations obvious in this review, an enterprise we all should welcome.[58]

Critics in the North of Ireland were less circumspect. Damian Smyth, writing in *North* magazine, dismissed all three pamphlets out of hand, warning that 'the reader can expect to be staggered more often by incoherence and ostentation than by truly penetrat-ing argument'. Kiberd he regarded as

an intellectual sucking at the dugs of the Dublin Government: for who else, with any knowledge of our wee six, would claim that the Dublin Forum was an example of the Irish living 'in the foreglow of a golden future'. . . . Someone should tell the Dublin regime and their press editors that the Forum was a waste of time, and that its effect in the North and in Britain was precisely nil: then, perhaps, they might shoulder some real responsibility.

Seamus Deane, though, was the real villain of the piece for Smyth, who wrote of him that 'More than either of the others, Mr. Deane's pamphlet displays how the first flowering of Catholic intellect in Ireland, north or south, is a bitter plant indeed.' Deane's purpose in introducing contemporary politics into a discussion of the Irish Revival was, according to Smyth, 'to lump the blame for the North-ern troubles onto the Anglo-Irish Ascendancy':

His basic premise is that, in 'reviving' Irish culture, the Anglo-Irish actually stole it. . . . We are not told just what this Irish culture was that was stolen;

he defines it only as 'cultural nationalism' which, because hijacked by the Ascendancy '. . . is thus transformed into literary unionism.'

The reason for the vehemence of Smyth's attack becomes clear by the end of his review. To his mind,

at the core of Deane's thought is an overwhelming sectarianism. For Ascendancy, read Protestant; for Irish, read Catholic. . . . As he sees it, because [Shaw, Parnell, Yeats, Hyde, and Lyons] were Protestant, they were not Irish, and so their immense contribution to this country is deemed an alien one.

He concluded, 'It is time to mock mockers such as these three and to affirm the vision of those who, like Connolly, are "Vilified now by the gangs of Catholic Action." '[59]

Edna Longley, who would rapidly establish herself as one of the most cogent and outspoken critics of Field Day, said similar things in more measured tones in the pages of *Fortnight*. Her review, printed along with a photograph of Seamus Deane with his eyes shut, began with the observation that 'I found the first three Field Day pamphlets largely a matter of old whines in new bottles.' Longley was no more impressed with the second three:

In line with static Nationalist views of history, Seamus Deane, Richard Kearney and Declan Kiberd project on to today a version of early twentieth-century literary history. Just as Brian Friel's *Translations* and Tom Paulin's *A New Look at the Language Question* ghost the lost cause of the Gaelic League (full linguistic independence); so these three pamphleteers identify the Irish Literary Revival as the source of all our woes.

I have argued that Paulin and Friel were in fact doing something very different, although their admirers may not always have understood what they were actually saying, but Longley was unwilling to acknowledge even an intention on the part of the Field Day writers to question old assumptions. Seamus Deane was selected for particular reproof:

Deane's argument, which looks faintly revisionist, in fact returns to Maoist first principles. The incurably absolutist thought-processes of even sophisticated Nationalists often recall the Irish countryman who, when asked the way, replies, 'If I were you, I wouldn't start from here.'

Like Smyth, Longley was most affronted by Deane's attack on Yeats, and she, too, attributed his attitude toward the poet to a political position:

Literary critics so insistent on 'history' should recognise that the roots of literature and history are too mysteriously intertwined for poets to invent, or people to accept, wholly untrue images. . . .

It may indeed be true, in ways Deane would repudiate, that Yeats's poetry has kept its foot in the door as a reminder of inconvenient complexities. He quotes Yeats's great statement of cultural conflict . . . and comments: 'The pathology of literary Unionism has never been better defined.'

Deane is fortunate in his own undivided certitude. And yet this pamphlet is tortured by something. The pathology of literary Nationalism, perhaps. It is sad, if logical, that 'Brits Out' can come to mean 'Yeats out'.

Despite the efforts of those who feel this way, though,

Big House poems and novels are somehow harder to get rid of than the houses themselves. This is because literature is not life, however Deane labours to remove the last distinction: the 'superiority' of a Yeats poem to one by Pearse is, he asserts, 'finally defensible only on the grounds of style'. That false separation between form and content indicates the risks run by literary critics when they dilute their obligation to the totality of a text, conscript texts for propaganda. They produce literal-minded, single-minded readings which respect the fine print of neither poetry nor politics.

Longley found Kiberd's literary analysis more convincing than Deane's. At least he quoted 'chapter and verse' to back up some of his pronouncements and 'he implicitly admits the cross-fertilisation that Deane denies'. His political arguments, however, seemed depressingly familiar to her:

He asks the English to understand 'what kind of people (they are) supporting in Ulster'. A good idea for some homework all round? No, Kiberd simply wants them to understand how nasty the Unionists are. Nasty they often are, but cross-cultural understanding (Field Day should try some) boomerangs like a paradox. You can't complain of 'British clichés' and then refer to 'that curious blend of resolution and hysteria, of barbarous vulgarity and bootfaced sobriety, which lies beneath the emotions of Ulster Protestantism'.

'Given a choice of stereotypes', she wryly observed, 'I'd sooner be a picturesque peasant.'

Like Smyth, Longley regarded Kearney's pamphlet as the least offensive. She noted that he discussed 'the actual condition of society in the Republic', while 'Deane and Kiberd are off fighting old wars against the English and Anglo-Irish, ignoring the real problem'. Nevertheless,

The *Crane Bag* editor's agony . . . seems excessive. Myth can be reduced to a minimum in public life, yet enrich spiritual, personal and imaginative worlds. When Kearney says 'without mythology, our hopes and memories are homeless; we capitulate to the mindless conformism of fact', he endorses that colonialist slur about the Celt's revolt against 'the despotism of fact'.

In short, Longley saw the pamphlets as 'more part of the problem than of the solution':

A curious aestheticism prevails, instead of the intended realism. Everything becomes a word or image within a uniformly determined situation. This reinforces both the oneness of myth and the myth of oneness. Kiberd's socialism, Kearney's rationalism undergo schizophrenic strain rather than abandon the forms of thought which politico-religious myth exacts. And one sentence of Deane's renders most of his others unnecessary: 'The acceptance of a particular style of Catholic or Protestant attitudes or behaviour, married to a dream of a final restoration of vitality to a decayed cause or community, is a contribution to the possibility of civil war.'[60]

Even some of those who were sympathetic towards Field Day had to admit that, on the evidence of the pamphlets, the directors were not themselves exempt from some of the limiting attitudes they pointed out in, for example, 'British' people. These essays made it clear that they operated on a number of assumptions themselves, which they did not always subject to the same scrutiny that they applied to the basic beliefs of others. Damian Gorman expressed this view when he remarked,

I think their colours are obvious enough. These are my own colours: pink and pastel green—those of the armchair leftie and 'no bombs' nationalist, and I have a lot of time for them. . . .

This is fair enough, but there are other Ulster perspectives. . . . Perhaps the problem in relation to Field Day is that its directors (and those I know are the very best of people) are a bit too similar in their hues.

A dash of pure orange in the ranks would do no harm.[61]

People like Gorman and Terence Brown were issuing a challenge to Field Day—a challenge that would be taken up in the next set of pamphlets.

6

Things Done and Left Undone:
The Fourth Field Day Tour

UP until 1983 it would have been possible to describe Field Day as a Northern Irish touring theatre company that produced Brian Friel plays. The directors of the company were eager, however, to broaden their scope to include new Irish plays by other playwrights. In keeping with their goal, announced publicly in the programmes for *Three Sisters* and *The Communication Cord*, to question old assumptions in the interest of forging a more inclusive notion of Irish identity, they were especially anxious to present the work of Protestant dramatists who might approach the issue of Irish identity from an angle that differed from traditional nationalist feelings about it. With this aim in mind, Friel contacted David Rudkin early in 1982 to ask if he would be interested in writing a play for Field Day.

Rudkin was a logical choice. He lived in England and his work had earned a wide exposure there, but his mother was an Ulster Protestant and he had spent a significant portion of his childhood and youth in County Armagh. Although Rudkin himself was a nationalist who believed that the Irish nation had been falsely identified with Irish Catholicism since the time of Daniel O'Connell, his Irish relatives were Orangemen. He had chosen to make his home in England, but the Irish Question remained a deeply personal one for Rudkin and pervaded much of his best work. He also shared a number of basic beliefs with the Field Day directors: for him, everything is political on some level. Language, political in its essence, both oppresses human beings and can liberate them. Myth, while it can awaken the mind and sensibility, must be broken away from to make true growth possible.

His first full-length stage play, *Afore Night Come*, produced by the Royal Shakespeare Company (RSC) in 1962, depicted the sacrificial murder of an Irish tramp by farm workers near Birmingham.

A 1973 radio play later staged by the RSC, *Cries from Casement as His Bones are Brought to Dublin*, explored the Irish nationalism of Roger Casement and located the energies behind it in the homosexuality which alienated him from his professional, orthodox society and self. His television play, *Penda's Fen* (1974), was written as a companion piece to *Cries from Casement* and subjected English nationalism to a similar scrutiny. In the award-winning stage play *Ashes*, also 1974, Rudkin exposed the political dimensions of virility in a culture which feels itself to be under siege[1] and made of one couple's infertility a symbol for the Troubles in Northern Ireland which in turn became a metaphor for a more universal death wish in human beings. Through the late 1970s and early 1980s Rudkin had had a number of stage plays produced—*The Sons of Light* (Newcastle 1976, RSC 1977), a version of *Hippolytus* (RSC 1978), *Hansel and Gretel* (RSC 1980), *The Triumph of Death* (Birmingham 1981)—and at the time he was approached by Friel he was working on *Across the Water*, a television nightmare quest in which an Ulster Protestant living in England goes home to Ireland to try to find his adopted daughter who has been stolen by her natural father, a Northern Catholic.

Rudkin was surprised and intrigued by Friel's suggestion. He was familiar with the personalities involved in Field Day and had assumed that they were green nationalists who would not be interested in the kinds of things he had to say about Ulster. He decided to visit Friel in Donegal. The older playwright had just put the finishing touches to *The Communication Cord*, that year's Field Day production, but confided his worry that the company was regarded as merely a vehicle for his own work—people had begun referring to it as 'Friels on Wheels'. What Field Day needed, he said, was input from other voices, particularly Protestant ones. When Rudkin left Friel's house he had accepted the commission. He had had an idea for another stage play in the back of his mind for some time, and talking with Friel about writing for Field Day had 'crystallized it'. He saw the request as an opportunity to take part in a dialogue about the future of what he still regarded as his country.

Rudkin's personal agenda for the play had several planks. Impatient with the slack, melodramatic strain he detected in much Irish acting, he wanted to write a play that would force Irish actors to adopt a more disciplined approach toward their roles. Believing that most of the plays arising out of the Troubles were too journalistic and that they allowed audiences to leave the theatre with their prejudices intact, he attempted to present a non-naturalistic response to the crisis that would be far enough removed from the actual situation to enable people to see it in a new way. Aware of the peculiar restrictions on Field Day, he sought to rise to the dramaturgical challenge of writing for a touring company with a low budget. Perhaps most important, he wished to articulate dramatically how it felt to be an Ulster Protestant.

Rudkin researched and wrote *The Saxon Shore* in the autumn and winter of 1982–3 and sent the final instalment to Field Day at the end of May.[2] He believed he had achieved all of his goals and succeeded in writing an objective play about the 'plantation mentality'.[3] The device he had settled upon was an elaborate historical metaphor. The play is set in Britain near the end of the Roman Empire and centres on two communities living on what was called the 'Saxon Shore'. Rudkin, who read Classics at St Catherine's College, Oxford, speculates that this name probably had two connotations—the shore faced the Saxon menace to the east and it was inhabited by Saxons resettled by Rome, as was usual imperial practice, to defend against a convergence of threats from Scottish and Irish Celts and from Saxons from the North Sea. 'So,' he writes,

whatever the later 'Saxons' did in this island to deserve the bad press the early Celtic literature gives them (and 'Saxon' remains to this day the basic Celtic word for an 'Englishman'), the likelihood almost certainly is that the very first 'Saxons' to come here were brought by Rome and planted here: uprooted from their own lands, brought in misery and bondage to a neighbouring island to serve the Empire's cause; then, when Empire's need of them was done, abandoned against the aftermath.[4]

The Saxons of Rudkin's play are made to act as a 'Defence Regiment: Part time' guarding the country south of Hadrian's Wall against the Celts north of it who still cherish memories of their 'Lost Britain, yet to be rewon. The struggle' (17, 23).

As drama critic Lynda Henderson points out, the parallel between the Saxons and the Ulster Protestants is precise. Many of the Protestants thrust on to the Northern Irish scene in the mid-seventeenth century 'were not British themselves in the first place but Huguenot French, and they had come to Scotland when they were driven out of France after the religious persecutions there, and then they became the people who were planted by the English in Ireland to try and essentially keep down the Celts'.[5] Rudkin reinforces the parallel primarily through language and accents. For the Saxon language he fuses 'certain Northern English "tunes" with Northern Irish idiom, and vice versa', and for the Celtic language he blends 'Welsh and Southern Irish tune and idiom in a similar way' (50). Rudkin also uses Latinate English for the 'Roman' element in the society. The British (Celts) are understood to be speaking their own language, Cumric, throughout, although most of the time they speak English so that the audience can understand them. There is even a deliberate echo and extension of the Yolland–Maire scene in *Translations* where the Saxon protagonist, Athdark, meets Ceiriad, a British princess, and the two communicate despite the fact that they do not speak the same language. Late in the play, after 'the separation between the two cultures is made unbridgeable', Rudkin writes a scene for the Celts in which he attempts to reconstruct a smattering of Cumric from the earliest recorded sources.

The terms of the historic analogy are made clear in other ways, too, particularly on the Saxon side. Central to the psyche both of Northern Protestants and of Rudkin's Saxons is a sense of crisis, of insecurity, and of being dependent on the whim of an imperial power that does not care about them. The threat that overhangs the play, finally realized in its conclusion, is that Rome, faced with problems of its own closer to home, will withdraw its army and support from Britain, leaving the Saxons at the mercy of the people they have been used to suppress. Their vulnerable position makes them preternaturally aware of both the British north of the wall and the Romans across the sea. Agricola, the Saxon pastor, preaches their predicament with the rich, biblical imagery familiar to Ulster Protestantism. Prefacing his remarks with the story of King Ahab and his wife, Jezebel, who stole from the upright Naboth the garden that was his heritage, he continues:

High in these cold windscourged hills of Northern Britain have we our garden. . . . Our heritage. THEY, that were here before us, had done nothing. THEY had not broken this hard high land. THEY had not tilled nor sown, nor wrought, nor husbanded, as we. Yet THEY, in their slums and

hovels of Turfmires, Pigsty Valley and Crooked Glen, look out like Ahab upon our garden we have made, and smoulder in their hearts. 'Oh,' says Jezebel, 'the land was THEIRS to start with.' Whose was any land, 'to start with'? The beasts'! And forest was its first estate. Is that God's Law, that we must all remain in first estate? Are we to lie on our backs, waiting for God's Grace alone to feed us? God gave me hands. By Will, I raise myself above the beasts. By Will, I rise from first estate. By Will, I break the rock and make a garden. By God's Grace, that garden grows. . . .
Brothers. Sisters. Yet we stand three times a stranger in our garden. We are Romans. We are Saxons. We are British. We are all, yet none of these. We are Roman, by covenant with Rome. Yet southward, along all that road to Rome, her order crumbles. In Rome herself there is worm at the heart. . . . We are Saxons, and Saxons no more. We are British, by land, by dwelling, and by husbandry. Yet THEY, around us and amongst us, those older, darker British, scowl and mutter, hating us to death. How else, indeed? So we are British; but not to THESE.
Be glad. We have a goodly garden. And it is not ours to give. Long ago, Rome brought our fathers here; when she was strong. Gave us her covenant; when she was strong. Now Rome might weary. We do not. No worm is at our heart. Gaul's light goes out. Spain, Danube, Africa. Our light does not go out. . . . Here on this Wall alone the flame burns steady. . . . And in our hands is the light of the earth (6–7).

The Saxon Shore is not an allegory, reliant on any rigid series of correspondences. It is internally consistent as an historical drama, and Rudkin's only conscious bendings of historical background for the purposes of the play were to move the Saxon community further north than it probably would have been and to compress the events of the last four years of the Roman Empire into one winter. Nevertheless, as most literature does, it aspires to a more universal meaning—to say something about the state of mind of 'settlers'. In a Northern Irish context, certain words, phrases, and speeches would have been politically resonant to local audiences. In the sermon cited above, for example, 'Northern Britain' would inevitably suggest 'Northern Ireland', Hadrian's Wall would remind theatre-goers of Derry's Walls, the dissolution of the Roman Empire would recall British imperial decline, the names of the Celtic 'slums' would echo with 'the Bogside' and 'Turf Lodge', the Saxons' determination to safeguard a Roman connection that the Romans were prepared to forget would highlight the importance of being British to many unionists, and the emphasis on what is now called the Protestant work ethic would no doubt also strike a chord with many in the North. Like the (British) Northern Irish Protestants, who need all four words to describe their condition, the Saxons cannot take refuge in any simple notion of their cultural identity. They do not feel as though they fully belong anywhere. They are not accepted by the Romans as Roman citizens with the same rights as those at home, but they are regarded as part of the imperial enemy by the Celtic tribes who seek to reconquer the entire island. Athdark expresses the curious envy the Saxons have of the dispossessed native British: 'They know who they are. Who am I?!' (40). Nevertheless, at the same time that the play sets up such associations in the minds of audience members it also disrupts familiar categories by showing them in an unfamiliar context. Thus, the British are the native Celts, and Rome is the imperial power.

The fantastic element which features so prominently in many of Rudkin's plays is not absent from this one. In order to present a balanced picture of the 'plantation mentality' Rudkin needed to come to terms with its repressive, violent side. Perhaps he was thinking of loyalist paramilitaries, of the ruthlessness of the B-Specials, or of the infamous RUC raid on the Bogside that precipitated some of the worst violence in Derry when he decided that his Saxons would turn into werewolves at night and prey on the British beyond the wall.[6] The wolf hairs grow inward during the day, and the Saxons are not even aware, in daylight, of what they have been doing at night. The British naturally retaliate with counter-raids, and seem to the beleaguered Saxons inhuman themselves. As Athdark muses, on duty on the Wall,

Brit . . . Brit . . . The name's a dread. Since I were a child. All his names. Welshman. Cumri . . . Come in child, or the Welshman'll get thee. Don't go down Cumri town. Don't stray west of Grindon Lough. Brit land. Bad land. Brit, Welsh, Cumri, I've dreamed of them, creeping at dusk like vampires from their graves. To fire our farms, kill victims of us they have chosen, stone by stone tak' Roman bridge apart. Not heard. Not seen. Shapes of night, that melt into the daybreak. Only their havoc showing they had been. 'They were over last night. Those ones.' Welsh. Brit. Cumri . . . And nowt of vampire I might see about him. Bastard, that can't be told from a man! (18–19).

Athdark discovers what has been going on when a wound inflicted on him by night mysteriously presents itself by day, and from then on the play records his private struggle to control the wolf side of his nature. The gash in his side that he received as a wolf prevents him from holding himself completely upright, and this illustrates dramatically his stunted personality. Rudkin has described *The Saxon Shore* as 'a play about a man learning to stand', and the last image in the play is of Athdark finally straightening himself as, after killing Ceiriad in his wolf-state, he resolves to give up savagery for good:

All this land now. Foe to me. How shall I be neighbour, who have been such fiend to these? There were such damage. There were such bloody slaughter done. And I killed the lovely lady. She was healing me . . . I do as the Good Word bids me. Spathum, sword, I make a blade of you. To shear the clay (49).

Rudkin's final stage direction is 'He is standing now, the beginnings of a man' (49).[7] The implication for Northern Ireland seems clear: Protestants should look to the land in which they live for their future, together with the people with whom they share it.

Two or three months after Rudkin sent the script to Field Day, he received a polite letter from Brian Friel informing him that the company would not be producing his play after all, although he would be paid for it and the copyright would be returned to him. The script, the directors had decided, was not suitable for them at that time. No other explanation was offered to him.[8] Rudkin felt 'immensely betrayed' by Field Day and concluded that they were not as interested in the Protestant point of view as they professed to be. He assumed that the decision not to stage his play was political—the directors were afraid of what 'their' (that is, nationalist) audiences would make of it.[9] For him personally the decision was a devastating one. He had had his heart set on an Irish production for this play, and when Field Day turned it down he offered it to the Lyric Theatre in Belfast, which declined to produce it.[10] Rudkin felt shut out of the debate in his other country—he has not written about Ireland since.[11] Eventually, in 1986, *The Saxon Shore* was put on at the Almeida Theatre in London, where it received favourable, albeit puzzled reviews. Hardly any of the critics made the connection with Northern Ireland.[12]

The temptation to speculate on Field Day's reasons for refusing to stage a play that the company had, after all, commissioned is irresistible. *The Saxon Shore* was exactly what one might have expected from David Rudkin at that time. Virtually everything he had ever written, from *Afore Night Come* to *Hippolytus*, had had as its crisis the explosion of irrational forces normally suppressed in acts of shocking violence. In some of his earlier plays he had even begun tentative experiments with the motif of supernatural transformation.[13] His fascination with history and language fit in with Field Day's concerns. The play was also written specifically for a small touring company such as Field Day. Rudkin points out that it requires no set at all, and its projected cast of nine[14] (it was eventually done with seven actors in the Almeida production) would have been smaller than that required for *Translations* (ten) and *Three Sisters* (fourteen) and only one more than had been needed for *The Communication Cord*. In short, *The Saxon Shore* appears to meet the criteria David Hammond says the Field Day directors consider in choosing a play:

Whatever plays we had in mind for a production we had to bear in mind the practical demands of a touring company and a company that never had enough money—so casts had to be small and stage sets easily handled, for instance.

About the plays themselves we always thought that we should do things excellently. That we should try to get new plays, that we should be attracting the best of writers, established as well as new.

In addition, Hammond remarks, the Field Day directors in those early years would have been particularly careful when commissioning a new play, because 'On a small island like Ireland everybody knows everybody else so the idea of having to turn down a commissioned play, or even a play submitted voluntarily, presents real difficulty.'[15]

Moreover, there is considerable evidence that Field Day was solicitous to air 'the Protestant point of view'. Stephen Rea, in particular, was outspoken about the need to speak to that segment of the population. An article in May 1983 contained this account of an interview with him:

Rea says that the hard nut which has to be cracked concerns the Northern Ireland Protestant 'who has to find his future in the context of Ireland. And in some feeble, pathetic way, Field Day is helping.'

He hopes that the theme of the psyche of the northern Protestant conscience—'it's more complex than ditching the border'—will be dealt with in their next production, in a new play commissioned from David Rudkin.[16]

In an interview given the previous month, Rea had also mentioned the commission to Rudkin and commented,

In political terms, I know that Ireland should exist as one entity, and the sooner the loyalist people in the North stop looking to Britain for any solution, the better. And if we can make some kind of statement that those people can identify with in any kind of way . . . that's what we're in it for.[17]

Finally, Field Day's abrupt change of plans must be considered in light of the considerable trauma and inconvenience it caused them. Because of it, the company nearly lost its grant from the Northern Ireland Arts Council for that year (probably, Rea explains, because they 'seemed to be dithering').[18] In practical terms, this would have meant no Northern tour at all in 1983. Field Day had always thought of itself as primarily a Northern enterprise, so clearly the directors must have felt very strongly about the 'unsuitability' of *The Saxon Shore* to refuse to produce it. As Rea puts it, 'Believe me, we needed that play, and if we'd felt that it had been what we wanted we would have done it.'[19]

Why, then, was *The Saxon Shore* not what Field Day wanted? In the absence of any real explanation, Rudkin drew his own conclusions—his views did not conform exactly to those of the Field Day directors, so once again, as a Protestant, he was not being allowed to speak as an Irishman. Other informed observers were reluctant to believe that the decision was a political one. Lynda Henderson, former editor of *Theatre Ireland*, notes Rudkin's opinion on the matter but says that she cannot agree with his interpretation of the rejection:

had the play been wholly sympathetic towards the Protestant culture I would have believed him, because I don't think that Field Day would have been sympathetic to that and I don't really see why they should have been, either, because there are faults on both sides, that's always the case. But the play is particularly hard-hitting. It's *finally* sympathetic to the position of the Protestant culture because it's a thankless position to be in, and they are people who have—well, *we* are, because I'm one of them . . . I'm not religious, but . . . my background is Protestant—but they are a people who have dual capacities and it's a case of which one they choose to emphasize. Every person has dual capacities. But because the play ... showed the Protestant culture as werewolves with a savage capacity it's not, it just is not in any way anything other than objective in terms of the fact that both sides have savaged each other. So I don't really think that—it doesn't seem to me likely that Field Day have a political objection to the play.[20]

Henderson prefers to locate the decision in practical considerations:

I think that they probably felt it would have been extremely hard to cast, which it would. That it would have been very expensive to produce, which it would because it's quite a big cast. And also possibly the earlier draft of the play wasn't as good as the final one.[21]

David Hammond, however, a member of the Field Day board, confirms one's suspicion that the decision must have been political in order to justify the trouble and expense of making it. He recalls that 'The David Rudkin episode was a very awkward one. You have to remember that none of us had been accustomed to offering commissions, let alone accepting or rejecting them. Rudkin was the first playwright that we commissioned, and when the text arrived it wasn't suitable.' The issues for Hammond, though, were very different from those Rudkin might have imagined. When asked why the text 'wasn't suitable', Hammond replied,

The Saxon Shore was about the colonisation and I thought that the image of northern protestantism was a bit askew. The misrepresentation of people and events in the Northern Ireland troubles over the last twenty-five years has been considerable. That's dangerous but almost inevitable when you're dealing with visiting journalists and other media people.

But you expect more of an artist than you do of a journalist. It was just that David Rudkin's northern protestants were not the people I knew. There was general agreement, from what I remember unanimous, on the decision not to accept the text.[22]

Stephen Rea protests that, if there were political objections to The Saxon Shore, they were not his. He insists that he simply did not think it worked as a play:

I think that Rudkin is a fabulous writer, and the things that were implicit in his work were all the things about Northern Protestantism that we would have quite liked to have addressed, but somehow, because it was a Field Day play, I think it was a bit over-stated. Somehow it didn't have the same dramatic charge of—his other plays always seemed intensely personal, and that's what I liked about his writing, loved about his writing. And I just didn't feel that play worked as well as his other work.

Rea concedes that Brian Friel, for example, might have had other considerations in mind:

I think that Brian would have been more sensitive about them being portrayed as ravening wolves . . . than I would. That isn't a problem for me. But for Brian as a Catholic maybe he felt that he didn't want to say that about those people, feel it was useful, maybe that might have been his attitude. My attitude was that the play didn't really dramatically work, although there was wonderful writing in it.[23]

Tom Paulin felt that the play suggested that the Saxon characters, who were analogous to the loyalists in Northern Ireland, did not have a right to their land, and he firmly resisted any implication that Protestants in the North should still be regarded as colonial 'settlers'. He also had misgivings about the werewolf metaphor, remembering that 'I just didn't fancy the idea of putting werewolves on stage in Magherafelt.'[24]

It would certainly be ironic if Field Day rejected *The Saxon Shore* to avoid offending Protestants, because the decision, inasmuch as it was publicly known at the time, probably had just the opposite effect. In the absence of any convincing explanation to the contrary they might well assume, as Rudkin himself did, that his play had embodied too forcefully a point of view that Field Day preferred to ignore. The timing of the refusal was particularly unfortunate as it came in the same year that the company published its first set of pamphlets, the writers of which did not always display the same tender concern for Protestant and unionist sensibilities. Although these expressed no beliefs that the directors had not had from the start, they stated things more directly and were easier to pin down than plays. Many reviewers (and more people would read reviews than would actually read the pamphlets) reacted to them, as we have seen, as old-fashioned nationalist propaganda, and from that time on the company would have to contend with the outright suspicion of that segment of its potential audience that did not share those opinions. This was arguably the part of the population of Ireland that Field Day most needed to reach if it were not to occupy itself in preaching to the converted, and from 1983 on its task was made much more difficult. It would have been making an important statement for Field Day to provide a platform for a Protestant playwright at that time, which is no doubt why the directors commissioned Rudkin in the first place. They had chosen, however, a Protestant who was very critical of certain aspects of his heritage, and they were put in the awkward position of finding themselves unwilling to be held responsible for some of his views.

In fairness, the Field Day directors were not simply being paranoid. The tour in 1983 included Ballymena, the birthplace of Ian Paisley and the heart of his constituency, and the sensitivities of Paisleyite unionists are difficult to exaggerate. When Field Day workers arrived in that town to publicize *Boesman and Lena*, the play that replaced *The Saxon Shore*, the local Arts Council nearly refused them permission to put up their posters because they contained words in Irish: 'An Chomhairle Ealaion', the official name of the Arts Council of the Republic. Then again, a Paisleyite unionist would be highly unlikely to have anything to do with Field Day in the first place. When *Boesman and Lena* eventually played Ballymena, hardly anyone in the tiny audience came from the town itself; nearly all were from the surrounding countryside.[25]

A more surprising feature of the dispute is the spectacle of artists and critics on both sides of the religious divide reducing altogether a dramatic work to politics. *The Saxon Shore* did not depict *Ulster Protestants* as ravening wolves—Northern Ireland was not even mentioned in the play. The incident illustrates the deeply sectarian nature of perceptions in the North, together with the conspiracy of silence precluding any open discussion of the problem. Rudkin was a nationalist and a Protestant, yet it did not occur to him that his nationalism rather than his Protestantism might be the cause for worry. Lynda Henderson, too, assumed that if Field Day did have a political objection to the play it must be because it was too sympathetic to the settlers. The Field Day directors were consciously trying to break away from such automatic reactions, and if they did reject *The Saxon Shore* on the basis that it might be offensive to Protestants this is evidence that they were in fact attempting to view the situation objectively—yet none of them explained this to David Rudkin. I have tried where possible, in the present history, to use political labels ('unionist' and 'nationalist') rather than sectarian ones ('Protestant' and 'Catholic'), but we must never lose sight of the fact that, in the Northern context, the two correspond more often than not. Though politics may be a matter of choice, sectarian association is not and, in a conflict between the two, will often turn out to be rooted more firmly in the psyche.

With hindsight, it seems unfortunate that Field Day decided against staging the first play it had commissioned. *The Saxon Shore* might well have offended Protestants or Catholics or both, but this would not necessarily have been a bad thing. If Field Day was serious about challenging its audience, this was certainly the play to do it. At any rate, the view of the world expressed in it was David Rudkin's—it did not necessarily have to be 'the management's' as well. One thing seems certain: a new play by a Northern playwright would have aroused more interest and controversy than the South African play Field Day elected to produce instead.

Rudkin found it ironic that the play Field Day chose to replace his on their 1983 tour was by Athol Fugard, a playwright with whom he feels a certain affinity. As a white South African, Fugard, says Rudkin, 'is the next best thing to an Ulster Protestant'.[26] With a father descended from English immigrants and an Afrikaner mother, Fugard's, like Rudkin's, was a mixed heritage. The first of Fugard's plays to be well known outside South Africa, *The Blood Knot* (1961), is about two coloured brothers, one light and one dark. Fugard suggests that race is as much a social and psychological construct as an objective reality. This theme would reappear again and again in his work.

The Blood Knot also set the pattern for several subsequent Fugard plays, including *Hello and Goodbye* (1965), *People are Living There* (1968), and *Boesman and Lena* (1969). All of these had small casts of marginal characters and were first performed in non-establishment settings. Like Stephen Rea, Fugard saw the actor as central. He wrote in 1961 about what he called 'the pure theatre experience' which required nothing more than

the actor and the stage, the actor *on* the stage. Around him is space, to be filled and defined by movement and gesture; around him is also silence to be filled with meaning, using words and sounds, and at moments when all else fails him, including the words, the silence itself.[27]

In the early 1970s Fugard experimented with forms of theatre that allowed actors a bigger role in the 'writing' of plays. One result of such collaboration with actors was the series of *Statements* plays of the early 1970s, which were performed together in the United Kingdom during the Royal Court Theatre's South African Season of 1973–4. These plays are dramatic expositions of the effects of particular apartheid laws. *Sizwe Bansi Is Dead* (1972) deals with the influx control laws, *The Island* (1973) with laws forbidding political opposition, and *Statements After an Arrest Under the Immorality Act* (1974) with the law prohibiting miscegenation. Since the mid-1970s, Fugard's work had taken a more private and less explicitly political turn, although his latest play '*Master Harold*'...*and the Boys* (1982), based on an autobiographical incident, had almost been banned in South Africa.[28]

Fugard would have appealed to the Field Day directors for a number of reasons. Like them, he was committed to taking theatre out of established venues to reach people who might otherwise have no access to it. Like them, he believed that art and politics had a necessary relationship with each other, and he wrote out of the experience of a society that was, like Northern Ireland's, deeply divided. One of Field Day's aims was to approach the problems of Ireland from a more international perspective, and the comparison with South Africa implied in their choice of a Fugard play was a suggestive one. Fugard agreed with the Field Day directors on the importance of local roots and accents in drama, even if it later acquired an international audience. He spoke first to the people in his own corner of the world, but at the same time, through his theatrical work, he made that society a bit more comprehensible to outsiders. As he reflected in his notebook during the writing of the play Field Day chose,

> an important aspect of my writing is an element of 'translation'.... Particularly conscious of it this time with Boesman and Lena. To begin with phrases were all in Afrikaans—some are still, and still defy 'translation'.[29]

When Field Day decided to produce a Fugard play the directors originally had in mind *The Island*, about political prisoners on Robben Island. The Northern Ireland Arts Council, however, indicated unofficially that this might not be a very politic choice, so they turned instead to the earlier *Boesman and Lena*. Though this was a less overtly 'political' play, it was by no means devoid of political content—about the same time that Field Day was making plans to stage *Boesman and Lena*, the Cape school board was ordering that its copies of the play be burned, fearing its 'corrupting' effect upon white youth.[30]

Perhaps the most subversive aspect of *Boesman and Lena* is that it shows with pitiless clarity the suffering that results directly from the apartheid system. The title characters are 'coloured' shanty-dwellers, and we meet them at the end of a long day that began with their shack being levelled by the whiteman's bulldozer in the name of slum clearance. This is not the first time such a thing has happened. Indeed, they have been forced to move so often that the woman, Lena, is unable to remember where they have been. Running throughout the play is her unsuccessful attempt to recall the long progression of places in their proper order, as if doing so would give her some clue as to who she is. Boesman, her husband, knows but is not telling. He insists that the past does not matter, anyway: 'What difference does it make? To anything? You're here now!'[31] 'Here' is Swartkops, a desolate mudflat where, as Lena complains, there is 'Not even a dog to look at us.' She desperately wants someone to see her, to listen to her, which Boesman resolutely refuses to do: 'Look at you! Listen to you! You're asking for a lot, Lena. Must I go mad as well?' (200).

Lena finds someone who will listen when an old black African wanders near the camp and Lena, in her desperate loneliness, calls him over to share their fire. He speaks one of the native African languages; Lena speaks Afrikaans; neither can understand the other's words, but Lena enters into the 'illusion of conversation' (215) with him. Although neither she nor the audience can understand what the old man is saying, the sense of his words as given by Fugard in a 1971 edition of the play closely parallels the story of hardships that Lena is telling him.[32] The playwright seems to imply, as Friel does in plays like *Translations* and *The Communication Cord*, that the most important part of communication is beyond language. For Lena, the contact with 'Outa'[33] is the main thing, not the literal meaning of what he is trying to tell her. She talks, he listens—just like the dog she had in Korsten who would come in to the hut every night after Boesman had gone to sleep:

All the things I did—making the fire, cooking, counting bottles or bruises, even just sitting, you know, when it's too much . . . he saw it. *Hond!* I

called him *Hond*. But any name, he'd wag his tail if you said it nice
(216).

Boesman, in contrast, talks to the world with his fist (218). The
violent, withholding side of his nature becomes more and more
apparent as the evening wears on. First he refuses to share his
knowledge of where they have been with Lena, then he declines to
speak to Outa although he knows a little bit of the old man's
language. He will not allow Lena to open one of their bottles of
wine or to split their loaf of bread three ways, and he rejects her
suggestion that they let the visitor sleep with them in their new hut.
Finally he allows Lena the choice of sleeping with him in the shack
or with the old man outside.

Boesman's shock when Lena opts for the latter is the first sign of
doubt on his part. His physical domination of her has been the only
secure thing in his life, but her affection and allegiance is, after all,
something he cannot command. When she disappears off stage in
search of firewood, Boesman communicates with Outa in the only
way he knows, by grabbing back the blanket Lena has given him
and pushing him off his seat on to the ground. By now Boesman is
afraid of his wife, though, and he returns the blanket before she
comes back, participating in the fiction that Lena and the old man
can understand each other's speech by threatening Outa, 'If you tell
her, I'll kill you' (224).

Lena, paradoxically, has found a glimmer of hope now that she
has someone with whom to share her despair. She tells Outa, and
herself, that 'As long as it doesn't rain it won't be so bad. The
blanket will help. Nights are long, but they don't last for ever. This
wind will also get tired' (224–5). Act I ends on a sacramental note,
as Lena shares her supper with her guest: 'Look at this mug,
Outa ... old mug, hey. Bitter tea, a piece of bread. Bitter and
brown. The bread should have bruises. It's my life' (225). Boesman
is shut out of their fellowship, or shuts himself out.

In Act II we see Boesman's threatened sense of self emerging once
again in violence. The act begins with him forcing Lena to re-enact
the scene that morning when their home was destroyed, making her
talk to him as if he were the white 'baas'. Lena, however, cuts this
charade short by calling him 'Whiteman's dog' and reminding him
that he had abased himself utterly at the time. Boesman insists
defiantly that 'Whiteman was doing us a favour':

... I went back to the place where our *pondok* had been. It was gone! You understand that? Gone! I wanted to call you and show you. There where we crawled in and out like baboons, where we used to sit like them and eat, our head between our knees, our fingers in the pot, hiding away so that the others wouldn't see our food. . . . I could stand there! There was room for me to stand straight. You know what that is? Listen now. I'm going to use a word. Freedom! *Ja*, I've heard them talk it. Freedom! That's what the whiteman gave us. I've got my feelings too, sister. It was a big one I had when I stood there. That's why I laughed, why I was happy. When we picked up our things and started to walk I wanted to sing. It was Freedom! (229)

Unfortunately, this mood had not lasted as long as the day: 'Freedom's a long walk. But the sun was low. Our days are too short.' There they are, with another *pondok*. Boesman vents his frustration with a shout, 'It's no use, *baas*. Boesman's done it again. Bring your bulldozer tomorrow and push it over!' (230).

With these speeches Boesman becomes as real and human for us as Lena. As he challenges her later, 'You think I haven't got secrets in my heart too?' (237). During the composition of the play Fugard had warned himself

To be careful that I do not pitch Boesman at a level of monotonous hatred and abuse. Not just the technical problem of variety of tone and tempo— the more basic issue that it is not as simple as Lena being the victim and Boesman the oppressor. Both are ultimately victims of a common, a shared predicament, and of each other. Which of course makes it some sort of love story. They are each other's fate.

So for Boesman as total a statement as for Lena. What is mutilated and why? The key I am sure is to reveal and dramatize his self-hatred as focused on Lena. What he really hates is himself.[34]

Boesman has absorbed the view that 'We're whiteman's rubbish. That's why he's so *beneukt* with us. He can't get rid of his rubbish. He throws it away, we pick it up. Wear it. Sleep in it. Eat it. We're made of it now. His rubbish is people' (231). Lena, who had earlier compared her life to 'Something that's been used too long. The old pot that leaks, the blanket that can't even keep the fleas warm' (198), now has no patience for Boesman's similar reasoning. 'Throw yourself away and leave us alone', she tells him (231). In reaching out to the old man, Lena has found that she has something of value to offer. Now she is the one who insists that she will take each moment as it comes:

You're right, Boesman. It's here and now. This is the time and place. To hell with the others. They're finished, and mixed up anyway. I don't know why I'm here, how I got here. And you won't tell me. Doesn't matter. They've ended *now*. The walks led *here*. Tonight. And he sees it (232).

In this mood Lena is even able to summon the strength to dance while Boesman watches gloweringly.

He finally finds a way to disperse her fleeting good spirits by telling her that he broke the bottles that he had beaten her for breaking that morning. When she asks him why he punished her for something she did not do, he finally admits to Lena and to himself that he beats her in protest against his own emptiness. As he remembers Lena's still-born children and their child who lived only six months, their own lives seem to him equally pointless:

One day your turn. One day mine. Two more holes somewhere. The earth will get *naar* when they push us in. And then it's finished. The end of Boesman and Lena.

That's all it is, tonight or any other night. Two dead *Hotnots* living together (238).

Moments after this declaration, however, the old man is discovered to have died during their argument—a forceful reminder that no matter how bad things are there is a vast difference between life and death, and they are still alive. Boesman is worried that people might discover the body and ask questions ('Why don't they ask some questions when we're alive?' Lena inquires bitterly), and the two are immediately involved once again in the business of living. He hurriedly starts packing their things and motions to Lena to come, but she holds on to her moment of rebellion. 'Why must I go with you? Because you're Boesman and I'm Lena?' (241, 244).

Abruptly, though, her mood changes. Going over to the old man, she talks to him again:

Outa, why the hell you do it so soon? There's things I didn't tell you, man. And now this as well. It's still happening! [Softly.] . . . *Moer moer moer*. Can't throw yourself away before your time. Hey, *Outa*. Even you had to wait for it (246).

Boesman hands her their bucket for her to put on her head, and she remarks, 'Hasn't got a hole in it yet. Might be whiteman's rubbish, but I can still use it' (246). As they walk off stage, Boesman and Lena begin to talk with rather than at each other, as he finally answers her question about where they have been. Lena has to admit that 'It doesn't explain anything', but she finds some comfort in the fact that 'Anyway, somebody saw a little bit. Dog and a dead man' (247).

The audience, of course, has also seen 'a little bit'. *Boesman and Lena* is, in the end, a play about survival and about witnessing. Lena's preoccupation with history, with how she came to be where she is, was a concern that was shared in Ireland, and her conclusion that the present and future are ultimately more important was one with which the Field Day directors concurred. In addition, the basic story of two people who are bound together by a tie almost more powerful than love—who might fight, sometimes even hate each other, but who define themselves in relation to the other—was one with obvious parallels in the North of Ireland where Protestants and Catholics, unionists and nationalists know who they are partly because they know what they are not.

Kader Asmal, in a programme note for the Field Day production, indirectly drew attention to a broad similarity between South Africa and Northern Ireland when he wrote that 'Nothing in South Africa is non-political. Race touches, blights and destroys every aspect of life.'[35] In Northern Ireland religion, not race, is used to classify and divide members of the society, but a consciousness of which side people belong on likewise permeates most aspects of life. Colour would seem to be a more obvious means of discrimination, but race is a matter of such fine degrees in the South African context that, in a case noted by Asmal, the race of a foundling infant three weeks old was decided by a police officer on the basis of one strand of hair. The apartheid laws then in effect would dictate who the foster parents of the infant could be, where she could live, go to school, attend university, which trains, hotels, restaurants, cinemas, and theatres she could enter, whom she could marry, what her political rights would be, what sort of job she could have, what pension she would get, and, finally, where she could be buried.

This notion of the extreme determining effect of such social distinctions as race and religion in a polarized society probably lay

behind Field Day's decision to stage *Boesman and Lena*. Different
directors no doubt found the play appropriate for Field Day for
different reasons. Brian Friel, according to the *Derry Journal*, 'said
that Athol Fugard's play was chosen not only because of its own
merits but also because Fugard is a very important playwright, who
has not received the attention he deserves'.[36]

In choosing a South African play Field Day was not attempting
to make any kind of crude equation between the position of blacks
under apartheid and the position of Northern Irish Catholics,
although there were certainly suspicions of that in some quarters.[37]
The decision was taken not to force any supposed parallels between
Northern Ireland and South Africa, but rather to let the play speak
for itself. The actors did not use make-up to change their colour,
but they did adopt South African accents and mannerisms for the
roles.[38] The cast was coached by a language expert from England
and advised by Kader Asmal.[39]

Besides the thematic and artistic reasons for producing *Boesman
and Lena*, there were obvious practical considerations. Due to its
change of plans, the company was even more than usually short
of both time and money. David Hammond recollects that the
directors decided to produce *Boesman and Lena* 'because we were
up against things. In order to get support from the Arts Councils we
had to fit in with their patterns of financing. We had no clear idea
of the play we wanted to do but we felt that if we decided not to do
a play, we'd lose that year's subvention and maybe disqualify
ourselves for future years.'[40] *Boesman and Lena* required only three
actors and very little in the way of a set, so it was well-suited to
touring. Some wondered whether audiences would accept white
Irish actors in these roles, but it was pointed out that in South
African terms 'coloured' did not apply only to people with black or
brown skin.[41] Fugard himself had played Boesman in the original
production and on other occasions had taken 'coloured' roles in his
plays.[42]

Rehearsals began at the end of August, three and a half weeks
before the show was due to open, with Stephen Rea in the role of
Boesman. For the first time Field Day employed an English director,
Clare Davidson, with whom Rea had worked in London. The
company also had a new manager, Julie Barber, who had handled
publicity for *The Communication Cord*. A four-week tour was
scheduled, avoiding Dublin and Belfast because touring companies

did not receive money to play these centres. Instead, the company concentrated on smaller venues both North and South. Money from the Arts Council of the Republic had been the first to be approved that year and was, for a time, Field Day's only assured source of support, so the tour in the North was short with only six one-night stands apart from the opening five performances in Derry. These were fitted in later in the tour than usual, after the play had already visited seven places in the Republic. Several new stops were added, as Field Day visited both the South East and the South West for the first time.[43] In Newcastle West the company was particularly welcome, as the town had not been visited by a professional touring company since the roving theatre manager Anew McMaster played there thirty years before.[44]

The result of the company's hard work and dedication was a stunning production. Critics all around Ireland loved Field Day's *Boesman and Lena*. David Nowlan of the *Irish Times* called it 'a parable set in the most distressing reality of homeless humanity in South Africa' and acknowledged that 'It might not, at first thought have much to do with the Field Day Theatre Company's avowed intent of seeking new cultural identities in Ireland.' The parable, though, was 'universal': 'It has a great deal to say about the abyss of alienation and its resultant loss of identity, a phenomenon not unknown on this island.' He pointed out that, although this was the first non-Friel play the company had produced, there were 'strong echoes of Friel' as 'one of its characters speaks only a language which the others do not understand, and there are litanies of place-names recited as the others try to make out where they have been and, through such identification, who they might really be.' He praised all three actors for their 'superb performances'.[45] Fintan O'Toole also mentioned the affinities with Friel's work and praised the actors' interpretations of their roles:

Rea plays a man trying to forget his humanity, taking refuge in animal gestures and movements; Donnelly a woman trying to remember her humanity, tentative in her movements, probing and searching. They combine into an emotional blowtorch, stripping away the comfortable familiarity of pain and humiliation to suggest the crumbling residue of self-awareness beneath.[46]

A reviewer for the *Derry Journal* commented that, at first, *Boesman and Lena* seemed an 'unusual' choice for Field Day,

But although the play gives an insight into the apartheid problem in South Africa, it is not a commentary on apartheid, it is more a love story as the characters of Boesman and Lena develop. It is also a reflection of life in general and the uncertainty, despair and loneliness faced by under-privileged people throughout the world.[47]

The *Belfast Telegraph*'s critic called the choice of a South African play a 'bold step': 'Field Day's vision has extended far beyond Ireland and its problems.'[48] A writer in the *Dungarvan Observer* referred to the 'soul-disturbing intensity' of the three performances, and Eugene Moloney expressed the view in the *Irish News* that 'the company once again have a triumph on their hands'.[49] Paddy Woodworth in the *Irish Press* praised both the play and the pro-duction in the strongest terms:

The play works superbly well at the ordinary human level—Boesman and Lena ask questions of themselves and each other that any couple might ask in crisis, and are finely drawn as individuals. . . . But their questioning is grotesquely distorted by the overpowering burden of apartheid. Fugard succeeds in making political lessons emerge unobtrusively from authentic human experience. At the end, he leaves just enough hope to go on, but no more. . . .

   That white people can give us the heart of this play without embarrass-ment or condescension is a credit to their theatrical commitment.

He implicitly wondered, however, 'whether audiences around the country will rise to the considerable demands made on their concentration'.[50]

   This was a reasonable worry. In the case of *Boesman and Lena* there appears to have been a vast discrepancy between the views of the critics and the opinions of less-experienced play-goers, as people all around the country stayed away in large numbers. It was evident from the first night that Field Day was going to meet some resistance. Part of the reason that there was less interest than in previous years was simply due to the fact that the play was not new, was not Irish, and was not by Brian Friel. After attending the opening in Derry, Woodworth noted that

Perhaps because it was not a Friel world première, the audience last night was not as studded with celebrities from the arts and public life as in previous years. But while there was less of a gala atmosphere the reception the play received was enthusiastic, and deservedly so.[51]

Nowlan confirmed this impression and hinted at a more political explanation. The Guildhall opening was, he said, different from the three previous Field Day first nights:

Less than half the members of the City Council were there, and there were no Unionist councillors there at all, nor any clergy from either side of the Irish divide.

I suppose it could have been just a manifestation of the coolness that had developed in the past year between the two main traditions in Derry politics, what with the SDLP deciding not to offer the mayoralty to a Unionist this year, where previously there had been a happy annual alternation between the parties. Or was the whole Guild Hall audience this time predominantly a nationalist gathering identifying itself with the coloured outcasts of Fugard's divided society? I hope not.

He concluded, however, that 'More likely the lower level of "buzz" this year was simply the result of there not being a new work from Brian Friel. But that means that, in just three years, Field Day has come of age as a theatre company and must now attract its audiences with plays other than those written by one of Derry's favourite sons.'[52]

David Hammond concedes that, for whatever reason, 'the play didn't do well on its tour and we had to make up a lot of ground thereafter'.[53] A critic who saw the play in Enniskillen asserted that it 'deserved better than the sprinkling of the 60 or so people who made up the audience'. He observed that

Field Day's last three plays . . . all enjoyed large audiences in Enniskillen. All were solidly set within the Irish context, as was *Children of the Dead End*, by the Donegal playwright Patrick Magill. This 'tale of Irish navvy life' attracted an audience of over 200 at Enniskillen High School some weeks ago. What a pity Fermanagh audiences cannot be a little less parochial. What they missed last Thursday was a theatrical experience that we will be lucky to see here again.[54]

In Newry, it may be safely assumed that the Arts Festival organizers, who had 'attempted to provide a light and entertaining programme' for their patrons and booked *Boesman and Lena* into the same large hall that had been filled to capacity for *The Communication Cord*, did not get what they had expected.[55]

Part of the confusion and disappointment over the play may be traced to Field Day's billing it as 'a love story' or 'a tale of love and discovery'.[56] Although this was true of *Boesman and Lena* in a qualified sense, and it is difficult to see how else the company could have tried to sell it, such a description could hardly have prepared audiences for what they actually witnessed on stage. The *Derry Journal* even reported before the play opened that Clare Davidson 'points out that the play has a good deal of humour as well as pathos', a claim that is rather misleading.[57]

Ian Starrett of the *Sunday News* must have spoken for many members of the audience when he complained,

Field Day Theatre Company are getting away above our heads. Mine anyway. . . .

The latest effort, their fourth, is Athol Fugard's *Boesman and Lena*, set in South Africa which for starters is unlikely to entice a bundle of laughs.

The Première night PR blurb promised the play would be laced with humour. All I can say is there weren't many laughs around seat G 17. . . .

. . . in the view of this apprentice stage reviewer there was too much shouting and as the girl at my shoulder put it so subtly you would have needed a crash course in Swahili to have understood some of it.

Starrett, who described the play as 'the bewildering ramblings of a scruffy African' and 'his loud mouthed woman', commented that 'There are subject matters much closer to home like the Troubles and unemployment that might put more posteriors on seats than an Irish interpretation of a South African playwright's views.'[58]

A writer for the *Derry Journal* was also curious to know why a Derry-based theatre company that declared itself to be engaged with politics had not as yet dealt directly with the open sectarian strife in Northern Ireland. Brian Friel, he reported, replied that

this is not as the result of a conscious decision on their part as there are many works about the troubles available. He points out that both *Boesman and Lena* with its references to the effects of apartheid on the individual and *Translations* with its theme which dealt with the passing of Irish place names, do have obvious modern references and the group have no set policy on the question of dealing with the troubles.[59]

Field Day ended 1983 with vague hopes of touring America and Europe some time in the future. In a change from previous rhetoric, Stephen Rea had begun to talk about international standards. He told an interviewer for *Company* that 'It's important to operate on the highest theatrical level. One way to test yourself is to look outside the island. I'd love to do something that people found theatrically exciting, not just an interesting Irish phenomenon.'[60] The Field Day directors were concentrating at this point on keeping the focus of their dramatic work, as opposed to their publishing, strictly theatrical, with the 'politics' implicit rather than explicit. Their avoidance of potentially divisive subject-matter in *The Saxon Shore* and their decision to keep *Boesman and Lena* in a South African idiom both demonstrate their cautiousness in this respect.

The publication of the pamphlets, however, authored by three of the directors themselves, would make it harder and harder to dodge the issue of where exactly they stood on the 'National Question'. A kind of postscript to 1983 was Stephen Rea's wedding to Dolours Price, one of two sisters convicted for their role in 1973 IRA car-bombings in London.[61] This, of course, had nothing to do with Field Day, but the company was naturally mentioned in connection with Rea and his marriage inevitably influenced the way it was regarded in Ireland and Great Britain. The impression that Field Day was a traditional nationalist organization was the product partly of the suspicion and closed-mindedness of those who did not believe that any middle ground existed, but it was also the result of the statements and actions of people associated with the company. Erroneous or not, this impression would prove impossible to dispel.

Poets as Playwrights: Field Day's Double Bill

THE main business of Field Day in 1984 was, as it had always been, its theatrical tour. This year the company had plans to perform in seventeen venues in less than two months, visiting Ballycastle and Limavady for the first time. In a departure from previous years the programme was a double-bill, two short plays commissioned from two Northern Irish poets. As Friel had reworked *Three Sisters*, so Tom Paulin produced a version of Sophocles's *Antigone* in Irish-English, and Derek Mahon did a verse translation of a Molière play, *The School for Husbands*. Though radically different in style and tone, the plays were related in the Field Day production through the use of the same cast of nine and the highlighting of a common theme.

Paulin's play, *The Riot Act*, was performed first. Stephen Rea played Creon and directed, a role he had taken over when it was decided that the original director, Simon Stokes, had a style that was not suited to the production. The staging strove for stark visual effect. The characters, in grey and black modern dress (Creon wore a business suit), moved in front of grey drapes inscribed with classical architectural lineaments. White light on a bare stage created shifting patterns of shadows, and the movements of the cast were precisely choreographed and described by more than one critic as 'balletic'. Creon also melted into and out of the chorus. Reviewers were divided as to the effectiveness of the production, but several agreed with Colm Cronin that 'Rea's direction . . . in striving for technical excellence seemed to drain the characters of any humanity'.[1]

Field Day considered part of its mission to be the popularization of the classics, and the decision to stage *Antigone* fitted in with that. As Paulin explained to a reporter from *North* magazine, the story of the girl who buries her slain brother in defiance of a royal edict expresses all the principal conflicts in the condition of man—men versus women, age versus youth, society versus the individual, the living versus the dead, and men versus the gods. In the course of these ongoing conflicts, the pairs define themselves as they define each other.[2]

Paulin's intense interest in the Antigone myth also owed something to a disagreement with Conor Cruise O'Brien over the interpretation of it. Back in 1968, already convinced that no matter what else the civil rights movement might achieve 'much blood would be shed',[3] O'Brien published an essay in *The Listener* in which he reflected on the claims of justice versus the desirability of keeping the peace. When violence is almost certain to result from non-violent protest, he wondered, is the protest worth it? He used *Antigone* to illustrate the dilemma. Creon's decision to forbid the burial of Polynices, he said, was 'rash'—but so was Antigone's action in flouting his order:

Creon's authority, after all, was legitimate, even if he had abused it, and the life of the city would become intolerable if citizens should disobey any law that irked their conscience. Ismene, who was Polynices' sister just as much as Antigone was, would not risk life for the sake of her brother's dead body. It was Antigone's free decision, and that alone, which precipitated the tragedy. Creon's responsibility was the more remote one of having placed this tragic power in the hands of a headstrong child of Oedipus.

O'Brien concluded that, uncompromising though Antigone may be, she must be allowed her say:

We should be safer without the trouble-maker from Thebes. And that which would be lost, if she could be eliminated, is quite intangible: no more, perhaps, than a way of imagining and dramatising man's dignity. It is true that this way may express the essence of what man's dignity actually is. In losing it, man might gain peace at the price of his soul.[4]

In *States of Ireland* (1972), O'Brien reprinted his *Listener* piece and confided that

Reading that essay now, three years afterwards, I find myself no longer in sympathy with the conclusion. . . . after four years of Antigone and her under-studies and all those funerals—more than a hundred dead at the time of writing—you begin to feel that Ismene's commonsense and feeling for the living may make the more needful, if less spectacular element in 'human dignity'.[5]

Tom Paulin took issue with this in 'The Making of a Loyalist', a scathing critique of O'Brien which he published in the *Times Literary Supplement* on 14 November 1980 and reprinted in *Ireland and the English Crisis* (1984). In his review, Paulin pointed out the contradictions, inconsistencies, and shifts in O'Brien's thought over the years as reflected in his writings. He was particularly contemptuous of the Southerner's gloss on *Antigone* in *States of Ireland*, commenting that 'Here Antigone (i.e. Bernadette Devlin and the Civil Rights movement) becomes responsible for "all those funerals". This means that the Unionist State is virtually absolved of all responsibility and Creon's hands appear to be clean.' Paulin implied that he himself adopted Hegel's view of the play as a conflict between 'the instinctive Powers of Feeling, Love and Kinship' and 'the daylight gods of free and self-conscious, social and political life'. In that interpretation, 'neither the right of family, nor that of the state is denied; what is denied is the absoluteness of the claim of each'. It is in these two opposing 'rights', Paulin claimed, that the tragedy resides. O'Brien, in his opinion, saw 'the political conflict in the play as one of unequal values and unequal personal responsibilities'.[6] By favouring Creon, he distorted the proper equilibrium of the play.

Paulin in his own version of *Antigone* would presumably attempt to redress the balance between Creon and Antigone. It is intriguing, then, that one of the most telling criticisms levelled against Paulin's version of the play was that he had cheapened the character of Creon, reducing tragedy to what Michael Billington described as 'political melodrama'. Billington commented, 'When Creon at the end cried "Pity me if you can, blind and thick" I simply felt an Ulster demogogue was receiving his come-uppance.' Several other critics reached similar conclusions.[7]

Paulin did not actually stray far from Sophocles. Most of the originality of his adaptation came from his rendering of the play in Northern Irish vernacular. Nevertheless, a closer examination of the script bears out the initial impression that the changes he did make had the effect of tipping the balance away from Creon and toward Antigone at the outset. This is perhaps hardly surprising, given Paulin's own political views. It is clear from his poetry and other writings that he has little patience with those who would choose stability over justice.

Stephen Rea likewise believed that an important element of the conflict between Antigone and Creon was that between the claims of abstract justice (the Law of the gods) and the laws of men, which should approximate the divine Law but often do not. Shortly before the play opened in Derry, Rea cited

> dismissal of the legitimacy of the miners' case in Britain by right wing opinion and the confrontational international stance by the US in Central America as examples of the plight of those who stand up and protest. Similar to the plight of the character of Antigone in the play which he directs—she is unwilling to remain silent in the face of injustice.[8]

Sometimes such earthly disputes centre around what exactly it is that the gods require. Creon believes that the gods would hardly countenance honouring Polynices with elaborate burial rites when he had returned to Thebes with an enemy army prepared to burn the city to the ground and their shrines with it. Antigone retorts that the quarrel of Polynices and Eteocles died with them:

> Who knows but that the dead
> can lie in peace together?[9]

Her justification for her action is that Death demands the same rites for everyone. Paulin implicitly acknowledged that there might be debate over the imperatives of Justice in any particular case when he told an interviewer from the Irish *Sunday Independent*, 'I hope people will read it in different ways. Some may say that Antigone is Bernadette Devlin. Others may see the character as Ian Paisley.'[10]

Nevertheless, as Paulin and Hegel recognized, there is another, equally valid, way of defining the principal conflict in the play. It is possible to read *Antigone* as a debate between the values of tribal solidarity and the newer idea of allegiance to a larger community in the form of the city-state. This may, in fact, be the only way to make sense of Antigone's puzzling speech as she is led to her death:

> But if I'd a husband
> or a child even
> and they dead, dead but not buried,
> I'd have laid no earth on them
> if the law forbade me.

And why? It's simple.
I might wed some other man,
have child by another,
but no one, now,
can make me a new brother.
(Paulin, 47)

Here she contradicts her earlier statements about the equality of the
dead and acknowledges that her deepest motives owe more to
private feeling than to universal principles. She buried her brother
when she would not have buried a husband or a child because
she regards the degree of consanguinity as higher. Various commentators (including Goethe) have deplored this abandonment of
principle, but it need not reflect badly on Antigone to admit the
possibility that both religious conviction and familial loyalty played
a part in her action.

Bernard Knox, in an illuminating introduction to Robert Fagles's
translation of *Antigone*, outlines the likely political implications of
the play for Sophocles's audience. The myth upon which it is based,
he writes, dates from a time long before the primacy of the city-
state, but the play is deliberately set 'against the background of
the city'. Creon at the beginning of the play would seem to have the
balance of right on his side because he speaks for the welfare of the
city as a whole, although the particular action he recommends may
not be a wise or humane one. He forfeits the sympathy of the
audience as the play continues by making it clear, when his policy
is questioned, that he considers the city to be his private property
and by ignoring until it is too late the warnings of Tiresias that the
gods are displeased with him. Nevertheless, the values of civil
relationship that he defends at the start of the play must carry equal
weight with Antigone's loyalty to her brother if we are to regard
their conflict as tragically balanced.[11] As Creon concludes his first
speech to the chorus in Fagles's translation,

our country *is* our safety.
Only while she voyages true on course
can we establish friendships, truer than blood itself.
(Fagles, 49)

The tension between tribal fidelity and individually reasoned
political positions in civic life is obviously one with a great deal of
resonance in Northern Ireland. This is not, however, the interpret-

ation of *Antigone* that emerges in *The Riot Act*. The basis for it was not readily available either to Tom Paulin or to his audience. In part the problem was due to the necessity of translating the play across centuries and into an entirely different cultural context. The idea of the city which lies behind Sophocles's play is something more organic than any modern state could be. If *Antigone* is summarized as a depiction of the conflict between an individual and the state, what this connotes to a modern European reader or audience member is some kind of confrontation between a citizen and his or her government. What is missing from this conception is a feeling for the civil community represented by the Greek city-state.

This general difficulty is exacerbated in Northern Ireland, where the legitimacy of the state itself is continually in question. The minority community as a whole has never really accepted the right of the government to exist, and since direct rule was instituted in 1972 the rest of the population has likewise felt shut out of the political process in the province. In any case, the elements of participation and identification so prominent in fifth-century Athens are lacking in the North. Paulin would have had a particularly difficult time conveying this aspect of the drama because in his own lexicon the word 'state' is almost invariably a negative one.[12]

In *The Riot Act* we are given a clear view of Creon's shortcomings without a corresponding sense of the dangerous limitations of Antigone's frame of reference. Creon is suspect from the start, so there is never any genuine contest between him and Antigone for our allegiance. Paulin obviously had fun with Creon's first speech to the citizens of Thebes:

For my own part, I have always held that one of the soundest maxims of good government is: *always listen to the very best advice*. And in the coming months I shall be doing a very great deal of listening, sounding opinions and so forth. However, let me say this, and say it plainly right at the very outset, that if ever any man here should find himself faced with a choice between betraying his country and betraying his friend, then he must swiftly place that friend in the hands of the authorities. That is the only right and proper decision and we must all abide by it.

If I might further add—and I know that Zeus will support me here—that if ever I should see this country heading for disaster I would be quite incapable of standing idly by and saying nothing. Nor could I conceive of having even the slightest personal friendship with anyone who wished my country ill. For we must at all times be vigilant and be prepared to speak up and lend a hand. If that should not be the case, then it would be most unwise to predict that our present peace and prosperity, with all the opportunities that accompany them, will last for very much longer. (Paulin, 16)

Even in Sophocles's time this speech was probably meant to sound like a verbal collage of stock political phrases, but for his audiences those phrases still had meaning—Knox points out that Creon's first speech anticipates, sometimes almost verbatim, the Funeral Oration of Pericles.[13] In Paulin's version of it, however, Creon is a figure of derision from his first appearance. Contemporary reviewers detected shades of discredited leaders from Richard Nixon to Jack Lynch to 'Humphrey Atkins/Brian Faulkner' to any one of 'those unfortunate British politicians who get Mrs. Thatcher's plum job in Northern Ireland'.[14] While the speech by itself is a highly successful comic turn—indeed, a number of critics thought it the best thing in Paulin's version—in the context of the play as a whole it weakens *The Riot Act* in relation to *Antigone*. As Fintan O'Toole put it in a review of the production for the *Sunday Tribune*,

> Rea's first speech is a brilliant parody of a Northern Ireland Office political functionary appealing for public support. It is enormously enjoyable to spot the Irish parallels and to smile. But it immediately draws the theatrical sting of the play. *Antigone* works as a play because we are also interested in Creon as a man, concerned with his dilemma and the way he tries to cope with it. Sophocles' Creon is a tragic hero as well as a villain. By satirising him from the start, the drama of his conflict with Antigone is rendered impossible.[15]

O'Toole went on to suggest that the real problem was that Paulin had not carried through the political parallels suggested by the speech. Instead of changing the overall structure of the play to make it into his own political parable, Paulin made mostly local changes. Thus, 'As Creon's tragedy mounts ... we are expected to switch from satire to sympathy, an impossible transition.' As another critic noted, the 'linguistic Ulsterization policy doesn't really seem to strike a blow for anything or anybody in particular'.[16]

Unevenness is a problem with the script as a whole. Paulin often realizes his intention of demonstrating that vernacular speech has within it the capacity to contain classic and universal ideas. Most of the time the language is spare and simple, colloquial without being distracting. The first scene between Antigone and Ismene shows Paulin's technique serving his purpose admirably. Ismene tries to calm her sister with the thought that things cannot get much worse,

> What's fretting you?
> They're both dead—
> dead in the one day.
> There's no worse grief than that.
>
> (Paulin, 9)

Here the language is natural and warm without being intrusive. Even in this scene, though, there is the odd word or phrase that jars. When Antigone warns Ismene

> When you talk that way
> it's like you're sour
> on everything that's sacred
>
> (Paulin, 14)

the word 'sour' seems woefully inadequate to express the idea of blasphemy that lies behind her utterance.

Threadbare language in *The Riot Act* is most often assigned to Creon. Even a critic who reviewed the play favourably commented that Creon was given 'the crudest most trite language in the play' (she thought he deserved it).[17] At the end of the play, when Creon's life disintegrates around him, he castigates himself thus:

> Wicked, cack-handed,
> that's Creon.
> Made a right blood-mess,
> did Creon.
> And where's the end of it?
> Ask Creon.
>
> (Paulin, 62)

Here the vocabulary is simply not capable of embodying his moment of tragic realization.

Paulin's strategy is most successful in the lighter speeches of the play, particularly those of the guard, whose vernacular also reinforces his status in the society. When he returns to the palace after having captured Antigone he explains the circumstances of the arrest to Creon:

Your honour, I could've sworn blind you'd seen the last of me entirely, but after I left here—well, I was dead lucky. I feel grand now. Tell you the truth, I was that scared by all you said . . . but that's no matter. I'd just slipped over for a last look—thought I'd give it one more try, I did—when: would you believe it? There's this wee girl spreading the dust on him and pouring wine on the ground. So I nabbed her straight. (Paulin, 24–5)

The speech is replete with Ulster vocabulary and constructions— 'grand', 'that scared', 'I did', 'wee'—without collapsing under the weight of them. The effect is funny and immediate. Slang that seems inappropriate in the mouth of a member of the royal family of Thebes convinces us in this context.

Aside from his 'Ulsterization' of the lines, Paulin compressed the script in a number of places. Antigone's confrontation with Creon, one of the most riveting exchanges in the play, is radically short-ened and curiously deflated. Paulin's Antigone defies Creon with the words

> It was never Zeus
> made that law.
> Down in the dark earth
> there's no law says,
> 'Break with your own kin,
> go lick the state.'
> We're bound to the dead:
> we must be loyal to them.
> I had to bury him.
>   (Paulin, 27)

In Sophocles's play this speech is several times longer, and in it Antigone develops her most powerful defence of her action on the grounds of abstract right and wrong. The first ten lines of Fagles's translation (seventeen others follow) give some sense of what is missing in Paulin's rendering of this speech:

> It wasn't Zeus, not in the least,
> who made this proclamation—not to me.
> Nor did that Justice, dwelling with the gods

beneath the earth, ordain such laws for men.
Nor did I think your edict had such force
that you, a mere mortal, could override the gods,
the great unwritten, unshakable traditions.
They are alive, not just today or yesterday:
they live forever, from the first of time,
and no one knows when they first saw the light.

(Fagles, 64)

It is odd, given his evident sympathy for Antigone and his belief that Creon has sinned against the gods,[18] that Paulin should so truncate his heroine's great moment. Presumably he did so to speed the pace of the drama, but effective dramatic timing is not just a matter of keeping the dialogue flowing. Sometimes the action needs to be brought to a standstill so that the audience can listen, and carefully, to what a character is saying.

Paulin treats the choruses most freely of all, shortening and reshaping them to make them more modern-sounding in the belief that they are basically 'undramatic'.[19] Modern audiences might find long chorus speeches tedious, but the chorus was an integral part of the drama in Sophocles's time, serving as a representative of the audience on stage and guiding its reaction to the spectacle presented. Modifying the choruses subtly changes the moral balance of the play. In an ode after the discovery that someone has been interfering with the corpse of Polynices, for example, the Greek chorus sings man's praises: he has harnessed the waves, subdued the earth, hunted some wild beasts and domesticated others, and learned to use language and live in cities. Only death, says the chorus, has defeated him. The speech ends with a reflection on man's capacity for good or evil and on the necessity for respecting both the laws of the city and the laws of the gods. The dangerous man is one who, reckless and daring, asserts his own will, and the city casts him out.[20] Paulin's replacement is quite different in tone:

There are many wonders on this earth
and man has made the most of them;
though only death has baffled him
he owns the universe, the stars,
sput satellites and great societies.

Fish pip inside his radar screens
and foals kick out of a syringe:
he bounces on the dusty moon
and chases clouds about the sky
so they can dip on sterile ground.

By pushing harder every way,
by risking everything he loves,
he makes us better, day by day:
we call this progress and it shows
we're damned near perfect!
                    (Paulin, 23–4)

He has found good modern equivalents for the accomplishments celebrated by Sophocles, but the overall effect is brasher. We get a clear impression of man's ingenuity, but not of the premium value placed on civil life in the original. The idea of the city as one of man's highest achievements, something towards which he has evolved, is missing. This robs the speech of any relevance to what is going on onstage. In the original, the chorus chooses this particular time to celebrate man's flowering in social life precisely because the stability of the city is perceived to be threatened. The ode expresses the citizens' disapproval of whoever menaces the security of the civil community. Furthermore, in Paulin's version the ambiguity of the original is lost. Sophocles's chorus hints at a failing, reckless daring, that is understood at the time to refer to whomever has buried Polynices. Later in the play, however, it will be seen to apply equally well to Creon, who refuses to admit that he has made a mistake. The mention of law likewise appears to condemn the defier of the king's proc-lamation, but it later becomes apparent that Creon has ignored the laws of the gods and is equally culpable. The chorus speech, coming where it does, both comments appropriately on the action up to that point and deftly foreshadows what is to come. Paulin's chorus does not serve this function. The endeavours it celebrates are all materialistic; man's responsibility as a moral being is left out of the scheme of things. The speech itself is a lyric interlude, having very little to do with the action of the play.[21] Something has been lost here in terms of the drama as a whole.

In other places, Paulin's adjustments to the choruses are gains in modern terms. After Creon orders the execution of Antigone the chorus has a long speech about the curse of Oedipus carrying on from generation to generation and the futility of trying to escape fate. Human happiness is merely an illusion that the gods can shatter any time they wish if a man is marked out for destruction.[22] Paulin's version drops the emphasis on one doomed house and opens itself up to universal significance immediately. The chorus leader reflects,

Ever since the day I first made this speech—it was in another time and place, and in a different language too—the grief I was speaking of then has grown and multiplied. It's got more and more.

What I'd say now is simply this—the world is a very, very old place, but the people in it, they're very young still, and if you've never grieved then you're lucky.

Generation after generation has suffered, and every time we think to get free of what happened before and will surely happen after, then we find there's something in our road, like a ramp maybe, that we can never get over, that we can never push past.

So we give up because we know it's taking us nowhere. (Paulin, 35)

For one or two minutes, the actors leave ancient Greece behind and join their twentieth-century audience. Oblique references to the play's classic status remind watchers that what they are seeing is a play about something that happened thousands of years ago, but the speech at the same time helps to bring the characters' suffering home. By thus situating *Antigone* in time, Paulin confirms its timelessness. The Greek notion of fate is transformed into an awareness of the inescapability of trouble in this life. The direct, conversational tone draws the audience in, and the use of the pronoun 'we' encourages an identification with the people on stage. In Northern Ireland in 1984, with hope of a purely political solution to the Troubles ever more anaemic, this statement of tragic inevitability must have found some hearers who could understand what that meant.

Perhaps one's judgement of Tom Paulin's rendering of *Antigone* will, in the end, be largely a matter of taste. His version does not capture all of the nuances of the original, but this was not what he had set out to do. Paulin's aim was to 'reapply' the myth in a Northern Irish context through the employment of a local idiom.[23] A final question remains: Why *Antigone*? What correspondence did

Paulin and Field Day perceive between the play and the condition of Ireland at that time?

A hint may be found in the speech of the messenger who returns to Thebes to announce the deaths of Antigone and Haemon, Creon's son who was to have married her and who kills himself in grief when he finds her dead. His theme is that there is nothing certain in life:

> Take Creon now—that man, he wanted for nothing, he'd everything you could want. He saved his country from its enemies, shared power with no man, had lovely children.
> There was nothing and no one that wasn't under his thumb.
> But that's all gone now. And d'you know why? I'll tell you.
> He could neither bend nor listen. He held firm just that shade too long. There was no joy nor give in him ever. (Paulin, 56)

In translations of the play the speech ends with the idea that, no matter how much money Creon has, he will never again be a happy man. Paulin cuts this conclusion and invents his messenger's interpretation of events. Creon has been brought low by his rigidity and stubbornness. These are failings that also characterize the hard-liners on both sides of the Northern Irish divide, but the reference to sharing power seems to point especially to unionists. There are also parallels with the position of the British government during the hunger strikes. In that situation, as in *Antigone*, a ruling power was shaken by the wilful self-destruction of its opponents.

The damaging effect of inflexibility was also the serious message underlying the comedy of *High Time*, Derek Mahon's translation of *The School for Husbands* by Molière. The second half of Field Day's double-bill was in other ways the reverse of the first. *High Time* was as raucous and colourful as *The Riot Act* had been muted and grey. Whereas the actors in the first play had been described by one critic as 'talking heads',[24] the same performers became, after the interval, virtual acrobats. The first production strove for classical restraint; the second indulged in unashamed 'pantomime antics'.[25] Nevertheless, *High Time* replayed in a comic framework what *The Riot Act* had set out in a tragic one.

Derek Mahon, a Northern Irish Protestant living in London, was regarded as one of the foremost figures in the Ulster poetry revival. By 1984 he had already published over ten volumes of his own poetry as well as translating work by the French poet Nerval and editing a book of *Modern Irish Poetry*.[26] Meanwhile, Mahon had worked as a theatre critic for the *Listener* and a poetry editor for the *New Statesman*. More recently he had turned his hand to screenplays, with the adaptation he made for television of Jennifer Johnston's novel *How Many Miles to Babylon?* selected as the BBC's 1981 nomination for the Emmy awards in New York.[27] Politically, Mahon was a 'secular, republican socialist'[28] who avoided making a fetish of his Ulster roots. As he told a writer for the *Sunday Independent*,

I try not to do too much Northern stuff. I may be from the North, but I consider myself an Irishman, an inhabitant of what Conor Cruise O'Brien calls 'this archipelago.' I try not to get drawn into Northern identity in any sort of confining way. I look for other kinds of things.[29]

Mahon had for some time been considering translating something by Molière and, as he explained in a programme note for the Field Day production, 'when Brian Friel provided the opportunity I leapt at it'. He quickly decided on *The School for Husbands*, partly because he did not believe that that play had ever been translated into English verse, although Molière himself wrote in rhyme.[30] First performed in 1661, *L'École des Maris* was, Mahon noted in a preface to the published script of his own version, the most frequently produced of Molière's plays during the Revolutionary period.[31] The story is that of two middle-aged brothers, each the guardian of one of two young sisters. The girls' dying father instructed the men to either marry his daughters themselves when they came of age or else find them suitable husbands among their acquaintance. The older brother treats his ward indulgently, allows her ample freedom, and makes it clear that she may marry whomever she chooses when the time comes. The younger brother, determined to marry his ward himself, keeps her under lock and key and does not trust her out of his sight. A young man who lives nearby sees the girl and falls in love with her before he even has the chance to exchange a word with her. She returns his love and, driven to heights of desperation and ingenuity by her incarceration, contrives to use her guardian as a go-between to inform her young suitor of the state of her feelings. In a bravado act of deception, the young people are wed, with the over-protective guardian himself unwittingly procuring the magistrate and notary to solemnize the match. The other sister declares her eternal fidelity to the older brother, whose more relaxed approach to his office is thus vindicated.

Mahon transported the action from seventeenth-century Paris to present-day Ireland. He acknowledges that in his approach to the play 'There were shadows of Seamus Heaney's idea of Ireland as female and England as masculine.'[32] He had originally planned to set the play in the late 1960s, with the young people as 'gentle hippies':

I liked the idea of May, 1968, partly because there was this background of student revolt and educational reform (educational theory is an important theme in the play), but more particularly because that student revolt, ancient history though it seems now, had interesting side-effects in Ireland. There was 'student unrest' everywhere then—in New York, Berlin—and eventually, in 1969, there was student unrest in Belfast and Derry. The young became political, *seriously* so, and heads got broken: the rest we know.[33]

The directors of the Field Day production, however, insisted that they wanted the show to be immediate rather than nostalgic, and the youths in *High Time* became punks instead.

Mahon modernized various details—references to styles of dress, for example, and social relationships (servants metamorphosed into friends and flatmates). He Anglicized the names of the characters— Sganarelle, the strict guardian, became Tom; his brother, Ariste, Archie; Valère, the young suitor, Val; his man Ergaste, Ernie; Ariste's ward, Léonor, Helen; her woman Lisette, Liz; and the stifled ward, Isabelle, Isabel. One or two jokes that were no doubt amusing to Molière's contemporaries but would have elicited blank stares in present-day Ireland were dropped. Otherwise, Mahon followed closely *The School for Husbands*.

A comparison of *High Time* with a prose translation by Allan Clayson reveals how Mahon updates the play while remaining within the confines of Molière's scenario. In one scene, Valère, trying to strike up a conversation with Sganarelle, asks him whether he has heard the latest gossip from court and, when that does not work, follows up with, 'Surely you're going to see the fireworks display in honour of the birth of our Dauphin?'[34] In *High Time*, Val strolls up to Tom and says, 'who do you think'll win the Cup?'

(Mahon, 24). Where Clayson's Isabelle pretends that Valère has sent her a box with a letter inside 'folded the way love-letters usually are' (Clayson, 70), Mahon's Isabel flourishes 'an immense, elaborate Valentine envelope' (Mahon, stage direction, 29). Clayson renders one of Lisette's lines thus:

I find the way you treat her shocking. Anyone would think we were a lot of Turks to keep our women locked up like this. They say the Turks keep their women locked up like slaves, and that's why they've angered the Lord. (Clayson, 58–9)

Mahon's Liz says,

> Why all the argument, for Jesus' sake?
> (*to* ISABEL)
> You'd think you were in some place like Iraq
> to be locked up and let out, by his grace,
> once daily, with a veil over your face.
> (Mahon, 17)

The effect is brisk and funny, while conveying more exactly than a reference to 'Turks' the sense of the original.

'Sake'—'Iraq' is only one of many outrageous rhymes among hundreds of what the *Irish Times* critic termed 'unheroic couplets'.[35] Tom tells Val

> she's more than just my ward. It's her good fortune
> to be my *wife* before the end of June.
> (Mahon, 28)

Mahon frequently splits contractions for the sake of the rhyme, as in Val's

> I think she's been entirely fair, and I
> 'll go now and set her mind at rest. Goodbye.
> (Mahon, 46)

Sometimes the rhyme depends on the deformation of words or a Northern Irish accent, or both:

> VAL. Who told you, sir, of this new subterfyoosh?
> TOM. Isabel; let's not beat about the bush.
> (Mahon, 41)

These sorts of rhymes are introduced for deliberate comic effect, but they do not dominate the script.

Mahon does not force rhyme where doing so would distort the meaning. A large proportion of his couplets, particularly in the more important speeches, rely on near-rhymes or similar consonant sounds only. Liz taunts Tom with the lines

> Anyway, do you think all your precautions
> would hold us if we started having notions?
> When a girl gets an idea in her skull
> the wisest man's no better than a fool.
> These chains are the result of cowardice;
> better for you to put your trust in *us*.
> Our instinct is to fight back, and the bloke
> who ties us down is risking his own neck.
>
> (Mahon, 17)

Archie approves her sentiments, warning his brother that

> Vigilance, locked doors and constricted lives
> don't make obedient girls or virtuous wives;
> only good faith can hold them to their trust,
> not the intransigence they see in *us*.
> Frankly, a woman who maintained discretion
> under duress would be a strange creation:
> we can't control their movements step by step;
> to win their hearts and minds is our one hope.
>
> (Mahon, 17)

In both speeches there is an underlying sense of pattern that avoids being overwhelming. The verse never becomes sing-song; audience members would not be so carried away by the music of the lines that they would forget to listen to what the characters were actually saying. Instead, they would learn to listen for the rhyme without necessarily expecting to hear it every time.

Without sacrificing meaning, Mahon does manage to find a remarkable number of full and fresh rhymes. After Tom 'returns' the unopened valentine (really a love-letter from Isabel) he comes back to see how Val is taking the rejection and to rub it in:

> but you see how your advances are received;
> she's unimpressed, indeed distinctly peeved.
> Believe me, it's a waste of time; she knows
> fine words butter no parsnips, nor weird clothes.
>
> (Mahon, 35)

The virtuosity of Mahon's technique is displayed most clearly in exchanges between characters, sometimes several lines long, in which he expertly fits short questions and answers into the overall pattern of his rhythm and rhyme. When Archie announces that it is not his intention to restrict Helen's freedom even if she does decide to marry him, Tom is incredulous:

TOM
Will you allow her still to wear
those frightful clothes, and do *that* to her hair?

ARCHIE
Of course.

TOM
And run around, like a half-wit,
to pubs and discos?

ARCHIE
If she wishes it.

TOM
You'll let her boyfriends in the house?

ARCHIE
I will.

TOM
To smoke their cannibis and drink their fill?

ARCHIE
Sure.

TOM
And you won't mind if they flirt with her?

ARCHIE
Not in the least.

TOM
So, you'll put up with their
impertinent calls, as if you were their friend?

ARCHIE
Certainly.

TOM
You must be round the bend.
(Mahon, 19–20)

In the Field Day production, the same actors took roles in both Paulin's play and *High Time*. The cross-casting is indicative of the parallels Field Day wished to suggest between the tragedy and the comedy. Stephen Rea played Creon and Tom, Veronica Quilligan Antigone and Isabel, and Hilary Reynolds took the part of her sister in both plays. *High Time* was directed for Field Day by Mark Long and Emil Wolk, both known for a highly physical type of theatre. Long was one of the founders of the People Show in 1966 and had been travelling all over the world with it ever since. Wolk had been with the People Show for the previous eight years, but prior to that he had worked with a circus family and a Romanian tumbler and studied mime with the teacher of Marcel Marceau.[36] The production they designed for Field Day reflected their experience. They embellished on the script in countless ways, adding a backstage counterpart to Molière's world and interpolating scenes for which one searches in vain in the published script. All of this was enhanced by music composed and played by Keith Donald, a saxophonist with the Irish band Moving Hearts, who had also provided incidental music for *The Communication Cord*.

Contemporary reviews provide hints as to what Field Day's audiences actually heard and saw. The *Guardian*'s Michael Billington reported that the directors

usher us right away into a louche backstage world (reminiscent of the Marx Brothers) where the voracious star lures girls into his dressing room, where an actress only goes out with actors who've got big parts and where the whole cast is likely to lapse into the Madison.[37]

A reviewer for the *Galway Advertiser* wrote,

Every device is used to highlight Molière's conversations: the phone, the car, the gymnasium, the garden; one stunt excels the other, and the whole thing becomes alive and is highlighted by modern disco music, lighting and dress.[38]

Another critic noted that 'the girls have some wild adventures in a club, in a restaurant, in a night-time garden with a hilarious balcony scene, and in a day-time garden'.[39]

A writer for *North* expressed the view that Mahon's script 'plays a discordant second fiddle to the glaring, protuberant set-pieces and the blaring, mottled costumery. Forty per cent Godawful slapstick, sixty per cent genuinely maverick refractory comic lambence.'[40] Michael Coveney echoed this estimate of the percentage of hits and misses among the 'veritable battery of sight gags, scenic jokes and unruly asides' but took a more tolerant view of what he called 'an exhilarating attempt to marry the purely visual world of the People Show to the textual satire of Molière'. In his opinion, 'It very nearly comes off.'[41] In a programme note, Mark Long justified the treatment that he and his partner had given the play:

Molière's company, the Illustre Théâtre, had to adapt continually to the differing natures of the spaces they played in. The company's material changed from day to day as the cast reacted to the social and political nuances of any particular place or time. The plays we have received as written by Molière are purely texts taken down by scribes on a particular evening. They do not reflect the continually changing nature of the work, a process that added so much to its comedy. It is this original flux of feeling that we are trying to recapture.[42]

Mahon, for his part, admitted that he was surprised on opening night: 'I'd seen various parts in the script where a bit of fun could be had guying the rhymes. . . . But I'd no idea they'd do with it what they did. They took it way over the top. I was completely taken aback.' Nevertheless, he conceded, 'It all works marvellously well. If Molière were alive today it's the sort of thing he might have done. It's impossible in this day and age to deliver verse drama with a straight face.'[43]

Most of the critics agreed with him. Lynda Henderson, editor of *Theatre Ireland*, thought *High Time* was the best thing from a theatrical standpoint that Field Day had yet done. The play, she observed, 'manages to deliver the statutory Field Day message of political import—here a warning of the destructive consequences of a siege mentality (Ulster protestants, take note)—in a highly entertaining and light handed form'.[44] David Nowlan felt that 'It doesn't all quite hang together, but here is a crack theatre company revelling in sheer theatricality, and to hilarious effect,' and Colm Cronin agreed that the acting was 'hamming of the most professional order'.[45] Fintan O'Toole remarked that the 'artificial style' of Long and Wolk was 'a kind of modern equivalent of the stylisation that Molière himself would have employed, and their production is entirely in keeping with the playfulness of Mahon's brilliant translation'.[46] The *New Galway Observer* informed its readers that those looking for a good night out would probably prefer the 1984 programme to *Boesman and Lena*:

Field Day's last visit was with a very bleak South African play which caused quite a few whispers when one of its cast, an old, dirty tramp made his entrance very slowly through the audience, for all the world like a curious vagrant strolling in off the street. But the menu this time 'round is much more lively, and colourful with two one-act plays sprinkled with frolics, jokes, music, dance and acrobatics.[47]

In general, *High Time* received better reviews than *The Riot Act*, although critics tended to expend more time and space in discussing the latter.[48] That was probably to be expected, since most people find comedy inherently more enjoyable than tragedy. The political inflections of *High Time* were also less obvious, and the production gave a clearer impression of existing simply as an end in itself. As a writer for the *Northern Constitution* put it:

Molière would have thoroughly approved an iconoclasm which never concealed love. Thoroughly enjoyable.

The adaptation of Antigone presented altogether more problems. . . .

It wasn't Sophocles liberated into the modern milieu, it was Sophocles chained to a rather ugly parish pump.[49]

The reviewer for the *Sunday Press* declared, 'Nobody with a sense of humour could resist the second part of the programme, but the first is a near-disaster which I think will only be approved by northerners or those closely involved with the northern political situation.'[50] 'Last Tuesday's performance at Enniskillen High School, adapted by Tom Paulin, from a Greek tragedy, could have been a tragedy for Field Day's popularity with Fermanagh audiences,' announced Chris Donegan in the *Impartial Reporter*.

What redeemed Field Day and probably assured its continued support by Fermanagh theatre-goers was the second play, *High Time*; living up to its title for both the audience and cast. . . .

Field Day would do well to remember its audience and the need to be entertained.[51]

The more sophisticated critics went beyond contrasting the two halves of the double-bill in order to consider how they worked together. Fintan O'Toole remarked that

Though they are theatrically the starkest contrast imaginable, the two halves of Field Day's new production have a certain thematic coherence. If *The Riot Act*, based on Sophocles' *Antigone*, is essentially about the self-destructiveness of excessive severity, *High Time*, based on Molière's *The School for Husbands* repeats as comedy what we have already seen as tragedy. But *High Time* gains considerably more from the association than *The Riot Act* does. . . .

[The fact that the same actors play Tom-Creon and Isabel-Antigone] gives an unconscious sense of substance to a production that is a delight of lunacies, full of style and exuberance and riotous humour.[52]

For David Nowlan, the production neatly captured 'the built-in conflicts of the purposes of this fine company. It is a double bill, half sermon and half frolic, half relevant and half sheer entertainment, all stylish and ever so slightly out of kilter.'[53] Lynda Henderson mischievously observed that

At a philosophical level, there is an extent to which the two adaptations cancel each other out. The message of *The Riot Act* is, 'what will be, will be', where *High Time* takes a more positive stance in its concluding address to the audience: 'If you have any bossy husbands, send them to us and we'll sort them out'. As has become usual with Field Day, the line upon which they stand is (deliberately?) left obscure and their audience is unsure as to what, if any, action is being called for.[54]

Colm Cronin also wanted to know what it all had to do with Field Day's lofty aspirations:

even allowing for the frothy fun of *High Time*, it struck me that a company, which set out to create a consciousness of itself as a movement involved not just in theatre but also in the life of the country, had gone off the rails even before this tour began. If this trend continues it will not even merit a footnote in the history books—*Translations* apart.[55]

In 1984 the directors of Field Day themselves had to decide whether, as Julie Barber, the company's administrator, put it, the whole thing was 'still a viable venture or not'. Finance was as much of a problem as ever. A complete tour cost at that time £100,000, and the company was operating with a deficit of £20,000. Sixty per cent of Field Day's funding still came from the two Arts Councils on an equal basis, but as Field Day looked to the future it was launching a more concerted campaign for corporate patronage, with large businesses and cultural organizations being asked to consider pledging fixed amounts of money for three years at a time.[56] In August, the Derry branch of the Bank of Ireland had become the first 'Corporate Patron' of Field Day with a cheque for £500 and a promise of the same for the next two years.[57] It was joined by the Allied Irish Bank, the American-Irish Foundation, and the Ireland Fund by the time the programme for the 1984 tour was printed.

Barber reported that, after discussing Field Day's general situation, the directors had decided that 'there was no doubt that the company is a going concern and they wanted to stick with it'.[58] As its fifth anniversary came and went, Field Day announced its plans for the next five years. Barber's position had finally been made a year-round, full-time one, and she would be overseeing development for the group. The directors had commissioned plays from Stewart Parker and Thomas Kilroy and chosen a theme—the Protestant idea of liberty—for the next set of Field Day pamphlets. They also had long-term plans to publish a major anthology of Irish writing. There was talk of Van Morrison, the Belfast rock musician, recording for Field Day, and Friel was hopeful that the company would soon be able to tour two or even three plays in a year. Field Day's first five years were not going to be its last.

Conclusion
Five Years of Field Day—
Fifth Province or Fifth Column?

BY 1985 Field Day was no longer a daring and precarious experiment but an established part of the Irish cultural landscape. With six theatrical productions, six pamphlets, and a book of poetry to its credit the company had come of age, and, rather than simply reviewing individual plays or publications, critics began attempting to impose some pattern on the group's activities as a whole. Seamus Deane's query 'What is Field Day?' had been premature in 1981. Now, after the company had had five years in which to define itself, critics around Ireland addressed themselves to this question. Since 1980, three tensions latent in the project since its inception had become more apparent. The most basic fault line was that between art and criticism. By 1985 this split was most clearly reflected in the difference between Field Day plays and Field Day pamphlets, but it was also evident in statements by the directors, in interviews and programme notes, about the company. Such off-stage comments highlighted the difficult issue of 'Field Day' versus the individuals who direct it. This problem was exacerbated as more directors became visibly involved through the publishing wing, and it was clear by this time that Field Day had not been able for long to transcend sectarian politics. These three tensions—between the artistic and the critical impulses within Field Day, between individual directors and the group, and inherent in Field Day's desire to articulate a Northern voice in Irish cultural politics without being regarded as simply a northern nationalist voice—underlay discussion of the company as it completed its fifth year.

John Gray, in the *Linen Hall Review*, was one of the first to question the connection between Field Day's publishing and its theatrical work. The company's founders, apparently, were not in agreement themselves about what the combination of two such different activities under the same umbrella might mean for Field Day. Rea, he reported, believed that the pamphlets 'release the theatrical side of Field Day from being overtly political'. Friel saw their value in 'opening debate' but acknowledged that 'a vision is not best articulated in this form', saying that 'if there is any political spillage from the one to the other it is going to come from the pamphlets'.[1]

Some 'spillage' might also have been expected from disquisitions by directors on the subject of Field Day's mission. One of these was offered around the same time by Seamus Deane, who, charac-teristically, attempted to explain the relationship between Field Day's social criticism and its drama in more programmatic terms:

What Field Day is saying is based on two things: (1) That the existing political arrangements on this island have only a very limited future; (2) That in the present interval, before the formal changes take place, that we should in some way try to re-member, re-understand a very complex heritage which has been simplified and reduced into sectional and sectarian patterns. That's in theory, and you can see it in practice in the Field Day plays.[2]

We are at liberty to question this description of the partnership. Theatre and polemics work by different means to different ends. Whereas plays suggest, pamphlets assert and thus, in a divided society such as that of Northern Ireland, may appear more confron-tational than challenging.

Here, again, the question of audience is crucial. A driving force behind the decision of Friel and Rea to start the company was a populist desire to bring quality theatre to as many people around Ireland as possible, and Field Day had succeeded in the intervening years in mounting five professional tours which included places like Maghera and Tralee along with Derry, Dublin, and Belfast. The pamphlets, on the other hand, were written by and for an academic clique. The arguments advanced in them were often reworkings of articles the writers had previously published and which therefore had been current in intellectual circles for several years before Field Day came into existence. The publishing side of the company was merely one more forum to add to publications such as *The Crane Bag* and the Lyric Theatre's *Threshold*, but marshalling such essays together under the Field Day aegis gave the pamphlet series the spurious appearance of a party platform. This impression was reinforced by the fact that the first six pamphlets came from a broadly similar, and basically nationalist, point of view. By the time the third set of pamphlets on *The Protestant Idea of Liberty* was published in 1985, people had already formed opinions as to where Field Day stood in political terms. We have also seen that, inasmuch as the debate over the pamphlets filtered into the popular press through book reviews and the like, it was not of a sort that was likely to make readers regard Field Day's offerings with open minds.

The company's plays were consequently being viewed more politically, so that by 1984, in a review of *High Time*, Lynda Henderson could refer to 'the statutory Field Day message of political import'.[3] One symptom of this change in focus on the company was a reappraisal of *Translations* in the light of what was seen as Field Day's later development. Received relatively uncritically in 1980, the play had since been quoted incessantly by fifth provincials and was firmly enshrined as Field Day's central text, so it was an obvious target. Brian McAvera, who identified himself as 'a Catholic born and bred in Andersonstown', reiterated historical objections to the play in the Belfast review *Fortnight* in March 1985: the Ordnance Survey, far from contributing to the erosion of Irish, actually helped to preserve much information about the language and culture of Ireland that would otherwise have been lost, and the official violence depicted in the play's ending was anachronistic.[4] McAvera argued that, far from offering a new perspective on an old problem, *Translations*

actually shores up a dangerous myth—that of cultural dispossession by the British—rather than what I take to be the historical actuality, the abandonment of the language. This obviously has political overtones and in terms of nationalism, the play worries me.

In applying *Translations*, as Deane had suggested, to the present day, he had an even bigger reservation. The characters generally assumed to have abducted and killed Yolland never appear on stage. 'Why did we never meet the Donnelly twins?' McAvera asked. In keeping the men of violence off-stage Friel, in his view, was 'carefully ignoring a crucial element in nationalism'.[5] This line of criticism was essentially the product of a reading of *Translations* by both Field Day's supporters and its detractors less as a piece of drama than as a cultural manifesto. Second thoughts about this play reflected changing public perceptions of the company as a whole.[6]

Another result of the association between Field Day's pamph-
leteering and its plays was just discernible by 1985. Tom Paulin's
The Riot Act had been the first Field Day play to be written with
the pamphlets in mind. This influence became more pronounced
after the production of Thomas Kilroy's *Double Cross* in 1986,
which had been written, as the author explained, in lieu of a
pamphlet promised but never delivered. Other instances of Field
Day's polemic insinuating itself into the company's plays would be
Friel's *Making History* (1988) and Terry Eagleton's *St Oscar*
(1989).

In addition to the tension between the Critic as Artist and the
Artist as Critic within the Field Day project, there was another rich
source of confusion about the enterprise inherent in its very nature.
The fact that the company had managed to put together theatrical
tours in five successive years in addition to issuing a series of beautifully produced pamphlets gave it a more coherent public image
than a closer examination justifies. Field Day was never more than
a loose coalition of artists dismayed by the political stalemate in
Ireland and eager to intervene in a creative fashion to try to open
people's eyes to other possibilities. Beyond pointing to this basic
common attitude, it would be extremely difficult to characterize the
Field Day directors collectively in terms that would be equally
fitting for all of them. Since each of them also has his own career
outside the company, it seems reasonable to suggest that none of
them can be taken as speaking for Field Day every time he puts pen
to paper. Ireland is so small, however, and the personalities involved with Field Day were so well known even before the foundation of the company, that the board of directors has always been
implicitly regarded in Irish intellectual circles as a Gang of Six (just
think, for example, of how often Field Day was and is referred to
as 'they' rather than 'it').

Often there is little or no distinction made between Field Day as
a corporate body, as a board of directors with limited responsibilities and aims, and the individual directors in their private and
professional lives. Thus Edna Longley, in a major essay on 'Poetry
and Politics in Northern Ireland' (1985), attempted to prove her
contention that 'Field Day itself has enacted the process whereby
political fixity shuts off imaginative possibility, the ideological tail
wags the creative dog' by arguing, in effect, that Seamus Deane
and Tom Paulin are not very good poets. That may or may not be

true, but, strictly speaking, it has very little to do with Field Day. If Longley wanted to argue that nationalist ideology had had a destructive effect upon the creative work sponsored by Field Day, she needed to find her evidence in the plays themselves, but these, apart from *Translations* and *The Communication Cord* (dismissed in one line as 'a farce which comfortably fails in its intention to subvert the pieties of *Translations*'), she did not consider at all. She discussed the pamphlets, but, with the exception of Heaney's, these are critical essays rather than works of art. Similarly, it conveyed a partial view of the company to quote Paulin on the subject of Ulster Protestantism as being representative of Field Day without at the same time mentioning David Hammond's sympathetic films on John Hewitt and other Ulster writers and artists when both Hammond and Paulin were directors of Field Day.[7]

Nevertheless, Longley's conflation of Deane, Paulin, and Field Day is readily understandable and not entirely the product of a selective reading of the company's career. By 1985 Seamus Deane, largely because he was more willing than the other directors to discuss the project in abstract terms, had become Field Day's unofficial spokesman. His opinions, consequently, were commonly taken to reflect company policy. In actual fact, the directorate was never willing (or sufficiently organized) to commit itself on paper to any clear set of aims. In the absence of an official statement of policy, individual directors parried questions about the company as they saw fit—and Deane leapt into the fray with more abandon than his colleagues.

The impact of this internal development on Field Day's reputation has proved immeasurable, because Deane is an inveterate controversialist. He is also, although he would doubtless dispute this, the deepest-dyed nationalist on the Field Day board. His political assumptions, largely unconscious, permeated his remarks on the company at this time. For example, after a talk on Field Day given by Deane in February 1985 at Magee College, the *Derry Journal* reported that

Field Day are working to achieve a sense of assent by building a sense of Irish culture which embraces all the diverse groups in the country. . . .

Field Day are hoping to show in a variety of ways how the political and cultural failure of modern Ireland inter-relate and how they adversely affect the whole people.

Professor Deane said Field Day hope to redress the present situation and begin to create the possibility of a cultural synthesis in Ireland. This is urgently needed for the kind of political settlement which will ensure that Ireland's history and future does not continue in the same tragic way.[8]

'Assent' for what? Why, a united Ireland, of course (or, in words which the readers of the *Derry Journal* would have no difficulties translating, 'the kind of political settlement which will ensure that Ireland's history and future does not continue in the same tragic way'). In another recent article quoted by Gray, Deane continued in the same vein:

the central crisis of the island has reached such an advanced stage that it seems irresponsible to avoid the opportunity to provide a sense or vision of the island's cultural integrity which would operate as a basis for an enduring and enriching political settlement.[9]

Again, to speak of the 'integrity' (wholeness) of 'the island' is clearly to come from a nationalist perspective. Whether the reader approved or disapproved of that would depend entirely on his or her own political views, but such a statement was less likely to make people consider the 'crisis' in a new light than to provoke a replay of old arguments on both sides of the nationalist/unionist divide.

A few months later, in the final issue of the *Crane Bag*, Deane participated in a round-table discussion with Jennifer Fitzgerald, Frank McGuinness, and Joan Fowler. In response to McGuinness's accusation that Field Day seemed to be over-fond of the colour green, Deane expressed the opinion that art should represent 'a rainbow', but acknowledged when pressed that Field Day had not yet managed to do that. He expounded extempore on the need to demythologize 'this society' (immediately begging the question 'which society?'—the Republic? Northern Ireland? Ireland as a whole?):

demythologise it in such a way that those sects and groupings within the society that form the basis of our disagreements also will find that there is in fact the possibility of a vision; a vision, if you like, a unity of culture, in which they all can share.[10]

Deane might have been chagrined if he stopped to remember where that last phrase originated.

Deane's various comments accentuate the most paradoxical

tension in the whole Field Day endeavour—the pursuit of an essentially political goal by non-political means. Stephen Rea in 1984 had described the company's purpose in these terms: 'What we're trying to do is build a body of work which establishes something different from the received English view and this takes time.... [W]e're trying to build a body of work removed from political action'.[11] The pamphlets project, however, had signalled an intention to deal with cultural issues in a manner more explicitly political, and the ideas disseminated in them had been widely discussed in Ireland, especially in academic circles. Assessment of Field Day on the occasion of its fifth anniversary, accordingly, focused on politics and followed a pattern established by the reception of the first two sets of pamphlets. The debate was dominated by intellectuals on both sides of the border who prided themselves on having eschewed hereditary assumptions in favour of more 'progressive' views. Now and again a doctrinaire nationalist would weigh in, but an impenetrable silence enfolded the ranks of hard-line unionism. Committed unionists evidently interpreted talk about Field Day's politics, like those of the New Ireland Forum, as a squabble within nationalism and, as such, of little interest to them.

At the centre of debate about Field Day at this time was the idea of the 'fifth province'. Shortly before Field Day began its fifth tour, Brian Friel elaborated upon the purposes of the company in terms similar to those he had used in 1982:

We're a Northern accented group . . . with a strong political element (small p) and that would concern itself with some sense of disaffection most of us would feel at the state of two nations, which is strongly reflected in the work we are doing this year. I would say that all six of us are not at home in Northern Ireland and indeed all six would probably not be at home in the 26 counties.

We appropriated (from Richard Kearney) the phrase 'Fifth Province', which may well be a province of the mind, through which we hope to devise another way of looking at Ireland, or another possible Ireland, and this really is the pursuit of the company. . . .

Field Day is a forum where a more generous and noble notion of Irishness than the narrow inherited one can be discussed.[12]

The following year, Friel defined the fifth province as 'a place for dissenters, traitors to the prevailing mythologies in the other four provinces'.[13]

Opinion was sharply divided as to whether or not Field Day had succeeded in distancing itself equally from all the 'prevailing mythologies'. Edna Longley, for instance, declared that she was opposed, not to the 'admirable notion' of the fifth province, but to

the Field Day version, and its acceptance as the genuine article. . . .

It is pointless to forge a new conscience of the race without putting the entire *fourth* province on the anvil. And might not 'the fifth province' be Scotland or Dalriada?[14]

Longley's objections testify to the fact that, by 1985, the fifth province was disputed territory. Moreover, rhetorically at least, it had been effectively annexed by liberal nationalists. As Frank Callanan cynically observed in *New Hibernia*,

For the new nationalist intelligentsia, identity crises are de rigueur as each writer strives autobiographically to enact the national travail. . . .

The taking of the oath of allegiance to the 'fifth province' is, like the identity crisis, de rigueur. The 'fifth province' is perhaps the most characteristic contrivance of the neo-nationalist idiom—a new frontier of the intelligentsia, a never-never land between politics and imagination.[15]

The word 'revisionist' was overtaken by a like fate, though from a different quarter. It had, by this time, become a kind of shorthand for 'anti-nationalist'.[16]

Longley's commentary on Field Day is of particular interest because, on the face of it, she had a great deal in common with the Field Day directors. Like them, she was a perennial outsider. Her father left the Catholic Church to teach at Trinity College, Dublin, then still subject to the Catholic Hierarchy's ban on what was considered a Protestant institution, and Longley herself attended TCD, where she met her husband, the poet Michael Longley. They moved to Belfast, Michael's native city, when she accepted a lectureship at Queen's University. Longley had lived there ever since, but she would always be a foreigner of sorts because she came from the Republic and suspect in some quarters because she instinctively assumed an all-Ireland context in her own work.[17]

Behind Longley's attacks on Field Day was her sense of frustration at having constantly to re-establish her credentials to speak as an Irish person.[18] She divined in the attitude of the Field Day directors a variant of

the Republican viewpoint from which history stands still: that refuses to accept the internal Northern vendetta as at least a variation on the old colonial theme, that writes Northern Protestants out of history unless prepared to go back and start again in 1798.[19]

Longley herself was more comfortable with ambiguities. She asked, quite reasonably, why Northern Irish identity had to be either Irish or British rather than both. With reference to Heaney's pamphlet she wrote,

Nobody doubts Heaney's Irishness. But his or Field Day's exclusive insistence, like the triumphalism which wants Londonderry to obliterate Derry and now vice versa, denies other contexts which his poetry nourishes and which nourish it. Ulster poets have been appearing for years in anthologies of English, Irish and British poetry. The confusion is perhaps more accurate than any attempt to tidy it up.[20]

In her *Crane Bag* essay, Longley castigates Field Day for renovating nationalist myths. She begins with the ringing declaration that 'Poetry and politics, like church and state, should be separated.' By the next sentence, however, it emerges that it is not politics *per se* that she is worried about, but 'ideologies'. Moreover, since 'nobody can accuse Unionism of being an inspiration to poets', in practice what she criticizes is any conjunction of nationalism and poetry. If Conor Cruise O'Brien in warning against the 'unhealthy intersection' of literature and politics was more worried about the effect on politics, Longley is equally concerned about the effect on literature. She argues in this article that when poets such as Heaney, Paulin, Deane, and John Montague succumb to nationalist sentiments this has a deleterious effect on their creative processes. At times, however, her own anti-nationalism (which should not be confused with unionism) distorts her critical perceptions.

She uses *Translations* as a starting point for her argument. Referring to the much-quoted speech about the need to renew images of the past in order to keep from fossilizing, she submits that

The play does not so much examine myths of dispossession and oppression as repeat them. . . .

Friel . . . translates contemporary Northern Catholic feeling into historical terms. He does this very well. But the play is partly 'fossilised' because he explores the ethos of a particular community exclusively in relation to British dominion over the native Irish. . . . *Translations* refurbishes an old myth.[21]

This overview misses much of the point of the play. It makes no mention of the play's success as a piece of drama, concentrating instead on its supposed political subtext. On that score *Translations* is, in part, about the conflict of native Irish and imported English culture, but not 'exclusively'. It is just as much, if not more, about the tension between old and new modes of self-definition within Ireland itself, with the characters of Owen, Hugh, and Manus at the centre of this interpretation. It is this theme that connects it with the rest of Friel's work, from *Philadelphia, Here I Come!* to *The Mundy Scheme* and *The Gentle Island* to *Aristocrats* and *The Communication Cord*.

Within the nationalist tradition, Friel was actually overturning an old myth—that Irish speech and writing, minus the Irish language, must be forever handicapped in relation to England. This is the apprehension that Joyce plays with in the famous exchange between Stephen Dedalus and the dean of studies and that Seamus Deane tacitly endorses in his 1975 essay, 'Irish Poetry and Irish Nationalism' (mentioned by Longley). In that article Deane had asserted that

In Ireland, the problem of language as used by Irish writers is not in the end separable from the problem of the Irish language. A place deprived of its speech is rendered deaf to its traditions. . . . This perhaps explains the fondness of Irish writers for translations, adaptations, renovated versions of some of the more famous Gaelic lyrics and epics. It also reminds us again that the movement towards identity in politics and literature was associated with a movement for the recovery of the old language. The recovery of Irish is part of the dream of total nationhood. In its inevitable imperfection Irish writers in English can never entirely overcome the language problem.[22]

Translations was inspirational to the artists who later made up the Field Day board because it acknowledged the impossibility of returning to some pristine Gaelic past while at the same time affirming the hope that Irish people could make of the English language a 'new home'. Friel in effect replaced Deane's 'never' with 'maybe, sometime'. It is relatively easy for Edna Longley or another critic from a non-nationalist background to say and believe that it does not make that much difference whether Irish writers use Irish or English. For someone like Brian Friel to hint that the language shift might not be a permanent disability is altogether more significant. It is also worth noting that, although it had produced translations and versions in plenty, Field Day had not generally looked for its material to 'the more famous Gaelic lyrics and epics', although this was a choice available to the directors. Instead, its plays had come from Russia, Ancient Greece, France—but filtered through the rhythms of contemporary Irish speech.

Old-fashioned nationalist critics objected to this forward-looking current in the Field Day enterprise. In the same issue of the *Crane Bag* in which Longley's article appeared was another one by Nina Witoszek and Pat Sheeran expressing impatience with the cultural criticism exemplified by that journal and the Field Day pamphleteers which seemed to them to call for a break with the past and tradition in order to create a new, modern, European culture in Ireland. The writers objected to the way trendy critics wanted to put the blame for Ireland's problems on Irish people instead of where it belonged—on England. Like Longley, they resented the 'reductionist view of Yeats' promulgated by Kearney, Kiberd, and Deane, but for a different reason. They proposed that rather than abandoning the Romantic agenda Ireland should complete it, thus 'turning our anachronisms to a virtue'. This scheme was later enthusiastically endorsed by Desmond Fennell, a self-proclaimed anti-revisionist and former ideological adviser to Provisional Sinn Féin.[23]

That Field Day was attacked both for being nationalist and for being anti-nationalist was a positive sign in so far as it proved that the company was raising questions generally, but the fact that the debate had narrowed so quickly to the old terms indicated that Field Day was losing the moral and artistic high ground. Moreover, the emphasis on the unionist–nationalist divide meant that the controversy joined by the company was starting to seem more and more outmoded to commentators in the Republic, where unionism was a dead letter. Social critics there were asking other questions. For example, Fintan O'Toole, in a review of the second set of pamphlets, remarked:

The Field Day movement spawned by six northern intellectuals has dominated the debate about Irish identity in recent years . . . and they have, naturally, stated the question in the terms in which it is understood in the North—the old Anglo-Irish question—rather than the newer, more difficult, Irish-American question which is in many ways more relevant to the South.[24]

Similarly, the playwright Frank McGuinness confessed in 1985 that

I'm a bit worried about the neglect of diversities other than the Catholic-Protestant/Nationalist-Unionist ones in Field Day: the diversities between the needs of men and the needs of women, between the needs not simply of rich and poor, but within the middle class, and of the homosexual and the heterosexual. I feel a sense of comfort about Field Day: it is in danger of repeating itself.[25]

Not surprisingly, given its Northern slant and outlook, Field Day provoked the most heated arguments in its home territory. Perhaps it is also not very surprising that whether one saw Field Day as 'nationalist' or 'revisionist' appeared to depend largely on one's own background and political views.

One of the most measured contemporary explorations of the Field Day phenomenon came from John Wilson Foster in an address to the International Association for the Study of Anglo-Irish Literature at its meeting in Belfast that July.[26] As an Ulster Protestant based in Canada, Foster, along with the Field Day directors and Edna Longley, spoke both as an insider and an outsider about Northern Ireland. He sensed in the province at that time 'reversion, the return to respective corners, the equivalent in the intellectual sphere of that increasing polarisation we are witnessing in the political sphere' (47). Citing most of the Field Day pamphlets as 'chromatic and resourceful' 'variations on the nationalist theme' (45), Foster mentioned on the other side a collection of essays on the Protestant imagination in Ireland edited by Longley and Gerald Dawe (to which he himself had contributed) and, further along the Protestant spectrum, the historical work of Ian Adamson (47). These, said Foster, were the productions of 'the New Partisans: inheritors of a cultural identity and political stance pulling them one way, but academic practitioners of a discipline whose various imperatives and currencies pull them, by gravity of intellect, another way' (39).

In presenting his case he used the Field Day pamphlets as examples, looking in most detail at Deane's *Heroic Styles*, Kiberd's *Anglo-Irish Attitudes*, and the recently published *Liberty and Authority in Ireland* by Robert McCartney, the only Field Day pamphleteer to write from a unionist point of view.[27] Each, he said, proved his contention that political prejudice prevented critical thinking on the North. In the pamphlets of Kiberd, Deane, and

Paulin, for instance, the 'subtext' of 'repudiation of the political union of Great Britain and Northern Ireland' is at war with the logic of the text itself:

Deane's argument points us towards anti-nationalism, Kiberd's towards an undefined British federalism. Paulin's points us towards partition or UDI as convincingly as towards Irish federalism. . . . The moment at which the subtext threatens to surface is rather like the turn in a sonnet. In each case there is a brilliant octave on English-Irish cultural relations, followed by a disappointing sestet when Ulster is contemplated. Criticism flounders when political discourse subverts the splendidly deployed critical discourse of the octave (45).

Foster's own political position might best be described as contingent unionism. Unlike Longley, he urged the avoidance of politics more as a matter of policy than of principle, believing that to promote unity before there had been adequate cultural preparation would be to invite civil war:

'Culture, not politics' ought to be one of our slogans, 'Criticism, not politics' another, each implying the strategic pretence that these are separable activities. By politics I mean political and constitutional scenarios, prescriptions, blueprints, programmes—and an uncritical contempt for 'the other side'. We simply do not know enough at present to prescribe or forecast the political future of Ireland, certainly not an imminent united Ireland. . . .

To those of us who wish to see a unified Ireland, it is an immense but necessary forbearance for us to accept, as accept I believe we must, words borrowed by Arnold from another context: the existing order of things till right is ready (46, 55).

Despite Foster's use of the first person in this context, Joe McMinn, in an article for *Fortnight*, had no qualms about condemning him as a unionist 'begrudger'. McMinn answered the allegation that Field Day was nationalist by indirectly allowing that it was, but arguing that that was not necessarily a bad thing in and of itself:

Far from being a mystifying ideology, the language of contemporary Irish nationalism is critical and self-critical. Field Day is a cultural effect of that process of political self-examination, which is attributable to the present 'Troubles'.[28]

He believed that criticisms of Field Day's politics by the likes of Foster and Longley were 'themselves concealed political objections' because to advocate 'an apolitical analysis of Irish culture which will be sensible, moderate, rational, detached, unemotional, dispassionate, is to take up a political position without naming it. It is an extension of unionist political values into the cultural arena.'[29]

McMinn himself exposed the absurdity of this suggestion by going on to argue that nationalism is not necessarily irrational and unionism is not necessarily sensible:

It is usually assumed that 'nationalist' in the Irish context refers to Republicans, since they're the ones with the historical hang-ups about identity, flags, myths etc. But unionism, as a form of British patriotism, would be hard beat for its nationalist fervour. If 'nationalism' does mean 'republicanism', then I would suggest that it has developed a far greater degree of self-criticism, internationalism and secularisation than has unionism.[30]

Unionism has often taken the form of extreme British nationalism, but where does that leave Longley, Foster, and the others convicted on the basis of their 'sensible' approach? If the 'rational' criterion is accepted after all, would McMinn have been prepared to defend it in the case of Ian Paisley? Keenly aware of a spectrum of political opinion within 'nationalism', McMinn seemed to forget that a similar range of views exists on the other side.

Longley's response, in the next issue, demonstrated that she was subject to similar lapses of memory. She ably defended herself with the rejoinder that 'All that does not espouse romantic or unromantic republicanism, or regard 1798 as a viable working model for the future, is not *ipso facto* "unionist"—the unspeakable slur insinuated by Dr. McMinn.' When she turned to Field Day, however, she professed herself unable to see any difference between what the directors were saying and what ethnic nationalists had said at the turn of the century, complaining that its 'cultural politics' had already received 'attention somewhat in excess of their novelty. (For ancestral voices, see Daniel Corkery and D. P. Moran.)' She went on to suggest that the company was the voice of unreconstructed Irish nationalism: 'Indeed, Field Day may have been founded in reaction against what its members see as forms of historical and cultural "revisionism", particularly in the Republic.'[31]

Longley's attempt to set Field Day in opposition to the more self-critical currents in Irish intellectual life ignored the company's real efforts to arrive at some new and more open understanding of Land, Faith, and Nation (Corkery's three pillars of Irishness) in contemporary Ireland. Hers was not the only letter that *Fortnight* received in response to McMinn's article. Pádraig Ó Conchúir wrote that 'It was surprising to learn from your 9 September edition reviewers that the Field Day pamphlets are faulted for being nationalist. From the overall series I gained the impression of an Alliance-style quiescence.'[32] Field Day and Longley herself were trying in their different ways to move beyond stale arguments about who was more or less 'Irish'. Arguments about who is more or less 'revisionist' are not really any more illuminating.

I began with the suggestion that Field Day was one example of a more general attempt by Northern writers and artists to escape the confines of sectarian politics. The foundation of the company was *ad hoc*, its beginnings haphazard, but from the start Brian Friel and Stephen Rea tried to cultivate a sense of local attachment that might override the touchy issue of national allegiance. At the same time they hoped, by subtly emphasizing their Irishness along with their northernness, to encourage this identification in the minds of their audience. After the addition of the board of directors Field Day became increasingly self-conscious, and with the publication of the pamphlets its politics grew more overt. This development within the company itself was reflected in the public perception of it.

In 1980 the new company had been warmly welcomed by both communities in the North, who were equally embarrassed about the bloody reputation the province had acquired in Ireland and the rest of the world. By 1985, however, Field Day had come to be identified more closely with the minority, traditionally nationalist, community in the North. This was due more to the company's off-stage activities than to its theatrical productions. The inauguration of the pamphlet series and the repeated insistence of the directors, in interviews and programme notes, that they worked and thought in an all-Ireland context created the impression that they spoke as nationalists.

The perception of Field Day as a nationalist conspiracy focused on the fact that the directors regarded the whole of Ireland as a cultural unit (and some of them were on record as favouring its integration as a political unit as well) but was apt to overlook their aversion to other pieties of traditional nationalism. As Northerners, they were aware of varieties of Irish experience and outlook that citizens of the Republic had been able to ignore. Although none of them could be described as unionist, the Field Day directors found many attitudes in the South equally repellant. Furthermore, because they were trying to articulate something that they saw as new, it was vital to their aims that they not be identified with either of the old cultural/political positions in the North. Once they were seen to belong primarily to one side or the other their ability to change people's minds would be weakened.

To a certain extent, regrettably, this is what happened. Examination of the discussion about Field Day in 1985 reveals that within five years of its foundation the company was effectively regarded as a nationalist organization, albeit an enlightened one—a cultural analogue of the SDLP. At least part of the blame for this belongs to the directors themselves and their tendency to talk about what they were doing rather than letting the work speak for itself. Art and criticism were competing on the Field Day board, and the latter too often won out over the reservations of the former. The company might have had a better chance of influencing a cross-section of opinion in the North in this period if it had more consistently respected the wisdom of Seamus Heaney's dictum that 'It isn't the business of the germ to explain but to get on with the disease.'[33]

This labelling, however, although sometimes apparently justified by comments by individual directors or ill-considered remarks in pamphlets, may also be traced to a failure of imagination on the part of their critics. When faced with a cultural and political stance that was avowedly not unionist, they were apt to dismiss the whole project as 'nationalist' as if that were all that needed to be said about it. Field Day, in turn, adopted a defensive attitude toward these commentators, too often assuming that if someone was not for the company he or she must be against it.[34]

Above all, the peculiarities of the Northern situation itself were responsible for the rapid slotting of Field Day into a familiar political category. Field Day was gesturing in the direction of something for which there was, as yet, no name. The only politics that have any reality in Northern Ireland are the old politics of polarity, and the constitutional question continued to intrude itself at every opportunity. Field Day was not unionist, therefore it must be nationalist—its more persistent critics were not nationalists, ergo they must be unionists.

Neither of these assumptions stands up to scrutiny. Edna Longley, for example, was no more a 'unionist' than Field Day was 'nationalist' as those terms had been understood in Northern Ireland. Both operated in the grey area between the real ideologues on either side. Nevertheless, what should by the logic of almost all concerned have been a mapping of potential common ground would too often in the next five years look more like a struggle for possession of it.

Postscript
The Field Day Anthology of Irish Writing

THE present study has focused almost exclusively on the first five years of Field Day's existence, in the belief that those five years established features of and contradictions within the company that would continue to be prominent in future years. In the Conclusion I examined three tensions latent in the Field Day project five years after its inception: that between the artistic and the critical impulses in Field Day, which might also be stated as that between the theatrical and the publishing sides of the operation; that between individual directors and the group; and that between their wish to become a Northern voice in Irish culture without being associated with either of the old sides in the province (Catholic-nationalist or Protestant-unionist) and a competing wish to articulate an enlightened version of republicanism that would confront the colonial heritage of Ireland. In the years after 1985 these would become more pronounced. When asked in 1988 what he hoped history would say about Field Day, Seamus Deane answered, 'Field Day made a contribution towards the achievement of the peaceful, nonsectarian society that emerged in Ireland somewhere in the next century'.[1] Perhaps in the next century it will be possible to say that. Unfortunately, it also fell to the company's lot to register the increasing polarization in Irish intellectual and social life through the late 1980s and early 1990s. The opportunity that had seemed to be there in 1980 for co-operation between different groupings in the North in a common cause, be it only the production of a play, had largely evaporated by 1990. By this time things had come to such a pass that Edna Longley, who should have been a natural ally, was universally acknowledged as Field Day's Official Opposition, while Charles Haughey, not exactly a symbol of the New Ireland, was eulogized by Deane as a statesman combining 'de Valera's meticulously crafted republicanism with Seán Lemass's best possible blend of cosmopolitan modernity and ancestral loyalty for present-day Ireland'.[2] It would take another volume the length of this one to discuss in detail developments between 1985 and 1993, when the Field Day directors announced a six-month 'sabbatical'.[3] Instead, I propose to look briefly at one illustrative episode: the genesis and development of and the controversy finally surrounding *The Field Day Anthology of Irish Writing*.

The notion that Ireland was in need of 'a definition, in the form of a comprehensive anthology, of what writing in this country has been for the last 300–500 years' was first suggested by Seamus Deane in his second Field Day pamphlet. He believed that a 're-vision' of 'our prevailing notion of what it is that constitutes the Irish reality' was necessary as a prelude to any sort of lasting peace in the North.[4] The direction of his thinking in 1984 is indicated by statements he made in January in the course of a conversation with Richard Kearney and Ciaran Carty that was published in the *Sunday Independent*. Deane remarked,

I think part of the tragedy that is easily missed South of the border is that the Unionist mind has been reduced by circumstances to the point where Unionism stands now as nothing more than a political position and a win-all or lose-all position. It's very hard to persuade DUP or Official Unionists that they are members of a culture which of course embodies a great deal of British culture and Scottish culture but also owes a great debt to Irish culture and to which Irish culture itself owes a great debt.

If the unionists could just be made to realize 'the depths of their own culture', Deane believed, they might learn that 'Union-ism is not just saying No Surrender'.[5] Presumably, although Deane did not say so in so many words, if the 'unionists' felt more secure in their Irish cultural heritage they would no longer see the need for political unionism. That is to say, they would cease to be unionists.

Deane was curiously reluctant to talk about 'Protestants', but surely they were the Irish people he particularly wanted and needed to reach. We have seen that an important part of Field Day's brief up until that point had been to encourage an identification with Northern Ireland and indirectly with Ireland as a whole on the part of everyone who happened to live there, as against other cultural and political affinities. This was a crucial, though tiptoed-around, element in the early conception of the anthology as well. By the beginning of 1985 Field Day was officially committed to making Deane's platonic anthology a reality. After a talk Deane gave in Derry in February the *Derry Journal* recorded that

He said that the anthology will make accessible the total range of the Irish achievement in writing and thereby give a definitive vision of an Ireland which is a secure cultural entity that can accommodate Irishmen and women of almost every persuasion.

Deane saw the Northern crisis as central to his generation's experience, forcing as it did the realization that 'A lot of notions which had previously been taken for granted had to be questioned and alternatives offered. He felt there was a need for Irish nationalism and literature to come to terms with the situation and be more accommodating and generous to the diverse groups in the island.'[6] In a description of the project written later that year, Deane declared that the anthology 'will cover 500 years of Irish writing of every kind . . . literary, political, philosophical, social and scientific . . . and from every tradition. The aim is to provide a definition of what constitutes our tradition.' John Gray noted the apparent contradiction between 'every tradition' and 'our tradition' and commented, 'Deane expresses an objective akin to that of the alchemists of old: the "aim" is to provide a view of "the continuity and coherence, of the Irish achievement in letters".'[7]

Clearly the deep structure of the anthology was to be nationalist, a generous version of nationalism which sought to include elements of Irish society (particularly Northern Protestants) who had long been excluded—or had excluded themselves—from the Irish 'nation'. At no point were the directors very specific about the nature of the shared culture that they expected the anthology to reveal, with Brian Friel remarking hopefully but vaguely in 1986 that 'Once it is put together in a form, there would be some kind of recognised sound or recognised melody.'[8] Those who did not share his assumptions about the nature of Irish culture might well wonder why he did not say 'harmony'.

Indeed, the directors themselves seemed to oscillate in their thinking between seeing Protestant-unionist culture in the North as, on the one hand, central to their own view of Ireland and a challenge to the lazy self-satisfaction of the Republic and, on the other, as altogether the antithesis of their own vision of the island. In North America, where they tended to speak more freely about the subtext of their cultural activities, the raw edges of their thinking were sometimes more obvious. Self-contradiction is clearly apparent, for example, in a statement Tom Paulin made to reporter

Geoffrey Stokes during a fund-raising tour of the United States in 1987:

we would very much welcome, actually, articulate opposition, I mean, for example, a counter Field Day which would produce its own pamphlets and plays and so on, which might come out of, would have to come out of the Unionist community though we would hope to be able to embrace the values and traditions of that community.[9]

In the same interview, Seamus Deane stated in one breath that Field Day aimed to encourage unionists to articulate 'their cultural bases, how their culture is structured, and what it is', and with the next expressed the opinion that 'they've had no need for culture because they've had so much authority, and now that they're losing authority they find they have no culture'. The answer to the vexing question of how unionists were supposed to articulate something that they did not have is implicit in Deane's concluding remark, 'we hope this anthology, in fact, will provide some illumination on the Unionist culture'.[10]

'Unionists' could hardly be blamed for wanting to look such a gift horse in the mouth. In a much more oblique prospectus circulated around the same time, Deane promised that the anthology would show 'how the various groups, sects and races which have intermingled in Ireland have produced a literature which is unique to them and an achievement which makes manifest what they have in common'.[11] Edna Longley praised these liberal intentions but pointed out that 'the anthology might just as interestingly manifest what they *don't* have in common. Unitary preconceptions or assimilative impulses ("unique to them") pre-empt the reader's own judgment.'[12] Even some of those working on the anthology had reservations about the grand overview. John Wilson Foster, who edited the contemporary fiction section, mulled over some of his doubts in an unsent letter to Seamus Deane written shortly after he was asked to participate in the assembling of the anthology. How, he wondered, could Deane be so sure that the anthology would confirm the 'cultural unity' of Ireland 'before the immense amount of stuff, chosen by divers hands, is in'. He took an example from the second volume of the anthology as already outlined by Deane to question the premisses of the undertaking:

The years 1930 to 65 are entitled *The Counter-Revival*. But those years were an attempt on the part of writers to do another thing as well as counter the Revival: they wanted to counter the Catholic State: O'Connor, O'Faolain, Wall, Kavanagh, Broderick and McGahern were more exercised about this than about the Revival, it seems to me. And even this leaves out of account those wonderful women fiction writers exercised neither about the Revival nor about the Free State—Bowen, Mary Lavin, Kathleen Coyle, Kate O'Brien, Janet McNeill: the best fiction writers in Ireland 1930–65. A subtitle like 'Provincialism and Censorship' is an academic title, not a living literary title that permits the above writers intelligible representation.[13]

Foster's main concern at that time was whether or not he would be given a free hand by Deane to make the selections he wanted in the section for which he was responsible. This concern was addressed to his satisfaction in a subsequent phone conversation with Deane, and indeed all of the many sub-editors were given a large measure of autonomy within the parameters established by Deane from the start. The issues that Foster raised at this stage, though, regarding the slant of the anthology as a whole, would be raised later by others.

In articles written as the anthology was being compiled, Deane was clearly uncomfortable with the idea that he was engaged in constructing a canon of 'Irish' literature, but he was honest enough to covertly admit on numerous occasions that that was in fact what he was doing.[14] This coy denial and admission is replicated in his introduction to the finished anthology, which was finally published in co-operation with Faber and Faber in the United Kingdom and Norton in the United States in November of 1991. He declares that 'There is no attempt here to establish a canon.' On the next page, however, he allows that 'Selection is not made from a preordained "tradition"; it is selection which ordains the tradition(s).'[15] This is a fine brief description of the process of canon-formation, something Deane denies he is doing even as he is doing it. Earlier he straightforwardly asserts that

There *is* a story here, a meta-narrative, which is, we believe, hospitable to all the micro-narratives that, from time to time, have achieved prominence as the official version of the true history, political and literary, of the island's past and present.[16]

What is this 'meta-narrative'? Oddly enough, on this point Deane is very evasive. From statements he makes elsewhere in the General

Introduction to the three volumes, however, it emerges that he sees the unifying theme of Irish literature as the story of colonialism and of nationalist resistance to it. Thus the conflicting aims of 'accommodation' and exclusion of the 'British' elements of Irish life are embodied in the conception of the Field Day anthology. True to Deane's word, the 'various groups, sects and races' of Ireland are united in a single narrative, but the narrative chosen is one that by definition emphasizes disunity and discord. The polemical slant of the anthology (which itself does in fact contain a mass of heterogeneous material, much of which would challenge Deane's central thesis) achieves one of Field Day's aims (exposing the colonial dimension of 'Irish writing') at the expense of another (encouraging Northern Protestants to identify themselves with Ireland). In this, the anthology is emblematic of the Field Day movement as a whole.

In other ways as well the story of the anthology and its reception can be regarded as a metaphor for Field Day. In no way is this more true perhaps than in the bold conception of the project. The sheer scope and ambition of the anthology are staggering. One of the aims was the creation of a canon (however contingent) of Irish writing, or, as Deane told a radio interviewer in the United States shortly after it was published, the 'invention of a tradition'.[17] In an immense act of imagination and organization, the Field Day volumes recover the Irish context for many authors and works previously absorbed into a general English-language tradition, as well as making available in relatively compact form hundreds of rare or inaccessible texts.

As always with Field Day, there was a marked disparity between the grand public showing and the behind-the-scenes frenzy. The anthology quickly outgrew the organizational framework of the company, and Seamus Deane, as general editor, ended up doing virtually alone work that would have kept a team of ten busy: mapping out the area to be covered; commissioning sub-editors (twenty-one of them); editing or helping to edit twelve of the forty-three sections; checking in periodically with all of the sub-editors to offer suggestions for their sections and hassle them for selections and editorial copy; fund-raising; publicizing; negotiating with the publishers; proof-reading; indexing. The original projected date of publication was 1988; after a series of delays the three-volume set was issued in 1991. Meanwhile, the idea of the anthology expanded exponentially. The 300- to 500-year time-span originally proposed by Deane gradually stretched to 1,500 years; two volumes became three; the 1,200 pages projected in 1985 grew to 4,044 by 1991 (and thin, double-column pages at that); perhaps most significantly, the cost of the anthology to the individual purchaser, estimated by Deane at £50 in 1988,[18] became £150 by the time of publication.

It seems reasonable to wonder whether the exuberant size of the anthology does not in some ways militate against several of the goals for it laid out by the Field Day directors. The populist ethos behind the early Field Day project as a whole was also present in the conception at least some of the directors had of the niche the anthology could fill. As Brian Friel told a reporter from the *Irish News* in 1987, 'Hopefully it will be the kind of book that will end up in everyone's home like Tom Moore's Irish Melodies in the last century'.[19] Seamus Deane also said he wanted the books to appeal to the general reader as well as to students and academics.[20] Obviously, if one is trying to foment a revolution in popular consciousness, this is essential. The published anthology, however, is simply unaffordable for most Irish people. Another imagined audience, arguably as important to Field Day, was the American academic community. The official description of the project alluded to this:

Irish literature is now studied all over the world at both undergraduate and graduate level. However the scarcity of texts and the expense of modern reprints have impeded its growth as a field of study and research. The Field Day Anthology will alleviate this problem and point the way to further exploration of the material.[21]

Field Day self-consciously set out to provide the world (and particularly American college students and instructors) with what would amount to the *Norton Anthology of Irish Writing*, and the directors acknowledged as much in an interview for the US National Public Radio Network shortly after the anthology was issued.[22] Partly for this reason, they did a great deal of their fundraising for the project in the United States, with Seamus Heaney, Brian Friel, Seamus Deane, and Tom Paulin visiting Boston, New York, and Washington DC in the course of one memorable weekend in March, 1987.[23] Yet even in the land of plenty $150 (the anthology's cost in the United States) is a hefty sum to expect the average undergraduate to expend on books for one course. It remains to be seen whether the anthology as it stands will prove amenable to redaction into the kind of one- or two-volume paperback form that might actually make it a commercial and popular success in that market. In the meantime, the anthology will be a useful reference for professors and graduate students, a sourcebook for libraries, or a decoration for particularly sturdy coffee-tables.[24]

Whether or not the published anthology accomplished the ends the directors had in mind, another feature of the ongoing project that was no doubt painfully familiar to them was the way in which critics lined up to attack it when it was still no more than a glimmer in Seamus Deane's eye. Eiléan Ní Chuilleanáin was probably the first to question the rationale for the anthology, in a review of the second set of Field Day pamphlets. Deane, she wrote, claimed that it would show 'the political ideas behind and expose the myth of Irishness'. It was her belief, however, that 'Anthologies do not work like that; and especially in the educational sphere which is Deane's home ground they reinforce the curriculum and promote a monolithic orthodoxy, the opposite of the provocative, occasional insights which at their best the Field Day Pamphlets represent.'[25] Edna Longley seconded this opinion on several occasions, going so far as to say in a debate with Deane in April of 1989 that 'all anthologies are ipso facto exclusive, and are a metaphor for the selectivities of Irish politics'.[26]

Certainly the real issue for Longley, as for those given the difficult task of reviewing this behemoth, was the question of what Field Day, in the anthology, took to be 'Irish'. In the words of Roy Foster, 'what qualifies as "Irish" literature, given that so many of its recoverable products, from the eighteenth century on, are written in English?'[27] Although the early assessment of Brian Fallon in the *Irish Times* that the anthology 'seems unlikely to be challenged for decades' proved overly sanguine, most of the reviewers paid tribute to its 'immense contribution to our perception of Irish writing, whether we build on that contribution or react against it'.[28] Of such reactions against the anthology, the charge of political nationalism was the most expected. It was also no surprise to see Edna Longley, Roy Foster, and Damian Smyth leading the charge from this quarter.[29] Smyth, in his review in *Fortnight*, stated this position most straightforwardly:

The meta-narrative, far from being, in Deane's terms, 'hospitable'—an interesting word, faking accommodation but in reality a gesture toward a stranger who is part-owner of the house and will not be cast out—is one of disappointment. . . . with the absence of conformity, of that coinciding complex of nation/state/culture which seems to be the editors' view of the complete, fulfilled political entity at the end of history.

It was clear to Smyth that Deane *et al.* regarded the fact of colonization as the source of this lack of 'politico-cultural identity'.[30] The organization of the anthology around questions of colonialism and nationalism does leave it open to this criticism. Roy Foster observed that the selections seemed marshalled to prove Deane's earlier contention (in *Civilians and Barbarians*) that Irish experience 'inhabits the highly recognizable world of modern colonialism'. This led to an editorial policy that was extremely flexible in some ways but rigid in others. Famous writers such as Swift, Burke, Sterne, and Goldsmith are reclaimed for Ireland, despite their 'Anglo' flavour. Occasionally English writers are included, too, because they wrote in or about Ireland, but in these cases the principles of selection are more obviously influenced by the framing thesis. Thus Cromwell is included but Gladstone is not. Foster questioned the basis for some of these decisions by wondering, 'Might it be the case that what Spenser and Cromwell wrote about Ireland fits into the anthologists' view of "highly recognizable" colonial attitudes, whereas the views of Thackeray, Trollope and Gladstone do not?'[31]

The Field Day anthology's 'nationalist' slant was not an issue for other reviewers. A number saw it as a positive aspect of the set, and indeed it would have been rather unreasonable to expect anything else in an anthology of 'Irish' writing. A non-nationalist editor would be unlikely to conceive of such a project in the first place. Even generally sympathetic reviewers, however, recognized a polemical slant to the collection, which John Banville called 'an energetic attempt to put the case for a progressive and unbigoted nationalism'.[32]

How well does the anthology manage to do that? Occasioned as it was by the Northern crisis, the framing of the anthology yet carefully avoids any explicit discussion of the obstacles, chiefly sectarianism, in the way of a political settlement that would be to Seamus Deane's liking. There is evidence that he was aware of the problem and thought of the anthology as a part of the solution. In 1989, for example, he told a reporter from the Associated Press that the work was intended to provide material that will show the stupidity and the broken-hearted terminus to which sectarianism leads, and how sectarianism can only be justified by a certain kind of deliberate, fostered, nurtured ignorance of what in fact has happened, what contributions have been made by various groups over the centuries to the culture.[33]

Yet in his general introduction to the published volumes, which would be the first thing that anyone interested in the anthology as such would read, Deane makes only oblique references to sectarian division in Ireland and none at all to partition. Unionism is mentioned only once, in passing. It would be possible for the naïve reader to read this essay through without realizing by the end of it that there are people in Ireland (and, indeed, in the anthology) who do not consider themselves to be 'Irish' (or who other nationalists, less liberal than Deane, would refuse to accept as authentic Irish voices). Several reviewers commented on the lack of attention to religious conflict and to the different paths taken by the Republic and Northern Ireland since 1922.[34] Why, in an anthology that aimed to bring the North back into an 'Irish' orbit, were these central issues soft-pedalled? Maybe because sectarianism is an embarrassment to liberal nationalism: Protestant sectarianism because it challenges the idea that eliminating the border will solve the problem of the North; Catholic sectarianism because it arouses suspicions that unionism might be based at least in part on rational self-interest rather than mere prejudice and superstition.

It might also be, of course, that religious affiliation in itself is simply not something that Deane considers interesting or important. Perhaps the most telling indictment of the Field Day anthology from the standpoint of the future was that in focusing on the old question of Irish identity with reference to colonialism it failed to reflect other forms of diversity in Irish life. This was the criticism of Field Day broached by Frank McGuinness and Fintan O'Toole back in 1985. O'Toole reviewed the anthology, although he confined his remarks to the drama selections, and his verdict was that 'the new canon amounts very much to the old one':

if you look at the Contemporary Irish Drama section, you get the impression of a theatre inhabited only by gnarled farmers, people caught up in the Northern Troubles, and people acting out in one way or another the conflict between Britishness and Irishness.[35]

O'Toole objected to the 'writing out of the Irish-American axis' and the slighting of popular urban dramatic forms such as music-hall revues. Other reviewers wondered about the emphasis on national rather than class politics, or asked where the travellers, Jews, immigrants, homosexuals, scientists, and others not traditionally seen as 'typical' Irish people were.[36] Colm Tóibín shrewdly identified the source of such omissions as 'the view that Southern Ireland is contemptible and complacent, and thus the changes which have taken place here are nothing beside the great events which have rattled Northern Ireland'.[37]

The most significant critique of this nature was the feminist. Nuala O'Faolain set the ball rolling with an editorial in the *Irish Times*. Where, she asked, were the women writers, particularly in the contemporary sections? In an anthology so concerned with 'politics', where was the women's movement?

Our world includes a future for women radically different from anything that was available to them in the past. This is an historical fact of the greatest importance, and assisting it, watching it has been the drama of my life, and of many other women's lives. Even those who haven't been conscious of it have found their condition transformed. The texts that bear witness to this transformation, both literary and non-literary, exist. They would have leapt to the mind of a woman editor. But in this whole huge enterprise no woman editor was employed.[38]

O'Faolain concluded with a call for the revision of the anthology to reflect the female contribution to Irish life and letters, a call that was quickly taken up by angry women throughout Ireland.[39] Kevin Barry pointed out that, even as it stood, the anthology was the largest collection of Irish women's writing available, with the ratio of men to women comparing favourably with other recent collections. Nevertheless, he admitted, the anthology 'remains . . . on a level with the lamentable dearth of scholarship about women's writing in Ireland.'[40] The Field Day directors, suitably embarrassed, vowed to make amends with a fourth volume to concentrate on women's writing, which is currently in production. Ironically, the publication of the Field Day anthology and the vehement feminist reaction against it stand fair to be remembered as events of singular importance in raising awareness of gender issues in Irish Studies.

None the less, the feminist furore over the anthology highlights the way in which Field Day's politics had come to be construed almost entirely in national terms. In trying to get beyond the National Question, the company ended by circling obsessively around it. The narrowing range of Field Day's vision should be seen in relation to its theatre. In all the controversy over the anthology, there has been no discussion of the effect that the concentration on it may have had on Field Day's theatrical being, but there must have been some impact. Perhaps this can be measured only in opportunity costs—the time and energy put into the anthology that might have been used instead to expand Field Day's theatrical operations. Repeatedly throughout this period, Friel and Rea made public statements to the effect that they would like to see Field Day produce more plays—maybe three or four in a year—and spend more time in Derry, perhaps with a more permanent company of actors.[41] This has not yet happened, and it seems to me unfortunate since I hold the view that theatre is potentially more subversive of settled attitudes and unconscious prejudices than even the most effectively worded argument.

Instead, Field Day's profile became more and more international. *Double Cross* (1986), *Making History* (1988), *Saint Oscar* (1989), and *The Cure at Troy* (1990) all transferred to London in their Field Day productions after the Irish tour; *Making History* was even a joint production with the National Theatre in London, while *The Cure at Troy* was rehearsed in London rather than in Derry. The fifth set of Field Day pamphlets was authored by three non-Irish literary critics. The anthology itself was aimed as much at North America as at Ireland. Meanwhile, many people who actually lived in Derry were either indifferent to Field Day or growing resentful of the attention and civic funds that the company garnered. By 1991 when the anthology was issued Field Day was in acute danger of being perceived as precisely that which it was originally founded to counter: imported culture which lacked strong roots in the community (or communities). Indeed, the following year Field Day was refused a £65,000 grant from the Impact '92 festival in Derry, which it had counted on to stage a promenade performance of Friel's *The Freedom of the City* in the Guildhall. There was consequently no Field Day production at all in 1992.[42]

Most potentially damaging to Field Day's long-term prospects as a theatre company was the rift between its founders, Brian Friel and Stephen Rea, after Friel decided to give his play *Dancing at Lughnasa* (1990) to the Abbey Theatre in Dublin instead of to Field Day. The play became an international hit, which understandably intensified hard feelings. No one except Friel knows exactly why he chose to do this, but I suspect he felt constrained by the ideological framework Field Day had developed by 1989. *Dancing at Lughnasa* is simply not a 'Field Day play' as described by Rea in 1989 ('a play of ideas, involved with language, involved with looking at imperialism, and looking at men who have one foot in Ireland and one in England') or by Deane in 1990 ('a political crisis produces a clash of loyalties that is analyzable but irresolvable. . . . the dramatic analysis centers on anxieties of naming, speaking, and voice and the relation of these to place, identity, and self-realization.')[43] Sadly, 'Field Day' notions of what mattered in Irish identity had ceased to accommodate one of the company's founding members. Around the same time another director, Seamus Heaney, attempted to steer Field Day back toward earlier concerns with Northern Irish vernacular, 'translation' of the classics, and communal reconciliation with *The Cure at Troy*, a version of Sophocles's *Philoctetes*.

The increased strain put on the company by the completion of a project as ambitious as the anthology, along with the tensions between various directors' ideas of what Field Day should be and between their work for the collective and the demands of their own individual careers, was probably behind the group's decision to suspend its operations in 1993. Rumours of Field Day's death proved to be greatly exaggerated, however. Brian Friel officially resigned from the Field Day board in January of 1994, but the other directors had already decided to go ahead with a new production early in 1995—Chekhov's *Uncle Vanya* in a new version by Frank McGuinness, a playwright who grew up directly across the border from Derry. Despite the boost afforded to his international career by his starring role in Neil Jordan's 'The Crying Game', Stephen Rea remained committed to managing Field Day's theatrical enterprises and intended to take the role of Uncle Vanya himself. He still envisioned that someday Field Day might produce two or three plays in a year and become more involved in the local community through writing and theatre arts workshops. Meanwhile, work on the fourth volume of the anthology continued, with a projected publication date of 1995. It is too early, therefore, to offer conclusive statements here, and this study, like the Field Day anthology, must languish 'at the mercy of the present moment'.[44] What Field Day has been in the past is ultimately of less consequence than what it might become in the future.

Appendix
Productions of the Field Day Theatre Company, 1980–4

1980: *Translations* by Brian Friel

Tour: Derry, Belfast, Dublin, Newry, Dungannon, Magherafelt, Carrickmore, Armagh, Enniskillen, Sligo, Coleraine, Galway, Tralee, Cork

1981: *Three Sisters* by Anton Chekhov, in a version by Brian Friel

Tour: Derry, Belfast, Maghera, Carrickmore, Enniskillen, Dungannon, Newry, Armagh, Dublin, Portadown, Coleraine, Galway, Tralee, Limerick, Cork

1982: *The Communication Cord* by Brian Friel

Tour: Derry, Belfast, Dungannon, Craigavon, Maghera, Enniskillen, Armagh, Newry, Omagh, Coleraine, Galway, Sligo, Limerick, Dublin, Cork

1983: *Boesman and Lena* by Athol Fugard

Tour: Derry, Tralee, Dungarvan, Callan, New Ross, Carrick-on-Suir, Newcastle West, Galway, Dungannon, Ballymena, Downpatrick, Enniskillen, Newry, Armagh, Sligo, Westport, Clonbur, Ennis

Publications: *A New Look at the Language Question* by Tom Paulin, *An Open Letter* by Seamus Heaney, *Civilians and Barbarians* by Seamus Deane, and *Sweeney Astray* (a translation by Seamus Heaney)

1984: *The Riot Act* (a version of Sophocles's *Antigone*) by Tom Paulin and *High Time* (a version of Molière's *The School for Husbands*) by Derek Mahon

Tour: Derry, Dublin, Belfast, Carrickmore, Enniskillen, Magherafelt, Downpatrick, Armagh, Newry, Mullingar, Athlone, Galway, Ballycastle, Limavady, Coleraine, Limerick, Cork

Publications: *Heroic Styles: The Tradition of an Idea* by Seamus Deane, *Myth and Motherland* by Richard Kearney, and *Anglo-Irish Attitudes* by Declan Kiberd

Notes

INTRODUCTION

1. For an exposition of this perspective by one of the Field Day directors, see Seamus Deane's introduction to *Nationalism, Colonialism and Literature* (Derry, 1990).
2. Kevin Boyle and Tom Hadden, *Ireland: A Positive Proposal* (Harmondsworth, Middlesex, 1985).
3. By 'unionist' and 'nationalist' I refer only to the general political perspectives. 'Unionist' and 'Nationalist' are used to indicate the organized political parties by those names.
4. Longley, 'The Longley Tapes', interview by Robert Johnstone, *Honest Ulsterman*, 78 (Summer 1985), 24.
5. Heaney, 'Editor's Note', *Soundings '72* (Belfast, 1972), 6.
6. David Lehman and Donna Foote, 'The Ulster Renaissance', *Newsweek* (International Edition), 12 May 1986, 53.
7. Parker, *Dramatis Personae* (Belfast, 1986), 19.
8. Parker, 'Me and Jim', *Irish University Review*, 12.1 (Spring 1982), 34.

CHAPTER I

The quotation in the title is taken from Derry musician Phil Coulter's song by that name.

1. Elgy Gillespie, 'Festival Profile: Stephen Rea', *Irish Times*, 10 Oct. 1980.
2. Lynne Riddel, 'Why Friel and Rea are Having a "Field" Day', *Belfast Telegraph*, 15 Sept. 1980.
3. Liam Robinson, 'New Play to Set Fire to the Foyle?', *Evening Press*, 19 Sept. 1980; Ciaran Carty, 'Finding Voice in a Language Not Our Own', *Sunday Independent*, 5 Oct. 1980.
4. The Arts Council of Northern Ireland gave about £40,000, and that of the Republic added about £10,000. This set the pattern for future years, in which Field Day tours would be funded jointly by the two Arts Councils, both allocating money according to the number of weeks the company spent in each jurisdiction. 'World Premiere of Friel's *Translations* Tonight', *Derry Journal*, 23 Sept. 1980; letter to the author from Gary McKeone, Field Day Company Manager, 26 Feb. 1992.

5. 'World Première of Friel Play to be Staged in Derry', *Irish News*, 25 Aug. 1980.

6. Kavanagh wrote,

   'Parochialism and provincialism are opposites. The provincial has no mind of his own; he does not trust what his eyes see until he has heard what the metropolis—towards which his eyes are turned—has to say on any subject. This runs through all activities.

   The parochial mentality on the other hand is never in any doubt about the social and artistic validity of his parish. All great civilizations are based on parochialism—Greek, Israelite, English.' (Kavanagh, 'The Parish and the Universe', *Collected Pruse* (Worcester, 1967), 282.)

7. Friel, 'Talking to Ourselves', interview by Paddy Agnew, *Magill*, Dec. 1980, 60.

8. Noel McCartney, 'Derry Rallies behind Friel Play Première', *Irish Press*, 20 Sept. 1980, 5.

9. 'World Premier Special Night for Derry', *Belfast Newsletter*, 24 Sept. 1980.

10. 'Self-help', editorial, *Irish Times*, 11 Oct. 1980.

11. Chaillet, 'Translations: Londonderry', *The Times*, 26 Sept. 1980.

12. 'Friel's Winner', editorial, *Irish Press*, 26 Sept. 1980.

13. O'Grady, 'Derry-Do', *New Statesman*, 3 Oct. 1980.

14. D. McGarry, 'A Field Day for Derry', *Liberty*, Oct. 1980.

15. Riddel, *Belfast Telegraph*, 15 Sept. 1980.

16. John Hume, foreword, in Frank Curran, *Derry: Countdown to Disaster* (Dublin, 1986), 1.

17. W. J. McCormack has commented on the peculiarly Irish nature of the term 'the Troubles', which 'carries with it a sense of intimate possession. Unlike gangsterism, mugging, or "the consequences of alienation within a decaying urban environment", your Troubles are your own. Only the Italians with their Cosa Nostra rival the Irish in the possession of their unhappiness.' (McCormack, *The Battle of the Books: Two Decades of Irish Cultural Debate* (Gigginstown, Mullingar, Co. Westmeath, 1986), 14.)

18. Brian Lacy, *Siege City: The Story of Derry and Londonderry* (Belfast, 1990), 254. In the discussion that follows, I am particularly indebted to Lacy's book. I have also drawn on Paul Arthur and Keith Jeffery, *Northern Ireland Since 1968* (Oxford, 1988); Curran (1986); Ronan Fanning, *Independent Ireland* (Dublin, 1983); Brian Mitchell, *Derry: A City Invincible* (Eglinton, Co. Londonderry, 1990); R. F. Foster, *Modern Ireland 1600–1972*, 1988 (London, 1989); Eamonn McCann, *War and an Irish Town* (London, 1974; rev. edn. 1980); Paul Kingsley, *Londonderry Revisited: A Loyalist Analysis of the Civil Rights Controversy* (Belfast, 1989); F. S. L.

Lyons, *Ireland Since the Famine*, 1971 (London, rev. edn., 1973);
A. T. Q. Stewart, *The Narrow Ground: The Roots of Conflict in
Ulster*, 1977 (London, rev. edn. 1989); Ian Adamson, *The Identity of
Ulster* (Northern Ireland, 1982); and Bob Purdie, *Politics in the
Streets: The Origins of the Civil Rights Movement in Northern
Ireland* (Belfast, 1990).

19. Curran (1986), 24-5.
20. In the discussion that follows I am not arguing that there actually was
    a conspiracy afoot against Derry and the rest of the north-west.
    Rather, I am trying to describe what I believe to have been a popular
    perception in the city at that time, an interpretation of contemporary
    events which led to the conclusion that the Second City was being
    deliberately isolated. Speaking generally, this type of perception may
    or may not be borne out by the facts as they emerge in subsequent
    historical research, but, if it is held by people who are in a position
    to influence events as they unfold, then it, too, becomes a historical
    fact that must be taken into account.
21. Editorial, *Londonderry Sentinel*, 20 Jan. 1965, 14. The following
    account of the university campaign in Derry has been pieced together
    from accounts in the *Sentinel* and the nationalist *Derry Journal* from
    Jan. to Mar. 1965. Exact quotations are attributed separately.
22. Onlooker, 'Distressed Derry Needs More Than "Chequers" Sop',
    Derry Journal, 26 Jan. 1965, 4.
23. The Lockwood Committee consisted of four English and four
    prominent Northern Irish members.
24. 'United Demand for Varsity', *Londonderry Sentinel*, 10 Feb. 1965,
    12.
25. 'Derry is the Obvious Place—Mayor' and 'A City in Revolt', *Lon-
    donderry Sentinel*, 10 Feb. 1965, 16-17.
26. W. R. Boyd, quoted in 'Derry the Site for University MPs Told
    Premier', *Londonderry Sentinel*, 10 Mar. 1965, 24.
27. 'Derry Unionists Repeat Call for a University', *Londonderry Sentinel*,
    3 Mar. 1965, 7 and Jones, quoted in 'Bound by Govt. Rule, Says City
    MP', *Londonderry Sentinel*, 3 Mar. 1965, 17.
28. 'His Way Out', editorial, *Derry Journal*, 2 Mar. 1965.
29. e.g. in a speech at the annual dinner of St Columb's College Union on
    9 Feb. 1966, Roman Catholic Bishop Neil Farran said, 'I know that
    some people have criticized me for keeping so quiet on the great
    disappointment of not getting the university, but I felt that if I did
    speak out how disappointed I was, then the hidden body who are
    determined to keep Derry down would have sought to use it to allege
    that the Catholic Church was really behind the idea of a university
    for Derry. There would be harmony in Derry today and greater
    employment if non-Catholics in the city were allowed to act in what

they know is the proper way, and were not dragooned by the hidden force.' Curran (1986), 48.

30. Ibid. 34.
31. Ibid. 42–3. Hume explains the significance of the university *campaign* in different terms: 'The university campaign had shown that there were Protestants willing to treat Catholics as equals, prepared to dispense with the traditional philosophy of Protestant supremacy.' Ibid. 39.
32. Lacy (1990), 250.
33. Heaney, 'Out of London: Ulster's Troubles', *New Statesman*, 1 July 1966, 23.
34. Lacy (1990), 250–2.
35. Curran (1986), 53–4.
36. Mitchell (1990), 89.
37. Bob Purdie documents a great deal of agitation that took place in Derry before this event. For a full account of this see Purdie (1990), ch. 5.
38. Heaney, 'Old Derry's Walls', *Listener*, 24 Oct. 1968, 522.
39. McCann (1980), 45.
40. For a detailed account of the People's Democracy see Purdie (1990), ch. 6.
41. Mitchell (1990), 90.
42. Lacy (1990), 260.
43. Mitchell (1990), 92.
44. Lacy (1990), 264; Foster (1989), 589. The two would have been closely associated in many people's minds, anyway, since discrimination against Catholics had been used in anti-partitionist propaganda since the 1940s. Bob Purdie, 'The Irish Anti-Partition League, South Armagh and the Abstentionist Tactic 1945–58', *Irish Political Studies*, 1 (1986), 71–3.
45. Foster (1989), 590.
46. In the four months after internment, 32 soldiers, 9 policemen, 98 civilians, and 5 members of the Ulster Defence Regiment were killed. This compared with the deaths of 10 soldiers, 2 policemen, and 15 civilians in the seven months immediately preceding internment. Lyons (1973), 776.
47. Heaney, *Wintering Out* (London, 1972, 1973).
48. Lacy (1990), 265–7.
49. Friel, 'The Man From God Knows Where', interview by Fintan O'Toole, *In Dublin*, 28 Oct. 1982, 22.
50. Deane, 'After Derry, 30 January 1972', in his *Gradual Wars* (Shannon: Irish UP, 1972), 15–16.
51. Lacy (1990), 267.
52. Foster (1989), 591.

53. Lacy (1990), 268.
54. Boyle and Hadden (1985), 71–2.
55. Brian Friel, *Selected Plays of Brian Friel*, ed. Seamus Deane (London, 1984), 140.
56. 'Standing Ovation for Friel's *Translations*', *Derry Journal*, 26 Sept. 1980.
57. Robinson, *Evening Press*, 19 Sept. 1980.
58. 'World Premiere of *Translations*', *Derry Journal*, 19 Sept. 1980. This article includes two paragraphs on the proposed theatre development.
59. Riddel, *Belfast Telegraph*, 15 Sept. 1980.
60. McGarry, *Liberty*, Oct. 1980.
61. O'Grady, *New Statesman*, 3 Oct. 1980.
62. McGarry, *Liberty*, Oct. 1980; 'First Readings of Brian Friel's *Translations*', *Derry Journal*, 12 Aug. 1980.
63. Riddel, *Belfast Telegraph*, 15 Sept. 1980.
64. 'Guildhall Première for Friel Play in September', *Derry Journal*, 6 June 1980; 'Derry Première Pair', *Sunday Press*, 8 June 1980; *Belfast Telegraph*, photo of three actresses at the first rehearsal, 13 Aug. 1980; *Londonderry Sentinel*, publicity photo of Ray McAnally and Mick Lally, 20 Aug. 1980; 'Derry Actresses's [*sic*] Three Television Appearances', *Northern Constitution*, 23 August 1980; '*Translations*—Derry Connections', *Derry Journal*, 19 Sept. 1980.
65. 'Derry Women in *Translations*', *Derry Journal*, 12 Sept. 1980.
66. '*Translations* Preparations', *Derry Journal*, 9 Sept. 1980; 'Councillors in the Dark', *Londonderry Sentinel*, 10 Sept. 1980; *Londonderry Sentinel*, photograph of new stage, 17 Sept. 1980.
67. McCartney, *Irish Press*, 20 Sept. 1980.
68. Sheridan, 'Translated Logic . . .', *Irish Press*, 23 Sept. 1980.
69. McCartney, *Irish Press*, 20 Sept. 1980.
70. 'World Première of *Translations*', *Derry Journal*, 19 Sept. 1980.
71. 'Derry Women in *Translations*', *Derry Journal*, 12 Sept. 1980; 'World Première of Friel's *Translations* Tonight', *Derry Journal*, 23 Sept. 1980.
72. 'Friel's Winner', editorial, *Irish Press*, 26 Sept. 1980.
73. Oscar II, 'County Cameo: A World Première in Derry of a Friel Play', *Strabane Chronicle*, 27 Sept. 1980, 8.
74. Nowlan, 'Electric Love Affair as Play Opens in Derry', *Irish Times*, 24 Sept. 1980.
75. 'Derry Delight at Friel Play Triumph', *Sunday Independent Special Edition*, 28 Sept. 1980; O'Grady, *New Statesman*, 3 Oct. 1980.
76. Curran (1986), 31.
77. Barry White, 'A Recipe for Chaos', *Belfast Telegraph*, 2 Oct. 1980, 12.

CHAPTER 2

1. D. McGarry, 'A Field Day for Derry', *Liberty*, Oct. 1980.
2. Maev Kennedy, 'The Voices that will Linger on After Dublin', *Belfast Telegraph*, 18 Oct. 1980.
3. John Finegan, 'Buoyant Year', *Evening Herald*, 27 Dec. 1980; *Sunday Independent* 28 Dec. 1980; 'Theatre', *Belfast Telegraph*, 24 Dec. 1980.
4. The play was broadcast first on 31 Jan. 1982 and repeated on 25 Apr. 1989 on Radio Three. *Translations* was also broadcast on RTÉ Radio One in the Republic of Ireland in Dec. 1983 (letter to the author, 8 Jan. 1990, from Margaret Cox of the BBC Transcript and Tape Unit; Paddy Woodworth, 'Friel's Day', *RTÉ Guide*, 2 Dec. 1983).
5. Brian Friel, letter to the author, 12 Oct. 1989.
6. Sheridan, 'Friel Play a Watershed in Irish Theatre', *Irish Press*, 25 Sept. 1980.
7. Caroline Walsh, '£5,000 Award for Brian Friel', *Irish Times*, 15 Jan. 1981.
8. Brian Friel, *Translations* in *Selected Plays of Brian Friel*, ed. Seamus Deane (London, 1984), 377–451. Further page references to this work will be included parenthetically in the text.
9. In Irish, *baile beag* means 'small town'.
10. When Lancey tells the villagers that 'This enormous task has been embarked on so that the military authorities will be equipped with up-to-date and accurate information on every corner of this part of the Empire', Owen translates it simply as 'The job is being done by soldiers because they are skilled in this work' (406).
11. 'It is not the literal past that rules us, save, possibly, in a biological sense. It is images of the past. These are often as highly structured and selective as myths.' (George Steiner, *In Bluebeard's Castle: Some Notes towards the Re-Definition of Culture* (London, 1971), 13.)
12. Stephen Rea said about this ending, 'I don't think it's unresolved. As Beckett once said: "Listen to the music." That's not a cop-out; I see that speech as a final defiant cry from the grave.' (Elgy Gillespie, 'Festival Profile: Stephen Rea', *Irish Times*, 10 Oct. 1980.)
13. Friel says, 'Of course a fundamental irony of this play is that it should have been written in Irish.' (Friel, 'Talking to Ourselves', interview by Paddy Agnew, *Magill*, Dec. 1980, 59.) The approach also raises the question of whether the English and Irish would have been able to communicate any better if they had spoken the same language (as they do today). The idea that this was a deliberate effect is borne out by the fact that when Friel gave permission to Chomhlachas Náisiúnta Drámaíochta to produce *Translations* in Irish he did so

only on the condition that the entire play be translated. '*Translations* Le hAistriu—Go Gaeilge!*', *Inniu*, 16 Jan. 1981 (trans. by Marc Caball).

14. George Steiner, *After Babel* (Oxford, 1975), 21. Other examples of this 'translation' include: 'To remember everything is a condition of madness' (Steiner, 29); '[T]here will be in every complete speech-act a more or less prominent element of translation. All communication "interprets" between privacies' (Steiner, 198); 'Often, cultures seem to expend on their vocabulary and syntax acquisitive energies and ostentations entirely lacking in their material lives. Linguistic riches seem to act as a compensatory mechanism' (Steiner, 55). Compare Hugh's lines: 'certain cultures expend on their vocabularies and syntax acquisitive energies and ostentations entirely lacking in their material lives' (Friel, 418).

15. Steiner (1975), 45.

16. Ibid. 120.

17. Ibid. 217–18, 229.

18. Ibid. 231.

19. Ibid. 233.

20. Ibid. 407.

21. Kearney, *Transitions: Narratives in Modern Irish Culture* (Manchester, 1988), 155, 136.

22. Ibid. 138.

23. Simmons, 'Brian Friel, Catholic Playwright', *Honest Ulsterman*, 79 (Autumn 1985), 65–6.

24. Friel, 'Extracts from a Sporadic Diary', in Tim Pat Coogan (ed.), *Ireland and the Arts* (a Special Issue of *Literary Review*) (London, 1983), 60.

25. Ibid. 58.

26. Friel, interview with Christopher Morash in 'Flamethrowers: Contemporary Northern Irish Playwrights', M. Phil. diss., Trinity College, Dublin, 1986, 41.

27. Quoted in A. C. Hepburn, *The Conflict of Nationality in Modern Ireland* (London, 1980), 60–1 and P. S. O'Hegarty, *A History of Ireland Under the Union 1801 to 1922* (London, 1952), 617–19.

28. Ronan Fanning, *Independent Ireland* (Dublin, 1983), 80.

29. Ibid. 81.

30. Ibid. 140.

31. For a chronological discussion of Irish language revival in the Republic of Ireland see Terence Brown, *Ireland: A Social and Cultural History 1922–79* (London, 1981).

32. Coogan (1983), 11.

33. After an encounter with the dean of studies of his college Stephen thinks rebelliously, 'The language in which we are speaking is his

before it is mine. How different are the words *home, Christ, ale, master*, on his lips and on mine! I cannot speak or write these words without unrest of spirit. His language, so familiar and so foreign, will always be for me an acquired speech. I have not made or accepted its words. My voice holds them at bay. My soul frets in the shadow of his language.' (James Joyce, *A Portrait of the Artist as a Young Man* (1916; 1964) (Harmondsworth, Middlesex, 1976), 189.)

34. Montague, 'A Grafted Tongue', in his *Selected Poems* (Oxford, 1982), 110–11. Thomas Kinsella addresses the issue of a discontinuous tradition in Irish literature in his essay 'The Divided Mind' (1973) in Mark Storey (ed.), *Poetry and Ireland Since 1800: A Source Book* (London, 1988), 207–16.

35. Ciaran Carty, 'Finding Voice in a Language Not Our Own', *Sunday Independent*, 5 Oct. 1980.

36. Friel, 'Talking to Ourselves', 60–1. This attitude closely resembles that of Hugh in the final moments of *Translations*.

37. Kearney (1988), 124; 'New Friel Play Set in a Hedge School', *Sunday Independent*, 6 June 1980.

38. e.g. Sean Connolly, 'Dreaming History: Brian Friel's *Translations*', *Theatre Ireland*, 13 (1987), 42–4; Brian Friel, John Andrews, and Kevin Barry, 'Translations and A Paper Landscape: Between Fiction and History', *Crane Bag*, 7.2 (1983), 118–24; Edna Longley, 'Including the North', *Text and Context* (Autumn 1988), 17–24.

39. Patrick John Dowling, *The Hedge Schools of Ireland* (Dublin, 1935), 31.

40. Revd T. Corcoran, *State Policy in Irish Education, A.D. 1536 to 1816* (Dublin, 1916), 38.

41. William Carleton writes, 'I do maintain, that he who is intimately acquainted with the character of our countrymen, must acknowledge, that their zeal for book learning, not only is strong and ardent, when opportunities of scholastic education occur, but that it increases in proportion as these opportunities are rare and unattainable. The very name and nature of Hedge Schools are proof of this' (Carleton, *Traits and Stories of the Irish Peasantry* (London, 1881), 127). Another observer, Wakefield, noted in the early nineteenth century, 'The people of Ireland . . . are, I may almost say, *universally educated*. . . . I do not know any part of Ireland so wild, that its inhabitants are not anxious, nay, eagerly anxious for the education of their children' (Dowling (1935), 48). An early education reformer, Sir Thomas Wyse, expressed the opinion in 1830 that 'the lower class proportionally to their position are better educated than the middle and upper' (Norman Atkinson, *Irish Education: A History of Educational Institutions* (Dublin: Figgis, 1969) 48).

42. J. H. Andrews, *A Paper Landscape: The Ordnance Survey in Nineteenth-Century Ireland* (Oxford, 1975), 91.

43. 'Contemporary opinions of the hedge schoolmaster are interesting, even if they are usually adverse' (Dowling (1935), 109).

44. Ibid. 153.

45. 'That he was supported in this by the pupils' parents is but poor justification for the anti-national and anti-cultural outlook which such scholars as the Hedge Schoolmaster should have been the first to condemn. The method employed to ensure that no Irish was spoken by the child, even in his own home or outside the school walls, was well qualified to achieve its aims. It was customary for children to have small sticks or tablets suspended from their necks, and notches were cut in these every time the children spoke Irish at home. On coming to school the next day the master would see at a glance whether the pupil had been using the forbidden language or no. Each notch usually meant the reward of a stroke of the cane.' (Auchmuty, *Irish Education: A Historical Survey* (Dublin, 1937) 16.)

46. Atkinson (1969), 48.

47. 'English is always spoken in the country schools, as the parents are anxious their children should speak it' (Galway, 1824); 'No Irish is spoken in any of the schools, and the peasantry are anxious to send their children to them for the purpose of learning English' (Clare, 1808); 'English being taught at all the schools, it is understood by most of the younger part of the lower classes' (Kilkenny, 1802); 'the children, being most commonly sent to school, speak in general some English' (Mayo, 1802); in O'Hegarty (1952), 395–6.

48. Dowling (1935), 53.

49. 'The Irish people looked on the establishment of the National Schools as providing a glorious opportunity to further the anglicisation of their children' (Auchmuty (1937), 151).

50. Atkinson (1969), 97.

51. Ó Buachalla, 'The Language in the Classroom', *Crane Bag*, 5.2 (1981), 18.

52. F. S. L. Lyons, *Ireland Since the Famine*, 1971 (London, rev. edn., 1973), 82–9. See also Atkinson (1969), 91 and Auchmuty (1937), ch. 4.

53. Connolly, 'Dreaming History', 43. He also notes that more than half of the schools that were part of the national system in 1840 were in existence before 1831, and more than half of the teachers had been teaching before the system was instituted.

54. Auchmuty (1937), 145–6.

55. 'In its curricular regulations, its funding arrangements, its teacher training programmes and its inspectorial process, the National school system made no provision for that segment of the population

(319,602 in 1851), for whom Irish was a vernacular and only language, nor for the much larger group totalling 1.5 million in 1851 who were bilingual.' (Ó Buachalla, 'The Language in the Classroom', 18.)

56. Atkinson (1969), 155–6; Auchmuty (1937), 151.
57. Auchmuty (1937), 151; Atkinson (1969), 103.
58. Auchmuty (1937), 151.
59. Atkinson (1969), 102.
60. Ibid. 101.
61. Ó Buachalla, 'The Language in the Classroom', 21.
62. O'Hegarty (1952), 395. He also quotes the following poem, which appeared in the same reader:

> I thank the goodness and the grace
>> Which on my birth has smiled,
> And made me in these Christian days
>> A happy English child.

63. Friel, 'Translations and A Paper Landscape', 124.
64. In the discussion that follows I will be drawing mainly on the same source consulted by Friel when he was writing *Translations*, a book called *A Paper Landscape* by John Andrews.
65. Friel, 'Extracts from a Sporadic Diary', 57.
66. Andrews (1975), 1.
67. Soldiers rather than civilians were used because it was felt that they would be faster, more efficient, and cheaper. However, some civilian labourers were hired in Ireland, and by the end of 1826 there were 43 civilian Irish surveyors on the staff as well (ibid. 21, 39, 64).
68. In Friel's play, Lancey tells the villagers that 'Ireland is privileged. No such survey is being undertaken in England' (407). Actually, approximately one-third of England and Wales had been surveyed by 1820 (ibid. 2).
69. Ibid. 28, 92.
70. Ibid. 15.
71. Ibid. 88.
72. Friel, 'Translations and A Paper Landscape', 123.
73. Andrews, 'Translations and A Paper Landscape', 121.
74. Ibid. 120.
75. 'It had been made clear in 1825 that Ordnance Survey personnel would not be used for military or police purposes in Ireland and that they would be expected to "conciliate the inhabitants by every possible means". When in 1829 a Survey officer was asked to supply men for purposes of law enforcement by a local justice of the peace, he refused on the ground that "it may cause the service to become obnoxious to the inhabitants which is most carefully to be guarded

against". When in the same year two Survey employees were assaulted near Caledon, the director of the Ordnance Survey asked the chief secretary of Ireland for an assurance that the matter would be dealt with by the police. Later when squatters on common land in Co. Wexford offered resistance to the Survey, police protection was sought and obtained by application to a local magistrate. All Lancey's burnings, levellings, evictions and livestock-shootings are what Friel describes as "bruises inflicted on history".' (Andrews, 'Notes for a Future Edition of Brian Friel's *Translations*', *Irish Review*, 13 (Winter 1992–3), 101).

76. Andrews (1975), 122.
77. Atkinson (1969), 153; Seamus Fenton, *A Great Kilkennyman: John O'Donovan* (Kilkenny, 1942), 12. Also R. B. Walsh, 'John O'Donovan, The Man and the Scholar', in Cyril Byrne and Margaret Harry (eds.), *Talamh An Eisc: Canadian and Irish Essays* (Halifax, Nova Scotia, 1986), 119–39. The Annals of the Four Masters was a compilation by four seventeenth-century historians of Irish history in the Irish language.
78. Andrews (1975), 123.
79. Ibid. 120.
80. Fenton (1942), 3.
81. 'In a random sample of a hundred townland names of Irish derivation, for instance, it has been found that in forty-six cases O'Donovan ended with a spelling that differed from *all* the recorded authorities.' (Andrews (1975), 125.)
82. Ibid. 125–6.
83. Ibid. 123.
84. Larcom's instructions to his men sound more like those of an anthropology professor to his graduate students than the orders of an efficiency-minded military man:

> Habits of the people. Note the general style of the cottages, as stone, mud, slated, glass, windows, one story or two, number of rooms, comfort and cleanliness. Food; fuel; dress; longevity; usual number in a family; early marriages; any remarkable instances on either of these heads? What are their amusements and recreations; Patrons and patrons' days; and traditions respecting them? What local customs prevail, as Beal tinne, or fire on St. John's Eve? Driving the cattle through fire, and through water? Peculiar games? Any legendary tales or poems recited around the fireside? Any ancient music, as clan marches or funeral cries? They differ in different districts, collect them if you can. Any peculiarity of customs? Nothing more indicates the state of civilisation and intercourse.
>
> Emigration. Does emigration prevail? To what extent? And at what season? To what places? Do any return? What numbers go annually to get

harvest or other work in England or other parts of the kingdom? Do they take wives and families with them? Do they rent ground, and sow potatoes for their winter support? (Quoted by Barry, 'Translations and A Paper Landscape', 119.)

85. Sometimes the omission of these points of interest was a matter of religious prejudice foreign to such as Larcom: ' "I am constantly at my men about these matters," one officer complained, "but many of them are presbyterians from the north who care not for 'eremites and friars, white, black and grey, with all their trumpery." ' (Andrews (1975), 127.)

86. Revd Michael O'Flanagan (ed.), *Letters Containing Information Relative to the Antiquities of the County of Dublin Collected During the Progress of the Ordnance Survey in 1837* (Bray, typescript, 1927), 12. Housed in the Bodleian Library, Oxford.

87. Ibid. 32 (letter of 17 Aug. 1837).

88. Andrews (1975), 158.

89. Anyone who has read Andrews's book must recognize Colby's preface for the masterful piece of fence-sitting that it is. He gives Larcom complete responsibility for the project, but whether he intends this as praise or blame will depend entirely upon the official and popular response the book receives:

> The elaborate search of books and records required to settle the orthography of names to be used on the maps, led him to compare the progressive states of the country . . . and the organization framed for carrying on the Survey, affording means for collecting and methodizing facts, which were never likely to recur, Lieutenant Larcom conceived the idea, that with such opportunities, a small additional cost would enable him, without retarding the execution of the maps, to draw together a work embracing every species of local information relating to Ireland. . . . To him I have intrusted the execution, and the present volume is the first public result.' (Col. Thomas Colby (Superintendent), *Ordnance Survey of the County of Londonderry: Memoir of the City and North Western Liberties of Londonderry, Parish of Templemore* (Dublin, 1837), 5–6.)

90. Andrews (1975), 160–1.

91. Ibid. 161.

92. Ibid. 160.

93. Ibid. 167.

94. Fenton (1942), 4.

95. Andrews (1975), 168.

96. Fenton (1942), 11.

97. Friel acknowledges that at one point in the planning of the play he 'indulged in [a] . . . bizarre and dangerous speculation: I read into

O'Donovan's exemplary career as a scholar and orthographer the actions and perfidy of a quisling. (The only excuse I can offer for this short-lived delusion is that the political situation in the North was particularly tense about that time.) Thankfully that absurd and cruel reading of O'Donovan's character and career was short-lived. But it soured a full tasting of the man. And O'Donovan appears in the play as a character called Owen.' (Friel, 'Translations and A Paper Landscape', 123.)

98. Connolly, 'Dreaming History', 43.
99. Andrews, 'Translations and A Paper Landscape', 121–2.
100. Friel, 'Translations and A Paper Landscape', 123.
101. Kearney (1988), 155.
102. Connolly, 'Dreaming History', 42. Edna Longley reports, 'Talking to A-level candidates in England, I found *Translations* accepted as more or less factual and realist.' (Longley, 'Including the North', 20.)
103. Dantanus, *Brian Friel: The Growth of an Irish Dramatist* (Göteborg, 1985), 188.
104. Friel, 'Extracts from a Sporadic Diary', 58.
105. Ibid.
106. Friel, 'Talking to Ourselves', 61.
107. D. E. S. Maxwell, *A Critical History of Modern Irish Drama 1891–1980* (Cambridge, 1984), 203.
108. Deane (ed.), introduction, *Selected Plays of Brian Friel*, 22.
109. Kearney (1988), 142.
110. Dantanus (1985), 183–4.
111. Carty, *Sunday Independent*, 5 Oct. 1980.
112. Ibid.
113. Brook, *The Empty Space* (London, 1968), 127.
114. 'Standing Ovation for Friel's *Translations*', *Derry Journal*, 26 Sept. 1980.
115. Martin O'Brien, 'Impressive Translations', *Belfast Telegraph*, 30 Sept. 1980. Of course, the Opera House was capable of holding about twice as many people as the Guildhall, which seats about 550, so one should not read too much into the fact that it did not sell out the first night.
116. Lowry, 'Friel Play Makes It a Great Night in Derry', *Belfast Telegraph*, 24 Sept. 1980.
117. Rosenfield, 'Unusual and Erudite', *Belfast Newsletter*, 1 Oct. 1980.
118. Longley, 'Including the North', 20.
119. Chris Spurr, former Production and Company manager of the now-defunct Irish Theatre Company, recalls touring with that group in the 1970s, in circumstances that must have been similar to those faced by Field Day a few years later:

On one such tour we visited a parish hall in a town in Munster noted for its annual drama festival. The previous night's bingo had left the hall knee-deep in cards, sweet wrappers and butts—'Ah, but that won't be there when you come,' our guide assured us. The blackout curtains were hanging off the rails—'Ah, but that won't be there when you come.' And littered dressing rooms and broken lighting fittings produced the same reply. The stage was dark, and to see it properly we had to open up the tabs. Squarely in the centre of the stage, the last act of the last joker in the hall the night before, was a huge human turd. Nothing daunted, the hall caretaker insisted—'Now, that won't be there when you come!'

Other venues, invariably convent halls, were just as different with floors beautifully polished—including one in Co. Clare, where the nun in charge informed us straight-faced when we asked about putting up sets, that she would tolerate 'no screwing or banging' on her floor! (Spurr, 'Going down the Country', *Theatre Ireland*, 13 (1987), 24.)

120. David Heap, 'On the Road with *Translations*', *Sunday Tribune*, 2 Nov. 1980.
121. Ibid.
122. '*Translations* to have Extra Performance', *Coleraine Chronicle*, 25 Oct. 1980, 8.
123. 'Brian Friel's Masterpiece in Carrickmore', *Ulster Herald*, 1 Nov. 1980.
124. 'Brian Friel comes to Carrickmore', *Tyrone Democrat*, 9 Oct. 1980.
125. 'All Tastes Catered for at Arts Festival', *Armagh Guardian*, 25 Sept. 1980, 10.
126. '*Translations* Sell-Out To-morrow', *Ulster Gazette*, 23 Oct. 1980, 7.
127. ' "Fantastic Response" for Friel's *Translations*', *Impartial Reporter*, 30 Oct. 1980.
128. 'Translations', *Impartial Reporter*, 30 Oct. 1980.
129. '*Translations* in Enniskillen', *Fermanagh News*, 1 Nov. 1980, 6.
130. 'Brian Friel's Masterpiece in Carrickmore', *Ulster Herald*, 1 Nov. 1980.
131. 'Brian Friel's Play', *Impartial Reporter*, 25 Sept. 1980.
132. 'Opening Night', editorial, *Irish Times*, 22 Aug. 1980.
133. Sheridan, 'Translated Logic . . .', *Irish Press*, 23 Sept. 1980 and 'Triumph for Translations', *Irish Press*, 25 Sept. 1980, 4.
134. Dawe, 'Writing in the West', *Connacht Tribune*, 31 Oct. 1980.
135. Fanning (1983), 212.
136. John Finegan, 'Friel Returns to History—and Success', *Evening Herald*, 24 Sept. 1980. Desmond Rushe also complained that much of the dialogue was 'unintelligible': 'Guildhall acoustics are not particularly helpful, but a substantial neutralising of northern accents would

pay dividends.' (Rushe, 'Friel at His Pleasing and Astonishing Best', *Irish Independent*, 25 Sept. 1980.)

137. Nowlan, 'Friel Play Opens in Derry', *Irish Times*, 25 Sept. 1980.

138. Nowlan, 'The Year of the Playwright', *Irish Times*, 1–2 Jan. 1981.

139. 'A Play I Can Recommend', *Irish Catholic*, 31 Oct. 1980.

140. Houlihan, 'That Was the Festival That Was', *Evening Press*, 25 Oct. 1980 and 'Make Sure You See this Memorable Friel', *Evening Press*, 7 Oct. 1980.

141. O'Toole, 'Today: Contemporary Irish Theatre—The Illusion of Tradition', in Coogan (ed.), *Ireland and the Arts* (1983), 134.

142. Cronin, 'Disasters—and *Translations*', *Sunday Tribune*, 28 Dec. 1980.

143. Sheridan, 'Triumph for Translations', *Irish Press*, 25 Sept. 1980.

144. McGinley, 'A City to Rival Juno's', *Donegal Democrat*, 26 Sept. 1980.

145. Ibid.

146. 'Aistriúcháin', *Irish Times*, 15 Oct. 1980 (trans. Marc Caball).

147. Jordan, 'Triumphant Translations', *Hibernia*, 9 Oct. 1980.

148. Sheridan, 'Friel Play a Watershed in Irish Theatre' *Irish Press*, 25 Sept. 1980.

149. Rushe, *Irish Independent*, 25 Sept. 1980.

150. McGinley, *Donegal Democrat*, 26 Sept. 1980.

151. Smith, 'As Friel's Peasant Play Dominates Second Festival Week . . .', *Sunday Independent*, 12 Oct. 1980.

152. Cronin, *Sunday Tribune*, 28 Dec. 1980.

153. McClelland, '*Translations*', *An Phoblacht/Republican News*, 11 Oct. 1980.

154. Boland, 'Artcetera', *Evening Press*, 17 Jan. 1981, 6.

155. W. H. Auden, 'In Memory of W. B. Yeats', in his *Selected Poems*, ed. Edward Mendelson (New York, 1979), 81.

156. Esslin, 'Translations', *Plays and Players*, Nov. 1981, 36.

157. Coveney, 'Translations', *Financial Times*, 13 Oct. 1980, 13.

158. Wardle, 'Translations', *The Times*, 13 May 1981, 11.

159. Chaillet, 'Translations', *The Times*, 7 Aug. 1981, 13.

160. Dixon, 'Mapping Cultural Imperialism', report, *Guardian*, 27 Sept. 1980, 11.

161. Fenton, 'Ireland: Destruction of an Idyll', *Sunday Times*, 28 Sept. 1980, 40.

162. Ibid.

163. Coveney, *Financial Times*, 13 Oct. 1980.

164. Chaillet, 'Translations: Londonderry', *The Times*, 26 Sept. 1980.

165. Both the Irish and English critics appeared to assume that the mysterious Donnelly twins represent some kind of organized resistance movement. The script, however, never states this, and for all we

really know they might be mere thugs or else men who would resent the incursion of any strangers, English, Irish, or otherwise, upon their world.

166. Hill, 'Mapping Cultural Imperialism', review, *Guardian*, 27 Sept. 1980, 11.
167. Sean McMahon, 'Brian Friel: His New Plays Reviewed', *Ulster Tatler*, Nov. 1980.
168. Coveney, *Financial Times*, 13 Oct. 1980.
169. Radin, 'Joyful Scandal—Magical Translations', *Observer*, 19 Oct. 1980.
170. Shorter, 'Best Irish Play for Years', *Daily Telegraph*, 8 Aug. 1981, 9.
171. Amory, 'Word-Play', *Spectator*, 23 May 1981, 27.
172. Billington, 'Translations', *Guardian*, 14 May 1981, 11.
173. Young, 'Translations', *Financial Times*, 14 May 1981, 21.
174. Ibid.
175. Chaillet, *The Times*, 7 Aug. 1981.
176. Mark Amory, *Spectator*, 23 May 1981.
177. James Fenton, 'How Mr. Eliot's Doodles Got Into a Catsuit', *Sunday Times*, 17 May 1981, 39.
178. John Russell Taylor, 'Plays in Performance', *Drama*, 141 (Autumn 1981), 28.
179. Amory, *Spectator*, 23 May 1981.
180. Young, *Financial Times*, 14 May 1981.
181. Ibid.
182. Joyce, *Ulysses: The Corrected Text*, ed. Hans Walter Gabler (New York, 1986), 17.
183. Wardle, *The Times*, 13 May 1981.
184. Esslin, *Plays and Players*, Nov. 1981.
185. Chaillet, *The Times*, 7 Aug. 1981.

CHAPTER 3

1. Heaney, 'A Field Day for the Irish', *The Times*, 5 Dec. 1988.
2. Heaney, personal interview, 23 Oct. 1989.
3. Ray Comiskey, 'Rehearsing Friel's New Farce', *Irish Times*, 14 Sept. 1982, 8.
4. Niall Kiely, 'An Irishman's Diary', *Irish Times*, 17 Sept. 1981.
5. Hammond, letter to the author, 19 Aug. 1993.
6. Paulin, personal interview, 26 Jan. 1992.
7. Margaret Spillane, 'Friel's Ireland Avoids Getting Lost in *Translations*', *In These Times*, 14–20 Sept. 1988, 21.
8. Heaney, *The Times*, 5 Dec. 1988.

9. Friel, 'Plays Peasant and Unpeasant', *Times Literary Supplement*, 17 Mar. 1972, 306.
10. Friel, 'The Man From God Knows Where', interview by Fintan O'Toole, *In Dublin*, 28 Oct. 1982, 22, 20, 22.
11. Ibid. 22.
12. Ulick O'Connor, 'Friel Takes Derry by Storm', *Sunday Tribune*, 6 Sept. 1981.
13. Mary Holland, 'A Field Day for Irish Theatre', *Observer Magazine*, 30 Oct. 1988, 65.
14. Quoted by Thomas Flanagan in his introduction to *Seamus Heaney: Poems and a Memoir*, selected and ill. by Henry Pearson (New York, 1982), p. xii.
15. For a detailed discussion of the hunger strikes and their impact see Padraig O'Malley, *Biting at the Grave* (Belfast, 1990).
16. 'The Outer Limits of Prison Reform', editorial, *Fortnight*, 183 (Oct.–Nov. 1981), 3.
17. Domhnall MacDermott, 'Deane Spells Out Field Day's Role', *Derry Journal*, 8 Feb. 1985.
18. F. S. L. Lyons records:

> Mr Lynch's public stance, as enunciated in his speech of 12 August 1969, was that his government could no longer stand by (or 'idly by' in some versions) and see innocent people injured 'or perhaps worse'. The use of British troops in the north was not acceptable 'certainly not in the long term'. He announced the establishment of Irish Army field hospitals along the border and called for the dispatch of a United Nations peace-keeping force to Northern Ireland. He also added this pregnant sentence: 'Recognising, however, that the re-unification of the national territory can provide the only permanent solution of the problem, it is our intention to request the British Government to enter into early negotiations with the Irish Government to review the present constitutional position of the Six Counties of Northern Ireland.' (Lyons, *Ireland Since the Famine*, 1971 (London, rev. edn., 1973), 770). Indeed, when the British Army first arrived in Derry some residents of the Bogside were unclear as to which country these soldiers represented (Brian Lacy, *Siege City: The Story of Derry and Londonderry* (Belfast, 1990) 262).

19. Ronan Fanning, *Independent Ireland* (Dublin, 1983), 209.
20. Ibid. 210.
21. Deane, 'Postscript', *Crane Bag*, 3.2 (1979), 94.
22. O'Brien, 'Nationalism and the Reconquest of Ireland', *Crane Bag*, 1.2 (1977), 9, 12.
23. Clare O'Halloran, *Partition and the Limits of Irish Nationalism: An Ideology Under Stress* (Dublin, 1987), pp. xiv, xviii.

24. A. C. Hepburn, *The Conflict of Nationality in Modern Ireland* (London, 1980), 205–7.

25. Garret FitzGerald, *Towards a New Ireland* (London, 1972), 147 ff., 176.

26. Lyons (1973), 689.

27. O'Halloran (1987), 193.

28. O'Brien, *States of Ireland* (London, 1972).

29. Clare O'Halloran explores these in depth. To summarize, the Protestants were seen as 'orange bigots' responsible for the sectarian violence. The Northern Catholics, on the other hand, were regarded as slaves at the mercy of the Protestants and their protection a burden on the South arising out of partition and increasingly resented (O'Halloran (1987), pp. xv, xvi).

30. Yeats, quoted in Terence Brown, *Ireland: A Social and Cultural History 1922–79* (London, 1981), 286.

31. P. S. O'Hegarty, author of one of the standard histories of Ireland, stated in his preface: 'The main conclusions which I have drawn are, I believe, unchallengeable, and if the story that comes out of the book is not coherent, not the story of a people coming out of captivity, out of underground, finding every artery of national life occupied by her enemy, recovering them one by one, and coming out at last in the full blaze of the sun, then the fault is in the writing. For that is how I have seen it.' (O'Hegarty, *A History of Ireland Under the Union 1801 to 1922* (London, 1952).)

32. For a more detailed and polemical discussion of 'revisionism' than I can provide here, see Michael Laffan, 'Insular Attitudes: The Revisionists and their Critics', in Máirín Ní Dhonnchadha and Theo Dorgan (eds.), *Revising the Rising* (Derry, 1991), 106–21; R. F. Foster, 'History and the Irish Question' (1982), *Transactions of the Royal Historical Society*, 5th ser., 33 (1983), 169–92; Ronan Fanning, 'The Meaning of Revisionism' (1987), *Irish Review*, 4 (1988), 15–19; Desmond Fennell, 'Against Revisionism' (1987), *Irish Review*, 4 (1988), 20–6; and Brendan Bradshaw, 'Nationalism and Historical Scholarship in Modern Ireland', *Irish Historical Studies*, 26.104 (Nov. 1989), 329–51.

33. Editor's introduction to Father Francis Shaw, SJ, 'The Canon of Irish History—A Challenge', *Studies: An Irish Quarterly Review*, 61 (1972), 113–14.

34. Sheridan, 'Field Day Carries on its Consciousness of History', *Irish Press*, 15 Sept. 1981.

35. David Lehman and Donna Foote, 'The Ulster Renaissance', *Newsweek* (International Edition), 12 May 1986, 54.

36. William Cole, 'Tradewinds: United Artists', *Saturday Review*, Jan.–Feb. 1986, 64.

37. W. J. McCormack, *The Battle of the Books: Two Decades of Irish Cultural Debate* (Gigginstown, Mullingar, Co. Westmeath, 1986), 55, 17.

38. Hammond, letter to the author, 19 Aug. 1993.

39. Heaney, personal interview, 23 Oct. 1989.

40. Kathleen Corrigan, 'Field Day for Stephen Rea', *Company*, Oct. 1983, 44.

41. Friel, quoted in Eavan Boland, 'The Northern Writers' Crisis of Conscience', *Irish Times*, 12 Aug. 1970, 12.

42. Friel, quoted in Fintan O'Toole, 'Friel's Day', *Irish Times*, 7 Jan. 1989; D. E. S. Maxwell, *A Critical History of Modern Irish Drama 1891–1980* (Cambridge, 1984), 200.

43. Friel, 'Self-Portrait', *Aquarius*, 5 (published by Servite Priory, Benburb, Co. Tyrone, Ireland, 1972), 19.

44. Maxwell (1984), 200.

45. Friel, 'Self-Portrait', 19–20.

46. Ibid. 18.

47. Friel, *Philadelphia, Here I Come!* in *Selected Plays of Brian Friel*, ed. Seamus Deane (London, 1984), 77.

48. O'Toole, 'Brian Friel: The Healing Art', *Magill*, Jan. 1985.

49. Fergus Linehan, Brian Friel, Hugh Leonard, and John B. Keane, 'The Future of Irish Drama', *Irish Times*, 12 Feb. 1970, 14.

50. Friel, 'Self-Portrait', 21.

51. Friel, 'The Man From God Knows Where', 22.

52. Friel, *The Mundy Scheme* (New York, 1970), 45, 7, 63.

53. In much the same way as Thomas Kilroy's *The Death and Resurrection of Mr. Roche* (London, 1969).

54. Friel, *The Gentle Island* (London, 1973), 37.

55. Friel, 'The Man From God Knows Where', 22.

56. Friel, *The Freedom of the City* in *Selected Plays*, 128–9, 154, 155.

57. Friel, *Volunteers* (London, 1979), 19, 26.

58. Friel, 'The Man From God Knows Where', 21, 23.

59. Friel, 'Talking to Ourselves', interview by Paddy Agnew, *Magill*, Dec. 1980, 60.

60. Friel, quoted in Michael Sheridan, 'Friel's Sense of Conflict', *Irish Press*, 1 Oct. 1986.

61. Friel, 'The Man From God Knows Where', 22.

62. Eugene Moloney, 'From a Nursery to the Opera House', *Irish News*, 29 Sept. 1982.

63. Alex Renton, 'Ireland's Leading Rebel', *Illustrated London News*, Jan. 1989, 61; Ciaran Carty, 'The Confessions of a One-time Werewolf', *Sunday Independent*, 24 Mar. 1985.

64. Renton, *Illustrated London News*, Jan. 1989, 61; Fintan O'Toole,

'Stephen Rea: The Great Leap from the Abbey', *Sunday Tribune*, 23 Sept. 1984.

65. Renton, *Illustrated London News*, Jan. 1989, 61; Rea, quoted in Malachi O'Doherty, 'On the Eve of Pentecost', *Hype*, Nov. 1987, 30.

66. O'Toole, *Sunday Tribune*, 23 Sept. 1984.

67. Charles Hunter, 'Stephen Rea: Actor-Manager with a Mission', *Irish Times*, 19 Sept. 1987.

68. O'Toole, *Sunday Tribune*, 23 Sept. 1984.

69. Hunter, *Irish Times*, 19 Sept. 1987.

70. Christie Hickman, 'Stephen Rea, Fringe Actor Par Excellence', *Drama* (Autumn 1983), 24. The group 7:84 takes its name from the fact that 7% of the population of Britain owns 84% of the wealth (Peter Sheridan, 'The Theatre and Politics', *Crane Bag*, 1.1 (Spring 1977), 68).

71. O'Toole, *Sunday Tribune*, 23 Sept. 1984; Hickman, *Drama* (Autumn 1983), 24; Renton, *Illustrated London News*, Jan. 1989, 61.

72. O'Toole, *Sunday Tribune*, 23 Sept. 1984.

73. Hickman, *Drama* (Autumn 1983), 25.

74. Moloney, *Irish News*, 29 Sept. 1982.

75. See Deane, 'Why Bogside?', *Honest Ulsterman*, 27 (Jan.–Feb. 1971), 1–8.

76. Deane (ed.), introduction to *The Adventures of Hugh Trevor* by Thomas Holcroft (London, 1973), p. ix.

77. Deane, 'A Fable', *Rumours* (Dublin, 1977), 28–30.

78. Deane, 'Derry', *Gradual Wars* (Shannon, 1972), 29.

79. Deane, 'Bonfire', *Rumours*, 22–3.

80. Deane, 'The Victim', *Rumours*, 24.

81. 'Editorial', *Atlantis*, 1 (Mar. 1970), 5.

82. Deane, 'Mugwumps and Reptiles', *Atlantis*, 2 (Oct. 1970), 4–6.

83. Ibid. 7. Deane believed that the Republic itself had a colonial problem with respect to Great Britain: 'The spirit of Connolly and even of Pearse seems to have died with an abruptness which has shocked the younger generation in the (Catholic) North particularly. Ireland has totally yielded her identity to her capitalist master.' (Ibid).

84. Ibid. 8.

85. John Dillon, 'Editorial: Some Remarks on the New Ireland Concept', *Atlantis*, 5 (Apr. 1973), 6.

86. McCormack (1986), 11.

87. 'Editorial', *Atlantis*, 6 (Winter 1973–4), 5.

88. 'Editorial I/Endodermis', *Crane Bag*, 1.1 (Spring 1977), 4.

89. 'Editorial II/Epidermis', *Crane Bag*, 1.1 (Spring 1977), 89.

90. Richard Kearney, 'Beyond Art and Politics', *Crane Bag*, 1.1 (Spring 1977), 10.

91. 'Editorial', *Crane Bag*, 1.2 (1977), 6.

92. 'Editorial', *Crane Bag*, 2.1 and 2 (1978), 5–7.
93. A number of these essays were later collected in Deane, *Celtic Revivals: Essays in Modern Irish Literature 1880–1980* (London, 1985).
94. Deane, 'Irish Poetry and Irish Nationalism', in Douglas Dunn (ed.), *Two Decades of Irish Writing: A Critical Survey* (Chester Springs, Pa., 1975), 16–17.
95. Deane, 'Scholar II', *Rumours*, 43.
96. Seamus Heaney, *Preoccupations: Selected Prose 1968–1978* (London, 1984), 28–30.
97. Deaglán de Breádún, 'Comfortable Image Belies the Serious Poet', *Irish Times*, 13 Sept. 1984.
98. Heaney, 'On Irish Expressionist Painting,' *Irish Review*, 3 (1988), 35.
99. Heaney, 'Docker', in *Death of a Naturalist* (London, 1966), 41.
100. Heaney, 'Unhappy and at Home', interview by Seamus Deane, *Crane Bag*, 1.1 (Spring 1977), 61–2.
101. Bel Mooney, 'Poet, Pilgrim, Fugitive . . .', *The Times*, 11 Oct. 1984, 8.
102. Ibid.
103. Heaney, 'Unhappy and at Home', 65.
104. Heaney, 'Bogland', in *Door Into the Dark* (London, 1969), 56.
105. Heaney, preface to *Bog Poems*, ill. by Barrie Cooke (London, 1975).
106. Heaney, 'Navvy', in *Wintering Out* (London, 1972, 1973), 51.
107. Heaney, 'Punishment', in *North* (London, 1975), 38.
108. Heaney, quoted in 'Poet Wearing the Mantle of Yeats', *Observer*, 21 June 1987, 7.
109. Heaney, introduction to *Stations* (Belfast, 1975), 3.
110. Heaney, *Stations*, 14, 11, 15.
111. Heaney, 'Trial Runs', in *Stations*, 18.
112. Heaney, 'The Other Side', in *Wintering Out*, 36.
113. Heaney, 'Whatever You Say Say Nothing', in *North*, 59–60.
114. Heaney, *Preoccupations*, 34–5.
115. Heaney, 'Unhappy and at Home', 62–3.
116. Heaney, 'Hercules and Antaeus', in *North*, 52–3.
117. Heaney, 'The Harvest Bow', in *Field Work* (London, 1979), 58.
118. Fintan O'Toole, 'Heaney's Half-Century', *Irish Times*, 8 Apr. 1989.
119. Heaney, 'An Interview with Seamus Heaney', interview by James Randall, *Ploughshares*, 5.3 (1979), 8.
120. Heaney, 'Stump' from 'A Northern Hoard', in *Wintering Out*, 41.
121. Heaney, 'Exposure', in *North*, 73.
122. 'Hammond's Second Golden Harp Award', *Derry Journal*, 24 June 1986.
123. Hammond's albums included 'I Am the Wee Falorie Man', 'Songs of the Belfast Streets', 'Irish Songs of Remembrance', and 'The Singer's

House'. Albums he produced are 'Ulster's Flowery Vale', 'John Doherty', and 'Green Peas and Barley-O'.

124. Biographical information from David Hammond, letters to the author, 5 Jan. 1992 and 18 Feb. 1992.

125. Hammond, personal interview, 24 Aug. 1990.

126. Ibid.

127. 'Screen Study of Ireland Planned', *Belfast Telegraph*, 7 Mar. 1987.

128. Hammond, personal interview, 24 Aug. 1990.

129. Hammond, letter to the author, 5 Jan. 1992.

130. Hammond, personal interview, 24 Aug. 1990.

131. Paulin, 'Introduction', *Ireland and the English Crisis* (Newcastle upon Tyne, 1984), 16–18.

132. 'What the North Really Needs Is an Irish English Dictionary', *Sunday Independent*, 16 Sept. 1984; 'Poetry, the Other Northern Ireland Ferment', *The Times*, 13 Apr. 1985; Paulin, personal interview, 26 Jan. 1992.

133. 'What the North Really Needs Is an Irish English Dictionary', *Sunday Independent*, 16 Sept. 1984; 'Poetry, the Other Northern Ireland Ferment', *The Times*, 13 Apr. 1985.

134. Paulin, 'Surveillances', in *Personal Column* (Belfast, 1978), 7.

135. Deane, 'Black Mountain Jacobin', *Honest Ulsterman*, 74 (Winter 1983), 49.

136. Paulin, 'A Just State', in *A State of Justice* (London, 1977), 24.

137. Paulin, 'States', in *A State of Justice*, 7.

138. Paulin, 'A Partial State', in *The Strange Museum* (London, 1980), 19.

139. Paulin, 'Manichean Geography I' and 'Manichean Geography II', in *Liberty Tree* (London, 1983), 42–4. These poems were included earlier in *The Book of Juniper*, ill. by Noel Connor (Newcastle upon Tyne, 1981).

140. Paulin, 'A New Society', in *Theoretical Locations* (Belfast, 1975), 16–17.

141. Paulin, 'Settlers', in *A State of Justice*, 8.

142. Deane, 'Mugwumps and Reptiles', 3.

143. Paulin, in John Haffenden (ed.), *Viewpoints: Poets in Conversation with John Haffenden* (London, 1981) 159.

144. Paulin, 'Desertmartin', in *Liberty Tree*, 16–17. This poem appeared earlier in *The Book of Juniper*. An Ulster nickname for Ian Paisley is 'the Big Man'.

145. Cole, *Saturday Review*, Jan.–Feb. 1986.

146. Heaney, *The Times*, 5 Dec. 1988.

147. Friel, 'The Man From God Knows Where', 22.

148. 'Field Day Theatre Co. to Present Chekov's *Three Sisters*', *Derry Journal*, 19 June 1981, 5.

149. John Feeney, 'Ad Lib: Brian Friel's Present Work is Top Secret', *Evening Herald*, 15 Jan. 1981.

150. Liam Robinson, 'New Play to Set Fire to the Foyle?', *Evening Press*, 19 Sept. 1980.

151. Gillespie, 'The Saturday Interview: Brian Friel', *Irish Times*, 5 Sept. 1981.

152. Ibid.

153. Ibid.

154. Deane, 'What Is Field Day?' (programme note for Field Day's 1981 production, *Three Sisters*).

CHAPTER 4

1. Martin O'Brien, 'Friel Gives Chekhov's Vision New Meaning', *Belfast Telegraph*, 5 Sept. 1981.

2. 'Friel's Three Sisters', *Evening Press*, 22 Aug. 1981.

3. Cathal Póirtéir, 'Drámaíocht don bpobal', *Irish Press*, 9 Sept. 1981 (trans. Marc Caball).

4. Mel Gussow, 'From Ballybeg to Broadway', *New York Times Magazine*, 29 Sept. 1991, 56.

5. 'Friel's Three Sisters', *Evening Press*, 22 Aug. 1981.

6. Anton Chekhov, quoted in V. S. Pritchett, *Chekhov: A Biography* (London, 1990), 37.

7. Chekhov, letter to Alexey N. Pleshcheyev, 4 Oct. 1888, in Avraham Yarmolinsky (ed.), *The Portable Chekhov*, 1947 (New York, 1977), 605.

8. Chekhov, letter to Alexey S. Suvorin, 25 Nov. 1892, in Yarmolinsky (ed.), *The Portable Chekhov*, 624–5.

9. Chekhov, *The Note-Books of Anton Tchekhov Together with Reminiscences of Tchekhov by Maxim Gorky*, trans. S. S. Koteliansky and Leonard Woolf (Richmond, 1921), 55.

10. Chekhov, quoted in Pritchett (1990), 36.

11. Chekhov, *The Note-Books*, 29.

12. Chekhov, letter to Alexey S. Suvorin, 9 Dec. 1890, in Yarmolinsky (ed.), *The Portable Chekhov*, 622.

13. Heaney, 'Chekhov on Sakhalin', programme for Field Day's production of *Three Sisters* (1981). This poem was later reprinted, with some revisions, in his *Station Island* (London, 1984), 18–19.

14. Nicholas Moravčevich, 'Chekhov and Naturalism', in Eugene K. Bristow (trans. and ed.), *Anton Chekhov's Plays* (New York, 1977), 294–5.

15. Ibid. 298, 306.

16. Georgy Tovstonogov, 'Chekhov's *Three Sisters* at the Gorky Theatre', in Bristow (trans. and ed.), *Anton Chekhov's Plays*, 328.

17. Yarmolinsky (ed.), *The Portable Chekhov*, 9.

18. Deane, 'Remembering the Irish Future', *Crane Bag*, 8.1 (1984), 83–4.

19. Hingley, '[Chekhov's Russia]', in Bristow (trans. and ed.), *Anton Chekhov's Plays*, 226.

20. Chekhov, *The Note-Books*, 89.

21. Brian Friel, version of *Three Sisters* by Anton Chekhov (Dublin, 1981), 103. Further page references to this play will be given in parentheses in the text.

22. Chekhov, quoted in Robert Brustein, '[Chekhov's Dramaturgy in *The Three Sisters*]', in Bristow (trans. and ed.), *Anton Chekhov's Plays*, 376.

23. Chekhov, *The Note-Books*, 13.

24. Mme Litvinoff, quoted by Mary McCarthy in a 1943 review for *Partisan Review*, included in Victor Emeljanow (ed.), *Chekhov: The Critical Heritage* (London, 1981), 435.

25. Sean O'Faolain, 'Anton Chekov, or *The Persistent Moralist*', in his *The Short Story* (Cork, 1972), 103.

26. Constantin Stanislavski, *My Life In Art*, trans. J. J. Robbins (London, 1980), 373–4.

27. O'Faolain (1972), 126.

28. Donal O'Donnell, 'Friel and a Tale of Three Sisters', *Sunday Press*, 30 Aug. 1981.

29. Ibid.

30. Friel, 'Talking to Ourselves', interview by Paddy Agnew, *Magill*, Dec. 1980, 59.

31. Ulick O'Connor, 'Friel Takes Derry by Storm', *Sunday Tribune*, 6 Sept. 1981.

32. 'Soft, Strong and Very Long', *Sunday News*, 13 Sept. 1981.

33. 'Chekhov in Irish Idiom', *Derry Journal*, 28 Aug. 1981.

34. Oliver Sayler (ed.), *The Moscow Art Theatre Series of Russian Plays*, trans. Jennie Covan (London, 1922), 13; Elisaveta Fen (trans.), *Chekhov Plays* (Harmondsworth, Middlesex, 1959), 260.

35. Ronald Hingley (trans.), *Chekhov: Ivanov, The Seagull, and Three Sisters* (London, 1968), 131.

36. Fen (trans.), *Chekhov Plays* (1959), 275.

37. Magarshack, *The Real Chekhov* (London, 1972), 147.

38. 'Seeking a Sense of Ireland', *The Times*, 5 Oct. 1981.

39. 'Friel to Make Derry Comeback', *Irish Press*, 15 Jan. 1981.

40. Stephen Dixon, 'Brian Friel's Chekhov', *Sunday Tribune*, 25 Jan. 1981.

41. 'Field Day Theatre Co. to Present Chekov's *Three Sisters*', *Derry Journal*, 19 June 1981, 5.
42. Ibid. The Irish-language drama correspondent of the *Irish News* was surprised to find a press release, in Irish, inside an envelope bearing the stamp 'Londonderry City Council'. 'Aistriúchán nua Friel', *Irish News*, 9 Sept. 1981 (trans. Marc Caball).
43. Elgy Gillespie, 'The Saturday Interview: Brian Friel', *Irish Times*, 5 Sept. 1981.
44. 'Chekhov Gets the Friel Treatment', *Sunday News*, 28 June 1981.
45. O'Donnell, *Sunday Press*, 30 Aug. 1981.
46. 'A Prickly Problem', *Belfast Newsletter*, 3 Aug. 1981.
47. Noeleen Dowling, 'Lot to Admire, not Something to Rave About', *Evening Press*, 9 Sept. 1981.
48. 'Chekhov Play for Dungannon', *Dungannon Observer*, 12 Sept. 1981, 3.
49. Venues included Derry, Belfast, Maghera, Carrickmore, Enniskillen, Dungannon, Newry, Armagh, Dublin, Portadown, Coleraine, Galway, Tralee, Limerick, and Cork. 'Field Day's Autumn Date in Cork', *Cork Evening Echo*, 8 Aug. 1981.
50. Sheridan, 'Field Day Carries on its Consciousness of History', *Irish Press*, 15 Sept. 1981.
51. MacGoris, 'The Mary MacGoris Column', *Irish Independent*, 19 June 1981.
52. Dowling, *Evening Press*, 9 Sept. 1981.
53. Ó Gallchóir, '"Dráma" i nDoire', *Irish Press*, 19 Sept. 1981 (trans. Marc Caball).
54. Nowlan, 'New Friel Play Opens in Derry Guild Hall', *Irish Times*, 9 Sept. 1981.
55. Diane Herron, 'Not a "Translation" in the Accepted Sense', *Londonderry Sentinel*, 18 Sept. 1981.
56. e.g. David Nowlan, '*Three Sisters* in Derry Guildhall', *Irish Times*, 10 Sept. 1981; Michael Coveney, 'Three Sisters', *Financial Times*, 10 Sept. 1981; Dowling, *Evening Press*, 9 Sept. 1981; 'Whose Play Anyway', *Sunday Press*, 4 Oct. 1981.
57. Nowlan, *Irish Times*, 10 Sept. 1981. Dowling and Coveney made similar comments.
58. John Keyes, 'Major Playwright Sets the Scene for a Russian Classic', *Belfast Newsletter*, 10 Sept. 1981, 5.
59. Desmond Rushe, 'Faithful but not quite True Chekov', *Irish Independent*, 10 Sept. 1981, 22.
60. Herron, *Londonderry Sentinel*, 18 Sept. 1981.
61. Kathleen Corrigan, 'Field Day for Stephen Rea', *Company*, Oct. 1983, 45.
62. Cronin, 'Three Sisters: Gaiety', *Sunday Tribune*, 4 Oct. 1981, 19.

63. 'Three Sisters', *Sunday Journal*, 4 Oct. 1981.
64. 'Seeking a Sense of Ireland,' *The Times*, 5 Oct. 1981.
65. Byrne, 'The World of Gay Byrne', *Sunday World*, 4 Oct. 1981.
66. Tim Hastings, 'Audiences in Dublin Hit for Criticism', *Irish Press*, 30 Sept. 1981.
67. John Gray, 'Field Day Five Years On', *The Linen Hall Review* (Summer 1985), 5. Friel himself had commented in 1981 that the 'ideal translation would be by a playwright who speaks Russian', a description that fits Michael Frayn. Betty Lowry, 'The Man from Muff', *Belfast Telegraph*, 7 Mar. 1981, 6.
68. O'Donnell, *Sunday Press*, 30 Aug. 1981.
69. Gillespie, *Irish Times*, 5 Sept. 1981.
70. 'Another Major Friel Play Première in Derry', *Derry Journal*, 25 June 1982. A list of venues was printed in 'Field Day's First Farce', *Ulster Tatler*, Oct. 1982: Derry, Belfast, Dungannon, Craigavon, Maghera, Enniskillen, Armagh, Newry, Omagh, Coleraine, Galway, Sligo, Limerick, Dublin, Cork. The following year, a new production was mounted at the Hampstead Theatre in London, directed by Nancy Meckler and with Stephen Rea in the lead. Christopher Hudson, 'Razing the Roof', *Standard*, 9 May 1983. In 1982 Field Day skipped the Dublin Theatre Festival, playing the city afterwards. This prompted speculation that the company was still annoyed about the fate of *Three Sisters* the year before, but Friel insisted that there was nothing 'sinister' about the decision to miss the festival. Colm Cronin, 'Delayed Entrance for Friel Farce', *Sunday Tribune*, 5 Sept. 1982; Ray Comiskey, 'Rehearsing Friel's New Farce', *Irish Times*, 14 Sept. 1982, 8.
71. *Three Sisters* was estimated to have lost between £15,000 and £20,000. Paul Hadfield and Lynda Henderson, 'Field Day: Magical Mystery Tour', *Theatre Ireland*, 2 (Jan. 1983), 66.
72. Lynda Henderson, personal interview, 25 Sept. 1989.
73. 'Friel's Farce', *Belfast Newsletter*, 9 Sept. 1982.
74. 'Another Guildhall World Première', *Derry Journal*, 31 Aug. 1982, 7.
75. Maggie Stanfield, 'Response Cry—Variations of a Catastrophe', *Irish Press*, 17 Sept. 1982.
76. Comiskey, *Irish Times*, 14 Sept. 1982.
77. Kearney, *Transitions: Narratives in Modern Irish Culture* (Manchester, 1988), 147.
78. Brian Friel, *The Communication Cord,* 1983 (Loughcrew, Oldcastle, Co. Meath, 1989), 21. Future references to this play will be given in parentheses in the text.
79. Friel, 'The Man From God Knows Where', interview by Fintan O'Toole, *In Dublin*, 28 Oct. 1982, 21.
80. Ibid. 23.

81. Seamus Heaney, personal interview, 23 Oct. 1989.
82. Ibid.
83. O'Toole, 'Theatre', *In Dublin*, 28 Oct. 1982, 52.
84. Nora Dan, the most self-aware character, was very popular, especially in the North. Eugene Moloney wrote, 'Pat Leavy as Nora steals the show from everyone else in her portrayal of the local woman whose slow, but shrewd Donegal character enables her to take a hand out of all the confused characters around her.' Frank Curran averred that 'Anyone who knows the country at all, has met "Nora Dan" and Pat Leavy so obviously enjoyed playing a role that was so true to life that most people I am sure equated the character with a person they know.' (Moloney, ' "Cord" that Tilts the Fun-Bath Over All', *Irish News*, 23 Sept. 1982; Curran, 'Friel's *Communication Cord* Rings the Bell', *Derry Journal*, 24 Sept. 1982.)
85. Stanfield, *Irish Press*, 17 Sept. 1982.
86. Friel, 'The Man From God Knows Where', 21.
87. Eugene Moloney, 'Communication Cord Set to be a Signal Success', *Irish News*, 17 Sept. 1982, 4.
88. Kearney (1988), 147–8.
89. Deane, 'In Search of a Story', programme note to *The Communication Cord*, Field Day production, 1982.
90. Paulin, 'Commencement', programme note to *The Communication Cord*, Field Day production, 1982.
91. O'Toole, *In Dublin*, 28 Oct. 1982, 52.
92. 'Friel Play Brought 3,500 to the Guildhall', *Derry Journal*, 15 Oct. 1982; 'Memoranda: Shows Go On', *Irish Times*, 30 Oct. 1982.
93. Hadfield and Henderson, 'Field Day: Magical Mystery Tour', 66.
94. Desmond Rushe, 'Friel: Comedy with a Cutting Edge', *Irish Independent*, 23 Sept. 1982.
95. Coveney, 'Londonderry Airs, Belfast Blues', *Financial Times*, 25 Sept. 1982.
96. Nowlan, 'A Sold-out Festival?' *Irish Times*, 17 Sept. 1982.
97. 'Brian Friel's *The Communication Cord*', *Ulster Herald*, 16 Oct. 1982, 16.
98. Rushe, *Irish Independent*, 23 Sept. 1982.
99. 'Evening of Laughter', *Newry Reporter*, 14 Oct. 1982.
100. Friel, 'The Man From God Knows Where', 21.
101. Comiskey, *Irish Times*, 14 Sept. 1982.
102. Smith, 'French Farce in Donegal Cottage', *Sunday Independent*, 7 Nov. 1982; MacGoris, 'Too-Wordy Friel Farce', *Irish Independent*, 2 Nov. 1982.
103. Nowlan, '*The Communication Cord* at the Gaiety', *Irish Times*, 2 Nov. 1982.
104. Comiskey, *Irish Times*, 14 Sept. 1982.

105. McGinley, 'Humour is in the Eye of the Beholder', *Donegal Democrat*, 1 Oct. 1982, 17.
106. Brian Trench, 'Friel Has the Last Laugh', *Sunday Tribune*, 26 Sept. 1982.
107. Séamus Ó Cinnéide, 'Northern Group's Ingenious Presentation of Friel Farce', *Limerick Leader*, 27 Oct. 1982.
108. Nowlan, 'New Friel Fare at Derry Guildhall', *Irish Times*, 23 Sept. 1982.
109. Simmons, 'Brian Friel, Catholic Playwright', *Honest Ulsterman*, 79 (Autumn 1985), 66.
110. Cathal Póirtéir, 'Dráma nua Friel', *Irish Press*, 18 Sept. 1982 (trans. Marc Caball).
111. Hadfield and Henderson, 'Field Day: The Magical Mystery', *Theatre Ireland*, 2 (Jan. 1983), 64.
112. Nowlan, 'New Friel Play Applauded', *Irish Times*, 22 Sept. 1982.
113. Stanfield, *Irish Press*, 17 Sept. 1982.
114. 'Field Day's First Friel Farce for Newry', *Rathfriland Outlook*, 30 Sept. 1982, 19.
115. Comiskey, *Irish Times*, 14 Sept. 1982.
116. Eugene Moloney, 'From a Nursery to the Opera House', *Irish News*, 29 Sept. 1982.
117. Paulin, 'Commencement', and Deane, 'In Search of a Story', programme notes to the Field Day production of *The Communication Cord*, 1982.
118. Simmons, review of *The Communication Cord*, *Theatre Ireland*, 2 (Jan. 1983), 69.
119. Dawe, review of *The Communication Cord*, *Theatre Ireland*, 2 (Jan. 1983), 67.
120. Woodworth, 'Reasons for Having a Field Day', *Irish Press*, 1 Nov. 1982.
121. Hadfield and Henderson, 'Field Day: The Magical Mystery', 63–5.
122. Comiskey, *Irish Times*, 14 Sept. 1982.
123. Friel, 'The Man From God Knows Where', 21, 23.
124. Ibid. 23.
125. Comiskey, *Irish Times*, 14 Sept. 1982. Hadfield and Henderson believed that the amounts contributed by the Arts Councils, North and South, were more nearly balanced than Friel indicated, estimating that Field Day received £30,000 from the Arts Council of Northern Ireland and £25,000 from An Chomhairle Ealaion in 1982 (Hadfield and Henderson, 'Field Day: Magical Mystery Tour', 66).
126. Rea, quoted in Woodworth, *Irish Press*, 1 Nov. 1982.
127. Rea, quoted in Lynne Riddell, 'In Derry the Talk is All About a Farce in Donegal', *Irish Press*, 18 Sept. 1982.

CHAPTER 5

The quotation in the title is taken from Stephen Rea, quoted in Christie Hickman, 'Stephen Rea, Fringe Actor Par Excellence', *Drama* (Autumn 1983), 23.

1. 'New Lines From Theatre Company', *Belfast Telegraph*, 2 Sept. 1983.
2. Deaglán de Bréadún, 'Comfortable Image Belies the Serious Poet', *Irish Times*, 13 Sept. 1984.
3. 'Anyone Here Speak British?', *Books Ireland*, Nov. 1983.
4. Tom Paulin, *A New Look at the Language Question* in *Ireland's Field Day* (London, 1985), 3. Further references to Paulin's pamphlet are also taken from this edition and will be given in parentheses in the text.
5. Ian Adamson, *The Identity of Ulster* (Northern Ireland, 1982).
6. Jonathan Swift on opposition to his 'A Proposal for Correcting the English Tongue', quoted in Irvin Ehrenpreis, *Swift: The Man, His Works, and the Age* (London, 1967), 548.
7. Heaney, *An Open Letter* in *Ireland's Field Day* (London, 1985). Page references to Heaney's pamphlet are taken from this edition and will be given in parentheses in the text. Morrison and Motion (eds.), *The Penguin Book of Contemporary British Poetry* (Harmondsworth, Middlesex, 1982).
8. Ironically, 'English' might have been less contentious because, while it could be taken to describe the language in which the poetry is written, 'British' is generally used only to denote nationality.
9. 'Field Day to Publish Heaney's *Sweeney Astray*', *Derry Journal*, 18 Oct. 1983, 11. Field Day's first venture into this type of publishing had been the production of Friel's *Translations* in book form in 1980. 'Heaney's Sweeney', *Belfast Newsletter*, 19 Oct. 1983.
10. 'Heaney's *Sweeney Astray* Launched', *Derry Journal*, 15 Nov. 1983.
11. Flann O'Brien, *At Swim-Two-Birds*, 1939, 1960 (London, 1976), 89–128.
12. 'Heaney to Publish Epic Poem', *Derry Journal*, 6 Sept. 1983, 8.
13. Heaney, introduction to *Sweeney Astray* (Derry, 1983), p. vii. Further page references to *Sweeney Astray* will be placed in parentheses in the text.
14. In fact, says Bernard O'Donoghue,

> The resonances of the Sweeney story for contemporary Ulster are considerable, and the translation is an eloquent rejoinder to the view of Heaney as moving away from political statement. . . . In the battle of Magh Rath, Sweeney is fighting for an Ulster King at the head of a Scottish army against the High King of Ireland to whom 'the romantic accounts tell us that the

whole of Ireland rallied' (according to J. G. O'Keeffe in the introduction to the 1913 edition of the poem used by Heaney). Ronan, the 'holy and distinguished cleric' who imposes madness on Sweeney, refuses the reconciliation that Sweeney wants, asking God to renew the curse in a voice familiar from modern Ulster: 'Remember that you struck him for an example, a warning to tyrants that you and your people were sacred and not to be lightly dishonoured and outraged.' To set against this, one of the disembodied heads in Sweeney's grisly nightmare echoes the voice of the modern uncomprehending outsider: 'This is the Ulster lunatic. Let us drive him into the sea.' And Sweeney reflects in his misery and exile: 'it would be better to trust my people than to endure these woes forever'. (O'Donoghue, 'Heaney's Sweeney', *Poetry Review*, 74.1 (Apr. 1984), 62.)

15. Thomas McCarthy, 'Heaney's Sweeney', *Connacht Tribune*, 23–30 Dec. 1983, 8.

16. Harris, 'Field Day and the Fifth Province', *An Gael* (Summer 1985), 11.

17. O Drisceoil, 'Heaney's Sweeney', *Irish Press*, 10 Dec. 1983, 9.

18. Montague, 'Tarzan Among the Nightingales', *Fortnight*, 200 (Dec. 1983–Jan. 1984), 27.

19. For example, Nick Carter, who got 'no feeling of or for the original except aversion'. Carter, 'Briefs', *In Dublin*, 1 Dec. 1983.

20. Boland, 'Heaney's Sweeney', *Irish Times*, 10 Dec. 1983.

21. O'Donoghue, 'Heaney's Sweeney', 63.

22. Deane, *Civilians and Barbarians* in *Ireland's Field Day* (London, 1985), 33. Further references to Deane's pamphlet will be given in parentheses in the text.

23. 'Language and Politics', *Irish News*, 10 Sept. 1983, 5.

24. Mhac an tSaoi is both Conor Cruise O'Brien's wife and a well-known Irish-language poet.

25. Mhac an tSaoi, 'The Book Page', *Irish Press*, 29 Oct. 1983.

26. Edwards, 'An Open Letter: On Receiving Three Pamphlets from Field Day, with their Compliments', *Irish Times*, 10 Dec. 1983.

27. Boland, 'Poets and Pamphlets', *Irish Times*, 1 Oct. 1983, 12.

28. Johnstone, 'Guldering Unselfconsciously', *Honest Ulsterman*, 75 (May 1984), 85–91.

29. Paulin and Johnstone, 'Another Look at the Field Day Question', *Honest Ulsterman*, 76 (Autumn 1984), 40–3.

30. Brown, 'Calling the North's Muses Home', *Fortnight*, 198 (Oct. 1983), 22–3.

31. Ó Conchúir, 'Field Day Pamphlets', letter, *Irish Times*, 3 Feb. 1984.

32. Harmon, review, *Irish University Review*, 14.1 (Spring 1984), 129.

33. Ó Doibhlin, 'No Answer for the Angels?', *Furrow*, 35.1 (Jan. 1984), 35–6.

34. Sheehan and Kearney, letter, *Irish Times*, 25 Jan. 1984.
35. Kearney, 'Brian Friel and the Three Pamphleteers', *Magill*, Oct. 1983, 55.
36. Kathleen Corrigan, 'Field Day for Stephen Rea', *Company*, Oct. 1983, 44.
37. Ibid.
38. Deane, Richard Kearney, and Ciaran Carty, 'Why Ireland Needs a Fifth Province', *Sunday Independent*, 22 Jan. 1984, 15.
39. 'Pick of the Arts in 1983: The Second Sunday Independent Arts Awards', *Sunday Independent*, 1 Jan. 1984.
40. The actress Siobhan McKenna launched the second series in Derry on 25 May 1984. 'Field Day Wisdom', *Evening Herald*, 24 May 1984.
41. This volume doubled as the *Crane Bag* 8.1 and appeared in the first part of 1984, shortly before the second set of Field Day pamphlets.
42. Not everyone was pleased by this seeming collusion. A writer in the Dublin-based magazine *The Phoenix* moaned, 'It had to happen but what a pity it did—the second set of Field Day pamphlets has been hijacked by the UCD Arts Faculty mafia.' ('Elitist Pamphlets', *Phoenix*, 22 June 1984.)
43. Deane, 'Remembering the Irish Future', *Crane Bag*, 8.1 (1984), 83–4.
44. Ibid. 86.
45. Ibid. 88.
46. Ibid. 90.
47. Deane, *Heroic Styles: The Tradition of an Idea* in Ireland's Field Day (London, 1985), 58. Further references will be given in parentheses in the text.
48. W. B. Yeats, 'A General Introduction for my Work', in his *Essays and Introductions* (London, 1961), 519.
49. Kearney, 'Faith and Fatherland', *Crane Bag*, 8.1 (1984), 64, 65.
50. Kearney, *Myth and Motherland* in Ireland's Field Day (London, 1985), 61. Further references to Kearney's pamphlet will be given in parentheses in the text.
51. Kiberd, *Anglo-Irish Attitudes* in Ireland's Field Day (London, 1985), 83. Further references to Kiberd's pamphlet will be given in parentheses in the text.
52. Kiberd, 'Inventing Irelands', *Crane Bag*, 8.1 (1984), 12–13, 14.
53. Oliver MacDonagh, *States of Mind: A Study of Anglo-Irish Conflict 1780–1980* (London, 1983).
54. F. S. L. Lyons, *Culture and Anarchy in Ireland 1890–1939* (Oxford, 1979).
55. Michael Farrell, *Northern Ireland: The Orange State* (London, 1976); Eamonn McCann, *War and an Irish Town* (London, rev. edn., 1980).

56. Moran was probably thinking of Longley's 'North: "Inner Emigré" or "Artful Voyeur"?' in Tony Curtis (ed.), *The Art of Seamus Heaney* (Bridgend, Mid Glamorgan, 1982, 1985), 63–95.
57. Moran, 'Three More from Field Day', *Irish Literary Supplement* (Fall 1984), 21.
58. Brown, 'Having a Field Day', *Irish Press*, 14 July 1984.
59. Smyth, 'Stick to the Twenty-Six, and Rhyme, Seamus Deane, Seamus Deane', *North*, 3 (Oct. 1984), 18–19. Smyth is referring to W. B. Yeats's poem, 'Nineteen Hundred and Nineteen' and 'Eclogue from Iceland' by Louis MacNeice.
60. Longley, 'More Martyrs to Abstraction' *Fortnight*, 206 (July–Aug. 1984), 18, 20.
61. Gorman, 'Send in the Prods', *Belfast Review*, Sept. 1984.

CHAPTER 6

1. Probably not coincidentally, *Ashes* was banned in Israel and South Africa, where the ruling groups also know the fear of being overwhelmed by the enemy within the state.
2. Cover letter, David Rudkin to the Field Day directors, 31 May 1983.
3. The foregoing information is mainly from interviews with Rudkin on 26 and 28 Oct. 1991.
4. Rudkin, 'An Historical Note' to *The Saxon Shore* (London, 1986), p. vii. Further page references to *The Saxon Shore* will be given in parentheses in the Chapter. The Methuen text is not exactly the same as the script that was submitted to Field Day—the directors read an earlier version of the play. However, Rudkin has kept only the second part of that original draft; no copy of the entire script remains in his possession or in the possession of Field Day. I am quoting from the published text by default, and the reader should bear in mind that the original was looser and less polished than the final version. Nevertheless, the concept was present and more or less realized in the Field Day text, and it seems to have been that rather than any specific objections to particular lines that gave the directors pause. As Rudkin puts it, 'The question is: if I had submitted, in 1983, the "final text", would or would not the subsequent story have been the same?' (Letter to the author from Gary McKeone, Field Day Company Manager, 25 Feb. 1992; Rudkin, letter to the author, 5 Mar. 1992.)
5. Henderson, personal interview, 25 Sept. 1989.
6. This twist also helped him to achieve his private aim of writing a difficult play for Irish actors, because he specified that 'it can never be right to use wolfmasks or werewolf costume. These human charac-

ters *experience* themselves as wolves. . . . the transformation to werewolf is an "acting problem" ' (52).

7. This is not exactly the way the Field Day text ended. There, the image
used was one of wakening rather than standing. The implication in
the original draft and in the published script is the same, however: the
Saxons must make a new beginning involving reconciliation with
their British enemies.

8. Public comment on the change of plans can only be called terse. In
one article announcing the *Boesman and Lena* tour, Field Day conceded that 'The English-based Northern playwright David Rudkin
was approached and produced a script but the project fell through.'
('Field Day', *Sunday Tribune*, 18 Sept. 1983.)

9. What little later commentary there is on the incident has implicitly
taken this view. See, for example, Brian McAvera, 'Reject Set for a
World Stage', *Irish News*, 3 Mar. 1986; Shaun Richards, 'Field
Day's Fifth Province: Avenue or Impasse?', in Eamonn Hughes (ed.),
Culture and Politics in Northern Ireland (Milton Keynes, 1991),
143.

10. Rudkin, letter to the author, 1 Dec. 1991.

11. Interviews with David Rudkin, 26 and 28 Oct. 1991.

12. The reviews that mentioned the Ulster dimension were Michael
Billington, 'Howl on the Wilder Shores', *Guardian*, 5 Mar. 1986, 11
and Richard Allen Cave, 'The Past is Not Another Country', *Times
Higher Education Supplement*, 14 Mar. 1986, 15. Other reviewers
tended to see the play as an exploration of the evolution of the
English national character. See e.g. Milton Shulman, 'Keep Your
Eyes on the Woad', *London Standard*, 4 Mar. 1986, 28; Irving
Wardle, 'Confusion in the Werewolf Idiom', *The Times*, 5 Mar.
1986, 9; Michael Ratcliffe, 'Paradise Unhitched', *Observer*, 9 Mar.
1986, 25; John Barber, 'Poet's Dark Ages', *Daily Telegraph*, 5 Mar.
1986, 11; and Michael Coveney, 'The Saxon Shore', *Financial Times*,
4 Mar. 1986, 21.

13. In *The Sons of Light*, a village elder rises from his wheelchair on
foggy days to become the terrifying Fog King. In a later play, *The
Triumph of Death*, one character nearly turns into a werewolf, but
manages to master himself. (Rudkin, *The Sons of Light* (London,
1981) and *The Triumph of Death* (London, 1981), 49.)

14. Rudkin, letter to the author, 1 Dec. 1991; cover letter from Rudkin
to the Field Day directors, 31 May 1983.

15. Hammond, letter to the author, 19 Aug. 1993.

16. John Cunningham, 'Communication Chord', *Guardian*, 6 May
1983.

17. Christie Hickman, 'Stephen Rea, Fringe Actor Par Excellence',
Drama (Autumn 1983), 25.

18. Rea, personal interview, 18 April 1991. Julie Barber, then administrator of Field Day, explains that this is why the tour in 1983 went from Derry down to Tralee and from there to other venues in the Republic without going first to other towns in the North, as was more usual practice. (Barber, personal interview, 1 Aug. 1990.)

19. Rea, personal interview, 18 Apr. 1991.

20. Henderson, personal interview, 25 Sept. 1989.

21. Ibid.

22. Hammond, letter to the author, 19 Aug. 1993.

23. Rea, personal interview, 18 Apr. 1991.

24. Paulin, personal interview, 26 Jan. 1992.

25. Julie Barber, telephone interview, 6 Nov. 1991.

26. Rudkin, personal interview, 26 Oct. 1991. It was Fugard's theatre company that had planned to produce *Ashes* before it was banned by the South African government.

27. Fugard, introduction to Athol Fugard, John Kani, Winston Ntshona, *Statements: Three Plays* (Oxford, 1974).

28. Biographical information about Fugard taken, unless otherwise attributed, from Dennis Walder, introduction to Athol Fugard, *Selected Plays* (Oxford, 1987).

29. Fugard in Oct. 1967, *Notebooks 1960–1977*, ed. Mary Benson (London, 1983), 156.

30. Walder, introduction to Fugard, *Selected Plays*, p. xviii.

31. Fugard, *Boesman and Lena* in *Selected Plays*, 200. Future references to the play will be taken from this edition, unless otherwise stated, and given in parentheses in the text.

32. Fugard, *Boesman and Lena* (New York, 1971). In the text given in his *Selected Plays*, Fugard does not put down most of the old man's words, instead explaining in a note that

> The elderly black man who arrives at their fire out of the dark, 'Outa', speaks only his own language, which in this edition is Xhosa, local to Port Elizabeth and its surroundings: the audience is not meant to understand him, any more than Lena does, and so the language spoken may be (and has been) varied according to production and performer. In the main, it is a long tale of suffering and despair, of travelling from place to place as an outcast (249).

33. A glossary note to the text in *Selected Plays* explains that this is a common 'mode of address to an elderly, usually "Coloured" or African man, often by children as a mark of respect to an elderly servant' (254).

34. Fugard, journal entry for 19 July 1968, quoted in the introduction to his *Selected Plays*, p. xxviii.

35. Kader Asmal, programme note to the Field Day production of

Boesman and Lena. Asmal was born in South Africa, but had lived in Dublin for 20 years and was an Irish citizen. He was Dean of the Faculty of Arts (Humanities) at Trinity College Dublin and Chairman of the Irish Anti-Apartheid Movement.

36. '*Boesman and Lena* for the Guildhall', *Derry Journal*, 2 Sept. 1983, 7.

37. Stephen Rea said later that the play seemed often to provoke the response, 'do you think you are as oppressed as the blacks?' (John Gray, 'Field Day Five Years On', *Linen Hall Review* (Summer 1985), 5.)

38. Domhnall MacDermott, 'Behind the Scenes at *Boesman and Lena*', *Derry Journal*, 16 Sept. 1983; '*Boesman and Lena* for the Guildhall', *Derry Journal*, 2 Sept. 1983.

39. Kay Hingerty, 'An Unforgettable Night of Theatre in Derry', *Cork Examiner*, 27 Sept. 1983.

40. Hammond, letter to the author, 19 Aug. 1993.

41. '*Boesman and Lena* for the Guildhall', *Derry Journal*, 2 Sept. 1983.

42. Fugard, *Selected Plays*, 192, 52.

43. '*Boesman and Lena* Travel South', *Dungarvan Leader*, 30 Sept. 1983.

44. 'Newcastle West', *Limerick Leader*, 1 Oct. 1983.

45. Nowlan, '*Boesman and Lena* at Derry Guild Hall', *Irish Times*, 22 Sept. 1983, 8.

46. O'Toole, 'Voices On', *Sunday Tribune*, 25 Sept. 1983.

47. '*Boesman and Lena*: Bottom of the Social Ladder', *Derry Journal*, 23 Sept. 1983.

48. 'Powerful Production from Field Day', *Belfast Telegraph*, 21 Sept. 1983.

49. '*Boesman and Lena* at Friary Hall Theatre', *Dungarvan Observer*, 8 Oct. 1983; Moloney, 'Stark Contrasts', *Irish News*, 22 Sept. 1983.

50. Woodworth, 'A Black Play of Stunning Power', *Irish Press*, 22 Sept. 1983.

51. Woodworth, 'Field Day Success is Greeted', *Irish Press*, 21 Sept. 1983.

52. Nowlan, 'Beyond the Pale', *Irish Times*, 30 Sept. 1983, 8.

53. Hammond, letter to the author, 19 Aug. 1993.

54. 'Fermanagh People Missed a Theatrical Experience', *Impartial Reporter*, 20 Oct. 1983.

55. 'Something New at Newry Arts Festival', *Rathfriland Outlook*, 6 Oct. 1983.

56. 'Friel's Theatre in New Show', *Belfast Telegraph*, 13 Aug. 1983; 'Pamphlets on Politics and Arts in Ireland', *Irish News*, 3 Sept. 1983, 5.

57. '*Boesman and Lena* for the Guildhall', *Derry Journal*, 2 Sept. 1983.

58. Starrett, 'Missing Out on Pat's Big Night', *Sunday News*, 25 Sept. 1983.

59. 'Boesman and Lena for the Guildhall', Derry Journal, 2 Sept. 1983.
60. Kathleen Corrigan, 'Field Day for Stephen Rea', Company, Oct. 1983, 45.
61. Price had served 8 years of a life sentence before she was released on medical grounds from Armagh jail in 1981. She and her sister had conducted a hunger strike in 1974 in a plea to be transferred from jail in Britain to Armagh. Since her release from prison she had been working as a freelance journalist in Dublin. ('Dolours Price Marries Actor', Irish Times, 5 Nov. 1983; 'Price Sister Weds', Daily Mirror, 5 Nov. 1983; 'Dolours Price Marries Actor', Irish Press, 5 Nov. 1983; 'A Secret Cathedral Wedding for Dolours the Sister of Terror', Daily Mail, 5 Nov. 1983.)

CHAPTER 7

1. Colm Cronin, 'Theatre', New Hibernia, Nov. 1984; Liam McAuley, 'Inside the Arts with Liam McAuley', Sunday Independent, 19 Aug. 1984; John Peter, 'The Lessons of Love', Sunday Times, 7 Oct. 1984; Keith Jeffery, 'In Defence of Decency', Times Literary Supplement, 19 Oct. 1984; Catherine Crowe, review, In Dublin, 17 Oct. 1984; Adrian Maddox, 'Theatre', North, Oct. 1984, 25; David Nowlan, 'Field Day Double Bill at Derry Guild Hall', Irish Times, 20 Sept. 1984; Michael Billington, 'High Old Time', Guardian, 5 Oct. 1984; Fintan O'Toole, 'Field Day: On the Double', Sunday Tribune, 23 Sept. 1984; Falstaff, 'Visit of Field Theatre Company to Newry', Newry Reporter, 18 Oct. 1984, 30; Tim Harding, 'Tractarians 10, Drama Nil', Sunday Press, 30 Sept. 1984, 15.
2. Maddox, North, Oct. 1984.
3. Conor Cruise O'Brien, States of Ireland (London, 1972), 156.
4. O'Brien, 'Views', Listener, 24 Oct. 1968, 526.
5. O'Brien, States of Ireland, 159.
6. Paulin, 'The Making of a Loyalist', in his Ireland and the English Crisis (Newcastle upon Tyne, 1984), 27–8.
7. Billington, Guardian, 5 Oct. 1984. Also Lynda Henderson, 'The Riot Act/High Time', Theatre Ireland, 7 (Autumn 1984), 35; Crowe, In Dublin, 17 Oct. 1984; 'Memorable Molière—but Subverted Sophocles', Northern Constitution, 3 Nov. 1984, 18; O'Toole, Sunday Tribune, 23 Sept. 1984.
8. Patrick Quilligan, 'Field Day's New Double Bill', Irish Times, 18 Sept. 1984.
9. Paulin, The Riot Act (London, 1985), 30. Further page references will be given in parentheses in the text.
10. 'What the North Really Needs Is an Irish English Dictionary', Sunday

Independent, 16 Sept. 1984. An essay Paulin wrote on Ian Paisley reveals a sneaking admiration for his rebelliousness. When the preacher was jailed in 1966 for demonstrating outside the General Assembly of the Presbyterian Church he reportedly told Terence O'Neill that 'To Our Lord, puppet politicians are but grasshoppers with portfolios.' (Paulin, 'Paisley's Progress', in *Ireland and the English Crisis*, 160.)

11. Bernard Knox, general introduction and introduction to *Antigone* in *Sophocles: The Three Theban Plays*, trans. Robert Fagles (London, 1982), 11, 25.

12. See e.g. Paulin, 'A Just State' in his *A State of Justice* (London, 1977), 24, 'States' and 'Under the Eyes' in the same volume (7, 9), and 'Where Art is a Midwife' in *Personal Column* (Belfast, 1978), 4.

13. Knox, introduction to *Antigone* in *Sophocles: The Three Theban Plays* (1982), 11, 23.

14. Robert Johnstone, 'Antigone in Ulster Dialect' (review of the published script), *Fortnight*, 227 (21 Oct. 1985), 23; Harding, *Sunday Press*, 30 Sept. 1984; 'Field Day Premières are Superb', *Derry Journal*, 21 Sept. 1984; Jeffery, *Times Literary Supplement*, 19 Oct. 1984.

15. O'Toole, *Sunday Tribune*, 23 Sept. 1984.

16. Maddox, *North*, Oct. 1984.

17. Kay Hingerty, 'Field Day Theatre Co. Take Over at Everyman', *Cork Examiner*, 3 Nov. 1984, 11.

18. Paulin, *Ireland and the English Crisis*, 28.

19. Paulin, personal interview, 26 Jan. 1992.

20. See E. F. Watling (trans.), *Sophocles: The Theban Plays* (Harmondsworth, Middlesex, 1947), 148–9; Kenneth McLeish, trans., *Four Greek Plays* (London, 1964), 71; Dudley Fitts and Robert Fitzgerald (trans.), *The Antigone of Sophocles* (London, 1940), 25; Sir Richard C. Jebb (trans.), *The Tragedies of Sophocles* (Freeport, New York, 1904, repr. 1972), 138–9; and Robert Fagles (trans.), *Sophocles: The Three Theban Plays*, ed. Bernard Knox (London, 1982), 58–9.

21. Paulin later reprinted it as 'There are many wonders on this earth' in *Fivemiletown* (London, 1987), 29.

22. See e.g. Fitts and Fitzgerald (1940), 41–2; McLeish (1964), 78–9; Watling (1947), 155–6; Jebb (1904), 147–8; and Fagles (1982), 73–4.

23. Paulin, personal interview, 26 Jan. 1992.

24. O'Toole, *Sunday Tribune*, 23 Sept. 1984.

25. Jeffery, *Times Literary Supplement*, 19 Oct. 1984.

26. *Twelve Poems* (1965), *Night-Crossing* (1968), *Ecclesiastes, Beyond Howth Head* (1970), *Modern Irish Poetry* (ed.), *Lives, The Man*

Who Built His City in Snow (1972), *The Snow Party* (1975), *Light Music* (1977), *The Sea in Winter, Poems 1962–1978* (1979), *Courtyards in Delft* (1981), *The Chimeras* by Nerval (trans.), *The Hunt by Night* (1982).

27. 'The Right Mahon for a Farce', *Sunday Independent*, 30 Sept. 1984.

28. 'Poetry, the Other Northern Ireland Ferment', *The Times*, 13 Apr. 1985.

29. 'The Right Mahon for a Farce', *Sunday Independent*, 30 Sept. 1984.

30. Actually, there is at least one other versified version in existence, which was produced in New York in 1933. The adapters, however, turned the play into a musical, adding several new scenes and characters and inserting a ballet interlude based on another piece by Molière. Arthur Guiterman and Lawrence Langner, *The School for Husbands* (New York, 1933).

31. Mahon, preface, *High Time* (Dublin, 1985), 7. Further page references will be given in parentheses in the text.

32. Mahon, quoted in 'The Right Mahon for a Farce', *Sunday Independent*, 30 Sept. 1984.

33. Mahon, 'High Time', programme note for the Field Day production of *High Time*, 1984.

34. Clayson (trans. and adapter), *The School for Husbands with The Flying Doctor, The Uneasy Husband, and Love is the Best Remedy* (London, 1969), 63. Further references to this work will be given in parentheses in the text.

35. Nowlan, *Irish Times*, 20 Sept. 1984.

36. Programme note for the Field Day production of *High Time*, 1984.

37. Billington, *Guardian*, 5 Oct. 1984.

38. An tSiur Ailbhe, 'Two Plays by Field Day', *Galway Advertiser*, 1 Nov. 1984.

39. Hingerty, *Cork Examiner*, 3 Nov. 1984.

40. Maddox, *North*, Oct. 1984.

41. Coveney, 'Field Day/Lyric, Belfast', *Financial Times*, 3 Oct. 1984.

42. Long, 'Molière's Method', programme note for the Field Day production of *High Time*, 1984.

43. 'The Right Mahon for a Farce', *Sunday Independent*, 30 Sept. 1984.

44. Henderson, personal interview, 25 Sept. 1989 and *Theatre Ireland*, 7 (Autumn 1984).

45. Nowlan, *Irish Times*, 20 Sept. 1984; Cronin, *New Hibernia*, Nov. 1984.

46. O'Toole, *Sunday Tribune*, 23 Sept. 1984.

47. 'Cushy, Ritzy, Swingin' Disco!', *New Galway Observer*, 17 Oct. 1984.

48. The attitude seems to have been that expressed by the reviewer for the *Times Literary Supplement*: '*High Time* is an agreeable *bonne*

bouche to follow *The Riot Act* and it certainly lets the company display their virtuosity.' (Jeffery, *Times Literary Supplement*, 19 Oct. 1984.)

49. 'Memorable Molière—But Subverted Sophocles', *Northern Constitution*, 3 Nov. 1984.

50. Harding, *Sunday Press*, 30 Sept. 1984.

51. Donegan, '*The Riot Act* Less Fizzle Than Damp Match', *Impartial Reporter*, 18 Oct. 1984, 12.

52. O'Toole, *Sunday Tribune*, 23 Sept. 1984.

53. Nowlan, *Irish Times*, 20 Sept. 1984.

54. Henderson, *Theatre Ireland*, 7 (Autumn 1984).

55. Cronin, *New Hibernia*, Nov. 1984.

56. Lynne Riddel, 'The Ups and Downs, Bumps and Bruises, of the Field Day Theatre Company...', *Belfast Telegraph*, 18 Sept. 1984; Quilligan, *Irish Times*, 18 Sept. 1984.

57. Photo and caption, *Derry Journal*, 24 Aug. 1984.

58. Barber, quoted in Riddel, *Belfast Telegraph*, 18 Sept. 1984.

CONCLUSION

1. Gray, 'Field Day Five Years On', *Linen Hall Review* (Summer 1985), 7.

2. Seamus Deane, Jennifer Fitzgerald, Joan Fowler, and Frank McGuinness, 'The Arts and Ideology', *Crane Bag*, 9.2 (1985), 64–5.

3. Henderson, 'The Riot Act/High Time', *Theatre Ireland*, 7 (Autumn 1984), 35.

4. These ideas had first gained wide currency in an amicable discussion between Brian Friel and John Andrews, the Ordnance Survey historian, that was published as 'Translations and A Paper Landscape: Between Fiction and History', *The Crane Bag*, 7.2 (1983), 118–24.

5. McAvera, 'Brian Friel: Attuned to the Catholic Experience', *Fortnight*, 215 (3 Mar. 1985), 19–20. This article inspired a passionate letter in response from Brighid Bean Mhic Sheain, who objected to his cavalier dismissal of the idea of British cultural suppression. Her epistle, McAvera's reply, and her parting shot appear in *Fortnight* 217, 219, and 222.

6. For examples of this in future years see Sean Connolly, 'Dreaming History: Brian Friel's *Translations*', *Theatre Ireland*, 13 (1987), 42–4; Lynda Henderson, 'A Dangerous Translation', *Fortnight*, 235 (10–23 Mar. 1986), 24; Edna Longley, 'Including the North', *Text and Context* (Autumn 1988), 17–24; and J. H. Andrews, 'Notes for a Future Edition of Brian Friel's *Translations*', *Irish Review*, 13 (Winter 1992–3), 93–106.

7. Longley, 'Poetry and Politics in Northern Ireland', *Crane Bag*, 9.1 (1985), 26–40.
8. Domhnall MacDermott, 'Deane Spells Out Field Day's Role', *Derry Journal*, 8 Feb. 1985.
9. Deane, quoted in Gray, 'Field Day Five Years On', 10.
10. Deane, 'The Arts and Ideology', 63.
11. Rea, 'Private Property', interview by Julia Pascal, *City Limits*, 27 Apr.–3 May 1984, 14.
12. Patrick Quilligan, 'Field Day's New Double Bill', *Irish Times*, 18 Sept. 1984.
13. Gray, 'Field Day Five Years On', 7.
14. Longley, 'A Reply', *Crane Bag*, 9.1 (1985), 120.
15. Callanan, 'The Idiom of Irishry', *New Hibernia*, Apr. 1985.
16. See e.g. Edna Longley's use of the word in the letters column of *Fortnight* 225 (quoted later in this Chapter). Conor Cruise O'Brien, in a review that August of a book of essays by Seamus Deane, referred to the writer as an 'anti-revisionist', prompting the response a week later from Declan Kiberd that 'Even before Conor Cruise O'Brien began his assault on Irish nationalism, Deane had set about his deconstruction of the Irish revival.' Such partisan appropriation of the term would shortly provoke the exasperated reminder from Roy Foster that any historian worth his or her salt is continually re-examining received versions of the past. Logically, then, they all are, or should be, 'revisionists'. O'Brien, 'Cult of Blood', *Observer*, 18 Aug. 1985; Kiberd, 'Non-Protesting Protestants', *Sunday Tribune*, 25 Aug. 1985; Foster, '"We Are All Revisionists Now"', *Irish Review*, 1 (1986), 1–5.
17. Reviewing a collection of essays edited by Longley and Gerald Dawe, Enoch Powell commiserated with the Northern Protestants, 'whose literateurs, like their opposite numbers in the Republic, also love to bellyache about who they are, what they are and why they are. Naturally this is much petted and encouraged by those, in Great Britain and elsewhere, who want to bully the Northern Ireland electorate out of their settled conviction.' (Powell, 'Cultural Ballyaches', review of Edna Longley and Gerald Dawe (eds.), *Across a Roaring Hill: The Protestant Imagination in Modern Ireland*, *The Times*, 15 Aug. 1985, 9.)
18. Longley's mother was Scottish, and Longley herself was brought up in the Church of Ireland. She would write in 1986 that '"Irish" needs to be a chosen common name, not an imposed category, before it can become an allegiance. Nor should Protestants everlastingly have to work their passage to Irishness, while others live off unearned ethnic rents.' (Longley, 'Anglo-Irish Resurrection', *Honest Ulsterman*, 82 (Winter 1986), 106.)

19. Longley, 'Poetry and Politics in Northern Ireland', 29.
20. Ibid. 33.
21. Ibid. 28–9.
22. Deane, 'Irish Poetry and Irish Nationalism', in Douglas Dunn (ed.), *Two Decades of Irish Writing: A Critical Survey* (Chester Springs, Pa., 1975), 8.
23. Witoszek and Sheeran, 'From Explanations to Intervention', *Crane Bag*, 9.1 (1985), 83–6; Fennell, 'A Project that would End Mood of Paralysis', *Irish Times*, 8 July 1985.
24. O'Toole, 'Ireland Goes to Hollywood', *Sunday Tribune*, 16 Sept. 1984.
25. McGuinness, 'The Arts and Ideology', 65.
26. Foster, 'The Critical Condition of Ulster', *Honest Ulsterman*, 79 (Autumn 1985), 38–55. Further references to this article will be given in parentheses in the text.
27. The third set of Field Day pamphlets, *The Protestant Idea of Liberty*, was published in May 1985. Since these pamphlets are beyond the scope of the present study, I will confine my remarks as much as possible to what Foster made of the first two sets of pamphlets.
28. McMinn, 'In Defence of Field Day: Talking Among the Ruins', *Fortnight*, 224 (9 Sept. 1985), 20.
29. Ibid. 19.
30. Ibid.
31. Longley, 'Edna Longley on Field Day', letter, *Fortnight*, 225 (23 Sept. 1985), 15–16.
32. Ó Conchúir, letter, *Fortnight*, 228 (4–17 Nov. 1985), 17.
33. Heaney, quoted in David Lehman and Donna Foote, 'The Ulster Renaissance', *Newsweek* (International Edition), 12 May 1986, 53–4.
34. In a thoughtful commentary on the Field Day flap Robert Johnstone remarked, 'It is absurd and futile for Declan Kiberd, Tom Paulin, et al to direct their fury at those enlightened ones among us who are not of the Enoch Powell persuasion, especially when there are so many who are.' (Johnstone, 'A Wilful Deafness to the North's Self-Questioning', *Fortnight*, 230 (2 Dec. 1985), 20.)

POSTSCRIPT

1. Deane, quoted from 'History Boys on the Rampage', a BBC 2 Arena Documentary on Field Day, by Stephen Regan in 'Ireland's Field Day', *History Workshop*, 33 (Spring 1992), 36.
2. Deane, introduction to 'Political Writings and Speeches 1900–1988',

in Deane *et al.* (eds.), *The Field Day Anthology of Irish Writing* (Derry, 1991), iii: 685.

3. Gerry Moriarty, 'Field Day Future Uncertain as Board Takes "Sabbatical" ', *Irish Times*, 28 Apr. 1993, 1.

4. Deane, *Heroic Styles: The Tradition of an Idea* in *Ireland's Field Day* (London, 1985), 58.

5. Deane, Carty, and Kearney, 'Why Ireland Needs a Fifth Province', *Sunday Independent*, 22 Jan. 1984, 15.

6. Domhnall MacDermott, 'Deane Spells Out Field Day's Role', *Derry Journal*, 8 Feb. 1985.

7. Gray, 'Field Day Five Years On', *Linen Hall Review* (Summer 1985), 8.

8. Martin Cowley, 'Field Day Has Made a Permanent Mark', *Irish Times*, 5 May 1986.

9. Stokes, 'Field Day Tours America', *An Gael* (Summer 1987), 31.

10. Ibid.

11. Field Day, *Field Day: Theatre Company and Publishing House* (Derry, 1987).

12. Longley, 'Opening Up: A New Pluralism', *Fortnight* (Nov. 1987).

13. Foster, unsent letter to Seamus Deane, 24 Apr. 1986, collection of the author.

14. Good examples of this are seen in John McKenna, 'Marathon Trip Through Irish Writing', *Irish Times*, 7 Sept. 1988, 14; Deane, 'Hot House Flowers or Anthologica Hibernica', *Gown Literary Supplement* (Spring–Summer 1990), 19; Deane, 'Introduction', in Deane (ed.), *Nationalism, Colonialism and Literature* (Derry, 1990), 15.

15. Deane, 'General Introduction', in Deane *et al.* (eds.), *The Field Day Anthology of Irish Writing* (Derry, 1991), pp. xix–xx.

16. Ibid. p. xix.

17. '1,500 Years of Irish Writing', National Public Radio interview, 12 Dec. 1991.

18. McKenna, *Irish Times*, 7 Sept. 1988.

19. 'US Field Day for Begging Bowl Big Four', *Irish News*, 30 Mar. 1987.

20. McKenna, *Irish Times*, 7 Sept. 1988.

21. Field Day (1987).

22. '1,500 Years of Irish Writing', National Public Radio interview, 12 Dec. 1991.

23. Elgy Gillespie, 'Field Day in Search of American Funds', *Irish Times*, 24 Mar. 1987; 'US Field Day for Begging Bowl Big Four', *Irish News*, 30 Mar. 1987.

24. Brian McIlroy reports visiting a bookshop in Dublin where the one copy of the Field Day anthology was kept in a locked glass case, like the Book of Kells. When he asked to look at it, the shop assistant was

unable to find the key. (McIlroy, 'NewsLetter Editor's Corner', *Canadian Association for Irish Studies Newsletter*, 6.2 (Fall 1992), 3.)

25. Ní Chuilleanáin, review of the second set of Field Day pamphlets, *Cyphers* (Summer 1984).

26. Longley, 'Writing, Revisionism and Grass-seed: Literary Mythologies in Ireland', in Jean Lundy and Aodán Mac Póilin (eds.), *Styles of Belonging: The Cultural Identities of Ulster* (Belfast, 1992), 17.

27. Foster, 'Nations, Yet Again', *Times Literary Supplement*, 27 Mar. 1992, 5.

28. Fallon, 'A Field Day for Anthology Addicts', *Irish Times*, 20 Nov. 1991, 12; Peter Denman, review of vol. 2 of the anthology, *Irish Literary Supplement* (Fall 1992), 5.

29. Longley, 'Belfast Diary', *London Review of Books*, 9 Jan. 1992, 21; Foster, *Times Literary Supplement*, 27 Mar. 1992, 5–7; Damian Smyth, 'Totalising Imperative', *Fortnight*, 309 (Sept. 1992), 26–7.

30. Smyth, *Fortnight*, 309 (Sept. 1992), 26.

31. Foster, *Times Literary Supplement*, 27 Mar. 1992, 6.

32. Banville, 'Put Up What Flag You Like, It Is Too Late', *Observer*, 1 Dec. 1991, 66. See also John C. Greene, Patricia L. Haberstroh, and Adrian Frazier, 'Wealth, Gender, Politics: Three Views of *The Field Day Anthology of Irish Writing*, *Éire-Ireland*, 27.2 (Summer 1992), 111–31; and comments by Anthony Bradley, Edna Longley, and Colm Toibin in *Canadian Journal of Irish Studies*, 18.2 (Dec. 1992), 117–24. Against this dominant perception, Eileen Battersby and Kevin Barry have pointed out that individual section editors (including some like W. J. McCormack and John Wilson Foster, who do not share Deane's nationalist views) were given the freedom to do as they pleased in their own sections, so that the individual parts of the anthology contradict each other at times and there are certainly inclusions that challenge the overall editorial strategy. The anthology, like Field Day itself, is less of a monolith than may appear at first glance. (Battersby, 'Is Irish Writing Necessarily Political?', *Irish Times*, 20 Nov. 1991, 12; Barry, 'Anthology as History: The Field Day Anthology of Irish Literature', *Irish Review*, 12 (Spring–Summer 1992), 50–5.)

33. Robert Barr, 'Defining Irish Writing but Not "Irishness"', *Vancouver Sun*, 5 Dec. 1989, C5.

34. See e.g. Foster, *Times Literary Supplement*, 27 Mar. 1992; Longley, *London Review of Books*, 9 Jan. 1992; and Riana O'Dwyer, review of vol. 3, *Irish Literary Supplement* (Fall 1992), 5–7.

35. O'Toole, 'Having a Field Day', *Irish Times*, 30 Nov. 1991, 5.

36. See e.g. Siobhan Kilfeather, 'The Whole Bustle', *London Review of Books*, 9 Jan. 1992, 20; Foster, *Times Literary Supplement*, 27 Mar. 1992.

37. Tóibín, review of *The Field Day Anthology of Irish Writing, Canadian Journal of Irish Studies,* 18.2 (Dec. 1992), 122.

38. O'Faolain, 'The Voice that Field Day Didn't Record', *Irish Times,* 11 Nov. 1991, 14.

39. Some important articles and reviews documenting this gender critique of the Field Day anthology are Kilfeather, *London Review of Books,* 9 Jan. 1992, 20–2; Longley, *London Review of Books,* 9 Jan. 1992; Katie Donovan, 'Absence Stirs Anger Amongst Women', *Irish Times,* 27 Feb. 1992, 10; Haberstroh, review of vol. 2, *Éire-Ireland,* 27.2 (Summer 1992), 118–23; and O'Dwyer, review of vol. 3, *Irish Literary Supplement* (Fall 1992), 5–7.

40. Barry, *Irish Review,* 12 (Spring–Summer 1992), 53.

41. For instance, see Patrick Quilligan, 'Field Day's New Double Bill', *Irish Times,* 18 Sept. 1984; Martin Cowley, 'Field Day Has Made a Permanent Mark', *Irish Times,* 5 May 1986; John Vidal, 'Stronger than Fiction', *Guardian,* 5 Dec. 1988.

42. Moriarty, *Irish Times,* 28 Apr. 1993.

43. Kevin Jackson, 'Running Wilde on the Road', *Independent,* 15 Sept. 1989, 18; Deane, 'Introduction', *Nationalism, Colonialism and Literature,* 14–15.

44. Deane, 'General Introduction', in Deane *et al.* (eds.), *The Field Day Anthology of Irish Writing,* p. xxi.

Bibliography and Further Reading

Interviews, 'discussions', and co-authored works are mixed together in chronological order after individual works by individual authors.

ADAMSON, IAN, *The Identity of Ulster* (Northern Ireland: Baird, 1982).

AGNEW, PADDY, '"The Blue Skies of Ulster . . ."' *Magill*, 7 Nov. 1981, 24–30.

—— 'Talking to Ourselves', Interview with Brian Friel. *Magill*, Dec. 1980, 59–61.

AILBHE, AN TSUIR, 'Two Plays by Field Day', *Galway Advertiser*, 1 Nov. 1984.

ALLEN, MICHAEL, 'Full of Passionate Contradictions', *Fortnight*, 226 (7 Oct. 1985), 19–20.

AMORY, MARK, 'Word-Play', *Spectator*, 23 May 1981, 27.

ANDERSON, BENEDICT, *Imagined Communities: Reflections on the Origin and Spread of Nationalism* (London: Verso, 1983, rev. edn. 1991).

ANDREWS, J. H., *A Paper Landscape: The Ordnance Survey in Nineteenth-Century Ireland* (Oxford: Oxford UP, 1975).

—— 'Notes for a Future Edition of Brian Friel's *Translations*', *Irish Review*, 13 (Winter 1992–3), 93–106.

—— FRIEL, BRIAN, and BARRY, KEVIN, 'Translations and A Paper Landscape: Between Fiction and History', *Crane Bag*, 7.2 (1983), 118–24.

ANON., 'A Challenging View of Ireland', *Londonderry Sentinel*, 30 May 1984.

—— 'A City in Revolt', *Londonderry Sentinel*, 10 Feb. 1965, 16.

—— 'A "Field Day" with Chekhov', *Impartial Reporter*, 1 Oct. 1981.

—— 'A Play I Can Recommend', *Irish Catholic*, 31 Oct. 1980.

—— 'A Prickly Problem', *Belfast Newsletter*, 3 Aug. 1981.

—— 'A Secret Cathedral Wedding for Dolours the Sister of Terror', *Daily Mail*, 5 Nov. 1983.

—— 'Actors Take a Breather', *Londonderry Sentinel*, 21 Aug. 1985.

—— 'Aistriúcháin', *Irish Times*, 15 Oct. 1980 (trans. Marc Caball).

—— 'Aistriúchán nua Friel', *Irish News*, 9 Sept. 1981 (trans. Marc Caball).

—— 'All Set for *Three Sisters*', *Ulster Gazette*, 10 Sept. 1981.

—— 'All Tastes Catered for at Arts Festival', *Armagh Guardian*, 25 Sept.

1980, 10–11.

ANON., 'Another Field Day Triumph in Derry', *Derry Journal*, 11 Sept. 1981.

—— 'Another Friel Play', *Irish Times*, 11 Oct. 1980.

—— 'Another Guildhall World Premiere', *Derry Journal*, 31 Aug. 1982, 7.

—— 'Another Major Friel Play Premiere in Derry', *Derry Journal*, 25 June 1982.

—— 'Anyone Here Speak British?', *Books Ireland*, Nov. 1983.

—— 'Around Town', *Offaly Topic*, 18 Oct. 1984.

—— 'The Bard Inspires—so does Friel', *Sunday Independent*, 16 Aug. 1981.

—— '*Boesman and Lena* at Friary Hall Theatre', *Dungarvan Observer*, 8 Oct. 1983.

—— 'Boesman and Lena: Bottom of the Social Ladder', *Derry Journal*, 23 Sept. 1983.

—— '*Boesman and Lena* for the Guildhall', *Derry Journal*, 2 Sept. 1983, 7.

—— '*Boesman and Lena* Opens Tonight', *Derry Journal*, 20 Sept. 1983.

—— 'Boesman and Lena Travel South', *Dungarvan Leader*, 30 Sept. 1983.

—— 'Bound by Govt. Rule, Says City MP', *Londonderry Sentinel*, 3 Mar. 1965, 17.

—— 'Brian Friel comes to Carrickmore', *Tyrone Democrat*, 9 Oct. 1980.

—— 'Brian Friel's Masterpiece in Carrickmore', *Ulster Herald*, 1 Nov. 1980.

—— 'Brian Friel's Play', *Impartial Reporter*, 25 Sept. 1980.

—— 'Brian Friel's *The Communication Cord*', *Ulster Herald*, 16 Oct. 1982, 16.

—— 'Briefing', *Observer*, 24 May 1981, 31.

—— 'Briefing', *Observer*, 7 June 1981, 28.

—— 'Chekhov Gets the Friel Treatment', *Sunday News*, 28 June 1981.

—— 'Chekhov in Irish Idiom', *Derry Journal*, 28 Aug. 1981.

—— 'Chekhov Play for Dungannon', *Dungannon Observer*, 12 Sept. 1981, 3.

—— 'Cogar Scéil', *Amarach*, 16 Jan. 1981.

—— 'The Communication Cord', *Derry Journal*, 8 Oct. 1982.

—— 'Communication Cord', *Londonderry Sentinel*, 22 Sept. 1982.

—— 'Councillors in the Dark', *Londonderry Sentinel*, 10 Sept. 1980.

—— 'Cultural Conflict', *Workers Life*, Dec. 1980.

—— 'Cushy, Ritzy, Swingin' Disco!', *New Galway Observer*, 17 Oct. 1984.

—— 'Deane Talk on Field Day', *Derry Journal*, 18 Jan. 1985.

—— 'Derry Actresses's [*sic*] Three Television Appearances', *Northern Constitution*, 23 Aug. 1980.

—— 'Derry Celebration', *Irish Press*, 25 Sept. 1982.

—— 'Derry Company Breaking New Ground', *East Antrim Times*, 28 Sept. 1984.

—— 'Derry Delight at Friel Play Triumph', *Sunday Independent Special Edition*, 28 Sept. 1980.

—— 'Derry is the Obvious Place—Mayor', *Londonderry Sentinel*, 10 Feb. 1965, 17.

—— 'Derry Likes New Brian Friel Work', *Irish News*, 9 Sept. 1981.

—— 'Derry Première Pair', *Sunday Press*, 8 June 1980.

—— 'Derry the Site for University MPs Told Premier', *Londonderry Sentinel*, 10 Mar. 1965, 24.

—— 'Derry Unionists Repeat Call for a University', *Londonderry Sentinel*, 3 Mar. 1965, 7.

—— 'Derry Women in *Translations*', *Derry Journal*, 12 Sept. 1980.

—— 'Des is No Stranger to Derry!', *Derry Journal*, 16 Sept. 1983, 17.

—— 'Dollar Endorsement', *Books Ireland*, Oct. 1988.

—— 'Dolours Price Marries Actor', *Irish Press*, 5 Nov. 1983.

—— 'Dolours Price Marries Actor', *Irish Times*, 5 Nov. 1983.

—— 'Double Bill Follows up Translation Formula', *Irish News*, 14 Sept. 1984.

—— 'Dramatic Opening', *Irish Post*, 27 Sept. 1980.

—— 'Due Honour', editorial, *Irish Times*, 15 Jan. 1981.

—— 'Editorial', *Atlantis*, 1 (March 1970), 5–6.

—— 'Editorial', *Atlantis*, 6 (Winter 1973–4), 5.

—— 'Editorial', *Crane Bag*, 1.2 (1977), 4–7.

—— 'Editorial', *Crane Bag*, 2.1 and 2 (1978), 5–7.

—— 'Editorial', *Crane Bag*, 7.2 (1983), 3.

—— 'Editorial I/Endodermis', *Crane Bag*, 1.1 (Spring 1977), 3–5.

—— 'Editorial II/Epidermis', *Crane Bag*, 1.1 (Spring 1977), 89–92.

—— 'Editorial', *Londonderry Sentinel*, 20 Jan. 1965, 14.

—— 'Eighth Arts Festival is Opened', *Newry Reporter*, 20 Oct. 1983.

—— 'Elitist Pamphlets', *Phoenix*, 22 June 1984.

—— 'Evening of Laughter', *Newry Reporter*, 14 Oct. 1982.

—— 'Excellent Fare for Theatre-Goers', *Londonderry Sentinel*, 19 Sept. 1984.

—— 'Exciting Double Bill from Field Day Theatre', *Fermanagh Herald*, 20 Oct. 1984.

ANON., '"Fantastic Response" for Friel's *Translations*', *Impartial Reporter*, 30 Oct. 1980.

—— 'Fermanagh People Missed a Theatrical Experience', *Impartial Reporter*, 20 Oct. 1983.

—— 'Festival Honours List', *Evening Herald*, 18 Oct. 1980.

—— 'Field Day', *Sunday Tribune*, 18 Sept. 1983.

—— 'Field Day Back in Derry', *Donegal Democrat*, 14 Aug. 1981.

—— 'Field Day Back in the North-West', *Londonderry Sentinel*, 10 Oct. 1984.

—— 'Field Day '83 Tour', *Ulster Tatler*, Sept. 1983.

—— 'Field Day Events', *Irish Literary Supplement*, Fall 1985.

—— 'Field Day for Local Theatre Fans', *Antrim Guardian*, 6 Oct. 1983.

—— ' "Field Day" on the Road', *Carrickfergus Advertiser*, 18 June 1981.

—— 'Field Day Openings', *Sunday Tribune*, 16 Sept. 1984.

—— 'Field Day Pamphlets in Book Form', *Derry Journal*, 22 Nov. 1985.

—— 'Field Day Pamphlets Welcomed', *Derry Journal*, 29 May 1984.

—— 'Field Day Premières are Superb', *Derry Journal*, 21 Sept. 1984.

—— 'Field Day Present Chekhov's *Three Sisters*', *Derry People and Donegal News*, 22 Aug. 1981.

—— 'Field Day—The Derry Connection', *Derry Journal*, 17 Sept. 1982.

—— 'Field Day Theatre Co. to Present Chekov's *Three Sisters*', *Derry Journal*, 19 June 1981, 5.

—— 'Field Day Theatre's Double Bill', *Impartial Reporter*, 27 Sept. 1984.

—— 'Field Day to Publish Heaney's *Sweeney Astray*', *Derry Journal*, 18 Oct. 1983, 11.

—— 'Field Day Wisdom', *Evening Herald*, 24 May 1984.

—— 'Field Day's Autumn Date in Cork', *Cork Evening Echo*, 8 Aug. 1981.

—— 'Field Day's First Farce', *Ulster Tatler*, Oct. 1982.

—— 'Field Day's First Friel Farce for Newry', *Rathfriland Outlook*, 30 Sept. 1982, 19.

—— 'Field Day's Riot Act of Humour', *Londonderry Sentinel*, 17 Oct. 1984.

—— 'First Readings of Brian Friel's *Translations*', *Derry Journal*, 12 Aug. 1980.

—— 'Friel Gets $10,000 from New York Group', *Irish Voice*, 21 Jan. 1989.

—— 'Friel Leads in Hope', *Irish Press*, 6 Jan. 1981.

—— 'Friel Plans for Derry Theatre Movement', *Derry Journal*, 20 Jan. 1981.

—— 'Friel Play Brought 3,500 to the Guildhall', *Derry Journal*, 15 Oct. 1982.

—— 'Friel Play Enraptures Audience', *Evening Press*, 24 Sept. 1980.

—— 'Friel Play Premier in Guildhall', *Londonderry Sentinel*, 4 June 1980.

—— 'Friel to Make Derry Comeback', *Irish Press*, 15 Jan. 1981.

—— 'Friel's Farce', *Belfast Newsletter*, 9 Sept. 1982.

—— 'Friel's Farce Ready for World Premiere', *Derry Journal*, 17 Sept. 1982.

—— 'Friel's Theatre in New Show', *Belfast Telegraph*, 13 Aug. 1983.

—— 'Friel's Three Sisters', *Evening Press*, 22 Aug. 1981.

—— 'Friel's Winner', editorial, *Irish Press*, 26 Sept. 1980.

—— 'Gary Watches Field Day at Work', *Derry Journal*, 9 Sept. 1983.

—— 'Guildhall Premiere for Friel Play in September', *Derry Journal*, 6 June 1980.

—— 'Hammond's Second Golden Harp Award', *Derry Journal*, 24 June 1986.

—— 'Heaney Poem Takes a Swipe at "British" Tag', *Belfast Telegraph*, 10 Sept. 1983, 9.

—— 'Heaney Protest Poem over "British" Label', *Irish Press*, 10 Sept. 1983.

—— 'Heaney to Publish Epic Poem', *Derry Journal*, 6 Sept. 1983, 8.

—— 'Heaney's Sweeney', *Belfast Newsletter*, 19 Oct. 1983.

—— 'Heaney's *Sweeney Astray* Launched', *Derry Journal*, 15 Nov. 1983.

—— 'His Way Out', editorial, *Derry Journal*, 2 Mar. 1965.

—— 'Interview with Seamus Twomey', *Crane Bag*, 1.2 (1977), 21–6.

—— 'Language and Politics', *Irish News*, 10 Sept. 1983, 5.

—— 'Look Back in Anger', editorial, *Ulster Herald and Strabane Chronicle*, 2 Oct. 1982.

—— 'Memorable Molière—but Subverted Sophocles', *Northern Constitution*, 3 Nov. 1984, 18.

—— 'Memoranda: Shows Go On', *Irish Times*, 30 Oct. 1982.

—— 'Memorandum: An Arts Notebook', *Irish Times*, 12 Sept. 1981.

—— 'Mother . . . Stage and TV Director', *Londonderry Sentinel*, 7 Sept. 1983.

—— 'New Field Day Series Probes Irish Society', *Irish Press*, 28 May 1984.

—— 'New Friel Play Set in a Hedge School', *Sunday Independent*, 6 June 1980.

—— 'New lines from Theatre Company', *Belfast Telegraph*, 2 Sept. 1983.

—— 'Newcastle West', *Limerick Leader*, 1 Oct. 1983.

ANON., 'Night of High Drama Earns a Curtain Call from the Art World', *Belfast Telegraph*, 20 Sept. 1984.

—— 'Northern Notebook', *Irish Catholic*, 2 Oct. 1980.

—— 'Not British', *Irish Times*, 10 Sept. 1983.

—— 'October Theatre Festival at Hawk's Well', *Sligo Champion*, 30 Sept. 1983.

—— 'Omnibus', *Tuam Herald*, 15 Nov. 1980.

—— 'On Being Brown', *Donegal Democrat*, 7 Oct. 1983.

—— 'Opening Night', editorial, *Irish Times*, 22 Aug. 1980.

—— 'The Outer Limits of Prison Reform', editorial, *Fortnight*, 183 (Oct.–Nov. 1981), 3.

—— 'Ovation for Brian Friel at Guildhall', *Irish Independent*, 24 Sept. 1980.

—— 'Pamphlets on Politics and Arts in Ireland', *Irish News*, 3 Sept. 1983, 5.

—— 'Pick of the Arts in 1983: The Second Sunday Independent Arts Awards', *Sunday Independent*, 1 Jan. 1984.

—— 'Poet Wearing the Mantle of Yeats', *Observer*, 21 June 1987, 7.

—— 'Poetry, the Other Northern Ireland Ferment', *The Times*, 13 Apr. 1985.

—— 'Portrait of a Poet as Accomplished Tightrope Walker', *Sunday Times*, 14 May 1989, A14.

—— 'Powerful Production from Field Day', *Belfast Telegraph*, 21 Sept. 1983.

—— 'Price Sister Weds', *Daily Mirror*, 5 Nov. 1983.

—— 'The Publication of the Ordnance Survey Memoirs', *Linen Hall Review*, 7.1 and 2 (Summer 1990), 4–6.

—— 'The Right Mahon for a Farce', *Sunday Independent*, 30 Sept. 1984.

—— 'Riverside Reviews', *Coleraine Chronicle*, 8 Nov. 1980.

—— 'Screen Study of Ireland Planned', *Belfast Telegraph*, 7 Mar. 1987.

—— 'Searchlight', *Derry Journal*, 17 Sept. 1982.

—— 'Seeking a Sense of Ireland', *The Times*, 5 Oct. 1981.

—— 'Self-Help', editorial, *Irish Times*, 11 Oct. 1980.

—— 'September Start for Riverside's New Season', *Coleraine Chronicle*, 4 Aug. 1984.

—— 'The Simple Complications of The Communication Cord', *Derry Journal*, 7 Sept. 1982, 12.

—— 'Soft, Strong and Very Long', *Sunday News*, 13 Sept. 1981.

—— 'Something New at Newry Arts Festival', *Rathfriland Outlook*, 6 Oct. 1983.

—— 'Special Premier of New Friel Play', *Londonderry Sentinel*, 15 Sept. 1982.

—— 'Stage Set for 2nd Annual Arts Festival', *Ulster Herald*, 2 Oct. 1982.

—— 'Standing Ovation for Friel's *Translations*', *Derry Journal*, 26 Sept. 1980.

—— 'Theatre', *Belfast Telegraph*, 24 Dec. 1980.

—— 'Theatre Topics', *Westmeath Examiner*, 13 Oct. 1984.

—— 'Three Sisters', *Sunday Journal*, 4 Oct. 1981.

—— 'Three Sisters for Date in Galway', *Connacht Sentinel*, 29 Sept. 1981.

—— 'Translations', *Impartial Reporter*, 30 Oct. 1980.

—— '*Translations* Arrives in Cork', *Cork Evening Echo*, 8 Nov. 1980.

—— '*Translations* at Magherafelt', *Coleraine Chronicle*, 18 Oct. 1980.

—— '*Translations*—Derry Connections', *Derry Journal*, 19 Sept. 1980.

—— '*Translations* in Enniskillen', *Fermanagh News*, 1 Nov. 1980, 6.

—— '*Translations* Le hAistriu—Go Gaeilge!', *Inniu*, 16 Jan. 1981.

—— '*Translations* Preparations', *Derry Journal*, 9 Sept. 1980.

—— '*Translations* Sell-Out To-morrow', *Ulster Gazette*, 23 Oct. 1980, 7.

—— '*Translations* to have Extra Performance', *Coleraine Chronicle*, 25 Oct. 1980, 8.

—— 'Two New Plays as . . . Field Day Plans Visit', *Ulster Gazette*, 9 Aug. 1984.

—— 'Two New Plays in Derry', *Donegal Democrat*, 7 Sept. 1984.

—— 'United Demand for Varsity', *Londonderry Sentinel*, 10 Feb. 1965, 12.

—— 'Unreviewable', *Sunday Tribune*, 2 July 1989.

—— 'US Field Day for Begging Bowl Big Four', *Irish News*, 30 Mar. 1987.

—— 'US Windfall Keeps Field Day Afloat', *Cork Examiner*, 13 Jan. 1989.

—— 'Very Funny *High Time* Production', *Limerick Chronicle*, 30 Oct. 1984.

—— 'What the North Really Needs Is an Irish English Dictionary', *Sunday Independent*, 16 Sept. 1984.

—— 'Whose Play Anyway', *Sunday Press*, 4 Oct. 1981.

—— 'Why Stephen Rea's Heart is Still in the Theatre', *Irish Press*, 26 Oct. 1984.

—— 'World Premier Special Night for Derry', *Belfast Newsletter*, 24 Sept. 1980.

—— 'World Première of Friel Play to be Staged in Derry', *Irish News*, 25 Aug. 1980.

—— 'World Première of Friel's *Translations* Tonight', *Derry Journal*, 23 Sept. 1980.

ANON., 'World Première of *Translations*', *Derry Journal*, 19 Sept. 1980.
—— 'Z Cars Inspector Lynch for Armagh', *Armagh Observer*, 22 Aug. 1981.
ARTHUR, PAUL and JEFFERY, KEITH, *Northern Ireland since 1968* (Oxford: Blackwell, 1988).
ASMAL, KADER, programme note for the Field Day production of *Boesman and Lena*, 1983.
ATKINSON, NORMAN, *Irish Education: A History of Educational Institutions* (Dublin: Allen Figgis, 1969).
AUCHMUTY, JAMES JOHNSTON, *Irish Education: A Historical Survey* (Dublin: Hodges Figgis, 1937).
AUDEN, W. H., *Selected Poems*, edited by Edward Mendelson (New York: Random House, 1979).
BALLANTINE, DAVID, 'A Starkly Contrasting Double Bill at Lyric', *Belfast Telegraph*, 3 Oct. 1984.
BANVILLE, JOHN, 'Put Up What Flag You Like, It Is Too Late', *Observer*, 1 Dec. 1991.
BARBER, JOHN, 'Another Irish Problem', *Daily Telegraph*, 14 May 1981, 15.
—— 'Dublin Festival's *Three Sisters*', *Daily Telegraph*, 30 Sept. 1981.
—— 'Poet's Dark Ages', *Daily Telegraph*, 5 Mar. 1986, 11.
BARBER, JULIE, personal interview, 1 Aug. 1990.
—— telephone interview, 6 Nov. 1991.
BARR, ROBERT, 'Defining Irish Writing but Not "Irishness"', *Vancouver Sun*, 5 Dec. 1989, C5.
BARRY, KEVIN, 'Anthology as History: The Field Day Anthology of Irish Literature', *Irish Review*, 12 (Spring–Summer 1992), 50–5.
—— FRIEL, BRIAN, and ANDREWS, JOHN, 'Translations and A Paper Landscape: Between Fiction and History', *Crane Bag*, 7.2 (1983), 118–24.
BATTERSBY, EILEEN, 'Is Irish Writing Necessarily Political?', *Irish Times*, 20 Nov. 1991, 12.
BELL, JANE, 'A Field Day for Friel Farce', *Belfast Telegraph*, 23 Sept. 1982.
BERTHA, CSILLA, 'Tragedies of National Fate: A Comparison between Brian Friel's *Translations* and its Hungarian Counterpart, András Sütö's *A szuzai menyegzö*', *Irish University Review*, 17.2 (Autumn 1987), 207–22.
BILLINGTON, MICHAEL, 'Translations', *Guardian*, 14 May 1981, 11.
—— 'Don't Miss', *Guardian*, 14 Aug. 1981, 8.
—— 'High Old Time', *Guardian*, 5 Oct. 1984.

—— 'Howl on the Wilder Shores', *Guardian*, 5 Mar. 1986, 11.

BINNIE, ERIC, 'Brecht and Friel: Some Irish Parallels', *Modern Drama* (Sept. 1988).

BOLAND, EAVAN, 'The Northern Writers' Crisis of Conscience', *Irish Times*, 12, 13, 14 Aug. 1970, 12, 12, 12.

—— 'Poets and Pamphlets', *Irish Times*, 1 Oct. 1983, 12.

—— 'Heaney's Sweeney', *Irish Times*, 10 Dec. 1983.

—— 'Heaney's Fifth Station', *Irish Times*, 13 Oct. 1984.

BOLAND, JOHN, 'Artcetera', *Evening Press*, 17 Jan. 1981, 6.

BOYLE, KEVIN, and HADDEN, TOM, *Ireland: A Positive Proposal* (Harmondsworth: Penguin, 1985).

BRADLEY, ANTHONY, review of *The Field Day Anthology of Irish Writing*, *Canadian Journal of Irish Studies*, 18.2 (Dec. 1992), 117–19.

BRADSHAW, BRENDAN, 'Nationalism and Historical Scholarship in Modern Ireland', *Irish Historical Studies*, 26.104 (Nov. 1989), 329–51.

BRENTON, HOWARD, *The Romans in Britain* (London: Eyre Methuen, 1980).

BRISTOW, EUGENE K. (trans. and ed.), *Anton Chekhov's Plays* (New York: Norton, 1977).

BROOK, PETER, *The Empty Space* (London: MacGibbon: 1968).

BROOKE, PETER, 'Culture', *Linen Hall Review*, 2.1 (Spring 1985), 20.

BROWN, TERENCE, *Ireland: A Social and Cultural History 1922–79* (London: Fontana, 1981).

—— 'Calling the North's Muses Home', *Fortnight*, 198 (Oct. 1983), 22–3.

—— 'Having a Field Day', *Irish Press*, 14 July 1984.

—— 'Normalcy in Belfast', *Irish Literary Supplement*, Fall 1985, 7.

BROWNE, VINCENT, 'Editorial', *Magill*, Jan. 1985, 4–15.

BUDBERG, MOURA (trans.), *Three Sisters* by Anton Chekhov (London: Davis-Poynter, 1971).

BYRNE, GAY, 'The World of Gay Byrne', *Sunday World*, 4 Oct. 1981.

CALLANAN, FRANK, 'The Idiom of Irishry', *New Hibernia*, Apr. 1985.

CALLENDER, L., 'Are We Two Nations?', *Fortnight* (8 Mar. 1972), 8–9.

CAREY, JOHN, 'The Most Sensuous Poet to Use English since Keats', *Sunday Times*, 3 Apr. 1988, G9.

CARLETON, WILLIAM, *The Autobiography of William Carleton*, preface by Patrick Kavanagh (London: Macgibbon, 1968).

—— *Traits and Stories of the Irish Peasantry* (London: Ward, 1881).

CARSON, MARY, 'Field Day Lands a Leading Lady', *Londonderry Sentinel*, 19 Sept. 1984.

CARTER, NICK, 'Briefs', *In Dublin*, 1 Dec. 1983.

CARTY, CIARAN, 'Finding Voice in a Language Not Our Own', *Sunday Independent*, 5 Oct. 1980.

—— 'The Confessions of a One-time Werewolf', *Sunday Independent*, 24 Mar. 1985.

—— DEANE, SEAMUS, and KEARNEY, RICHARD, 'Why Ireland Needs a Fifth Province', *Sunday Independent*, 22 Jan. 1984, 15.

CASSIDY, CES, 'Playwright Who Stays in the Wings', *Irish Independent*, 2 Nov. 1982.

CATHCART, REX, *The Most Contrary Region: The BBC in Northern Ireland 1924–1984* (Belfast: Blackstaff, 1984).

CAVE, RICHARD ALLEN, 'The Past is Not Another Country', *Times Higher Education Supplement*, 14 Mar. 1986, 15.

CHAILLET, NED, 'Translations: Londonderry', *The Times*, 26 Sept. 1980.

—— 'Translations', *The Times*, 7 Aug. 1981, 13.

CHEKHOV, ANTON, *Letters on the Short Story, the Drama, and Other Literary Topics*, selected and edited by Louis Friedland (London: Vision, 1965).

—— *The Note-Books of Anton Tchekhov Together with Reminiscences of Tchekhov by Maxim Gorky* (translated by S. S. Koteliansky and Leonard Woolf) (Richmond: Hogarth, 1921).

CLAYSON, ALLAN (trans. and adapter), *The School for Husbands with The Flying Doctor, The Uneasy Husband, and Love is the Best Remedy* (London: Heinemann Educational, 1969).

COLBY, COL. THOMAS, Superintendent, *Ordnance Survey of the County of Londonderry: Memoir of the City and North Western Liberties of Londonderry, Parish of Templemore* (Dublin: Hodges, 1837).

COLE, WILLIAM, 'Tradewinds: United Artists', *Saturday Review*, Jan.–Feb. 1986, 64.

COMISKEY, RAY, 'Rehearsing Friel's New Farce', *Irish Times*, 14 Sept. 1982, 8.

CONNOLLY, SEAN, 'Dreaming History: Brian Friel's *Translations*', *Theatre Ireland*, 13 (1987), 42–4.

COOGAN, TIM PAT (ed.), *Ireland and the Arts*, special issue of *Literary Review* (London: Namara, 1983).

COONEY, JOHN, '$10,000 Award for Field Day Anthology', *Irish Times*, 12 Jan. 1989.

CORCORAN, SEAN, 'How Many Irish Traditions?', *Fortnight*, 222 (9–23 June 1985), 21.

CORCORAN, REVD T., *State Policy in Irish Education, A.D. 1536 to 1816* (Dublin: Fallon, 1916).

CORRIGAN, KATHLEEN, 'Field Day for Stephen Rea', *Company*, Oct. 1983.

COSTELLO, ROSE, 'Chekhov is Not for Changing', *Cork Examiner*, 30 Sept. 1981.

COVENEY, MICHAEL, 'Translations', *Financial Times*, 13 Oct. 1980, 13.

—— 'Translations', *Financial Times*, 7 Aug. 1981, 9.

—— 'Three Sisters', *Financial Times*, 10 Sept. 1981.

—— 'Londonderry Airs, Belfast Blues', *Financial Times*, 25 Sept. 1982.

—— 'Field Day/Lyric, Belfast', *Financial Times*, 3 Oct. 1984.

—— 'The Saxon Shore', *Financial Times*, 4 Mar. 1986, 21.

COWLEY, MARTIN, 'Field Day Has Made a Permanent Mark', *Irish Times*, 5 May 1986.

COX, MARGARET, letter to the author, 8 Jan. 1990.

CRONIN, CLARE, 'Field Day Delights at Everyman', *Cork Examiner*, 6 Nov. 1984.

CRONIN, COLM, 'Disasters—and *Translations*', *Sunday Tribune*, 28 Dec. 1980.

—— 'Three Sisters: Gaiety', *Sunday Tribune*, 4 Oct. 1981, 19.

—— 'Delayed Entrance for Friel Farce', *Sunday Tribune*, 5 Sept. 1982.

—— 'Ghosts in the Greenroom', *New Hibernia*, Oct. 1984.

—— 'Theatre', *New Hibernia*, Nov. 1984.

CROWE, CATHERINE, review, *In Dublin*, 17 Oct. 1984.

CUNNINGHAM, JOHN, 'Communication Chord', *Guardian*, 6 May 1983.

CURRAN, FRANK, 'Friel's *Communication Cord* Rings the Bell', *Derry Journal*, 24 Sept. 1982.

—— 'Time is Running Out for Northern Protestants', *Fortnight*, 199 (Nov. 1983), 6.

—— *Derry: Countdown to Disaster* (Dublin: Gill, 1986).

DANTANUS, ULF, *Brian Friel: The Growth of an Irish Dramatist* (Göteborg, Sweden: Acta Universitatis Gothoburgensis, 1985).

DAVIS, E. E. and SINNOTT, RICHARD, 'Attitudes in Republic to Northern Ireland Problem', *Irish Times*, 16 Oct. 1979, 4.

DAWE, GERALD, 'Writing in the West', *Connacht Tribune*, 31 Oct. 1980.

—— Review of *The Communication Cord* by Brian Friel, *Theatre Ireland*, 2 (Jan. 1983), 67.

—— 'Literature', *Linen Hall Review*, 2.3 (Autumn 1985), 25.

—— and LONGLEY, EDNA (eds.), *Across a Roaring Hill: The Protestant Imagination in Modern Ireland* (Belfast: Blackstaff, 1985).

DEANE, EAMONN, 'Northern Ireland: Community Work in the 70s', *Crane Bag*, 4.2 (1980–1), 71–8.

DEANE, JOHN, 'Poetry', Review of *Station Island* and *Sweeney Astray* by Seamus Heaney. *Linen Hall Review*, 1.4 (Winter 1984–5), 18.

DEANE, SEAMUS, *While Jewels Rot* (Belfast: Festival Publications, 1967).

—— 'The Old Coach Road', *Threshold*, 23 (Summer 1970), 51–3.

—— 'Mugwumps and Reptiles', *Atlantis*, 2 (Oct. 1970), 3–10.

—— 'Why Bogside?', *Honest Ulsterman*, 27 (Jan.–Feb. 1971), 1–8.

—— *Gradual Wars* (Shannon, Ireland: Irish UP, 1972).

—— (ed.), *The Adventures of Hugh Trevor* by Thomas Holcroft (London: Oxford UP, 1973).

—— 'Irish Politics and O'Casey's Theatre', *Threshold*, 24 (Spring 1973), 5–16.

—— 'The Writer and the Troubles', *Threshold*, 25 (Summer 1974), 13–17.

—— 'Irish Poetry and Irish Nationalism', in Douglas Dunn (ed.), *Two Decades of Irish Writing: A Critical Survey* (Chester Springs, Pa: Dufour, 1975), 4–22.

—— *Rumours* (Dublin: Dolmen, 1977).

—— 'Yeats, Ireland and Revolution', *Crane Bag*, 1.2 (1977), 56–64.

—— 'Synge's Western Worlds', *Threshold*, 29 (Autumn 1978), 25–42.

—— 'An Example of Tradition', *Crane Bag*, 3.1 (1979), 41–7.

—— 'Exemplary Dramatists: Yeats and O'Casey', *Threshold*, 30 (Spring 1979), 21–8.

—— 'Postscript', *Crane Bag*, 3.2 (1979), 92–4.

—— 'Brian Friel', *Ireland Today*, 978 (July–Aug. 1981), 7–10.

—— 'What Is Field Day?', programme note for the Field Day production of *Three Sisters*, 1981.

—— 'Introduction: The Longing for Modernity', *Threshold*, 32 (Winter 1982), 1–7.

—— 'In Search of a Story', programme note for the Field Day production of *The Communication Cord*, 1982.

—— 'Black Mountain Jacobin', *Honest Ulsterman*, 74 (Winter 1983), 49–51.

—— *History Lessons* (Dublin: Gallery, 1983).

—— *Civilians and Barbarians* (1983), in *Ireland's Field Day* (London: Hutchinson, 1985), 31–42.

—— 'Derry: City Besieged Within the Siege', *Fortnight*, 198 (Oct. 1983), 18–19.

—— 'Remembering the Irish Future', *Crane Bag*, 8.1 (1984), 81–92.

—— (ed.), *Selected Plays of Brian Friel* (London: Faber, 1984).

—— *Heroic Styles: The Tradition of an Idea* (1984), in *Ireland's Field Day* (London: Hutchinson, 1985), 43–58.

—— *Celtic Revivals: Essays in Modern Irish Literature 1880–1980* (London: Faber, 1985).

—— 'The Protestant Mind in Irish Writing', review of Edna Longley and Gerald Dowe (eds.), *Across a Roaring Hill: The Protestant Imagination in Modern Ireland. Irish Times*, 14 Sept. 1985.

—— letter to John Wilson Foster, 3 Mar. 1986.

—— 'Canon Fodder: Literary Mythologies in Ireland' (1989), in Jean Lundy and Aodán Mac Póilin (eds.), *Styles of Belonging: The Cultural Identities of Ulster* (Belfast: Lagan, 1992), 22–32.

—— (ed.), *Nationalism, Colonialism and Literature* (Derry: Field Day, 1990).

—— *General Introduction* (Derry: Field Day, 1990).

—— 'Hot House Flowers or Anthologica Hibernica', *Gown Literary Supplement* (Spring–Summer 1990), 19.

—— 'Silence and Eloquence', *Guardian*, 12 Dec. 1991, 23.

—— 'Unhappy and at Home', interview with Seamus Heaney, *Crane Bag*, 1.1 (Spring 1977), 61–7.

—— and FITZPATRICK, BARRÉ, 'Interview with John Hume', *Crane Bag*, 4.2 (1980–1), 39–43.

—— CARTY, CIARAN, and KEARNEY, RICHARD, 'Why Ireland Needs a Fifth Province', *Sunday Independent*, 22 Jan. 1984, 15.

—— FITZGERALD, JENNIFER, FOWLER, JOAN, and McGUINNESS, FRANK, 'The Arts and Ideology', *Crane Bag*, 9.2 (1985), 60–9.

—— *et al.* (eds.), *The Field Day Anthology of Irish Writing*, 3 vols. (Derry: Field Day, 1991).

DE BREÁDÚN, DEAGLÁN, 'Comfortable Image Belies the Serious Poet', *Irish Times*, 13 Sept. 1984.

—— 'Writers in Irish and English Win $50,000 Awards', *Irish Times*, 9 Sept. 1988.

DENMAN, PETER, review of vol. 2 of *The Field Day Anthology of Irish Writing*, *Irish Literary Supplement* (Autumn 1992), 5.

DE PAOR, LIAM, 'The Ambiguity of the Republic', *Atlantis*, 3 (Nov. 1971), 3–9.

DEVITT, JOHN, 'Field Day's First Publications', *Irish Literary Supplement*, 3.1 (Spring 1984), 19.

DILLON, JOHN, 'Editorial: Some Remarks on the New Ireland Concept', *Atlantis*, 5 (Apr. 1973), 5–7.

DIXON, STEPHEN, 'Mapping Cultural Imperialism', report, *Guardian*, 27 Sept. 1980, 11.

—— 'Brian Friel's Chekhov', *Sunday Tribune*, 25 Jan. 1981.

DONEGAN, CHRIS, 'The Riot Act Less Fizzle Than Damp Match', Impartial Reporter, 18 Oct. 1984, 12.

DONOGHUE, DENIS, 'A Playwright, Three Poets, an Actor and a Walking Saint', Inside Tribune, 2 Oct. 1983.

DONOVAN, KATIE, 'Absence Stirs Anger Amongst Women', Irish Times, 27 Feb. 1992, 10.

DOOLEY, SUSAN, 'Literature along the Liffey', Washington Post Book World, 3 June. 1984.

DORAN, PETER, 'Chekhov Goes Irish!', Sunday World, 6 Sept. 1981.

DOWLING, NOELEEN, 'Lot to Admire, not Something to Rave About', Evening Press, 9 Sept. 1981.

—— 'A Play to Dispel the Prevailing Mood in Bomb-Scarred Derry', Evening Press, 22 Sept. 1982.

DOWLING, PATRICK JOHN, The Hedge Schools of Ireland (Dublin: Talbot, 1935).

DUNNIGAN, ANN (trans.), Chekhov: The Major Plays (New York: Signet, 1964).

DURCAN, PAUL, 'The World of Derek Mahon', Magill, Christmas 1984, 38–46.

EDWARDS, OWEN DUDLEY, 'An Open Letter: On Receiving Three Pamphlets from Field Day, with their Compliments', Irish Times, 10 Dec. 1983.

EDWARDS, RUTH DUDLEY, An Atlas of Irish History, maps by W. H. Bromage (London: Methuen, 1973).

EHRENPREIS, IRVIN, Swift: The Man, His Works, and the Age (London: Methuen, 1967).

EMELJANOW, VICTOR (ed.), Chekhov: The Critical Heritage (London: Routledge, 1981).

ESSLIN, MARTIN, 'Translations', Plays and Players, Nov. 1981, 36.

ETHERTON, MICHAEL, Contemporary Irish Dramatists (London: Macmillan, 1989).

EVANS, JOHN, 'Born on the Island', In Dublin, 20 Oct. 1983.

EVANS, SIAN, 'Second's Out in the Derry Arts', Irish News, 12 Sept. 1985.

FAGLES, ROBERT (trans.), Sophocles: The Three Theban Plays, edited by Bernard Knox (London: Lane, 1982).

FALLON, BRIAN, 'A Field Day for Anthology Addicts', Irish Times, 20 Nov. 1991, 12.

FALSTAFF, 'Visit of Field Theatre Company to Newry', Newry Reporter, 18 Oct. 1984, 30.

FANNING, RONAN, Independent Ireland (Dublin: Helicon, 1983).

—— 'The British Dimension', *Crane Bag*, 8.1 (1984), 41–51.

—— 'The Meaning of Revisionism' (1987). *Irish Review*, 4 (1988), 15–19.

FARRELL, MICHAEL, *Northern Ireland: The Orange State* (London: Pluto, 1976).

FARREN, RONAN, 'Broadway? Who Cares!', *Evening Herald*, 28 Aug. 1980.

—— 'Festival a Success—Despite Strike', *Evening Herald*, 17 Oct. 1980.

FEENEY, JOHN, 'Ad Lib: Brian Friel's Present Work is Top Secret', *Evening Herald*, 15 Jan. 1981.

FEN, ELISAVETA (trans.), *Chekhov Plays* (Harmondsworth: Penguin, 1959).

FENNELL, DESMOND, 'The Last Years of the Gaeltacht', *Crane Bag*, 5.2 (1981), 8–11.

—— 'Choosing Our Self-Image (The Problem of Irish Identity)', *Crane Bag*, 7.2 (1983), 191–6.

—— 'Some Notes on Field Day's Margin', *Sunday Press*, 9 Oct. 1983.

—— 'How Not to See Ireland', *Crane Bag*, 9.1 (1985), 92–3.

—— 'A Project that would End Mood of Paralysis', *Irish Times*, 8 July 1985.

—— 'Against Revisionism' (1987), *Irish Review*, 4 (1988), 20–6.

—— *Whatever You Say, Say Nothing: Why Seamus Heaney is No. 1*, (Dublin: ELO, 1991).

FENTON, JAMES, 'Ireland: Destruction of an Idyll', *Sunday Times*, 28 Sept. 1980, 40.

—— 'How Mr. Eliot's Doodles Got Into a Catsuit', *Sunday Times*, 17 May 1981, 39.

FENTON, SEAMUS, *A Great Kilkennyman: John O'Donovan*, Kilkenny, *Kilkenny People*, 1942.

FIELD DAY, *Field Day: Theatre Company and Publishing House* (Derry: Field Day, 1987).

FINEGAN, JOHN, 'Friel Returns to History—and Success', *Evening Herald*, 24 Sept. 1980.

—— 'Record-Breaker Spins to a Big Conclusion', *Evening Herald*, 18 Oct. 1980.

—— 'Buoyant Year', *Evening Herald*, 27 Dec. 1980.

FITTS, DUDLEY, and FITZGERALD, ROBERT (trans.), *The Antigone of Sophocles* (London: Oxford UP, 1940).

FITZGERALD, CHARLES, 'Taking the Cosy Option', *Belfast Newsletter*, 29 Sept. 1982.

FITZGERALD, GARRET, *Towards a New Ireland* (London: Knight, 1972).

FITZPATRICK, BARRÉ, 'Editorial', *Crane Bag*, 4.2 (1980–1), pp. i–iii.

—— 'The Politics of Pluralism, Interview with Garret FitzGerald', *Crane Bag*, 5.1 (1981), 50–4.

FOLEY, MICHAEL, 'Can You Spot Them?', *Fortnight* (20 Nov. 1970), 11.

—— '*Crane Bag* to Cease Publication in Autumn', *Irish Times*, 20 May 1985.

FOSTER, JOHN WILSON, 'The Critical Condition of Ulster', *Honest Ulsterman*, 79 (Autumn 1985), 38–55.

—— letter to Seamus Deane (unsent), 24 Apr. 1986.

—— letter to Seamus Deane, 27 May 1986.

FOSTER, R. F., 'History and the Irish Question' (1982). *Transactions of the Royal Historical Society*, 5th ser., 33 (1983), 169–92.

—— ' "We Are All Revisionists Now" ', *Irish Review*, 1 (1986), 1–5.

—— *Modern Ireland 1600–1972* (1988) (London: Penguin, 1989).

—— 'Nations, Yet Again', *Times Literary Supplement*, 27 Mar. 1992, 5–7.

FOX, MAUREEN, 'A Moving Painting', *Cork Examiner*, 16 Oct. 1981.

FRAYN, MICHAEL (trans.), *Three Sisters* by Anton Chekhov (London: Methuen, 1983).

FRAZIER, ADRIAN, Review of vol. 3 of *The Field Day Anthology of Irish Writing*. *Éire-Ireland*, 27.2 (Summer 1992), 124–31.

FRIEL, BRIAN, *The Enemy Within* (1962) (Dublin: Gallery, 1979).

—— *The Loves of Cass McGuire* (1966) (London: Faber, 1967).

—— *Lovers* (1967) (London: Faber, 1968).

—— *Crystal and Fox* (1968) (London: Faber, 1970).

—— *The Mundy Scheme* (1969) (New York: French, 1970).

—— *The Gentle Island* (1971) (London: Davis-Poynter, 1973).

—— 'Plays Peasant and Unpeasant', *Times Literary Supplement*, 17 Mar. 1972, 305–6.

—— 'Self-Portrait', *Aquarius*, 5 (1972), 17–22, published by Servite Priory, Benburb, Co. Tyrone, Ireland.

—— *Volunteers* (1975) (London: Faber, 1979).

—— *Three Sisters* (a version of the play by Anton Chekhov) (Dublin: Gallery, 1981).

—— *The Communication Cord* (1982, 1983) (Loughcrew, Oldcastle, Co. Meath: Gallery, 1989).

—— 'Address at Opening of Annaghmakerrig', *Threshold*, 33 (Winter 1983), 58–9.

—— 'Extracts from a Sporadic Diary', *Ireland and the Arts*, Special Issue of *Literary Review*, edited by Tim Pat Coogan (London: Namara, 1983), 56–61.

—— *Selected Plays of Brian Friel*, edited by Seamus Deane (London: Faber, 1984).

—— Letter to the author, 12 Oct. 1989.

—— LINEHAN, FERGUS, LEONARD, HUGH, and KEANE, JOHN B., 'The Future of Irish Drama', *Irish Times*, 12 Feb. 1970, 14.

—— 'Talking to Ourselves', interview by Paddy Agnew, *Magill*, Dec. 1980, 59–61.

—— 'The Man From God Knows Where', interview by Fintan O'Toole, *In Dublin*, 28 Oct. 1982, 20–3.

—— ANDREWS, JOHN, and BARRY, KEVIN, 'Translations and A Paper Landscape: Between Fiction and History', *Crane Bag*, 7.2 (1983), 118–24.

FUGARD, ATHOL, *Boesman and Lena* (New York: French, 1971).

—— *Boesman and Lena and Other Plays* (Oxford: Oxford UP, 1978).

—— *Notebooks 1960–1977*, edited by Mary Benson (London: Faber, 1983).

—— *Selected Plays*, edited by Dennis Walder (Oxford: Oxford UP, 1987).

—— KANI, JOHN, and NTSHONA, WINSTON, *Statements: Three Plays* (Oxford: Oxford UP, 1974).

GIBBONS, IVAN, 'A Theatre for Derry', *Fortnight* (6 June 1975), 14.

GILLESPIE, ELGY, 'Festival Profile: Stephen Rea', *Irish Times*, 10 Oct. 1980.

—— 'The Saturday Interview: Brian Friel', *Irish Times*, 5 Sept. 1981.

—— 'Field Day in Search of American Funds', *Irish Times*, 24 Mar. 1987.

GORMAN, DAMIAN, 'The Stuff of Argument', *Belfast Review*, Winter 1983.

—— 'Send in the Prods', *Belfast Review*, Sept. 1984.

—— 'Reading, Writing and Pauline Rhetoric', *Belfast Review*, Mar.–Apr.–May 1985.

GRAY, JOHN, 'Field Day Five Years On', *Linen Hall Review* (Summer 1985), 4–10.

GREEN, ARTHUR, 'Unionist Horizons', *Irish Review*, 4 (1988), 27–32.

GREENE, JOHN, review of vol. 1 of *The Field Day Anthology of Irish Writing*. *Éire-Ireland*, 27.2 (Summer 1992), 111–18.

GUITERMAN, ARTHUR and LANGNER, LAWRENCE, *The School for Husbands* (New York: French, 1933).

GUSSOW, MEL, 'From Ballybeg to Broadway', *New York Times Magazine*, 29 Sept. 1991, 56.

GUTHRIE, TYRONE and KIPNIS, LEONID (trans.), *The Three Sisters* by Anton Chekhov, edited by Henry Popkin (New York: Avon, 1965).

HABERSTROH, PATRICIA, Review of vol. 2 of *The Field Day Anthology of Irish Writing, Éire-Ireland*, 27.2 (Summer 1992), 118–23.

HADFIELD, PAUL, 'From Devlin to Sophocles', *Fortnight*, Oct. 1984, 29.

—— and HENDERSON, LYNDA, 'Field Day: Magical Mystery Tour', *Theatre Ireland*, 2 (Jan. 1983), 65–6.

—— —— 'Field Day: The Magical Mystery', *Theatre Ireland*, 2 (Jan. 1983), 63–5.

HAFFENDEN, JOHN (ed.), *Viewpoints: Poets in Conversation with John Haffenden* (London: Faber, 1981).

HAMMOND, DAVID, personal interview, 24 Aug. 1990.

—— letter to the author, 5 Jan. 1992.

—— letter to the author, 18 Feb. 1992.

—— letter to the author, 19 Aug. 1993.

HARDING, TIM, 'Tractarians 10, Drama Nil', *Sunday Press*, 30 Sept. 1984, 15.

HARMON, MAURICE, review, *Irish University Review*, 14.1 (Spring 1984), 126–31.

HARRIS, MITCHELL, 'Field Day and the Fifth Province', *An Gael* (Summer 1985).

HASTINGS, TIM, 'Audiences in Dublin Hit for Criticism', *Irish Press*, 30 Sept. 1981.

HEALY, CRICHTON, 'Friel's New Play at the Opera House', *Cork Examiner*, 10 Nov. 1980.

HEALY, JOHN, 'Literary Excitement in Derry', *Irish Times*, 12 Sept. 1983.

HEANEY, SEAMUS, *Death of a Naturalist* (London: Faber, 1966).

—— 'Out of London: Ulster's Troubles', *New Statesman*, 1 July 1966, 23–4.

—— *Eleven Poems*, (Belfast: Festival Publications, 1967).

—— 'Old Derry's Walls', *Listener*, 24 Oct. 1968, 521–3.

—— *Door Into the Dark* (London: Faber, 1969).

—— 'The Poetry of John Hewitt', *Threshold*, 22 (Summer 1969), 73–7.

—— (ed.), *Soundings '72* (Belfast: Blackstaff, 1972).

—— *Wintering Out* (London: Faber, 1972, 1973).

—— *North* (London: Faber, 1975).

—— *Stations* (Belfast: Ulsterman, 1975).

—— *Bog Poems*, illustrations by Barrie Cooke (London: Rainbow, 1975).

—— *Field Work* (London: Faber, 1979).

—— *Ugolino*, lithographs by Louis Le Brocquy (Dublin: Carpenter, 1979).

—— 'A Tale of Two Islands: Reflections on the Irish Literary Revival', in P. J. Drudy (ed.), *Irish Studies 1* (Cambridge: Cambridge UP, 1980), 1–20.

—— *Preoccupations: Selected Prose 1968–1978* (1980) (London: Faber, 1984).

—— '. . . English and Irish', *Times Literary Supplement*, 24 Oct. 1980, 1199.

—— 'Chekhov on Sakhalin', programme note for the Field Day production of *Three Sisters*, 1981.

—— *Seamus Heaney: Poems and a Memoir*, selected and illustrated by Henry Pearson, introd. by Thomas Flanagan (New York: Limited Editions Club, 1982).

—— 'Forked Tongues, Ceilís and Incubators', *Fortnight*, 197 (Sept. 1983), 18–21.

—— *An Open Letter* (1983). In *Ireland's Field Day* (London: Hutchinson, 1985), 19–30.

—— *Sweeney Astray* (Derry: Field Day, 1983).

—— *Station Island* (London: Faber, 1984).

—— 'On Irish Expressionist Painting', *Irish Review*, 3 (1988), 34–9.

—— 'A Field Day for the Irish', *The Times*, 5 Dec. 1988.

—— 'Unhappy and at Home', interview by Seamus Deane, *Crane Bag*, 1.1 (Spring 1977), 61–7.

—— 'An Interview with Seamus Heaney' by James Randall, *Ploughshares*, 5.3 (1979), 7–22.

—— 'Interview with Seamus Heaney', *Gown Literary Supplement*, 31.4 (Summer 1985).

—— 'An Interview with Seamus Heaney' by Patricia McGovern King, *An Gael* (Summer 1985), 2–4.

—— 'Poetry and Politics: A Conversation between Seamus Heaney and Joseph Brodsky', edited by Fintan O'Toole, *Magill*, Nov. 1985, 40–8.

—— personal interview, 23 Oct. 1989.

—— Telephone interview, 22 Feb. 1994.

HEAP, DAVID, 'On the Road with *Translations*', *Sunday Tribune*, 2 Nov. 1980.

HEDERMAN, MARK PATRICK, ' "Far-off, most secret, and inviolate Rose" ', *Crane Bag*, 1.2 (1977), 29–34.

—— '*The Crane Bag* and the North of Ireland', *Crane Bag*, 4.2 (1980–1), 94–103.

—— 'Poetry and the Fifth Province', *Crane Bag*, 9.1 (1985), 110–19.

—— and KEARNEY, RICHARD (eds.). *The Crane Bag Book of Irish Studies 1977–1981* (Dublin: Blackwater, 1982).

HENDERSON, LYNDA, 'Failed Languages of Farce', *Fortnight* (Dec. 1982), 31.

—— 'A Wealth of New Ulster Writing', *Fortnight* (Feb. 1984), 28–9.

—— 'The Riot Act/High Time', *Theatre Ireland*, 7 (Autumn 1984), 35.

—— 'A Dangerous Translation', *Fortnight*, 235 (10–23 Mar. 1986), 24.

—— 'Not Even a Name: *The Saxon Shore* by David Rudkin', *Theatre Ireland*, 15 (May–Aug. 1988), 27–9.

—— 'Second Innings', Interview by Cavan Hoey, *Theatre Ireland*, 20 (Sept.–Dec. 1989), 45–8.

—— Personal interview, 25 Sept. 1989.

—— and HADFIELD, PAUL, 'Field Day: Magical Mystery Tour', *Theatre Ireland*, 2 (Jan. 1983), 65–6.

—— —— 'Field Day: The Magical Mystery', *Theatre Ireland*, 2 (Jan. 1983), 63–5.

HEPBURN, A. C., *The Conflict of Nationality in Modern Ireland* (London: Arnold, 1980).

HERRON, DIANE, 'Not a "Translation" in the Accepted Sense', *Londonderry Sentinel*, 18 Sept. 1981.

HEWISON, ROBERT, 'The Soldier's Tale', *Sunday Times*, 9 Aug. 1981, 30.

—— 'Behind the Lines in Ireland', *Times Literary Supplement*, 1 June 1984, 612.

HEWITT, JOHN, 'The Family Next Door', *Threshold*, 23 (Summer 1970), 14–19.

HICKMAN, CHRISTIE, 'Stephen Rea, Fringe Actor Par Excellence', *Drama* (Autumn 1983), 23–5.

HILL, IAN, 'Mapping Cultural Imperialism', review, *Guardian*, 27 Sept. 1980, 11.

HINGERTY, KAY, 'Northern Notebook: Friel For All!', *It*, Nov. 1981.

—— 'Northern Notes', *It*, Nov. 1982.

—— 'An Unforgettable Night of Theatre in Derry', *Cork Examiner*, 27 Sept. 1983.

—— 'Field Day Theatre Co. Take Over at Everyman', *Cork Examiner*, 3 Nov. 1984, 11.

HINGLEY, RONALD (trans.), *Chekhov: Ivanov, The Seagull and Three Sisters* (London: Oxford UP, 1968).

HOLLAND, MARY, '*Translations* Translates Well', *Sunday Tribune*, 5 Sept. 1982.

—— 'Fifth Province', review of *Ireland and the English Crisis* by Tom Paulin, *Observer*, 20 Jan. 1985.

—— 'A Field Day for Irish Theatre', *Observer Magazine*, 30 Oct. 1988, 60–5.

HOLLY, PATTI, 'Field Day's First Double Act', *Derry Journal*, 31 Aug. 1984, 17.

HOULIHAN, CON, 'Make Sure You See this Memorable Friel', *Evening Press*, 7 Oct. 1980.

—— 'That Was the Festival That Was', *Evening Press*, 25 Oct. 1980.

—— 'Turning Chekov Gold into Base Metal', *Evening Press*, 29 Sept. 1981.

HUDSON, CHRISTOPHER, 'Razing the Roof', *Standard*, 9 May 1983.

HUGHES, EAMONN, '"To Define Your Dissent": The Plays and Polemics of the Field Day Theatre Company', *Theatre Research International*, 15.1 (Spring 1990), 67–77.

—— (ed.), *Culture and Politics in Northern Ireland 1960–1990* (Milton Keynes: Open UP, 1991).

HUNTER, CHARLES, 'Seamus Heaney: Keeping a Steady Watch', *Irish Times*, 20 June, 1987.

—— 'Stephen Rea: Actor-Manager with a Mission', *Irish Times*, 19 Sept. 1987.

IMHOF, RÜDIGER, review of *Ireland and the English Crisis* by Tom Paulin, *Irish University Review*, 15.2 (Autumn 1985), 250–2.

JACKSON, KEVIN, 'Running Wilde on the Road', *Independent*, 15 Sept. 1989.

JEBB, SIR RICHARD C. (trans.), *The Tragedies of Sophocles* (Freeport, NY: Books for Libraries, 1904; repr. 1972).

JEFFERY, KEITH, 'In Defence of Decency', *Times Literary Supplement*, 19 Oct. 1984.

JOHNSTONE, ROBERT, 'We Still Believe What We Hear', *Fortnight* (Dec. 1979–Jan. 1980), 20–1.

—— 'Happy Boys and Angry Young Men', *Fortnight*, 176 (May 1980), 21.

—— 'Guldering Unselfconsciously', *Honest Ulsterman*, 75 (May 1984), 85–91.

—— 'Antigone in Ulster Dialect', *Fortnight*, 227 (21 Oct. 1985), 23.

—— 'A Wilful Deafness to the North's Self-Questioning', *Fortnight*, 230 (2 Dec. 1985), 19–20.

—— 'Picture Postcards, Poetic Springs', *Honest Ulsterman*, 81 (Spring–Summer 1986), 28–30.

—— and PAULIN, TOM, 'Another Look at the Field Day Question', *Honest Ulsterman*, 76 (Autumn 1984), 40–3.

JOHNSTONE, ROBERT, 'The Longley Tapes', interview with Michael Longley, *Honest Ulsterman*, 78 (Summer 1985), 13–31.

JORDAN, JOHN, 'Triumphant Translations', *Hibernia*, 9 Oct. 1980.

—— 'Irish Catholicism', *Crane Bag*, 7.2 (1983), 106–16.

JOYCE, JAMES, *A Portrait of the Artist as a Young Man* (1916; 1964). (Harmondsworth: Penguin, 1976).

—— *Ulysses: The Corrected Text*, edited by Hans Walter Gabler (New York: Random House, 1986).

KAVANAGH, PATRICK, *Collected Pruse* (Worcester: MacGibbon, 1967).

KEARNEY, RICHARD, 'Beyond Art and Politics', *Crane Bag*, 1.1 (Spring 1977), 8–16.

—— 'Myth and Terror', *Crane Bag*, 2.1 and 2 (1978), 125–39.

—— 'The IRA's Strategy of Failure', *Crane Bag*, 4.2 (1980–1), 62–70.

—— 'Between Politics and Literature: The Irish Cultural Journal', *Crane Bag*, 7.2 (1983), 160–71.

—— 'Brian Friel and the Three Pamphleteers', *Magill*, Oct. 1983, 53–5.

—— 'Faith and Fatherland', *Crane Bag*, 8.1 (1984), 55–66.

—— *Myth and Motherland* (1984). In *Ireland's Field Day* (London: Hutchinson, 1985), 59–80.

—— 'Between Conflict and Consensus', *Crane Bag*, 9.1 (1985), 87–9.

—— *Transitions: Narratives in Modern Irish Culture* (Manchester: Manchester UP, 1988).

—— 'Myth as the Bearer of Possible Worlds', interview with Paul Ricoeur, *Crane Bag*, 2.1 and 2 (1978), 112–18.

—— and HEDERMAN, MARK PATRICK (eds.), *The Crane Bag Book of Irish Studies 1977–1981* (Dublin: Blackwater, 1982).

—— DEANE, SEAMUS, and CARTY, CIARAN, 'Why Ireland Needs a Fifth Province', *Sunday Independent*, 22 Jan. 1984, 15.

KEARNEY, TIMOTHY, 'Beyond the Planter and the Gael: Interview with John Hewitt and John Montague on Northern Poetry and the Troubles', *Crane Bag*, 4.2 (1980–1), 85–92.

—— 'Editorial', *Crane Bag*, 5.1 (1981), 3–4.

KENDRICK, IAN, 'Poetry', review of *High Time* by Derek Mahon, *Linen Hall Review*, 2.4 (Winter 1985), 16.

KENNEDY, DOUGLAS, 'Brian Friel: Delighting in Mischief, Wary of Praise', *Irish Times*, 4 July 1987.

KENNEDY, LIAM, 'Modern Ireland: Post-Colonial Society or Post-Colonial Pretensions?', *Irish Review*, 13 (Winter 1992–3), 107–21.

KENNEDY, MAEV, 'The Voices that Will Linger on After Dublin', *Belfast Telegraph*, 18 Oct. 1980.

—— 'Prompts from London: Friel Nationalised', *Irish Times*, 31 July 1981.

—— 'Theatre', *Image*, Nov. 1987, 6.

KENNELLY, BRENDAN, 'Soaring from the Treetops', *New York Times Book Review*, 27 May 1984.

KENNER, HUGH, 'There's Music in the Ould Sod Yet', *The New York Times Book Review*, 26 Jan. 1992.

KEYES, JOHN, 'Major Playwright Sets the Scene for a Russian Classic', *Belfast Newsletter*, 10 Sept. 1981, 5.

KIBERD, DECLAN, 'Writers in Quarantine? The Case for Irish Studies', *Crane Bag*, 3.1 (1979), 9–21.

—— 'The Fall of the Stage Irishman', in Ronald Schleifer (ed.), *The Genres of the Irish Literary Revival* (Norman, Okla.: Pilgrim, and Dublin: Wolfhound, 1980), 39–60.

—— 'Editorial: The Irish Language', *Crane Bag*, 5.2 (1981), 4–6.

—— 'Inventing Irelands', *Crane Bag*, 8.1 (1984), 11–23.

—— *Anglo-Irish Attitudes* (1984), in *Ireland's Field Day* (London: Hutchinson, 1985), 81–105.

—— 'Non-Protesting Protestants', *Sunday Tribune*, 25 Aug. 1985.

—— 'Insecurity, Local Piety and Ulsterisation', *Fortnight*, 227 (21 Oct.–3 Nov. 1985), 18–20.

KIELY, NIALL, 'An Irishman's Diary', *Irish Times*, 17 Sept. 1981.

KILFEATHER, SIOBHAN, 'The Whole Bustle', *London Review of Books*, 9 Jan. 1992, 20–2.

KILROY, THOMAS, *The Death and Resurrection of Mr. Roche* (London: Faber, 1969).

—— 'Writing in the West', *Connacht Tribune*, 31 Oct. 1980.

KING, PATRICIA McGOVERN, 'An Interview with Seamus Heaney', *An Gael* (Summer 1985), 2–4.

KINGSLEY, PAUL, *Londonderry Revisited: A Loyalist Analysis of the Civil Rights Controversy* (Belfast: Belfast Publications, 1989).

KINSELLA, THOMAS, 'The Divided Mind' (1973), in Mark Storey (ed.), *Poetry and Ireland Since 1800: A Source Book* (London: Routledge, 1988), 207–16.

—— *Fifteen Dead* (Dublin: Dolmen, 1979).

KIRK-SMITH, IAN, 'Another Striking Friel Translation', *Belfast Telegraph*, 9 Sept. 1981.

KNOX, BERNARD (ed.), *Sophocles: The Three Theban Plays* (translated by Robert Fagles) (London: Lane, 1982).

LACY, BRIAN, *Siege City: The Story of Derry and Londonderry* (Belfast: Blackstaff, 1990).

LAFFAN, MICHAEL, 'Two Irish States', *Crane Bag*, 8.1 (1984), 26–37.

—— 'Insular Attitudes: The Revisionists and their Critics', in Máirín Ní Dhonnchadha and Theo Dorgan (eds.), *Revising the Rising* (Derry: Field Day, 1991), 106–21.

LEHMAN, DAVID and FOOTE, DONNA, 'The Ulster Renaissance', *Newsweek* (International Edn.), 12 May 1986.

LENNON, PETER, 'Adrift on the Flood', *Guardian*, 12 Dec. 1991, 23.

LINEHAN, FERGUS, LEONARD, HUGH, KEANE, JOHN B., and FRIEL, BRIAN, 'The Future of Irish Drama', *Irish Times*, 12 Feb. 1970, 14.

LOCKWOOD COMMITTEE, *Higher Education in Northern Ireland*, Cmd. 475 (Belfast: Her Majesty's Stationery Office, 1965).

LONG, MARK, 'Molière's Method', programme note for the Field Day production of *High Time*, 1984.

LONGLEY, EDNA (ed.), *The Selected James Simmons* (Belfast: Blackstaff, 1978).

—— 'Stars and Horses, Pigs and Trees', *Crane Bag*, 3.2 (1979), 54–60.

—— 'Heaney—Poet as Critic', *Fortnight*, 179 (Dec. 1980–Jan. 1981), 15–16.

—— (ed.), *A Language Not to be Betrayed: Selected Prose of Edward Thomas* (Manchester: Carcanet New, 1981).

—— '*North*: "Inner Emigré" or "Artful Voyeur"?', in Tony Curtis (ed.), *The Art of Seamus Heaney* (Bridgend, Mid Glamorgan: Poetry Wales, 1982, 1985), 63–95.

—— (ed.), *The Selected Paul Durcan* (Belfast: Blackstaff, 1982).

—— 'Sweet Dreams or Rifles', *Fortnight*, 196 (Summer 1983), 19–21.

—— 'More Martyrs to Abstraction', *Fortnight*, 206 (July–Aug. 1984), 18–20.

—— 'The Writer and Belfast', in Maurice Harmon (ed.), *The Irish Writer and the City* (Gerrards Cross: Smythe, 1984), 65–89.

—— 'Poetry and Politics in Northern Ireland', *Crane Bag*, 9.1 (1985), 26–40.

—— 'A Reply', *Crane Bag*, 9.1 (1985), 120–2.

—— 'Casting the Cold Eye', *Fortnight*, 223 (8 July–8 Sept. 1985), 18.

—— 'Edna Longley on Field Day', letter, *Fortnight*, 225 (23 Sept. 1985), 15–16.

—— 'Anglo-Irish Resurrection', *Honest Ulsterman*, 82 (Winter 1986), 102–8.

—— *Poetry in the Wars* (Newcastle upon Tyne: Bloodaxe, 1986).

—— 'Progressive Bookmen: Politics and Northern Protestant Writers since the 1930s', *Irish Review*, 1 (1986), 50–7.

—— 'Opening Up: A New Pluralism', *Fortnight* (Nov. 1987).

—— 'Including the North', *Text and Context* (Autumn 1988), 17–24.

—— 'Writing, Revisionism and Grass-Seed: Literary Mythologies in Ireland' (1989), in Jean Lundy and Aodán Mac Póilin (eds.), *Styles of Belonging: The Cultural Identities of Ulster* (Belfast: Lagan, 1992), 11–21.

—— *From Cathleen to Anorexia: The Breakdown of Irelands* (Dublin: Attic, 1990).

—— 'Belfast Diary', *London Review of Books*, 9 Jan. 1992, 21.

—— 'Hospitable Meta-Narrative or Hegemonic Bid?', *Canadian Journal of Irish Studies*, 18.2 (Dec. 1992), 119–21.

—— and DAWE, GERALD (eds.), *Across a Roaring Hill: The Protestant Imagination in Modern Ireland* (Belfast: Blackstaff, 1985).

—— Personal interview, 20 Sept. 1989.

LONGLEY, MICHAEL, 'The Longley Tapes', interview by Robert Johnstone, *Honest Ulsterman*, 78 (Summer 1985), 13–31.

LOWRY, BETTY, 'Friel Play Makes It a Great Night in Derry', *Belfast Telegraph*, 24 Sept. 1980.

—— 'The Man from Muff', *Belfast Telegraph*, 7 Mar. 1981, 6.

LUNDY, JEAN and MAC PÓIILIN, AODÁN (eds.), *Styles of Belonging: The Cultural Identities of Ulster* (Belfast: Lagan, 1992).

LYONS, F. S. L., *Ireland Since the Famine* (1971) (London: Fontana; rev. edn., 1973).

—— *Culture and Anarchy in Ireland 1890–1939* (Oxford: Clarendon, 1979).

McAUGHTRY, SAM, 'Having a Field Day', *Irish Times*, 13 May 1987, 13.

McAULEY, LIAM, 'Something Stirs in the Londonderry Air', *Sunday Times*, 21 Sept. 1980, 14.

—— 'Inside the Arts with Liam McAuley', *Sunday Independent*, 19 Aug. 1984.

McAVERA, BRIAN, 'Brian Friel: Attuned to the Catholic Experience', *Fortnight*, 215 (3 Mar. 1985), 19–20.

—— 'Friel on Language', letter, *Fortnight*, 219 (13–26 May 1985), 16.

—— 'Reject Set for a World Stage', *Irish News*, 3 Mar. 1986.

McCANN, EAMONN, *War and an Irish Town* (1974) (London: Pluto, rev. edn. 1980).

McCARTHY, THOMAS, 'Heaney's Sweeney', *Connacht Tribune*, 23–30 Dec. 1983, 8.

McCARTNEY, NOEL, 'Derry Rallies behind Friel Play Première', *Irish Press*, 20 Sept. 1980, 5.

McClean, Dr Raymond, *The Road to Bloody Sunday* (Swords, Co. Dublin: Ward River, 1983).

McClelland, Martha, 'Translations', *An Phoblacht/Republican News*, 11 Oct. 1980.

McCormack, W. J., *The Battle of the Books: Two Decades of Irish Cultural Debate* (Gigginstown, Mullingar, Co. Westmeath, Lilliput, 1986).

MacCurtain, Margaret, review of vol. 1 of *The Field Day Anthology of Irish Writing*, *Irish Literary Supplement* (Fall 1992), 4.

MacDermott, Domhnall, 'Behind the Scenes at *Boesman and Lena*', *Derry Journal*, 16 Sept. 1983.

—— 'Deane Spells Out Field Day's Role', *Derry Journal*, 8 Feb. 1985.

MacDonagh, Oliver, *States of Mind: A Study of Anglo-Irish Conflict 1780–1980* (London: Allen, 1983).

—— 'What Was New in the New Ireland Forum?', *Crane Bag*, 9.2 (1985), 166–70.

McDowell, Lindy, 'Another Suitcase, Another Hall . . .', *Belfast Telegraph*, 5 Oct. 1984.

McDowell, Michael, 'Removing the British Guarantee—A Policy Based on Rigour or Rhetoric?', *Crane Bag*, 4.2 (1980–1), 34–8.

McEvoy, James, 'Catholic Hopes and Protestant Fears', *Crane Bag*, 7.2 (1983), 90–105.

McGarry, D., 'A Field Day for Derry', *Liberty*, Oct. 1980.

McGinley, Frank, 'A City to Rival Juno's', *Donegal Democrat*, 26 Sept. 1980.

—— 'Humour is in the Eye of the Beholder', *Donegal Democrat*, 1 Oct. 1982, 17.

MacGoris, Mary, 'The Mary MacGoris Column', *Irish Independent*, 2 Sept. 1980.

—— 'The Mary MacGoris Column', *Irish Independent*, 19 June 1981.

—— 'Too-Wordy Friel Farce', *Irish Independent*, 2 Nov. 1982.

McGrath, F. C., 'Introducing Ireland's Field Day', *Éire-Ireland*, 23.4 (Winter 1988), 145–55.

McIlroy, Brian, 'NewsLetter Editor's Corner', *Canadian Association for Irish Studies Newsletter*, 6.2 (Autumn 1992), 3.

McIntyre, Tom, 'Tribal Treasure', *Inside Tribune*, 4 Dec. 1983.

McKenna, David, 'Me Tonto', *In Dublin*, 3 Oct. 1980.

McKenna, John, 'Marathon Trip Through Irish Writing', *Irish Times*, 7 Sept. 1988, 14.

McKeone, Gary, Letter to the author, 25 Feb. 1992.

—— Letter to the author, 26 Feb. 1992.

McKITTRICK, DAVID, 'The Class Structure of Unionism', *Crane Bag*, 4.2 (1980–1), 28–33.

McLEISH, KENNETH (trans.), *Four Greek Plays* (London: Longmans, 1964).

McMAHON, SEAN, 'Brian Friel: His New Plays Reviewed', *Ulster Tatler*, Nov. 1980.

McMINN, JOE, 'In Defence of Field Day: Talking Among the Ruins', *Fortnight*, 224 (9 Sept. 1985), 19–20.

MacNAMARA, JOHN, 'The Irish Language and Nationalism', *Crane Bag*, 1.2 (1977), 40–4.

McQUAID, CARMEL, 'Just What Were You Trying to Say, Brian?', *Sunday News*, 28 Sept. 1980.

McWHIRTER, GEORGE, 'Odd Bods: Seamus Simmons and James Deane', *Honest Ulsterman*, 82 (Winter 1986), 109–12.

MADDOX, ADRIAN, 'Theatre', *North*, Oct. 1984, 25.

MAGARSHACK, DAVID, *The Real Chekhov* (London: Allen, 1972).

MAHON, DEREK, 'Un Beau Pays, Mal Habite', *Magill*, Feb. 1979, 18–22.

—— *Poems 1962–1978* (Oxford: Oxford UP, 1979).

—— *High Time* (1984) (Dublin: Gallery, 1985).

—— 'High Time', programme note for the Field Day production of *High Time*, 1984.

MARTIN, AUGUSTINE, 'What Stalked through the Post Office?', *Crane Bag*, 2.1 and 2 (1978), 164–77.

—— 'Observe the Sons of USNA', Review of *Ireland and the English Crisis* by Tom Paulin, *Sunday Press*, 7 Apr. 1985.

MAXWELL, D. E. S., 'Imagining the North: Violence and the Writers', *Éire-Ireland*, 8.2 (1973), 91–107.

—— *A Critical History of Modern Irish Drama 1891–1980* (Cambridge: Cambridge UP, 1984).

MEMMI, ALBERT, *The Colonizer and the Colonized* (1957) (translated by Howard Greenfeld) (New York: Orion, 1965).

MHAC AN TSAOI, MAIRE, 'The Book Page', *Irish Press*, 29 Oct. 1983.

MHIC SHEAIN, BRIGHID BEAN, letter, *Fortnight*, 217 (1 Apr. 1985), 16.

—— 'Further Linguistic Disputes', letter, *Fortnight*, 222 (24 June 1985), 10–12.

MITCHELL, BRIAN, *Derry: A City Invincible* (Eglinton, Co. Londonderry: Grocers' Hall, 1990).

MOLIÈRE, *L'École des Maris*, edited by Peter Nurse (London: Harrap, 1959).

MOLIÈRE, *The School for Husbands with The Flying Doctor, The Uneasy Husband, and Love is the Best Remedy*, translated and adapted by Allan Clayson (London: Heinemann Educational, 1969).

MOLONEY, EUGENE, 'Communication Cord Set to be a Signal Success', *Irish News*, 17 Sept. 1982, 4.

—— ' "Cord" that Tilts the Fun-Bath Over All', *Irish News*, 23 Sept. 1982.

—— 'From a Nursery to the Opera House', *Irish News*, 29 Sept. 1982.

—— 'Stark Contrasts', *Irish News*, 22 Sept. 1983.

MONTAGUE, JOHN, 'Foreword', *Threshold*, 23 (Summer 1970), 1.

—— *Selected Poems* (Oxford: Oxford UP, 1982).

—— 'Tarzan Among the Nightingales', *Fortnight*, 200 (Dec. 1983–Jan. 1984), 27.

MOODY, T. W., 'Irish History and Irish Mythology', *Hermathena*, 124 (Summer 1978), 7–24.

MOONEY, BEL, 'Poet, Pilgrim, Fugitive . . .', *The Times*, 11 Oct. 1984, 8.

MOORE, BRIAN, 'Rewriting Ireland', *Independent on Sunday*, 24 Nov. 1991, 36–7.

MORAN, DERMOT, 'Wandering from the Path', *Crane Bag*, 2.1, 2 (1978), 96–102.

—— 'Three More from Field Day', *Irish Literary Supplement* (Fall 1984), 21.

MORASH, CHRISTOPHER, 'Flamethrowers: Contemporary Northern Irish Playwrights', M.Phil. diss. Trinity College, Dublin, 1986.

MORIARTY, GERRY, 'A Field Day of Tragedy and Farce', *Evening Press*, 15 Sept. 1984.

—— 'Field Day Future Uncertain as Board Takes "Sabbatical" ', *Irish Times*, 28 Apr. 1993, 1.

MORRISON, BLAKE and MOTION, ANDREW (eds.), *The Penguin Book of Contemporary British Poetry* (Harmondsworth: Penguin, 1982).

MULLEN, FIONA, 'Poetry', review of Edna Longley and Gerald Dawe (eds.), *Across a Roaring Hill: The Protestant Imagination in Modern Ireland*, *Linen Hall Review*, 2.3 (Autumn 1985), 30.

MURPHY, JOHN, 'Further Reflections on Irish Nationalism', *Crane Bag*, 2.1, 2 (1978), 156–63.

MURRAY, CHRISTOPHER, review of *Translations*, *Irish University Review*, 11.2 (Autumn 1981), 238–9.

—— review of *Selected Plays of Brian Friel* and *A Critical History of Modern Irish Drama* by D. E. S. Maxwell, *Irish University Review*, 15.2 (Autumn 1985), 244–8.

MYERS, KEVIN, 'An Irishman's Diary', *Irish Times*, 4 Sept. 1980.

NEARY, PETER, 'The Failure of Economic Nationalism', *Crane Bag*, 8.1 (1984), 68–76.

NÍ CHUILLEANÁIN, EILÉAN, review of the second set of Field Day pamphlets, *Cyphers*, Summer 1984.

NORTHERN IRELAND, Government, *Higher Education in Northern Ireland*, Cmd. 480 (Belfast: Her Majesty's Stationery Office, 1965).

NORTHERN IRELAND, Parliament, *Parliamentary Debates (Hansard)*, vol. 59: 501–7 (10 Feb. 1965), 1338–1428, 1442–1658 (3–4 Mar. 1965) (Belfast: Her Majesty's Stationery Office, 1965).

NOWLAN, DAVID, 'Theatre Group in Search of Sponsorship', *Irish Times*, 2 Sept. 1980.

—— 'Electric Love Affair as Play Opens in Derry', *Irish Times*, 24 Sept. 1980.

—— 'Friel Play Opens in Derry', *Irish Times*, 25 Sept. 1980.

—— 'Theatre Festival Breaks Box-Office Records', *Irish Times*, 8 Oct. 1980.

—— 'Theatre Festival: The Summing-Up', *Irish Times*, 24 Oct. 1980.

—— 'The Year of the Playwright', *Irish Times*, 1–2 Jan. 1981.

—— 'New Friel Play Opens in Derry Guild Hall', *Irish Times*, 9 Sept. 1981.

—— '*Three Sisters* in Derry Guildhall', *Irish Times*, 10 Sept. 1981.

—— 'The Fringe and Beyond', *Irish Times*, 3 Sept. 1982.

—— 'A Sold-out Festival?', *Irish Times*, 17 Sept. 1982.

—— 'New Friel Play Applauded', *Irish Times*, 22 Sept. 1982.

—— 'New Friel Fare at Derry Guildhall', *Irish Times*, 23 Sept. 1982.

—— '*The Communication Cord* at the Gaiety', *Irish Times*, 2 Nov. 1982.

—— '*Boesman and Lena* at Derry Guild Hall', *Irish Times*, 22 Sept. 1983, 8.

—— 'Beyond the Pale', *Irish Times*, 30 Sept. 1983, 8.

—— 'Field Day Double Bill at Derry Guild Hall', *Irish Times*, 20 Sept. 1984.

—— 'Politics in the Theatre', *Irish Times*, 27 Sept. 1984.

O'BRIEN, CONOR CRUISE, 'Views', *Listener*, 24 Oct. 1968, 526.

—— *States of Ireland* (London: Hutchinson, 1972).

—— 'An Unhealthy Intersection', *New Review*, 2.16 (July 1975), 3–8.

—— 'Politics and the Poet', *Irish Times*, 21 Aug. 1975, 10.

—— 'Eradicating the Tragic Heroic Mode', *Irish Times*, 22 Aug. 1975, 10.

—— 'Nationalism and the Reconquest of Ireland', *Crane Bag*, 1.2 (1977), 8–13.

—— 'Cult of Blood', *Observer*, 18 Aug. 1985.

O'Brien, Flann, *At Swim-Two-Birds* (1939; 1960) (London: Hart-Davis, 1976).

O'Brien, Martin, 'Impressive Translations', *Belfast Telegraph*, 30 Sept. 1980.

—— 'Friel Gives Chekhov's Vision New Meaning', *Belfast Telegraph*, 5 Sept. 1981.

Ó Buachalla, Séamas, 'The Language in the Classroom', *Crane Bag*, 5.2 (1981), 18–31.

Ó Cinnéide, Séamus, 'Northern Group's Ingenious Presentation of Friel Farce', *Limerick Leader*, 27 Oct. 1982.

O'Clery, Conor, 'The People's Democracy: Revolution by Protest', *Fortnight* (4 Dec. 1970), 13–14.

Ó Conchúir, Pádraig, 'Field Day Pamphlets', letter, *Irish Times*, 3 Feb. 1984.

—— letter, *Fortnight*, 228 (4–17 Nov. 1985), 17.

O'Connor, Ulick, 'Friel Takes Derry by Storm', *Sunday Tribune*, 6 Sept. 1981.

O'Doherty, Malachi, 'On the Eve of Pentecost', *Hype*, Nov. 1987, 29–30.

Ó Doibhlin, Breandán, 'No Answer for the Angels?', *Furrow*, 35.1 (Jan. 1984), 34–8.

O'Donnell, Donal, 'Friel and a Tale of Three Sisters', *Sunday Press*, 30 Aug. 1981.

O'Donoghue, Bernard, 'Heaney's Sweeney', *Poetry Review*, 74.1 (Apr. 1984), 62–3.

O'Donoghue, Robert, 'Translations: A Tour De Force', *Cork Evening Echo*, 15 Nov. 1980.

—— 'Contrast from Field Day', *Cork Evening Echo*, 10 Nov. 1984.

O Drisceoil, Proinsias, 'Heaney's Sweeney', *Irish Press*, 10 Dec. 1983, 9.

O'Dwyer, Riana, Review of vol. 3 of *The Field Day Anthology of Irish Writing*, *Irish Literary Supplement* (Fall 1992), 5–7.

O'Faolain, Sean, *The Short Story* (1948) (Cork: Mercier, 1972).

O'Faolain, Nuala, 'The Voice that Field Day Didn't Record', *Irish Times*, 11 Nov. 1991, 14.

O'Flanagan, Revd Michael (ed.), *Letters Containing Information Relative to the Antiquities of the County of Dublin Collected During the Progress of the Ordnance Survey in 1837*, Bray, Ireland, typescript, 1927, Bodleian Library, Oxford.

Ó Gallchóir, Dónall, ' "Dráma" i nDoire', *Irish Press*, 19 Sept. 1981 (trans. by Marc Caball).

O'Grady, Timothy E., 'Derry-Do', *New Statesman*, 3 Oct. 1980.

O'Halloran, Clare, *Partition and the Limits of Irish Nationalism: An Ideology under Stress* (Dublin: Gill, 1987).

O'Hegarty, P. S., *A History of Ireland Under the Union 1801 to 1922* (London: Methuen, 1952).

O'Leary, Olivia, 'The John Hume Show', *Magill*, Mar. 1984, 16–23.

—— 'Haughey at the Forum', *Magill*, May 1984, 10–14.

O'Malley, Padraig, 'Beyond the Real World of Awful Bitterness?', *Fortnight*, 227 (21 Oct.–3 Nov. 1985), 8–10.

—— *Biting at the Grave* (Belfast: Blackstaff, 1990).

Onlooker, 'Distressed Derry Needs More Than "Chequers" Sop', *Derry Journal*, 26 Jan. 1965, 4.

Oscar II, 'County Cameo: A World Premiere in Derry of a Friel Play', *Strabane Chronicle*, 27 Sept. 1980, 8.

O'Toole, Fintan, 'Theatre', *In Dublin*, 28 Oct. 1982, 52.

—— 'Today: Contemporary Irish Theatre—The Illusion of Tradition', in Tim Pat Coogan (ed.), *Ireland and the Arts* (London: Namara, 1983), 132–7.

—— 'Voices On', *Sunday Tribune*, 25 Sept. 1983.

—— 'Ireland Goes to Hollywood', *Sunday Tribune*, 16 Sept. 1984.

—— 'Field Day: On the Double', *Sunday Tribune*, 23 Sept. 1984.

—— 'Stephen Rea: The Great Leap from the Abbey', *Sunday Tribune*, 23 Sept. 1984.

—— 'Brian Friel: The Healing Art', *Magill*, Jan. 1985, 31–5.

—— 'What Paisley and Reggae Have in Common', review of *Ireland and the English Crisis* by Tom Paulin, *Sunday Tribune*, 3 Feb. 1985.

—— 'Friel's Lost Tribe', *Sunday Tribune*, 24 Mar. 1985.

—— 'Seamus Heaney: Beyond the Normal Niceties', *Colour Tribune*, 10 Apr. 1988.

—— 'Friel's Day', *Irish Times*, 7 Jan. 1989.

—— 'Heaney's Half-Century', *Irish Times*, 8 Apr. 1989.

—— 'Having a Field Day', *Irish Times*, 30 Nov. 1991, 5.

—— 'The Man From God Knows Where', interview with Brian Friel, *In Dublin*, 28 Oct. 1982, 20–3.

—— (ed.), 'Poetry and Politics: A Conversation between Seamus Heaney and Joseph Brodsky', *Magill*, Nov. 1985, 40–8.

Parker, Stewart, 'Me and Jim', *Irish University Review*, 12.1 (Spring 1982), 32–4.

PARKER, STEWART, *Dramatis Personae* (Belfast: John Malone Memorial Committee, 1986).

PASCAL, JULIA, 'Private property', interview with Stephen Rea, *City Limits*, 27 Apr.–3 May 1984, 14.

PAULIN, TOM, *Theoretical Locations* (Belfast: Ulsterman, 1975).

—— *A State of Justice* (London: Faber, 1977).

—— *Personal Column* (Belfast: Ulsterman, 1978).

—— *The Strange Museum* (London: Faber, 1980).

—— *The Book of Juniper*, illustrated by Noel Connor (Newcastle upon Tyne: Bloodaxe, 1981).

—— 'Commencement', programme note for the Field Day production of *The Communication Cord*, 1982.

—— *Liberty Tree* (London: Faber, 1983).

—— *A New Look at the Language Question* (1983), in *Ireland's Field Day* (London: Hutchinson, 1985), 1–18.

—— *Ireland and the English Crisis* (Newcastle upon Tyne: Bloodaxe, 1984).

—— *The Riot Act*, 1984 (London: Faber, 1985).

—— 'The Background to Antigone and The Riot Act', programme note for the Field Day production of *The Riot Act*, 1984.

—— *The Argument at Great Tew* (Dublin: Willbrook, 1985).

—— *Fivemiletown* (London: Faber, 1987).

—— and ROBERT JOHNSTONE, 'Another Look at the Field Day Question', *Honest Ulsterman*, 76 (Autumn 1984), 40–3.

—— personal interview, 26 Jan. 1992.

PETER, JOHN, 'The Lessons of Love', *Sunday Times*, 7 Oct. 1984.

PILKINGTON, LIONEL, 'Language and Politics in Brian Friel's *Translations*', *Irish University Review*, 20.2 (Autumn 1990), 282–98.

PINE, RICHARD, 'Finding the Right Words', *Sunday Press*, 25 Sept. 1983.

PÓIRTÉIR, CATHAL, 'Drámaíocht don bpobal', *Irish Press*, 9 Sept. 1981 (trans. Marc Caball).

—— 'Dráma nua Friel', *Irish Press*, 18 Sept. 1982.

POLLAK, ANDY, 'The State of the Press and Media in N. Ireland: A Short Survey', *Fortnight*, 229 (18 Nov.–1 Dec. 1985), 4–6.

POWELL, ENOCH, 'Cultural Ballyaches', review of Edna Longley and Gerald Dawe (eds.), *Across a Roaring Hill: The Protestant Imagination in Modern Ireland*, *The Times*, 15 Aug. 1985, 9.

PRITCHETT, V. S., *Chekhov: A Biography*, 1988 (London: Penguin, 1990).

PURDIE, BOB, 'The Friends of Ireland: British Labour and Irish National-ism, 1945–49', in Tom Gallagher and James O'Connell (eds.), *Contemporary Irish Studies* (Manchester: Manchester UP, 1983), 81–94.

—— 'The Irish Anti-Partition League, South Armagh and the Abstentionist Tactic 1945–58', *Irish Political Studies*, 1 (1986), 67–77.

—— *Politics in the Streets: The Origins of the Civil Rights Movement in Northern Ireland* (Belfast: Blackstaff, 1990).

QUILLIGAN, PATRICK, 'Field Day's New Double Bill', *Irish Times*, 18 Sept. 1984.

RADIN, VICTORIA, 'Joyful Scandal—Magical Translations', *Observer*, 19 Oct. 1980.

RANDALL, JAMES, 'An Interview with Seamus Heaney', *Ploughshares*, 5.3 (1979), 7–22.

RATCLIFFE, MICHAEL, 'Paradise Unhitched', *Observer*, 9 Mar. 1986, 25.

REA, STEPHEN, 'Private Property', interview by Julia Pascal, *City Limits*, 27 Apr.–3 May 1984, 14.

—— personal interview, 18 Apr. 1991.

REGAN, STEPHEN, 'Ireland's Field Day', *History Workshop*, 33 (Spring 1992), 25–37.

RENTON, ALEX, 'Ireland's Leading Rebel', *Illustrated London News*, Jan. 1989, 60–1.

REYNOLDS, STANLEY, 'Chekhov in Derry', *Guardian*, 5 Apr. 1983.

RICHARDS, SHAUN, 'Field Day's Fifth Province: Avenue or Impasse?', in Eamonn Hughes (ed.), *Culture and Politics in Northern Ireland* (Milton Keynes: Open UP, 1991), 139–50.

RIDDELL, LYNNE, 'Why Friel and Rea are Having a "Field" Day', *Belfast Telegraph*, 15 Sept. 1980.

—— 'In Derry the Talk is All About a Farce in Donegal', *Irish Press*, 18 Sept. 1982.

—— 'Can Derry Go a Stage Further?', *Belfast Telegraph*, 27 Aug. 1983, 10.

—— 'The Ups and Downs, Bumps and Bruises, of the Field Day Theatre Company . . .', *Belfast Telegraph*, 18 Sept. 1984.

ROBINSON, LIAM, 'New Play to Set Fire to the Foyle?', *Evening Press*, 19 Sept. 1980.

ROCHE, ANTHONY, 'Ireland's *Antigones*: Tragedy North and South', in Michael Kenneally (ed.), *Cultural Contexts and Literary Idioms in Contemporary Irish Literature* (Gerrards Cross: Smythe, 1988).

ROSENFIELD, JUDITH, 'Unusual and Erudite', *Belfast Newsletter*, 1 Oct. 1980.

RUDKIN, DAVID, *Afore Night Come*, in *New English Dramatists* 7, introd. J. W. Lambert (Harmondsworth: Penguin, 1963).

—— *The Grace of Todd* (London: Oxford UP, 1969).

—— *Ashes* (London: French, 1974).

—— *Cries from Casement as his Bones are Brought to Dublin* (London: BBC, 1974).

—— *Penda's Fen* (London: Davis-Poynter, 1975).

—— *Hippolytus* (London: Heinemann, 1980).

—— *The Sons of Light* (London: Eyre Methuen, 1981).

—— *The Triumph of Death* (London: Eyre Methuen, 1981).

—— 'Across the Water', first version, typescript, collection of the author.

—— 'Athdark and the Flood' (early version of *The Saxon Shore*), Act Two, typescript, collection of the author.

—— Letter to Field Day, 31 May. 1983.

—— *The Saxon Shore* (London: Methuen, 1986).

—— letter to the author, 1 Dec. 1991.

—— letter to the author, 8 Dec. 1991.

—— letter to the author, 5 Mar. 1992.

—— Personal interview, 26 Oct. 1991.

—— Telephone interview, 28 Oct. 1991.

RUSHE, DESMOND, 'Friel at his Pleasing and Astonishing Best', *Irish Independent*, 25 Sept. 1980.

—— 'Finest Play in Years', *Irish Independent*, 7 Oct. 1980.

—— 'Faithful but not quite true Chekov', *Irish Independent*, 10 Sept 1981, 22.

—— 'Superficial Chekhov Production Fails to Convince', *Irish Independent*, 29 Sept. 1981.

—— 'Friel: Comedy with a Cutting Edge', *Irish Independent*, 23 Sept. 1982.

RUSSELL, NOEL, 'Passion and Cold Douses', review of *Celtic Revivals* by Seamus Deane, *Irish News*, 10 Oct. 1985.

SAYLER, OLIVER (ed.), *The Moscow Art Theatre Series of Russian Plays*, translated by Jennie Covan (London: Brentano's, 1922).

SELLNER, EDWARD, 'New Books', *Furrow* (Sept. 1984), 601.

SHAW, FATHER FRANCIS, SJ, 'The Canon of Irish History—A Challenge', *Studies: An Irish Quarterly Review*, 61 (1972), 113–53.

SHEEHAN, RONAN and KEARNEY, RICHARD, letter, *Irish Times*, 25 Jan. 1984.

SHERIDAN, KATHY, 'Imprint', *Irish Times*, 10 Dec. 1983.

SHERIDAN, MICHAEL, 'Translated Logic . . .', *Irish Press*, 23 Sept. 1980.

—— 'Friel Play a Watershed in Irish Theatre', *Irish Press*, 25 Sept. 1980.

—— 'Triumph for Translations', *Irish Press*, 25 Sept. 1980, 4.

—— 'Gate: Translations by Brian Friel', *Irish Press*, 7 Oct. 1980.

—— 'Derry Hails Friel Version of Chekhov', *Irish Press*, 9 Sept. 1981.

—— 'Great Night in Guildhall as Derry Hails Friel's "Sisters"', *Irish Press*, 10 Sept. 1981.

—— 'Field Day Carries on its Consciousness of History', *Irish Press*, 15 Sept. 1981.

—— 'Another Triumphant Friel Translation', *Irish Press*, 29 Sept. 1981.

—— 'Friel Strikes a "Cord"', *Irish Press*, 23 Sept. 1982.

—— 'Friel's Sense of Conflict', *Irish Press*, 1 Oct. 1986.

SHERIDAN, PETER, 'The Theatre and Politics', *Crane Bag*, 1.1 (Spring 1977), 68–71.

SHORTER, ERIC, 'Best Irish Play for Years', *Daily Telegraph*, 8 Aug. 1981, 9.

SHULMAN, MILTON, 'The Key to Glory', *New Standard*, 13 May 1981, 26.

—— 'Keep Your Eyes on the Woad', *London Standard*, 4 Mar. 1986, 28.

SIMMONS, JAMES, 'Kinsella's Craft', *Fortnight* (11 May. 1972), 19.

—— Review of *The Communication Cord* by Brian Friel, *Theatre Ireland*, 2 (Jan. 1983), 69.

—— 'Brian Friel, Catholic Playwright', *Honest Ulsterman*, 79 (Autumn 1985), 61–6.

—— 'A Counterblast to Paddy Solemn', *Honest Ulsterman*, 81 (Spring–Summer 1986), 85–96.

SINGTON, ANNE, 'Behan and Friel in Paris', *Irish Times*, 20 Dec. 1984.

SMITH, GUS, 'As Friel's Peasant Play Dominates Second Festival Week . . .', *Sunday Independent*, 12 Oct. 1980.

—— 'Festival Concludes with Shocker Drama', *Sunday Independent*, 19 Oct. 1980.

—— 'Friel Behind Dynamic New Derry Movement', *Sunday Independent*, 18 Jan. 1981.

—— 'French Farce in Donegal Cottage', *Sunday Independent*, 7 Nov. 1982.

SMYTH, DAMIAN, 'Stick to the Twenty-Six, and Rhyme, Seamus Deane, Seamus Deane', *North*, 3 (Oct. 1984), 18–19.

—— 'Totalising Imperative', *Fortnight*, 309 (Sept. 1992), 26–7.

SPILLANE, MARGARET, 'Friel's Ireland Avoids Getting Lost in *Translations*', *In These Times*, 14–20 Sept. 1988, 21.

SPURR, CHRIS, 'Going down the Country', *Theatre Ireland*, 13 (1987), 23–5.

STANFIELD, MAGGIE, 'Response Cry—Variations of a Catastrophe', *Irish Press*, 17 Sept. 1982.

STANISLAVSKI, CONSTANTIN, *My Life in Art*, translated by J. J. Robbins (London: Eyre Methuen, 1980).

STARRETT, IAN, 'Missing Out on Pat's Big Night', *Sunday News*, 25 Sept. 1983.

—— 'Ratepayers Stage Demo Over Field Day Pay-day', *Sunday News*, 18 Feb. 1990.

STEINER, GEORGE, *In Bluebeard's Castle: Some Notes towards the Re-Definition of Culture* (London: Faber, 1971).

—— *After Babel* (Oxford: Oxford UP, 1975).

—— *Antigones* (University of Exeter, Twelfth Jackson Knight Memorial Lecture, 1979).

—— *Antigones* (Oxford: Oxford UP, 1984).

STEPHENS, ANNIE, 'A Column from Cork', *Newtownards Chronicle and Co. Down Spectator*, 15 Nov. 1984.

STEWART, A. T. Q., *The Narrow Ground: The Roots of Conflict in Ulster* (1977) (London: Faber, rev. edn. 1989).

STOKES, GEOFFREY, 'Field Day Tours America', *An Gael* (Summer 1987), 29–31.

STOLER, PETER, 'Singing of Skunks and Saints', *Time*, 19 Mar. 1984.

STYAN, J. L., *Chekhov in Performance: A Commentary on the Major Plays* (Cambridge, Cambridge UP, 1971).

TAYLOR, JOHN RUSSELL, 'Plays in Performance', *Drama*, 141 (Autumn 1981), 28.

THOMPSON, PETER, 'The Contrast is Only Astonishing', *Irish Press*, 25 Sept. 1984.

TIMM, EITEL F., 'Modern Mind, Myth, and History: Brian Friel's *Translations*', in Heinz Kosok (ed.), *Studies in Anglo-Irish Literature* (Bonn: Bouvier, 1982), 447–54.

TÓIBÍN, COLM, review of *The Field Day Anthology of Irish Writing*, *Canadian Journal of Irish Studies*, 18.2 (Dec. 1992), 121–4.

TRENCH, BRIAN, 'Friel Has the Last Laugh', *Sunday Tribune*, 26 Sept. 1982.

URIS, JILL and LEON, *Ireland: A Terrible Beauty* (London: Corgi, 1977).

VANDENBROUCKE, RUSSELL, *Athol Fugard: Bibliography, Biography, Playography* (London: TO Publications, 1977).

VARIOUS WRITERS, 'Field Day: *The Communication Cord*', *Theatre Ireland*, 2 (Jan. 1983), 66–9.

VERNON, MICHAEL, 'Brian Friel and the Road to Ballybeg', *Fortnight*, 181 (May–June 1981), 16–17.

—— 'The Language of Passion: David Rudkin's *Ashes*', *Fortnight*, 184 (Dec. 1981–Jan. 1982), 22–3.

—— 'Across the Dark Water', *Theatre Ireland*, 2 (Jan.–May 1983), 59–60.

VIDAL, JOHN, 'Stronger than Fiction', *Guardian*, 5 Dec. 1988.

WALSH, CAROLINE, '£5,000 Award for Brian Friel', *Irish Times*, 15 Jan. 1981.

WALSH, R. B., 'John O'Donovan, The Man and the Scholar', in Cyril Byrne and Margaret Harry (eds.), *Talamh An Eisc: Canadian and Irish Essays* (Halifax, Nova Scotia: Nimbus, 1986), 119–39.

WARDLE, IRVING, 'Translations', *The Times*, 13 May 1981, 11.

—— 'Confusion in the Werewolf Idiom', *The Times*, 5 Mar. 1986, 9.

WATERS, JOHN, *Jiving at the Crossroads* (Belfast: Blackstaff, 1991).

WATLING, E. F. (trans.), *Sophocles: The Theban Plays* (Harmondsworth: Penguin, 1947).

WATSON, G. J., *Irish Identity and the Literary Revival: Synge, Yeats, Joyce and O'Casey* (London: Croom Helm, 1979).

WHITE, BARRY, 'A Recipe for Chaos', *Belfast Telegraph*, 2 Oct. 1980, 12.

WHORF, AMY, 'Poetry Reading Benefits Irish Literature Project', *Patriot Ledger*, 24 Mar. 1987.

WILKINS, PAUL, 'Field Day for Friel', *Hibernia*, 25 Sept. 1980.

WITOSZEK, NINA and SHEERAN, PAT, 'From Explanations to Intervention', *Crane Bag*, 9.1 (1985), 83–6.

WOODWORTH, PADDY, 'Reasons for Having a Field Day', *Irish Press*, 1 Nov. 1982.

—— 'Field Day Success is Greeted', *Irish Press*, 21 Sept. 1983.

—— 'A Black Play of Stunning Power', *Irish Press*, 22 Sept. 1983.

—— 'Friel's Day', *RTÉ Guide*, 2 Dec. 1983.

—— 'Field Day's Men and the Re-Making of Ireland', *Irish Times*, 5 Nov. 1990, 10.

YARMOLINSKY, AVRAHM (ed.), *The Portable Chekhov* (1947) (New York: Penguin, 1977).

YEATS, W. B., *Essays and Introductions* (London: Macmillan, 1961).

YOUNG, B. A., 'Translations', *Financial Times*, 14 May 1981, 21.

YOUNG, STARK (trans.), *The Three Sisters* by Anton Chekhov (New York: French, 1941).

Index